Strategic Management for Public and Nonprofit Organizations

PUBLIC ADMINISTRATION AND PUBLIC POLICY

A Comprehensive Publication Program

Executive Editor

JACK RABIN
Professor of Public Administration and Public Policy
School of Public Affairs
The Capital College
The Pennsylvania State University—Harrisburg
Middletown, Pennsylvania

Additional Volumes in Preparation

Principles and Practices of Public Administration, edited by Jack Rabin, Robert F. Munzenrider, and Sherrie M. Bartell

Handbook of Developmental Policy Studies, edited by Stuart S. Nagel

Case Studies in Public Budgeting and Financial Management, edited by Aman Khan and W. Bartley Hildreth

Handbook of Conflict Management, edited by William J. Pammer, Jr., and Jerri Killian

Annals of Public Administration

1. *Public Administration: History and Theory in Contemporary Perspective*, edited by Joseph A. Uveges, Jr.
2. *Public Administration Education in Transition*, edited by Thomas Vocino and Richard Heimovics
3. *Centenary Issues of the Pendleton Act of 1883*, edited by David H. Rosenbloom with the assistance of Mark A. Emmert
4. *Intergovernmental Relations in the 1980s*, edited by Richard H. Leach
5. *Criminal Justice Administration: Linking Practice and Research*, edited by William A. Jones, Jr.

Strategic Management for Public and Nonprofit Organizations

Alan Walter Steiss

Virginia Polytechnic Institute and State University
Blacksburg, Virginia, U.S.A.

MARCEL DEKKER, INC.   NEW YORK · BASEL

Library of Congress Cataloging-in-Publication Data
A catalog record for this book is available from the Library of Congress.

ISBN: 0-8247-0874-1

This book is printed on acid-free paper.

Headquarters
Marcel Dekker, Inc.
270 Madison Avenue, New York, NY 10016
tel: 212-696-9000; fax: 212-685-4540

Eastern Hemisphere Distribution
Marcel Dekker AG
Hutgasse 4, Postfach 812, CH-4001 Basel, Switzerland
tel: 41-61-260-6300; fax: 41-61-260-6333

World Wide Web
http://www.dekker.com

The publisher offers discounts on this book when ordered in bulk quantities. For more information, write to Special Sales/Professional Marketing at the headquarters address above.

Current printing (last digit):
10 9 8 7 6 5 4 3 2 1

PRINTED IN THE UNITED STATES OF AMERICA

Preface

Modern organizations have been required to make significant transformations in response to an accelerating rate of change in technical, social, political, and economic forces. As a result of these changing forces, the management process has become more difficult, requiring greater skills aimed at guiding the future course of an organization in a rapidly evolving and uncertain world. These skills are the essence of strategic management.

Strategic management is concerned with deciding in advance what an organization should do in the future (strategic planning). It involves determining how the objectives of the strategic plan will be achieved and who will be responsible for carrying them out (resource management). And it entails monitoring and enhancing ongoing activities and operations to ensure that the strategic plan remains on track (control and evaluation). *Strategic planning* establishes overall strategic goals and objectives, selects appropriate policies for the acquisition and distribution of resources, and provides a basis for translating policies and decisions into specific action commitments. *Resource management* involves a determination of the particular configuration of resources (fiscal, personnel, materials, equipment, and time) to be employed and the judicious allocation of those resources to organization units that will carry out the plans and programs. Organizational structure and processes provide the means by which proposed strategies are implemented. *Control and evaluation* focus on internal requirements for implementing selected strategies. Performance is measured through various control mechanisms. Feedback from these evaluations is used to determine necessary modifications in the resource allocations and in the processes and structure of the organization. An assessment of the overall capability of the organization, as well as certain political considerations, helps to relate the organization to the demands of the external and internal environment.

Strategic management provides an interface between the performance capacity of an organization and the opportunities and challenges it must face in the broader environment. A primary aim of strategic management is to broaden the bases on which critical decisions are made. Strategic managers must attempt to (a) identify the long-range needs of the organization, (b) explore the ramifications of policies and programs designed to meet these needs, and (c) formulate strategies that maximize the positive aspects and minimize the negative aspects of the foreseeable future.

Many of the tasks identified in the strategic management process are currently assigned to various sectors in a complex organization. Planners plan, financial analysts prepare budgets, program personnel schedule and control resources for specific activities, and administrators monitor and evaluate. Some of these tasks are undertaken on a grand scale, while others are fairly routine. With the increasing complexity of organizational operations, however, the current division of labor established to deal with complexity may well become the major impediment to effective strategic management. Unless a more comprehensive framework is created to provide guidance and coordination, the sum of the component parts may be far less than an integrated whole.

Much of the material for this book is drawn from my experiences as Director of the Division of Research Development and Administration at the University of Michigan and, in particular, my participation in the M-Pathways Project. The M-Pathways Project was launched in 1996 in response to the university's commitment to implement the recommendations of a Strategic Data Plan. M-Pathways involved not only the development and installation of a new administrative information system, but, perhaps more importantly, a rethinking of how major functions and processes are conducted. M-Pathways changed how information is collected and used in every area of the university and also influenced how the university's administrators think about its overall organization.

Alan Walter Steiss

Contents

Strategic Management for Public and Nonprofit Organizations

1

Strategic Management

Strategic management involves the development of strategies and the formulation of policies to achieve organizational goals and objectives. In this process, attention must be given to both *external strategies* and *internal capabilities*. Strategic management offers a framework by which an organization can adapt to the vagaries of an unpredictable environment and uncertain future. An interface is provided between the performance capacity of an organization and the opportunities and challenges it must face in the broader environment. Strategic management is concerned with relating organizational resources to challenges and opportunities in the larger environment and determining a long-range direction relative to these resources and opportunities.

1 ORGANIZATIONAL STRATEGY

The term *strategy* is derived from the Greek *strategos*, meaning "general." In a military sense, strategy involves the planning and directing of battles or campaigns on a broad scale, that is, the responsibility of the general. In this context, strategy is distinguished from *tactics*, which involve the initiation of actions to achieve more immediate objectives. In the business world, however, "strategy" often is used to refer to specific actions taken to offset actual or potential actions of competitors. In a more fundamental sense, the term denotes linkages with the goal-setting process, the formulation of more immediate

1

objectives, and the selection of specific actions required in the application of resources to achieve these objectives. Richard Vancil has defined the concept of strategy as

> a conceptualization, expressed or implied by the organization's leader, of (1) the long-term objectives or purposes of the organization, (2) the broad constraints and policies ... that currently restrict the scope of the organization's activities, and (3) the current set of plans near-term goals that have been adopted in the expectation of contributing to the achievement of the organization's objectives [1].

As Bourgeois observed, "... the strategy concept has its main value, for both profit-seeking and non-profit organizations, in determining how an organization defines its relationship to its environment in the pursuit of its objectives [2]." Thompson and Strickland suggested that

> Objectives are the "ends" and strategy is the "means" of achieving them. In effect, strategy is the pattern of actions managers employ to achieve strategic and financial performance targets [3].

1.1 Strategic Decision Elements

Most complex organizations must deal with six strategic decision elements (see Table 1.1). Decisions along these six dimensions provide overall direction to all subsequent management activities within the organization [4]. These variables also act as constraints on future decisions. Thus, strategic decision elements (1) relate the total organization to its environment, and (2) provide unity and direction to all organizational activities.

TABLE 1.1   Strategic Decision Elements

Basic Mission	Basic purposes of the organization and its guiding principles for behavior.
Target Groups	Clientele or benefactors of program activities of the organization.

Goals and Objectives	What the organization seeks to accomplish through its programs:
	  Generally (goals) and
	  Specifically (objectives).

Program/Service Mix	Types of programs and administrative activities offered in order to accomplish the goals and objectives.
Geographic Service Area	Physical boundaries of the programs of the organization.
Comparative Advantage	"Differential advantage" desired over other organizations engaged in similar program activities.

Basic mission: Every organization must first determine its fundamental purpose and guiding principles for program activities. As Drucker observed,

> A business mission is the foundation for priorities, strategies, plans, and work assignments. It is the starting point for the design of managerial jobs and, above all, for the design of managerial structures. . . . Actually, "What is our business?" is almost always a difficult question and the right answer is usually anything but obvious. The answer to this question is the first responsibility of strategists. Only strategists can make sure that this question receives the attention it deserves and that the answer makes sense and enables the business to plot its course and set its objectives [5].

Specific decision issues to be addressed include

1. Major constituencies of the organization and the nature of the obligations to each constituency;
2. Relative emphasis placed on the various program activities that could be undertaken;
3. Role of the organization within its broader environment;
4. Any particular priorities that will shape the nature of the organization; and
5. Other decisions that represent broad commitments and directions for the development of the organization as a whole.

While focusing on broad purposes, this mission statement must also convey specific decisions about the priority given to various programs or services, the basic character of the organization as a whole, and expectations of support by participants in the organization. These "guiding principles" set the tone and direction for the organization as a whole.

Target groups: Specific decisions must be made about the target groups to be served by the organization within the context of its mission statement. These target groups or clientele should be described in terms of their needs and demographic characteristics. The term *stakeholder* frequently is used in connection with corporate strategic management and planning procedures. Stakeholders are claimants on the organization. They depend on the organization for the realization of some of their goals and thereby have an important stake in its activities. The organization, in turn, depends on these individuals and groups for the full realization of its purpose.

The principal stakeholders of many organizations are "members" who have made various tangible commitments to the programs of the organization. In other situations, the organization's "customers" are members of a broader public who avail themselves of the services of the organization on an "as needed" basis. The roles played by various institutions and agencies that may support and/or regulate the organization also must be identified (e.g., governments, foundations, industrial sponsors, and so forth). For most organizations, these external entities (organizations in themselves) continue to increase in importance. It is critical for management purposes to define the "needs" and characteristics of these entities along with the more traditional client groups.

Goals and objectives: Goals represent the end results that an organization seeks to achieve in order to fulfill its mission and meet the needs of its clientele or stakeholders. In general, it is useful to identify three categories of goals:

1. Goals for societal development—the results desired in terms of the contributions of the organization to its broader environment;
2. Goals for clienteles or stakeholders—outcomes that facilitate the development of target groups—economic, social, political, physical, emotional, intellectual, moral, and so forth; and
3. Goals for organizational development—the resource-related ends desired in order to facilitate goal attainment in the other two areas.

Decisions made in each of these categories help to further identify the unifying themes of a complex organization.

As will be discussed in greater detail in Chapter 3, there is also a hierarchy of objectives.

1. Strategic objectives define the expected change in conditions, welfare, or behavior as a consequence of the initiation of some program or activity and relate to the impact of the program or activity the organization's clientele or service groups (usually external).
2. Management objectives describe specific program actions in terms of *how* and *where* specific resources (project budgets) should be allocated, and identify the commitments required to translate a strategic objective into specific activities.
3. Operational objectives are associated with the implementation and control of specific tasks and the assignment of specific resources to achieve strategic and management objectives and frequently reflect explicit performance measures that can be adopted to monitor activities.

Program/service mix: The next step is to define the programs and services to be offered by the organization in order to accomplish its goals and objectives and thereby serve the needs of its clientele and fulfill its mission. In this context, there are three strategic decision issues:

1. The programs or services to be offered;
2. Relative emphasis (priorities) to be placed on the programs; and
3. Targets for new program development over an extended time horizon.

Many organizations typically have focused only on the first of these issues. The changing nature of the environment for most organizational activities, however, requires that increasing attention be given to the second and third decision issues as well.

Geographic service area: The fifth strategic decision element involves an identification of the geographic areas served by the various programs of the organization. Depending on the program, an organization may participate in varying degrees in local, state, regional, or national "markets." All of the strategic decision elements are highly interdependent, of course, but the issue of geography is particularly tied to the target groups or clientele identified by the organization.

Comparative advantage: Finally, an organization must seek to identify how it will gain a "competitive edge" or "differential advantage" over other organizations offering similar programs to similar target groups or markets. The key decision here involves the basis on which the organization will strive to differentiate itself from competitors. The basis for differentiation may well be in one or more of the other strategic decision areas; for example, the particular types of programs emphasized by the organization or the uniqueness of its particular goals and objectives. On the other hand, the basis for differentiation may be nonstrategic in nature; for example, the sense of exclusiveness that membership in the organization may suggest.

Strategic decision elements are interdependent. Where one "enters the circle" for strategic evaluation often is dictated by the needs and circumstances of the organization in question. In the case of a well-established organization, for example, the nature of the target groups traditionally served may determine the specific goals and objectives to be pursued, rather than the reverse being true. It simply may not be feasible to consider changing the definition of the target market in order to put a new set of goals and objectives into place.

1.2   Functional and Program Strategies

The mission statement identifies what an organization is and what it intends to do in a collective sense. *Functional strategies* must build on this mission statement by addressing in a systematic manner the "how" questions of the total organization. Functional strategies serve as the initial steps toward the implementation of an overall strategic plan for the organization by focusing on critical issues related to organizational structure, finance, membership size and recruitment, human resource development, and facilities. In short, functional strategies should *drive* decision-making regarding finances, facilities, and the like, rather than the other way around.

Functional strategies should be formulated in advance of program-level strategies to ensure that the more specific program strategies are guided by an internally consistent set of parameters. For example, any strategy formulated in support of a particular program must take cognizance not only of the decisions made as part of the total organizational strategy, but also the overall financial outlook of the organization, availability of personnel and facilities, and other contextual variables.

At the program level, each subunit should formulate competitive strategies that encompass the same dimensions included at the organizational level. The strategic plans for individual subunits should also include statements of resource requirements in order to facilitate the review process by higher levels of management. Decisions at the program level are constrained not only by organizational strategy but also by the functional strategies that permeate all areas of the organization.

The final level of strategy includes those actions that each subunit intends to implement in order to achieve its overall strategy. What kinds of recruitment strategies should be developed to attract the identified target or client groups? What program changes are necessary in order to serve the needs of the identified target markets? Will it be necessary to hire new personnel to give leadership to new program initiatives? What financial strategies must be employed in order to increase external support for programs? Given a new statement of program priorities, is there a need to re-evaluate the present distribution of funds among the subunits responsible for program implementation? These and other implementation strategies at the program level are analogous to the strategies of production, marketing, engineering, and so on, that are found within a division of any diversified firm.

2 A FRAMEWORK FOR STRATEGIC MANAGEMENT

Today's manager is faced with an accelerating rate of change in technical, social, political, and economic forces. Through all of these changes, the organization must be directed to meet unprecedented challenges. In the past, organizations often were relatively small and focused on one major product or service. Tremendous changes have taken place in the size and complexity of modern organizational operations. As a result of these changing forces, the management process has become more difficult, requiring greater skills in planning, analysis, and control. These skills, aimed at guiding the future course of an organization in a changing and uncertain world, are the essence of strategic management.

2.1 Strategic Management Defined

As applied in the private sector, Fred R. David defined strategic management as

> the art and science of formulating, implementing, and evaluating cross-functional decisions that enable an organization to achieve its objectives. As this definition implies, strategic management focuses on integrating management, marketing, finance/accounting, production/operations, research and

development, and computer information systems to achieve organizational success [6].

Advocating its application in the not-for-profit sector, the Alliance for Nonprofit Management asserts that

strategic management is the application of strategic thinking to the job of leading an organization.... It entails attention to the "big picture" and the willingness to adapt to changing circumstances, and consists of the following three elements:

- formulation of the organization's future mission in light of changing external factors such as regulation, competition, technology, and customers
- development of a competitive strategy to achieve the mission
- creation of an organizational structure which will deploy resources to success-fully carry out its competitive strategy [7].

Rowe, Mason, and Dickel suggested that strategic management should be

seen as a "total" system perspective and not merely as the process of choos-ing from among alternative long-range plans. It reflects the organization's "strategic capability" to balance the demands imposed by external and in-ternal forces and to integrate the overall functioning of the organization so as to allocate resources in a manner best designed to meet goals and objectives [8].

David suggested that the strategic management process consists of three stages [9]:

Strategy formulation: Developing a mission statement, identifying exter-nal opportunities and threats, determining internal strengths and weak-nesses, establishing long-term objectives, formulating alternative strate-gies, and selecting particular strategies to pursue.

Strategy implementation: Establishing annual program objectives, devising policies, motivating employees, and allocating resources to ensure the successful execution of formulated strategies; developing a strategy-sup-portive culture, creating an effective organizational structure, preparing budgets, and developing and utilizing information management systems.

Strategy evaluation: Reviewing external and internal factors that are the bases for current strategies; measuring program performance; and taking corrective actions [9].

In a similar vein, Thompson and Strickland identify the five tasks of strategic management as

1. Formulating a strategic vision of where the organization needs to be headed—providing a sense of purpose, a long-term direction, and a clear mission as to what is to be accomplished.

2. Converting the strategic vision and mission into measurable objectives and performance targets.
3. Developing and testing strategies designed to achieve the desired results.
4. Implementing and executing the chosen strategy efficiently and effectively.
5. Evaluating performance, reviewing new developments, and initiating corrective adjustments in long-term direction, objectives, strategy, or implementation in light of actual experience, changing conditions, new opportunities, and new ideas [10].

2.2 Basic Components of Strategic Management

Over the past 20 years, efforts have been made to develop mechanisms to more fully integrate the fundamental objectives of effectiveness, efficiency, and accountability. A *strategic management continuum* addresses these basic objectives through:

Strategic planning (effectiveness): Doing the right things.
Resource management (efficiency): Doing things right.
Control and evaluation (accountability): Being held responsible for what is done.

Strategic management is concerned with deciding in advance what an organization should do in the future (strategic planning), determining how it will be done and who will do it (resource management), and monitoring and enhancing ongoing activities and operations (control and evaluation). It involves the combined effect of these three basic components in meeting the goals and objectives of an organization (Figure 1.1).

Strategic planning identifies the specific actions required to carry out a given strategy. *Resource management* involves a determination of the particular configuration of resources to be employed and the allocation of those resources to units within the organization that will carry out the plan. Organizational structure and processes, and the allocation of resources, provide the means through which proposed strategies are implemented. *Control and evaluation* focus on internal requirements for the implementation of selected strategies. Feedback from various control mechanisms is used to determine any necessary modifications of the resource allocations and in the processes and structure of the organization to meet environmental demands and to ensure the success of a strategy. *Performance evaluation* ties the output of the organization to the requirements of the internal environment. An assessment of the overall capability of the organization, as well as certain political considerations, helps to relate the organization to the demands of the external and internal environments.

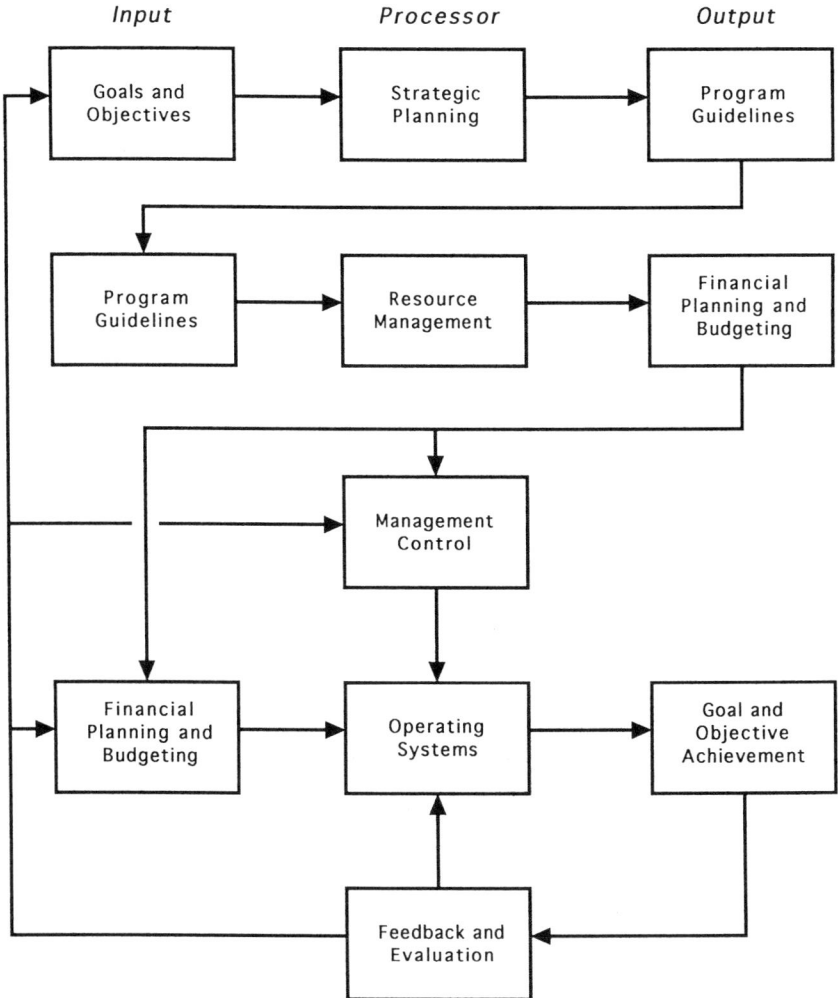

FIGURE 1.1 The strategic management process.

2.3 Strategic Planning

Various writers often have used the concepts of strategic planning and strategic management interchangeably. The Alliance for Nonprofit Management, however, has observed:

> Strategic planning is only useful if it supports strategic thinking and leads to strategic management—the basis for an effective organization. Strategic

thinking means asking, "Are we doing the right thing?" Perhaps, more precisely, it means making that assessment using three key requirements about strategic thinking: a definite purpose in mind; an understanding of the environment, particularly of the forces that affect or impede the fulfillment of that purpose; and creativity in developing effective responses to those forces [7].

Mark Moore asserted that "thinking strategically in the public sector requires managers to assign equal importance to substance, politics, and organizational implementation [11]."

As used here, strategic planning is that component of the strategic management system designed to (1) clarify goals and objectives, (2) determine policies for the acquisition and distribution of organizational resources, and (3) establish a basis for translating policies and decisions into specific action commitments. Strategic planners identify the long-range needs of an organization, explore the ramifications and implications of policies and programs designed to meet these needs, and formulate strategies to maximize the positive aspects and minimize the negative aspects of the foreseeable future. Strategic planning stresses the critical need to make strategic decisions that will ensure an organization's ability to successfully respond to an environment that is dynamic and changing (often in unpredictable ways). This emphasis stands in contrast to other long-range planning approaches, which assume that current knowledge about future conditions is sufficiently reliable to ensure the validity of the plan over the duration of its implementation. The primary output of strategic planning should be a series of guidelines within which more detailed plans and programs can be designed and implemented.

The concept of strategic planning has evolved over the past two decades as a response to the need for a more dynamic planning process—one that would permit continued efficacy of decisions to be tested against the realities of current conditions and, in turn, corrected and refined as necessary. As applied in government, it has been suggested that strategic planning

> is the process of identifying public goals and objectives, determining needed changes in those objectives, and deciding on the resources to be used to attain them. It entails the evaluation of alternative courses of action and the formulation of policies that govern the acquisition, use, and disposition of public resources [13].

A major purpose of strategic planning is to support decision making with the formulation of alternative courses of actions that will have long-term, desirable consequences. It should involve an examination of alternative courses of actions and the impacts and consequences that are likely to result from their implementation. Explicit provision should be made for dealing with the uncertainties of probabilistic futures. Strategic planning should be part of a continuous process that includes the allocation and management of resources, as well as performance evaluation and feedback. Peter F. Drucker defined strategic planning as

> the continuous process of making present entrepreneurial *(risk-taking) decisions* systematically and with the greatest knowledge of their futurity; organizing systematically the *efforts* needed to carry out these decisions; and measuring the results of these decisions against the expectations through organized, *systematic feedback* [13].

2.4 Resource Management

The resource management problem is as old as mankind. People have always been concerned with the allocation of scarce resources to achieve specific objectives. In theory, the problem is quite simple—it is difficult only in practice. One merely has to decide what is wanted (specification of goals and objectives), measure these wants (quantification of benefits sought), and then apply the available means to achieve the greatest possible value of the identified wants (maximize benefits). In contemporary society, the *means* become the financial resources of complex organizations, and, therefore, the problem is to *maximize benefits* (once specified and quantified) for any given set of financial inputs (i.e., specified and quantified costs).

Resource management involves (1) programming goals and objectives into specific programs, projects, and activities, (2) designing organizational processes to carry out approved programs and plans, and (3) staffing these processes and procuring the necessary resources to carry out the plans and programs. Effective resource management requires a continuous search for more productive ways to operate the organization and to assess its ability to meet changing environmental conditions. Resource management is the link between goals and objectives and the actual performance of organizational activities.

Strategic planning raises fundamental questions: What is the organization doing and why? These questions, in turn, force an examination of current practices and processes, and an identification of those activities that may be inappropriate, erroneous, or obsolete. Redesigning current processes in order to improve existing operations means getting to the root of things, not merely continuing to struggle with suboptimization. It may be necessary to disregard existing structures and procedures and invent new ways of accomplishing critical objectives. Resource management may rely upon continuous improvement programs, such as those fostered by total quality management (TQM) techniques, Hoshin planning, Quality Function Deployment, and other methods to enhance quality and productivity. Alternatively, resource management may require dramatic, holistic changes when an organization redesigns (or reengineers) its processes to achieve significant improvements in performance.

The common denominator among the various resources of any organization is the cost involved in their utilization. Therefore, the focus is often on financial resources. No decision is free of costs, whether or not it leads to the actual commitment of financial resources. However, the tendency is to think of costs strictly in terms of inputs—the resources required to support personnel, equipment, materials, and so forth. Costs that cannot be conveniently measured in dollar terms are all too often dismissed as noncost considerations. Future costs, however, may have important economic implications beyond their measurable monetary value. A basic tenet in strategic management is that costs should be incurred only if by so doing, the organization can expect to move toward the achievement of agreed-upon goals and objectives.

Primary outputs of the resource management process are analyses of the costs and benefits associated with various strategic alternatives and the financial plans and budgets required to implement the selected alternative. The *budget process* provides a primary linkage between resource requirements and strategic management by focusing on the application of analytical models for the allocation of scarce resources and the evaluation of alternative strategies at the program level. The traditional role of a budget has been to serve as a control mechanism to ensure financial integrity, accountability, and legal compliance. The budget, however, also can provide an important tool for management when used to ascertain operating economies and performance efficiencies. As a component of strategic management, the budget must reflect organizational goals and objectives and the overall effectiveness of programs in meeting client and community needs.

The most difficult part of strategic management and the least receptive to mechanical approaches involves the *management of change*. Many organizations focus their change management efforts on identifying and implementing innovations, especially in terms of the introduction of new technology. They mistakenly assume that the effects of technology are independent of the organizational structure and processes in which the technology is embedded. Research has shown that while investments in information technology often are associated with higher productivity, complementary changes in organizational processes and practices often are more important, and more difficult, to achieve.

2.5   Control and Evaluation

As Martin Gannon observed, "planning and control are intimately related and, in fact, represent opposite sides of the same coin. Without planning, there can be no control [14]." Control can do relatively little to reduce the uncertainty that surrounds many organizational activities. While programs may be carried out more efficiently, more important issues of effectiveness—the ability to achieve long-range objectives—may be left largely unresolved. On the other hand, without an adequate set of control mechanisms to monitor the continuously changing decision environment, long-range plans may become little more than a record of good intentions or worse yet, static fixtures that impede rather than advance the goals and objectives of the organization or community.

Early definitions of management control tend to emphasize the need for corrective action when deviations occur from some predetermined course of events. In one of the better-known definitions, Henri Fayol suggested that "Control consists of verifying whether everything occurs in conformity with the plan adopted, the instructions issued, and principles established. It has for an object to point out weaknesses and errors in order to rectify and prevent recurrence [15]." Robert Mockler placed greater emphasis on positive action in his definition of management control as

> a systematic effort to set performance standards consistent with planning objectives, to design information feedback systems, to compare actual performance with these predetermined standards, to determine whether there are any deviations and to measure their significance, and to take any action required to assure that all corporate resources are being used in the most effective and efficient way possible in achieving corporate objectives [16].

Accounting procedures have always been an important component of the control functions of organizations. The traditional role for accounting systems has been that of scorekeeping. In this function, reports of past performance are prepared for internal management as well as for outside groups such as stockholders, creditors, and the general public. These reports may pinpoint responsibility for deviations from previously approved plans. The extent to which these deviations can be attributed to specific components within the organization, however, depends on the degree of sophistication built into the accounting and related control mechanisms.

The role of public accounting is expanding as a consequence of the increased attention in recent years to the need for greater economy, efficiency, and effectiveness in government operations. There is growing recognition that, in addition to the functions of financial record keeping and external reporting, accounting systems can and should serve as a tool for strategic planning, resource management, and evaluation.

An *evaluation*, for the purposes of this discussion, is an assessment of the effectiveness of ongoing and proposed programs in achieving agreed-upon goals and objectives and an identification of areas needing improvement through program modification (including the possible termination of ineffective programs), which takes into account the possible influence of external as well as internal organizational factors. An evaluation can focus on the extent to which programs are implemented according to predetermined guidelines (*process evaluations*) or the extent to which a program produces change in the intended direction (*impact evaluations*).

Standard approaches for conducting an evaluation include (1) before and after comparisons, (2) time–trend–data projections, (3) with and without comparisons, (4) comparisons of planned versus actual performance, and (5) controlled experimentation. The selection of an appropriate approach will depend on the timing of the evaluation, the costs involved and resources available, and the desired accuracy. These approaches are not either/or choices. Some or all of the methods can be used in combination.

Evaluations can reduce uncertainty but cannot eliminate it totally. As Rossi observed, "Evaluations cannot influence decision-making processes unless those undertaking them recognize the need to orient their efforts toward maximizing the policy utility of their evaluation activities [17]." The full potential of such evaluation techniques as management and performance audits, sunset legislation, and program reconstruction has not yet been realized. Such techniques, however, provide additional incentives for administrators to undertake evaluations and apply the results in the improvement of program performance.

2.6 Information Management Systems

Contemporary strategic management activities are both information-producing and information-demanding. Important managerial feedback—soundings, scanning, and evaluations of changing conditions resulting from previous program decisions and actions—must be available to facilitate timely and effective decision making.

Such procedures also generate information intended to provide a basis for more informed decisions and actions over a range of time periods, locations, and perspectives. Feed forward information emerges from such components as projections and forecasts; goals, objectives, and targets to be achieved; program analyses and evaluations; and the projections of outcomes and impacts of alternative programs.

Timely information is essential to understand the circumstances surrounding any problem and to identify and evaluate alternative courses of action to resolve such problems. In this sense, information is incremental knowledge that reduces uncertainty in particular situations. Although vast amounts of facts, numbers, and other data may be processed in any organization, what constitutes information for strategic management depends on the problem at hand and the particular frame of reference of the manager. Traditional accounting data, for example, can provide information when arrayed appropriately in balance sheets and financial statements. Accounting data, regardless of how elaborately processed, may be relatively meaningless if the problem is related to an evaluation of the effectiveness of a new program. To contribute to improved decisions, the information available to management must be both timely and pertinent.

First and foremost, an information management system (IMS) involves processes to organize and communicate information in a timely fashion to resolve management problems. Many managerial decisions require information inputs that cannot be easily computerized. Thus, information management and decision-support systems must be designed to include explicit attention to nonquantifiable inputs as well as to data that may result from computerized applications. Hardware should be the last matter to be considered when thinking about an IMS. It is first necessary to decide what kind of information is needed—how soon, how much, and how often.

Large centralized data processing centers are not a prerequisite to or concomitant of an IMS. The desirability of such large "figure factories" or "number crunchers" depends more on the size and nature of the organization than on the purposes of the IMS. Many excellent systems are serviced by relatively simple, local data-processing operations, tailored to the particular needs of the users. Many organizations, sold on the notion that "bigger is better" have found that, with the rapid changes in computer technology, they are saddled with a "dinosaur" that consumes vast quantities of resources, but can not serve the expanding needs of particular users.

2.7 An Illustration of the Strategic Management Continuum

The strategic management continuum can be illustrated in the context of local government by the following. Assume that members of city council are aware of the problems of declining business in the downtown area due to congestion, lack of adequate parking, and the problem of access among various segments of the community (e.g., the elderly, low-income families, or handicapped). Various alternatives are considered and finally a decision is reached to inaugurate a public transit system in an effort to increase access and relieve some of the congestion.

A decision of this nature involves *strategic planning:* "The process of identifying public goals and objectives, determining needed changes in those objectives, and deciding on the resources to be used to attain them." The city council may also outline certain expectations regarding the overall ridership of the public transit system and the desirable ratio of costs to benefits to be attained by the transit system. When a plan or program fails to meet such broad standards, the remedies may be equally broad. They may include the recasting of goals and objectives, a reformulation of plans and programs, changes in organizational structure and improved internal and external communications. Strategic planning can assist decision makers in determining appropriate program adjustments when unpredicted changes occur in the broader environment of the organization.

The good intentions of the strategic plan are likely to go unrealized unless the process is further extended to include the techniques of *resource management.* A basic responsibility of management is to identify the appropriate processes required to carry out the plan, to budget the financial resources and personnel, and to provide a framework within which the use of these resources can be allocated and evaluated.

Using the public transit system to further illustrate this process, various modes of public transit might be examined in terms of costs and benefits, various route configurations analyzed, and budget priorities developed and evaluated. Resource management would likely involve the development and presentation of specific funding approaches and budget requests. The scheduling of resources must take into account the availability of funds, the sequence of activities or jobs, and the resource requirements and possible starting times for each activity. In the public transit example, resource scheduling would involve a determination of the timing of equipment acquisition, training programs for operators, the actual route designations, and the development of related public improvement projects.

Control involves the measurement and evaluation of program activities to determine if policies and objectives are being accomplished as efficiently and effectively as possible. Controls provide the basic structure for coordinating day-to-day activities and often try to anticipate possible deviations from established standards or criteria of performance. Continuous monitoring and evaluation of activities is appropriate to ensure that corrective action is taken on a timely basis. Output from an accounting system, for example, can provide managers with important performance-measurement information as decisions are made and actions taken that are expected to lead to desired results.

Continuing with the example of the transit system, studies would need to be made of the most effective means of implementation (city-operated versus privately-operated system), the routes to be served, number of personnel and facilities needed to operate the routes, and so forth. Service facilities would need to be acquired. Projections would be based on guidelines established in the strategic planning and resource management processes. Operating budgets must be established for the various routes, and these budgets, in turn, would serve as a basis to measure performance at various levels in the transit system.

Effective and comprehensive strategic planning may mean the difference between success and failure in the delivery of vital services. Successful resource management can mean the difference between the effective utilization of scarce resources and waste. The application of efficient management controls can mean the difference between "on time" and "late" in the achievement of a specific project.

2.8 Objective Methods and Subjective Ability

Strategic management can serve as both a conceptual framework for orches-trating the basic decision-making process and as a collection of analytical tools designed to facilitate the making of decisions. Assigning appropriate methodologies to the various stages in the decision process is a key responsibility of the strategic manager. Various analytical tools or approaches and their linkages to the three basic components of strategic management (as envisioned in this presentation), are shown Table 1.2.

TABLE 1.2 Analytical Tools for Strategic Management

Component of strategic management	Methodology
Strategic Planning	General systems theory
	Situation assessments (SWOT)
	Environmental analyses
	Multiple-policy matrices
	Objectives matrices
	Program analysis and evaluation
	Effectiveness measures
	Horizon planning
	Decision theory
	Simulation and gaming
	Dynamic programming
	Linear and nonlinear programming
	Enterprise resource planning
	Hoshin planning
Resource Management	Process reengineering
	Process mapping/event modeling
	Gap analysis
	Customer/user analysis
	Identifying core competencies
	Benchmarking
	Total quality management
	Activity-based costing
	Cost–benefit analysis
	Cost–effectiveness analysis
	Sensitivity and contingency analysis
	Strategic funds programming
	Financial ratio analysis
	Cash management
	Investment strategies
	Program budgeting
	Service level analysis
	Capital facilities planning
	Change management

(continued)

TABLE 1.2   (*Continued*)

Component of strategic management	Methodology
Control and Evaluation	Information management systems
	Decision–support systems
	Managerial and cost accounting
	Responsibility accounting
	Financial accounting
	Strategic control systems
	Formative and summative evaluations
	Network analysis (CPM and PERT)
	Work breakdown schedules
	Heuristics
	Feedback mechanisms

An objective of strategic management is to strike a balance between the polar pressures for methodological sophistication and ease of utilization. In applying a mixed bag of analytical techniques and methods to the variety of decision situations encountered in complex organizations, the primary focus of strategic management remains the integration of planning, analysis, management, and control in more productive harmony. In short, the functions of strategic management necessarily must be carried out as a balanced blend of objective methods and subjective ability.

3   SUMMARY

Effective strategic management must be a dynamic process, involving the blending and directing of available human, physical, and financial resources in order to achieve the agreed-upon goals and objectives of the organization. A basic purpose of strategic management should be to provide focus and consistency to the action programs of the organization. The effectiveness of such an approach must be measured by the results achieved and by the people served in terms of performance.

The concept of performance suggests a melding of the basic management objectives of efficiency and effectiveness. In this context, efficiency can be equated with doing things right, whereas effectiveness involves doing the right things. Moreover, effectiveness must be measured in terms of the response time required to make strategic adjustments when things go wrong. As a consequence, more systematic and responsive approaches to management are required. The objective is to achieve coordinated processes capable of yielding more rational decisions.

A primary aim of strategic management is to broaden the bases on which decisions are made. Strategic managers must attempt to (a) identify the long-range needs of the organization, (b) explore the ramifications of policies and programs designed to meet these needs, and (c) formulate strategies that maximize the positive aspects and minimize the negative aspects of the foreseeable future.

The following procedural definition identifies the scope of strategic management.

1. Establish overall strategic goals and objectives; select appropriate policies for the acquisition and distribution of resources; provide a basis for translating policies and decisions into specific action commitments (*strategic planning*).

2. Determine requirements to meet identified goals and objectives; determine the available resources (fiscal, personnel, materials, equipment, and time) required for organizational programs; establish the organizational processes, procedures, operations, and activities necessary to carry out the strategic plan; and judiciously allocate the resources of the organization in accordance with some system of priorities (*resource management*).

3. Schedule programs from the point of commitment to completion; exercise control by anticipating (and reacting to) deviations between predicted and actual performance; monitor activities to determine whether or not reasonable, feasible, and efficient plans and programs are being executed and if not, why not (*control and evaluation*).

Many of the tasks identified in this procedural definition are presently assigned to various sectors in a complex organization. Planners plan; financial analysts analyze costs and prepare budgets; program personnel schedule and control resources for specific activities; and administrators monitor and evaluate. Some of these tasks are undertaken on a grand scale, while others are fairly routine. With the increasing complexity of organizational operations, however, the "division of labor" established to deal with complexity may well become the major impediment to effective policy formulation and implementation. Unless a more comprehensive framework is created to provide guidance and coordination, the sum of the strategic management parts may be far less than an integrated whole.

The focus of strategic management, to date, has largely been on applications in a corporate setting. These concepts have yet to be extended to more general applications to public and nonprofit organizations. Selected case studies may be drawn from government, education, or health care. In the main, however, the public and nonprofit sectors represent new and virtually untapped areas for research and application of strategic management.

ENDNOTES

1. Richard F. Vancil. Strategy formulation in complex organizations. Strategic Planning Systems. Peter Lorange and Richard F. Vancil, eds. Englewood Cliffs, N.J.: Prentice-Hall, Inc., 1977, p. 4.
2. L. J. Bourgeois. Strategy and environment: a conceptual integration. Academy of Management Review. January 1980.
3. Arthur A. Thompson, Jr. and A. J. Strickland III. Strategic Management: Concepts & Cases. Boston, MA.: Irwin/McGraw-Hill, 1996, p. 6.
4. Robert C. Shirley. Strategic Planning in the Higher-Education Setting. National Center for Higher Education Management Systems, Boulder, CO, 1980.
5. Peter F. Drucker. Management: Tasks, Responsibilities, and Practices. New York: Harper & Row, 1974, p. 61.
6. Fred R. David. Strategic Management. New York: Macmillan Publishing Company, 1993, p. 5.
7. FAQ's. Alliance for Nonprofit Management. Washington, D.C., 2001. www.allianceonline.org.
8. Alan J. Rowe, Richard O. Mason, and Karl E. Dickel. Strategic Management and Business Policy: A Methodological Approach. Reading, MA.: Addison-Wesley Publishing Co., 1982, p. 2.
9. Fred R. David. Strategic Management. New York: Macmillan Publishing Company, 1993, pp. 5–6.
10. Arthur A. Thompson, Jr. and A. J. Strickland III. Strategic Management: Concepts & Cases. Boston, MA.: Irwin/McGraw-Hill, 1996, p. 3.
11. Mark H. Moore. Creating Public Value: Strategic Management in Government. Cambridge, MA.: Harvard University Press, 1995, p. 74.
12. Alan Walter Steiss. Public Budgeting and Management. Lexington, MA.: Lexington Books, 1972, p. 148.
13. Peter F. Drucker. Management: Tasks, Responsibilities, and Practices. New York: Harper & Row, 1974, p. 125.
14. Martin J. Gannon. Management: An Organizational Perspective. Boston, MA: Little, Brown, 1977, p. 140.
15. Henri Fayol. General and Industrial Management. New York: Pitman Corporation, 1949, p. 107.
16. Robert J. Mockler. The Management Control Process. New York: Appleton-Century-Crofts, 1972, p. 2.
17. Peter H. Rossi, Howard E. Freeman, and Sonia Wright. Evaluation: A Systematic Approach. Beverly Hills, CA.: Sage Publications, 1979, p. 283.

2

Organizational Decision Making: The Framework for Strategic Management

Decision making is one of the most pervasive functions of strategic management—whether in business or in government. If an organization is to achieve its goals and objectives, decisions must be made and action programs arising from these decisions must be planned, implemented, and controlled. However, studies of complex organizations often fail to give adequate attention to the more dynamic aspects of the decision process. By concentrating on a particular aspect or phase of decision making, these studies present a somewhat static picture, even though the dynamic characteristics of the decision process often are acknowledged. In the context of strategic management, decision making should be viewed as a multistage process involving the gathering, evaluating, recombining, and disseminating of information. It is a dynamic process, within which communication binds the process together and moves it from stage to stage in response to demands for both strategic and tactical decisions.

1 A DYNAMIC, OPEN, GOAL-DIRECTED, STOCHASTIC SYSTEM

Organization decision making can be considered an open system that seeks relative stability through a stochastic (trial-and-error) search process. An open system is one that receives inputs from its broader environment and/or acts on its environment through its outputs. Even though the decision-making process often appears to operate on a stochastic basis, its behavior is goal-directed. In the search process, the decision system of an organization may pass through a number of critical stages until eventually it settles down into a stable region, wherein conflict with some larger environment can be held to a minimum.

1.1 Adaptation to Change

An effective decision system does not merely seek equilibrium. The classic equilibrium model assumes that, in the face of change, a system is compelled by an overriding force to re-establish some pre-existing state of equilibrium. This traditional concept of equilibrium is incapable of describing important ranges of dynamic phenomena. An open system does not merely seek static continuity at some fixed point or level of equilibrium. Rather, in responding to forces of change, an open system frequently strives to create conditions that, under favorable circumstances, will permit some new level of stability to be achieved. At times, positive action may even be taken to destroy a previous equilibrium or even to achieve some new point of continuing disequilibrium. These dynamic qualities of open systems also require that a more thorough examination be given to the temporal sequences by which the structure of a system shapes its functions, and which, in turn, is altered by functional change.

Adaptation to change represents more than simple adjustments to events that impose themselves on the structure of the system. A primary characteristic of all open systems is that they are able to manifest a wide range of actions of a positive, constructive, and innovative sort for warding off or absorbing forces of displacement.

An organization, operating as a dynamic, open system, interacts continually with its broader environment. Expressed and unexpressed demands, emanating from the broader environment and from within the organization, continue to act as disturbances to the stability of the organization. These disturbances force the organization to develop and employ regulatory devices to counter these "dysfunctional" aspects.

The range of possible adjustments is governed by the relative number of responses available to the decision system when confronted by decision-demanding situations. In general systems theory, this condition is analogous to the Law of Requisite Variety—a set of regulators (R) can only be successful in warding off a set of disturbances (D) if the number of alternatives available to R (R's variety) is equal to, or greater than, those available to D (D's variety) [1]. It is possible to increase the range of variety available to regulatory devices through coupling, that is, the insertion of a regulator at some point between the disturbance and the system upon which it impinges. In this sense, coupling can be equated to increased access to information and channels of communication within the decision-making process.

1.2 A Decision Continuum

Clearly, not all decisions are of the same magnitude. In some instances, decision making may be a relatively simple task, and decisions may be reached as a matter of routine. In other areas, however, decision making may require the most demanding exercise of judgment, reasoning, and imagination. In the first instance, a decision is merely the mechanism that activates some pre-cast response—a regulatory device held in readiness for the advent of a decision-demanding situation. In more complex cases, however, a decision becomes a means of outlining a commonly acceptable response where none existed before. Such problem situations arise when (1) unfamiliar demands result in a lack of general agreement as to relevant patterns of response to achieve a particular objective, or (2) there is disagreement as to the objectives themselves. Such situations require creativity or innovation rather than the application of some pre-cast response. Thus, organizational decisions can be arrayed on a continuum, with *tactical decisions* at one extreme and *strategic decisions* at the other.

The majority of decisions handled effectively through the use of pre-cast responses are relatively routine, tactical decisions. If both the underlying conditions of the problem and the requirements that must be satisfied by the solution are known, programmed problem solving is the only approach necessary. In such cases, the task is merely one of choosing from among a few obvious alternatives. The decision criterion is usually one of economy (least cost). While many tactical decisions may be relatively complex and important, they invariably are unidimensional in nature and deal with matters of more immediate concern. Such short-term decisions, however, frequently have important long-term implications, which, if overlooked or ignored, may have serious repercussions for the organization and its client groups.

Decisions with far-reaching implications are generally decisions of *strategy*. To arrive at effective decisions in such instances, it is necessary: (1) to find out what the problem situation is, (2) to determine what alternative courses are open to change the situation, (3) to identify the most effective solution in light of available resources, and (4) to determine what additional resources might be necessary (and feasible) to achieve a more effective solution. A rational choice as to the course of action to be pursued can only be made after these steps have been taken.

The goals and objectives of an organization are established through strategic decisions. Decisions are made at the strategic level as to what kinds of services or products the organization will provide, who the beneficiaries will be, and what major capital and operating expenditures will be required to produce these services and products.

A third category must be inserted into the continuum of tactical–strategic decisions to account for decisions that may begin with programmed responses but require considerable reconstruction of program details. Such decisions might be identified as *adaptive decisions*.

Adaptive decisions seek to alleviate built-up pressures by removing the more immediate sources of demand or by providing a satisfactory alternative solution to that which is sought. Such decisions provide a means of modifying established patterns of response and, thereby, re-establish a flow of productive activity on a more or less stable basis. Since such adaptations may not eliminate the root causes of the problem, they are often only temporary solutions. As pressures of displacement continue to mount, adaptive decisions may no longer suffice, and in some instances, may even contribute to the total stress on the decision system.

Since accommodation is relatively less painful and less disruptive to the *status quo*, most activities that become dysfunctional to an organization are dealt with through adaptive rather than more innovative or creative solutions. Adaptive decisions lead to certain minor revisions in expectations, whereas more innovative decisions may lead to new or substitute expectations. The term expectations is used in this connection to denote the indigenous criteria against which persons affected by a particular decision may gauge its efficacy. The principal test of the efficacy of new patterns produced by a decision is their compliance with the minimal expectations sanctioned by the group, organization, community, or society.

When these expectations are met through adaptive decisions, fine adjustments are initiated that may lead to routinization of the response. The revised pattern gradually is "programmed" as a legitimized pattern of response, that is, as a regulatory device. Even though adaptive decisions may effectively dissipate those stresses that evoked the initial need for adjustment, such decisions may include some ill-conceived steps or unanticipated side effects, which, in turn, may produce new and unfamiliar stresses. In such cases, further adaptive decisions may be required to produce more satisfactory patterns.

1.3 Innovative Decisions

The structure of a decision is limited, however, in terms of its malleability. Adaptive adjustments must be devised within these limits. A major problem arises when the suggested accommodations call for changes that exceed these limits. Such situations require creative or innovative decisions to bring about major modifications in *ends* as well as *means*.

An innovative decision differs from an adaptive decision in the rate at which change comes about. A series of adaptive decisions may eventually introduce a substantial change in the structure of the system. An innovative decision, however, is a deliberate attempt to deal with a problem situation through a direct frontal attack rather than through oblique incremental operations.

This not to deny the value of incremental decisions. It may be said that the highest art of decision making is to know when to induce change in genuine increments and when to use the bold strokes of creativity and innovation. Situations requiring innovative (strategic) decisions usually involve issues that run to the roots of the organization—problems that are so central and compelling that they cannot be disposed of either obliquely or incrementally.

Once the need for an innovative decision is apparent and accepted, an overt appraisal should be made of the goals and objectives of the organization. The purpose of this assessment is to place the strategic innovation in its proper perspective. This appraisal often brings to the surface conflicting motives distributed among several otherwise discontinuous roles within the structure of the organization.

Decision making involves an aggregate of people collaborating through some imposed system—a system that they have inherited and continually remake. As a consequence, the goals and objectives of individuals frequently diverge and become inconsistent with the overall goals of the organization. So long as conflicting goals and objectives remain unstated (that is, are not explicitly held up to the light for examination), these inconsistencies may go unnoticed, even though they may be dysfunctional to the total system. However, when an innovative approach is introduced, an overt appraisal of the identifiable goals and objectives of the organization generally follows in an effort to place the strategic decision in its proper perspective. As goals and objectives are made more explicit, conflict may become more evident and must be dealt with if the organization is to retain its stability.

1.4   Rational and Nonrational Decisions

Organizational decisions often are judged to be "rational" or "irrational" (i.e., nonrational) depending on the particular perspective of individuals involved in the decision situation. Public decisions frequently do not appear rational in the sense that economic decisions generally are evaluated. Therefore, many writers have concluded that the criteria of rational decision processes often are not applicable to public decision situations.

Rational decisions result from a sequence of acts or flow of choices that are mutually related to the attainment of some objective or group of objectives. Rational decisions must be distinguished from *opportunistic decisions*, that is, decisions that are made as events unfold. Opportunistic decisions may not be mutually related, nor do they have a single, overriding design or plan. In short, opportunistic decisions do not entail planning, whereas rational decisions require the orderly, systematic procedures of planning. This statement does not preclude the possibility, however, that opportunistic decisions may have to be made during a planned, rational course of action.

A decision generally is defined as rational or nonrational according to some set of rules that delineate what actions are reasonable and consistent with a given set of premises. It is possible to identify four basic categories of *nonrational decisions:* (1) illogical decisions, (2) blind decisions, (3) rash decisions, and (4) ignorant action. These categories are illustrated by the following "decisions" made by a hypothetical local governing body in an effort to expand its economic base.

1. Our community needs more industry to provide jobs. Therefore, we have decided to zone that large tract of vacant land out by the bypass for industrial use. In this way, we will attract all the industry we need.

This is clearly an *illogical decision* since it confuses a possible outcome—the location of new industry—with a necessary consequence of the decision to zone for industrial use. The mere availability of land for development provides no guarantee that industry will select the designated location. In many parts of the United States, localities are significantly "overzoned" for industry, so that the aggregate supply of land is four to five times greater than the potential demand, even when this demand is projected far into the future.

2. The planning director suggested that site development and market feasibility studies should be undertaken before capital construction funds are invested in the improvement of our new industrial park. Such studies will take time, and, while we are waiting for the results, we could be reaping the benefits of new industry. Therefore, we have decided to go ahead with the extension of sewer and water improvements to the site.

This is an example of a *blind decision,* one that operates in the absence of complete information regarding the consequences of certain actions. The carrying capacity and configuration of the sewer system installed prior to the development of these proposed studies may prove to be inadequate or inappropriate to serve the needs of the future occupants of the industrial park. In the meantime, a considerable amount of public funds will be tied up in the construction project.

3. Since industry X has announced its intention to locate in this part of the state, we have decided to put up a shell building in the industrial park and offer them rent-free space. We are sure to get our investment back several times over in increased tax receipts.

This *rash decision* is made after an incomplete or hasty review of the discernible alternatives. Industry X may or may not be interested in a shell building (it may have its own unique space needs), and may or may not find the offer of rent-free space attractive. Also, there is no assurance that the community's investment in such a facility will be recouped in increased taxes.

4. Since we have limited funds for capital improvements, we have decided to put the money where the town is likely to get the best results. Forget about buying land for public recreation, extending street lighting in residential areas, or adding the wing to the public library. We're going to improve the facilities in the industrial park now and worry about those other things later, after we get the industry that can pay the taxes.

The proposed action ignores the fact that many of these community improvements are among the vary features that attract industry by making the community a more desirable place to live and, thereby, improving the competitive position of the community vis-a-vis other possible locations. Thus, it is *ignorant action* based on either mistakes about the facts or omissions of relevant facts.

Accepting the distinctions outlined above, it may be suggested that nonrational decisions are not completely devoid of consistency. Indeed, such decisions are perfectly consistent with their premises—it is the premises that are in error. Therefore, what may be judged as a nonrational or irrational action by an observer may seem totally rational to the decision maker, based on their set of premises. A principle objective of strategic management, therefore, should be to assist in making decisions more rational, that is, to circumvent the shortcomings brought about by these forms of nonrational action.

1.5 Incremental Decisions

Charles Lindblom and others have suggested that decision makers seldom face the clear-cut problems suggested by the rational model [2]. Moreover, information is scarce and therefore expensive, and decision makers seldom are willing or able to incur the high cost of data collection for the sake of complete rationality in their decisions.

Lindblom offers the concepts of *disjointed incrementalism* and *partisan mutual adjustments* as the basis for a counter-theory to the rational model. He argues that the only policy alternatives decision makers are willing to consider are those for which the consequences are known incrementally—those that vary only slightly from the status quo. Human ability to foresee the consequences of government action, according to this perspective, is so limited that objectives must be approached in small, manageable steps. Since the problems confronting the decision maker are continually redefined, incrementalism allows for countless adjustments that make the problem more manageable. Most decisions, therefore, are simply marginal adjustments to existing programs. The question of the ultimate desirability of most programs arises only occasionally.

Lindblom also suggests that people can coordinate with each other without anyone coordinating them, without a dominant common purpose, and without rules that fully prescribe their relations to each other. They achieve this coordination by mutually adjusting their positions from their individual partisan perspectives. Lindblom and his followers conclude that partisan mutual adjustment is a positive factor in the current system of decision making. By dividing an organizational structure into interacting areas, Lindblom suggests that competition among units will lead to optimal decisions and actions.

The concepts of disjointed incrementalism and partisan mutual adjustment have a certain pragmatic appeal and have been embraced by both academics and practitioners in the field of public administration. Decision making under the incremental approach can be carried on with the knowledge that few problems must be solved once and for all. Since there is no "right" solution to any given problem, the test of a good decision is that various analysts agree on it, without agreeing that the decision is the most appropriate means to an agreed objective.

Incremental decision making, however, is essentially remedial, geared more to the amelioration of present imperfections than to the promotion of long-range solutions.

Many problems brought before decision makers have no precedents and therefore cannot be examined solely in terms of incremental differences. Such problems require innovative solutions; incremental adjustments may only postpone the inevitable or may even exacerbate the problem. Unlike day-to-day operational decisions that can be corrected if the incremental approach proves incorrect, while more fundamental decisions require strategic decisions, arrived at through a more rational approach.

1.6 Satisficing Decisions

The concept of *satisficing*, as originally formulated by Herbert Simon, provides a strategy for narrowing the search and screening process without necessarily reverting to incrementalism [3]. Under the satisficing model, when a decision maker finds an alternative that is good enough—one that suffices or resolves the dilemma for the movement—he or she refrains from further search (i.e., is satisfied), thereby conserving time, energy, and resources. Under this approach, the decision maker is not necessarily concerned with the best or optimal solution, only with moving toward a better position or a more satisfactory state. Therefore, the path through which the decision-maker moves is characteristic of a trial-and-error process. Unfortunately, in some quarters Simon's model has become a normative defense of the status quo, since many political decisions to which it is applied rarely exhibit any evidence of long-range planning.

Although in his discussion of satisficing, Simon tends to be relatively indifferent to high-level goal-determination processes, he makes it clear that one can call an alternative "satisfactory" only if it meets some set of standards established prior to its selection. Such standards, however, must be equated with goals and objectives. If they themselves are not ultimate goals, they must be evaluated on the basis of their relation to some set of ultimate goals. This notion of formulating standards of adequacy at the outset of the search process is closely related to the concept of "means–ends chains" introduced by Simon in his examination of administrative behavior [4]. The process involved in balancing ideals, estimates of feasibility, and probable costs of further search is generally far more subtle than many of the interpretations of Simon's conceptual framework would suggest.

The concept of *successive approximations* seems appropriate in this respect. Using this approach, the standards established at the outset of the search and screening process serve as the mechanisms for evaluation of alternatives. Although certain alternatives in the initial set might be put aside temporarily, they would not be totally discarded. Subsequently, in the development of successive approximations, some of these alternatives or elements of them might be reconsidered and combined with other alternatives to form a new, more effective alternative. Such an alternative would more closely approximate the expectations established by these standards or objectives.

Etzioni offers an alternative theory in an effort to reconcile these different perspectives [5]. His *mixed scanning* approach implies that, when the decision maker has the time and information and perceives the problems to be of importance, he or she will pursue a more comprehensive approach. In other situations, the decision maker will simply "muddle through."

2 STAGES OF DECISION MAKING

While attempts have been made to analyze decision making as a universal process, considerable differences exist in the ways in which decision responses are handled in an organization. It is important to recognize these differences and to systematically examine the unique attributes of the general classes of regulatory devices and their impact on the decision process.

2.1 Demands as the Inputs of a Decision System

As a rule, the decision process becomes more orderly and identifiable at the stage in which alternative solutions are formulated and evaluated. Earlier stages of decision making often are characterized by a good deal of randomness, with considerable arbitrariness in the sequence of steps taken. A systematic approach is required, however, in the analysis of these early stages if meaningful insights are to be derived. As Northrup has so aptly pointed out, "One may have the most rigorous of methods during the later stages of investigation but if a false or superficial beginning has been made, rigor later will never retrieve the situation [6]."

It must be recognized that many aspects of the broader environment have important impacts on the organization with regard to decision demands. Decision demands enter the system in the form of inputs. Easton has defined a demand as "an expressed opinion that an authoritative allocation with regard to a particular subject matter should or should not be made by those responsible for doing so [7]." A demand does not necessarily reflect the value preferences of the demand maker. In fact, demands may be used to conceal true preferences, as when a program is promoted for the purposes of generating support for some other, unexpressed course of action.

Demands may also arise from dysfunctional conditions in a given situation without taking the form of expressed opinions. Such conditions may be interpreted from within the system as constituting demand inputs, even though in the larger environment the conditions have not been identified or verbalized as such.

A demand may be narrow, specific, and relatively simple; or it may be general, vague, and complex. Demands may be expressed as specific grievances associated with a particular situation, or they may be generalized. Such generalized demands seldom include proposals for specific courses of action, although they may embody ill-defined, all-encompassing programs. *Expressed demands* may be directed toward specific individuals or groups within an organization, or may be ubiquitously oriented. However, every expressed demand carries with it a set of expectations concerning the responses that should come from the organization.

Unexpressed demands also arise from a variety of sources and assume multifaceted characteristics. As with expressed demands, they are evidence that someone within the organization has recognized the existence of unacceptable conditions. In other words, before demands can gain entry as inputs into the decision system, they must be sensed as demands. Someone within the organization must recognize that the conditions giving rise to the demands are "out of phase" with some acceptable norm or conditions within the desired state of the organization.

It is this perception of a demand that sets the decision process in motion. Very often, this perception is merely a sense of uncertainty or doubt that exists because constituent elements of a segment of the broader environment are unsettled or are not unified. As Dewey observed, "It is the very nature of the indeterminate situation which evokes inquiry to be questionable ... to be uncertain, unsettled, disturbed [8]."

This concept of uncertainty is a positive one, meaning more than a mere subjective sense of absence or deprivation. The uncertainty that exists stems from a particular uncertain objective situation. Objective observations of the situation do not coincide with the definition of what *should be*—a concept that may be subjectively or objectively defined.

An individual's conceptual frame of reference, in large measure, governs the way in which they approach an uncertain situation. Furthermore, this frame of reference will contribute to the identification of a situation as being "out of phase" with the presently accepted system. Background and training may provide individuals with well-constructed sets of concepts that make them more sensitive to certain problems that others might pass over unobserved.

Thus, the role of the strategic manager can be identified more clearly. The strategic manager must continually appraise various aspects of the accepted system and identify any elements in the broader environment that may seem to be potential disturbances to the organization. This role might be likened to a regulator that acts as a warning device against disturbances that threaten to drive a system out of some desirable set of states.

Decision demands may originate from within the organization itself, as well as coming from sources external to the organization [9]. The manner by which these inputs or demands are handled within the organization, however, varies only slightly whether the sources of uncertainty are external or internal.

2.2 Screening Demands to Determine Intakes

Once a situation has been identified as uncertain, four responses are possible (see Figure 2.1). Each of these responses involves a different degree of commitment to the decision process.

The first possibility is to disregard the uncertain situation, that is, to decide to do nothing about it. Such a response is likely when the demand is below some threshold of tolerance. If for some reason—such as time, cost, or effort—this response is invoked, the decision process will be cut short. For the purposes of this discussion, we have no further interest in such negative behavior.

The second possible response is to identify the uncertain situation as one that can be handled through programmed decision mechanisms. This response would suggest that some sort of memory bank exists within the decision system in which these programmed decision mechanisms are stored and against which uncertain situations can be tested to determine if an appropriate programmed decision is available. Again, the decision process is cut short by the application of a programmed response.

If either of the two remaining possible responses is invoked, the decision process moves to the next stage—that of *classification and definition*. Inputs are screened to determine the actual intakes into the decision system. This screening filters out those demands for which no further action will be taken at present and those which can be handled through programmed mechanisms. The individuals responsible for this screening are analogous to the "gatekeepers" in Easton's conceptual schema.

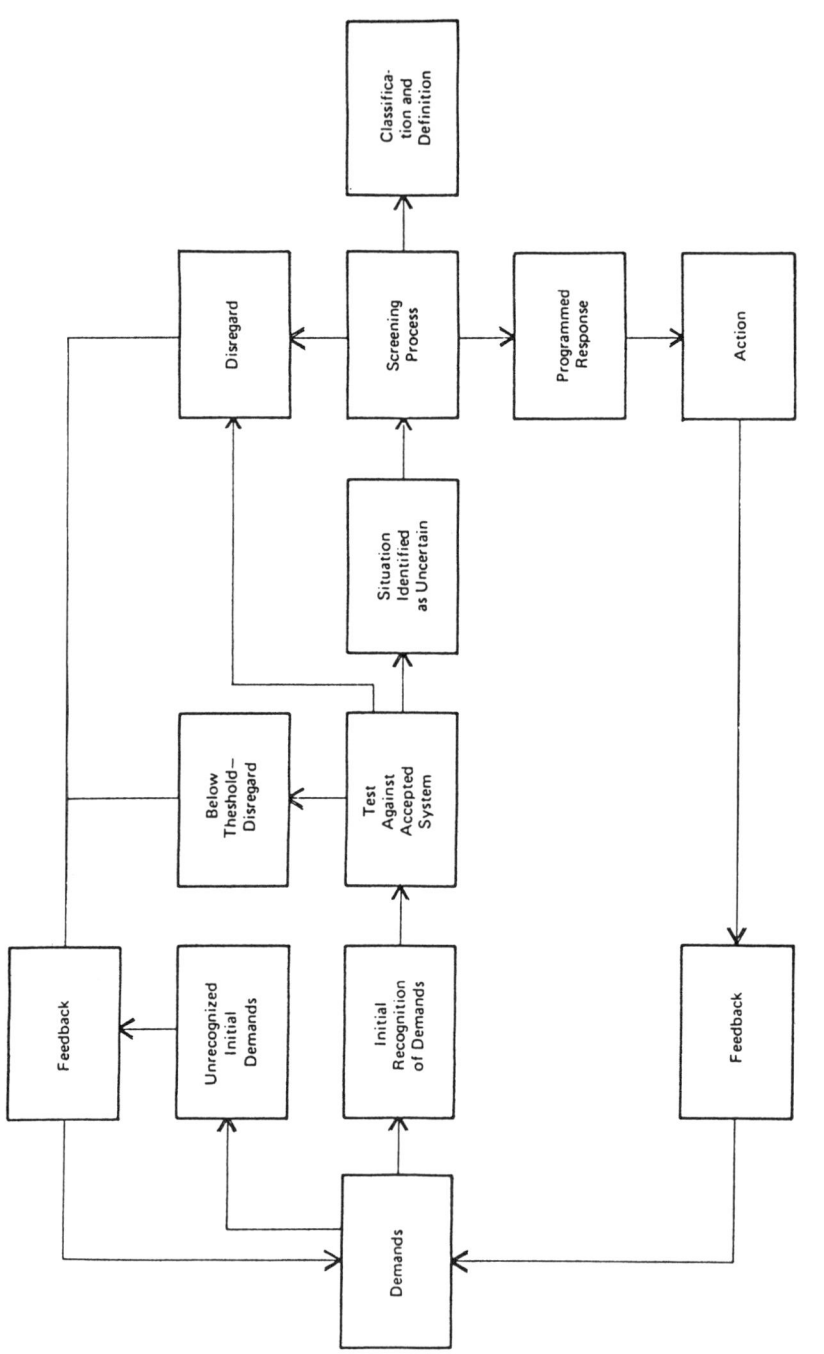

FIGURE 2.1 Screening demands to determine intakes.

Although uncertainty is essential to an initiation of the decision process, it is not sufficient to create a problematic situation, that is, one for which decision makers are likely to seek alternative solutions. As Dewey has observed, the uncertain situation "becomes problematic in the very process of being subjected to inquiry [10]." Under analysis, the problematic situation is made more explicit. As Rapoport noted, the first step in solving a problem is to state it.

> The statement usually involves a description of an existing state and desirable state of affairs where the factors involved in the discrepancy are explicitly pointed out. The success with which any problem is solved depends to a great extent on the clarity with which it is stated. In fact, the solution of the problem is, in a sense, a clarification (or concretization) of the objectives [11].

Vague statements of the situation lead to vague methods, where success is erratic and questionable. The more a given problem situation can be extended, the better the classification, and the greater the promise of a successful solution.

The first question to be asked about an uncertain situation is: Is this a symptom of a fundamental or generic problem or merely a stray event? A generic problem often can be handled through the application of programmed to adaptive responses. The truly exceptional event, however, must be handled as it is encountered [12].

Strictly speaking, a distinction should be made among four, rather than two, different types of problem sets. First, there is a truly *generic event*, of which the individual occurrence is only a symptom. Most of the problems confronting complex organizations fall into this category. As a rule, such generic situations require adaptive decisions. Frequently, programmed decision mechanisms are applied to the symptoms of a generic problem. Until the generic problem is identified, however, significant amounts of time and energy may be spent in the piecemeal application of programmed decisions to the symptoms without ever gaining control of the generic situation.

The second type of occurrence is one that, although unique in a given organization, is actually a generic event. For example, the choice of a location for a new sewage plant may be a unique situation as far as the current decision makers in a community are concerned. It is, of course, a generic situation that has confronted many other communities in the past. Some general rules exist for deciding on the best location for such facilities, and the decision makers can turn to the experience of others for these guidelines.

The third possible classification is the truly *unique situation*. In such cases, the event itself may be unique or the circumstances in which the event has occurred may be unique. For example, the huge power failure of November 1965, which plunged northeastern North America into darkness, was a true exception or unique event, at least according to the first explanations. On the other hand, the collision of two airplanes miles from any air terminal is a unique situation, not because airplanes do not run the risk of collision, but because the unique circumstances under which the event occurred.

The fourth type of event confronting the decision process is the *early manifestation* of a new generic problem. Both the power failure and the collision of the two airplanes, for example, turned out to be only the first occurrences of what are likely to become fairly frequent events unless generic solutions are found to certain basic problems of modern technology.

General rules, policies, or principles usually can be developed or adapted to deal with generic situations. Once an appropriate decision has been found, all manifestations of the same generic situation can be handled fairly pragmatically by adapting the rules or principles to the concrete circumstances of the situation. In short, such problems can be handled through adaptive decision making.

The unique problem and the first manifestation of a generic problem, however, often require greater innovation in the search for successful solutions. As illustrated in Figure 2.2, the relationships among these four categories can be described in terms of the two fundamental dimensions of *availability of rules and principles* for dealing with such problems and the *frequency of encounter* of these situations.

By far the most common mistake in decision making is to treat a generic problem as if it was a series of unique events. The other extreme, treating a unique event as if it was just another example of the same old problem to which the same old rule should be applied (that is, treating every problem incrementally), can have equally negative repercussions.

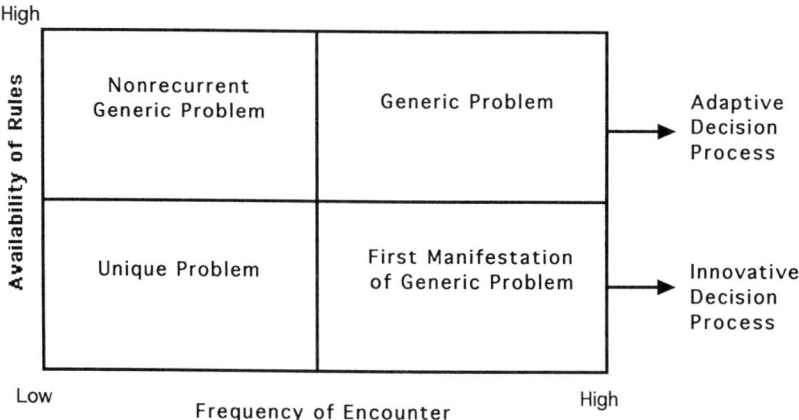

FIGURE 2.2 Classification and definitions of basic problems.

The role of the experienced strategic manager is to avoid incomplete solutions to problems that are only partially understood. The technical expertise of those closest to the situation should be used to classify the problem. Once a problem has been classified, it is usually relatively easy to define. A further danger in this step, however, is that of finding a plausible albeit incomplete definition of the problem. Safeguards against an incomplete definition include checking it against all observable facts and discarding the definition if and when it fails to encompass any of these facts.

The outcome of this analysis should be a clear definition of the problem. If the problem cannot be stated specifically, preferably in one interrogative sentence (including one or more objectives), then the analysis has been inadequate or of insufficient depth. Emotional bias, habitual or traditional behavior, and the human tendency to seek the path of least resistance may contribute to a superficial analysis, followed by a statement of the apparent rather than the real problem. An excellent solution to an apparent problem will not work in practice, because it is the solution to a problem that does not exist in fact. Short-circuiting this phase of the decision process may actually result in more time spent later to get at the real problem when it becomes painfully evident that further analysis is required.

2.3 Identification of Constraints and Boundary Conditions

The next major step in the decision process involves the clear specification of what the decision must accomplish. Five basic questions must be answered.

1. What objectives must be met and what are the minimum goals to be obtained?
2. What are the existing or potential constraints to an effective solution?
3. What measure of efficiency can be used relative to each of the objectives?
4. What standard can be applied for the evaluation of possible courses of action?
5. What definition of "most effective" is to be applied in evaluating the possible solutions to any given problem set?

These questions aid in the establishment of *boundary conditions*—the set of factors that define the field within which a feasible solution can and should be found. When techniques of operations research (such as linear or dynamic programming) can be applied, boundary conditions can be clearly identified and even given numerical values. In most organizational decision situations, however, the identification of boundary conditions may be a difficult undertaking.

Nevertheless, this stage of the decision process is crucial. A decision that does not meet the boundary conditions is worse than one that incorrectly identifies the problem. It is all but impossible to salvage a decision that starts with the right premise but stops short of the right conclusions. Furthermore, clear thinking about boundary conditions is essential to recognize when a course of action, brought about by a given decision, should be abandoned. Decision makers must be able to recognize a subsequent shift in objectives—in specifications—that may make a prior "right" decision suddenly inappropriate. As Drucker observed, "Unless the decision maker has kept the boundary conditions clear, so as to make possible the immediate replacement of the outflanked decision with a new and appropriate policy, he may not even notice that things have changed [13]."

Often the decision specifications to be satisfied are incompatible. In other words, to achieve objective A through the course of action prescribed by the decision may preclude the achievement of objective B, or at best, make this achievement highly unlikely. This dilemma represents the classic case in which boundary conditions were not fully and clearly identified. Similarly, decisions often are made which involve a gamble or so-called calculated risk. This type of decision, which may work if nothing whatsoever goes wrong, often emerges from something less rational than a gamble—a futile hope that two or more clearly incompatible specifications can be fulfilled simultaneously.

Determining boundary conditions requires a clear view of organizational goals and objectives. All too often, however, these goals are too vague to establish meaningful boundary conditions applicable to any particular decision situation. What is required is some mechanism whereby overall goals can be translated into more specific program objectives and through which identifiable boundary conditions can be tested against the more general (and more remote) organizational goals. Such mechanisms generally are available in deterministic decision situations. In stochastic situations, however, such mechanisms are more difficult to develop and apply.

2.4 Formulation of Alternatives

Several alternatives should be developed for every problem situation. Otherwise, there is a danger of falling into the trap of a false "either-or" proposition. There is a common confusion in human thinking between a true contradiction that embraces all possibilities, and a contrast that lists only two out of a number of possibilities. This danger is heightened by a tendency to focus on the extremes in any problem situation.

In adaptive decision making, for example, a standard set of alternatives may be selected for analysis with the outcome being limited to some initial set of "givens." This procedure tends to limit the evolutionary nature of alternative formulation. And as a consequence, this approach should be avoided, if possible, even in adaptive decision-making.

Alternative solutions are the primary means of bringing to light the basic assumptions concerning a given problem situation, thereby forcing an examination of their validity. Alternative solutions are no guarantee, however, of wisdom or the right decision. Nevertheless, an examination of alternatives can guard against making a decision that would have been seen to be wrong if the problem had been thought through more carefully.

Alternative approaches to a given decision-demanding situation differ according to the level of reflection reached. At first, they may be relatively vague, but as further observation is directed by the alternatives posed, they become more suitable for resolving the problem. As alternatives become more appropriate, empirical observations likewise become more acute. Perception and conception work together, the former locates and describes the problem, while the latter represents possible methods of solution [14].

The next step is to develop an understanding of the possible consequences, by-products, and side effects associated with each of the suggested alternatives (see Figure 2.3). This examination involves an identification of the implications of particular courses of action in relation to other aspects of the organization. This formulation leads to a proposition: if a given relation is accepted, then we are committed to other prescribed courses of action because of their membership in the same set. A series of such intermediate examinations leads to an understanding of the problem that often is more relevant to the decision-demanding situation than was the original conception.

The examination of suggested alternatives for their operational fitness involves an investigation of their capacity to direct further observations aimed at securing additional factual material. This examination may result in the rejection, acceptance, or modification of ideas in an attempt to arrive at more relevant alternatives. The possible range of alternatives will vary with the problem. It must be recognized, however, that alternatives, in part, are a function of the data and concepts at the disposal of the organization. When these are sufficient, useful alternatives are likely to emerge.

One possible alternative is always that of taking no action at all. This alternative seldom is recognized as a decision, although it is no less a commitment than any specific positive action. An unpleasant or difficult decision cannot be avoided by doing nothing, however. The potential consequences of a decision not to act must be clearly spelled out. By carefully considering the alternative of doing nothing, the traditional ways of doing things, which often reflect past needs rather than those of the present, may be examined more carefully.

Frequently an impasse is reached in the search for alternatives. In such cases, restructuring the problem may lead to new insights into possible courses of action. Problem restructuring involves the manipulation of the elements

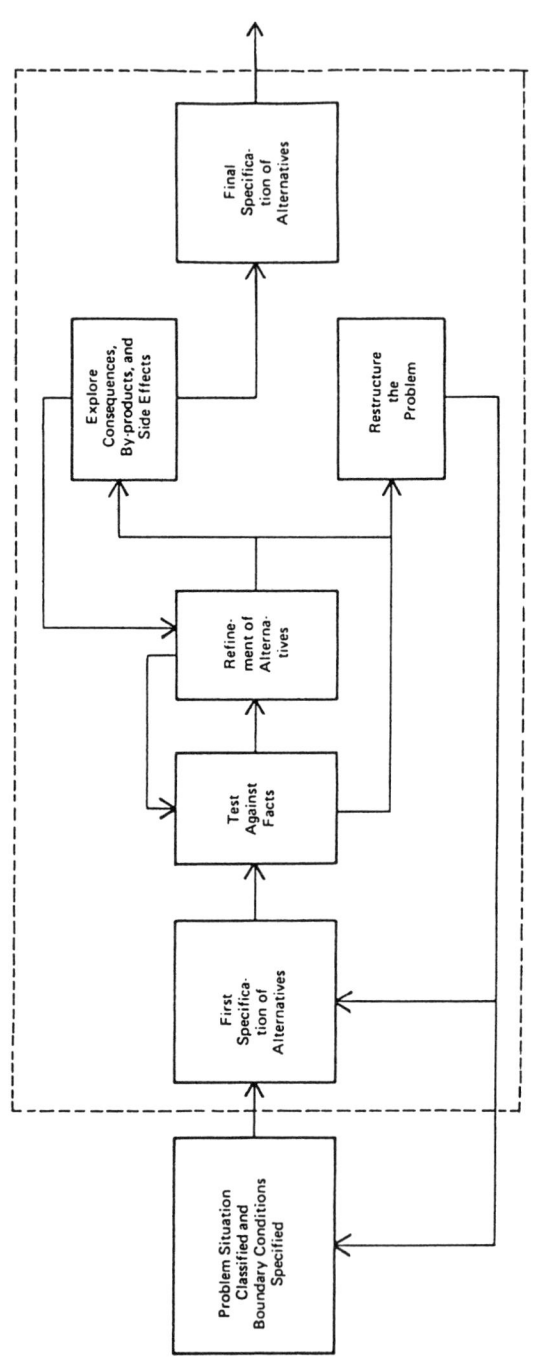

FIGURE 2.3   Formulation of alternatives.

of the problem. It may involve, for example, a change of viewpoint, or a permissible modification of objectives, or a re-arrangement of other problem elements. Framing and analyzing alternatives and their consequences in light of the problem and the relevant facts of the situation is a major part of all rational decision making. In spite of its primary role in the decision process, there are no simple hard-and-fast rules for hitting upon the right set of alternatives.

2.5   Search for the Best Solution

It is possible to determine the best solution only after a number of alternatives have been formulated and evaluated. If an adequate job has been done to this point, it likely will be found that there are several alternatives from which to choose. There may be half a dozen or so, all of which fall short of perfection but differ as to the area of shortcoming. It is a rare situation in which there is one and only one right solution. In fact, whenever analyses lead to this comforting conclusion, one may reasonably suspect the conclusion as being little more than a plausible argument for a preconceived idea.

There are two basic modes of operation for finding the best solution from among several alternatives (see Figure 2.4). The mode selected depends on the general class of decision sought: adaptive or strategic. Since adaptive decisions merely require that the alternative meet certain minimal expectations sanctioned by the organization, the best alternative can be selected on the basis of relatively straightforward criteria. The selected alternative should be one that provides a satisfactory solution to the problem (thereby alleviating the pressures created by the demand). At the same time, the selected course of action should create a minimum disturbance to established expectations. No single alternative may satisfy these conditions and, therefore, it may be necessary to combine elements from several alternatives to achieve these objectives.

A strategic decision requires more rigorous analysis and testing, since it ultimately will result in the modification or substitution of expectations. Several criteria may be useful in seeking the best strategic decision. These criteria deal with such issues as (1) uncertainty, (2) risk and expected gains, (3) economy of effort, (4) timing of alternatives, and (5) limitation of resources.

Most strategic decisions involve major conditions of uncertainty. In such cases, therefore, analyses of alternatives must provide for explicit treatment of uncertainty. Several techniques, applicable under varying circumstances, have been developed for this purpose. Since problems of uncertainty are so crucial to effective strategic decisions, a major section of Chapter 7 will be devoted to these techniques.

The risks associated with each proposed course of action must be weighed against expected gains. The terms "risks" and "gains" are used here rather than the more conventional concepts of "costs" and "benefits" for several reasons.

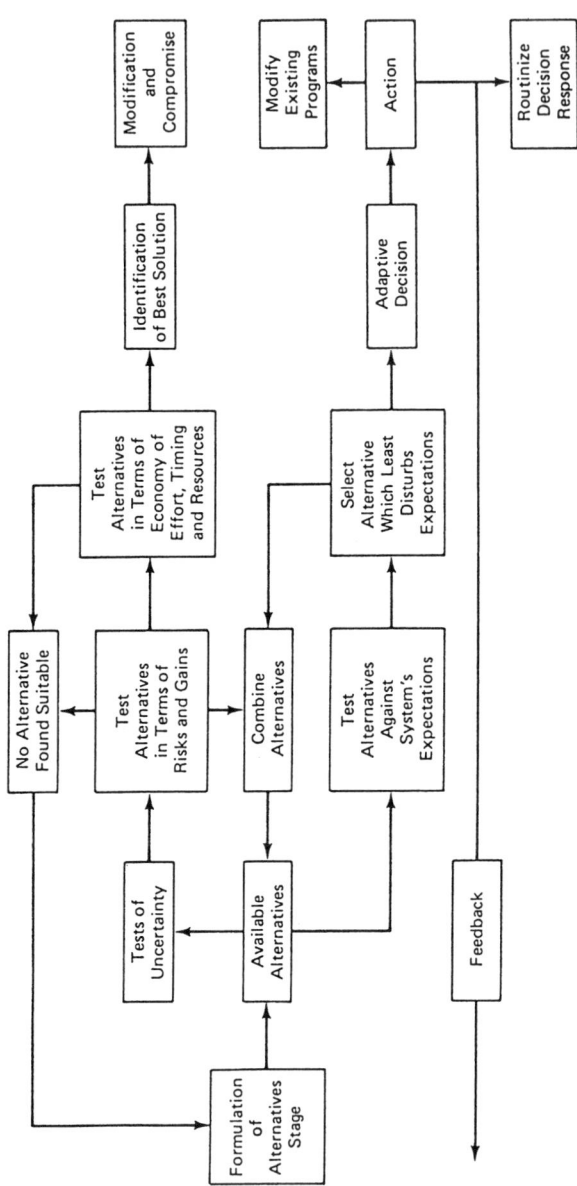

FIGURE 2.4 Finding the best solution.

Efforts to convert positive and negative aspects of any alternative into dollars and cents frequently results in too narrow a frame of reference. The concept of costs associated with strategic decision alternatives means something more than that which shows up on a profit and loss statement. In developing a cost–benefit analysis, items often are omitted because they are intangibles. Many of these intangibles are important risks that may seriously affect the outcomes of a strategic decision. Assessments of benefits, on the other hand, frequently involve a form of double counting. Direct benefits, for which dollar figures can be derived, often are counted again in terms of more indirect benefits. In arriving at a net gain figure, therefore, such indirect benefits must be discounted in order to avoid an unrealistic assessment.

There is no riskless action or even riskless nonaction. What is important, however, is neither the expected gain nor the anticipated risk, but the relationship between them. Every alternative should be evaluated on this basis. The value of such an analysis lies not in the end result but in the process pursued in arriving at this result.

The third criterion involves an assessment of the economy of effort. The various alternatives must be examined to determine which course of action will give the greatest results with the least effort. As Drucker observed, decision makers often use an elephant gun to chase sparrows or a slingshot against forty-ton tanks [15]. Grandiose schemes have many hidden risks which, if carefully considered, would reduce the overall economy of effort. By the same token, solutions that fail to set their sights high enough to produce optimal results may yield a series of incremental actions that, in the long run, will involve a much higher expenditure of effort.

The fourth criterion is concerned with the timing of the possible alternatives. If the situation is urgent, the preferable course of action may be one that dramatizes the decision and serves notice that something important is happening. If, on the other hand, long, consistent effort is needed, a slow start that gains momentum may be preferable. In some situations, the decision must be final and must immediately inspire those involved to seek new goals and objectives. In other situations, the first step is the most important—the final goal may be shrouded in obscurity for the time being.

Timing decisions is often extremely difficult to systematize; they may elude analysis and depend on perception. There is one guide however. Whenever a decision requires a change in vision to accomplish something new, it is best to be ambitious and to present the complete program and the ultimate aim. When a decision necessitates a change in people's long-standing habits, however, it may be best to take one step at a time, to start slowly and modestly, and to do no more at first than is absolutely necessary. These issues will be discussed further in Chapter 9 on the management of change.

The final criterion deals with the limitation of resources and is closely related to the notion of *systems readiness*—the capacity of the organization to undertake the proposed course of action. A basic problem of organizational decision making in both the public and private sectors is to achieve a balance in programs and the allocation of resources that will ensure a system readiness in the short- , medium- , and long-term futures. Achieving this objective requires flexibility in confronting a wide range of competing actions.

Decisions often are made, processes and procedures developed, and policies formulated without first asking: Are the means available for carrying out these actions? Perhaps the most important resource is the personnel who will be called upon to execute the decision. A less-than-optimal decision should not be adopted simply because the competence is lacking to do what is required. The best decision should always lie among genuine alternatives, that is, among courses of action that will adequately solve the problem. If such solutions demand greater competence, skill, and understanding than is available, then provision must be made to raise the capacity of those who must implement the programs associated with the best solution. All too often, substantial investments are made in organizational programs without adequate consideration given to the training of personnel necessary to effectively carry out the requisite activities.

2.6   Modification to Gain an Acceptable Decision

The effective decision maker must start with what is right or best rather than what is merely acceptable or possible because in the end compromises invariably will be necessary [16]. This factor relates back to the specification of boundary conditions. If it is not clearly known what will satisfy the boundary conditions, the decision maker can not distinguish between an appropriate and an inappropriate compromise. The decision maker gains relatively little if the decision process starts out with the question: What is acceptable? In the process of answering this question, important things usually are overlooked, and any chance of coming up with an effective solution—let alone the right answer—may be lost. The things that one worries about seldom happen, while difficulties no one initially thought about may turn out to be almost insurmountable obstacles.

After a best solution has been identified, the first step in seeking an acceptable decision is to make a reconnaissance of the expectations of those segments of the organization most likely impacted by this decision (see Figure 2.5). Unlike adaptive decisions, strategic decisions almost always require that expectations be altered or modified. Therefore, a careful appraisal must be made of expectations (both internal and external) to the organization. These expectations are relevant factors that must be accommodated by the decision.

Upon matching the proposed solution against the expectations of people within the organization, it may be anticipated that one of three conditions will

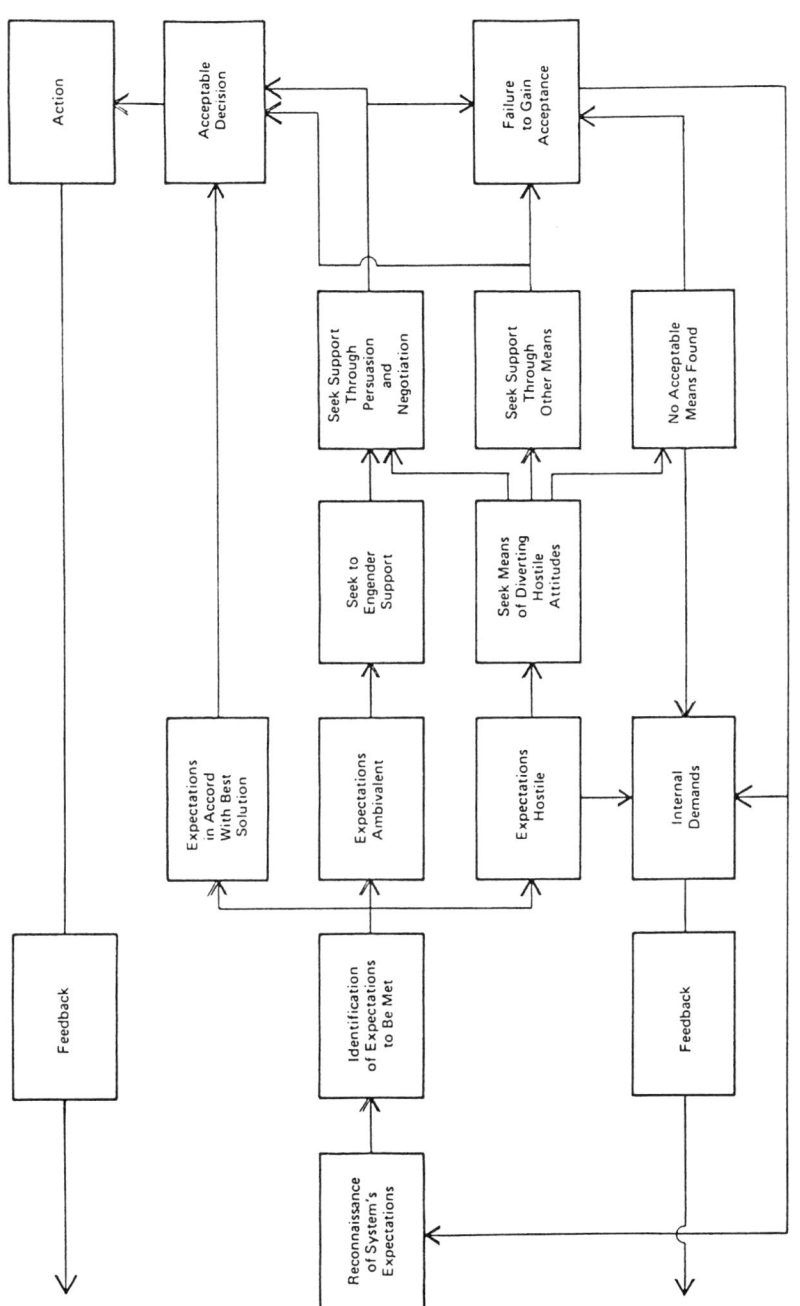

FIGURE 2.5 Achieving an acceptable decision.

prevail: (1) the expectations are in accord with the proposed solution, (2) the people are ambivalent with respect to the proposed solution, or (3) there is hostility with regard to the proposed solution. In the latter two cases, some means must be devised to divert the hostile attitudes and engender support for the proposed solution. If no acceptable means are found, internal demands will be heightened, and a further reconnaissance of the organization's expectations will be required.

This process of modification and compromise is somewhat akin to what other decision models have identified as "accommodating to the power structure." The more neutral notion of system expectations has been used here to give recognition to the role of the internal structure of the decision process, as well as to provide a model that is adaptable to both the power-structure and pluralistic approaches to decision making. The term expectations can include all factors, both internal and external, to the decision system.

2.7   Converting the Decision into Action

Although thinking through the boundary conditions may be the most difficult phase in the decision process, converting the decision into effective action is usually the most time consuming. Yet a decision will not become effective unless action commitments have been built in from the start. In fact, no decision has been made unless carrying it out in specific steps has become someone's work assignment. Until this is accomplished, the decision is only a good intention.

The flaw in many policy statements is that they contain no action commitments; they fail to designate specific areas of responsibility for their effective implementation. Converting a decision into action requires that four distinct questions be answered: (1) Who must know the decision?, (2) What action must be taken?, (3) Who is to take this action?, and (4) What must the action be, so that the people who must do it can do it? All too often, the first and last of these questions are overlooked with dire consequences.

Action commitments become doubly important when people must change their behavior, habits, or attitudes in order for the decision to become effective. Care must be taken to see that responsibility of the action is clearly assigned and that the people are capable of performing it. Measurement, standards for accomplishment, and incentives associated with the proposed action, must be changed simultaneously with the introduction of the decision.

2.8   Feedback Phase

Provision must be made throughout the decision process for feedback. Feedback occurs, intentionally or unintentionally, at many stages in the decision process. Much of this feedback is internal to the process, resulting in a recycling of a particular phase in order to achieve further refinements and modifications. The feedback that has an impact on the entire decision process generally occurs at two points: (1) after the decision has been made and action programs have been initiated, and (2) whenever internal demands are created within the organization. In both cases, new demands (inputs) may be generated, causing the process to recycle.

Information monitoring and reporting is particularly important after a decision has been reached. This feedback is necessary to provide continuous testing of expectations against actual results. Even the best decision has a high probability of being wrong. Even the most effective decision eventually becomes obsolete. Failure to provide for adequate feedback is one of the primary reasons for persisting in a course of action long after it has ceased to be appropriate or rational. The advent of the computer has made it possible to compile and analyze great quantities of feedback data in a relatively short time period. It must be recognized, however, that computers can handle only abstractions. Abstractions can be relied upon only if they are constantly checked against concrete results. Unless decision makers build their feedback around direct exposure to reality, their decision may result in sterile dogmatism [16].

A basic aspect of the decision process is the development of a predictive capacity within the organization to identify changing conditions that might necessitate modifications in the selected course of action. Controls should be developed for a given solution by:

1. Defining what constitutes a significant change for each variable and relationship that appears as a component in the decision;
2. Establishing procedures for detecting the occurrence of such changes; and
3. Specifying the tolerable range within which the solution can be modified if such changes occur and beyond which new solutions must be sought.

3 SUMMARY AND CONCLUSIONS

Although this prescriptive model of decision making is present in eight distinct stages, it would be misleading to assume that real-life problems are obliging enough to permit an easy, logical sequence of attention. As Joseph Cooper observed, problems

> conceal their true nature so that halfway down the path of a decision you may find that you must retrace your steps for a new beginning. Or you may have alternatives for decisions presented to you which, in your belief, are not the only and best possible courses. This, too, will send you back to the beginning [17].

Alternatives seldom are created by moving in an orderly sequence from the first stage to the last. It is not uncommon for new alternatives to occur from time to time while data are still being collected. Moreover, in a complex situation, different phases of the process may develop at different rates. For example, the stage of alternative formulation may be reached for one aspect of a complex problem, while other parts of the same problem are still at the stage of definition and analysis. Thus, in a complex, difficult problem situation, various stages may appear simultaneously in different aspects of the same problem. Nevertheless, it is necessary to approach the patterns of decision making stage by stage in order to adequately analyze the process. Only in this way is it possible to uncover meaningful and useful insights into how the process can be improved.

ENDNOTES

1. For a further discussion of general systems theory and its applications to organizations, see: Ludwig von Bertalanffy. General Systems Theory. New York: George Braziller, 1968; W. Ross Ashby. An Introduction to Cybernetics. New York: John Wiley & Sons, 1963; Alan Walter Steiss. Models for the Analysis and Planning of Urban Systems. Lexington, Mass.: Lexington Books, 1974, chapter 7; Alan Walter Steiss. Strategic Management and Organizational Decision Making. Lexington, Mass.: Lexington Books, 1985, chapter 2.
2. Charles E. Lindblom. The Intelligence of Democracy. New York: Free Press, 1965.
3. Herbert A. Simon. Administrative Behavior, 2nd edition. New York: Macmillan, 1957.
4. Herbert A. Simon. Administrative Behavior, 2nd edition. New York: Macmillan, 1957, chapter 9.
5. Amitai Etzioni. Mixed scanning: a third approach to decision making. Public Administration Review. Vol. 27, December 1967, pp. 309–390.
6. Filmer S. C. Northrup. The Logic of the Sciences and the Humanities. New York: Macmillan, 1947, p. 1.
7. David A. Easton. A Systems Analysis of Political Life. New York: John Wiley & Sons, 1965, p. 38.
8. John Dewey. Logic: The Theory of Inquiry. New York: Holt, Rinehart and Winston, 1938, p. 105.
9. David A. Easton. A Systems Analysis of Political Life. New York: John Wiley & Sons, 1965, p. 21. (Easton makes a distinction between inputs and withinputs, the latter referring to demands that are generated from within the organization.)
10. John Dewey. Logic: The Theory of Inquiry. New York: Holt, Rinehart and Winston, 1938, p. 105.
11. Anatol Rapoport. What is information? ETC: A Review of General Semantics. Vol. 10, Summer 1953, p. 252.
12. Peter F. Drucker. The effective decision. Harvard Business Review. Vol. 45, January–February 1967, pp. 92–104.

13. Peter F. Drucker. The effective decision. Harvard Business Review. Vol. 45, January–February 1967, p. 95.

14. Robert W. Morell. Managerial Decision-Making. Milwaukee, WI.: Bruce Publishing, 1960, p. 22.

15. Peter F. Drucker. The Practice of Management. New York: Harper and Brothers, 1954, p. 363.

16. Peter F. Drucker. The effective decision. Harvard Business Review. Vol. 45, January–February 1967, p. 95.

17. Joseph D. Cooper. The Art of Decision-Making. Garden City, N.Y.: Doubleday, 1961, pp. 15–16.

3

Strategic Planning: Mission, Vision, Goals, and Objectives

Strategic planning has been a vital ingredient of corporate decision making for some time. As King and Cleland explained, strategic planning in the private sector:

> involves the development of objectives and the linking of these objectives with the resources which will be employed to attain them. Since these objectives and resource deployments have impact in the future, strategic planning is inherently future-oriented. Strategic planning, therefore, deals primarily with the contrivance of organizational efforts directed to the development of organizational purpose, direction, and future generation of products and services and the design of implementation policies by which the goals and the objectives of the organization can be accomplished [1].

The term *strategic* is applied to these planning activities to denote linkages with the goal-setting process, the formulation of more immediate objectives to move an organization toward its goals, and the selection of specific actions (or strategies) required in the allocation of organizational resources to assist in achieving these objectives. The term also was adopted to distinguish the scope of this process from the forecasting and other piecemeal efforts undertaken in industry, business, and government in the name of "planning."

1 ORIGINS OF STRATEGIC PLANNING

Many organizations that undertake long-range planning place considerable emphasis on the extrapolation of expected developments into the future, so that top management can get a better understanding of where the organization is going. These forecasts of future performance are then compared with what might be desirable according to a set of goals and objectives for the organization. The discrepancy between desirable goals and objectives, and expected performance, is commonly called the *planning gap*. Forecasting is only one of the ingredients in the planning process, however. Forecasts involve educated guesses about the future. A major purpose of planning is to support strategic decision making by formulating alternative courses of action that will have long-term, desirable consequences.

1.1 Strategic Planning in the Private Sector

Strategic planning had its origins in the a private sector in a period of rapid growth and change that began in the late 1950s and early 1960s. As B.W. Scott observed in a 1965 publication of the American Management Association,

> Strategic planning is a systematic approach by a given organization to make decisions about issues which are of a fundamental and crucial importance to its continuous long-term health and vitality. These issues provide an underlying and unifying basis for all the other plans to be developed within the organization over a determinant period of time. Thus, a long-range strategy is designed to provide information about an organization's basic direction and purpose, information which will guide all of its operational activities [2].

When Robert S. McNamara left the presidency of the Ford Motor Company in 1961 to become Secretary of Defense in the Kennedy administration, he took with him a multi-year planning process that had helped him gain a perspective on the key strategic decisions in that company. McNamara's abilities as a manager and the role of long-range planning as an essential ingredient to this effectiveness were widely discussed in the media. As a consequence, managers of large organizations all over the country began to wonder if they too should attempt such a long-range planning effort.

While some companies attempted to formalize a planning process during the 1960s simply because "it was the thing to do," there were more substantial reasons for this movement toward a more comprehensive and long-range approach to organizational decisions. The 1960s were a period of steady economic growth and general prosperity, especially in the United States. Many corporate executives realized that they had to choose carefully from among numerous attractive opportunities for growth. During this period, many businesses chose to diversify, sometimes through acquisitions, and to enter into international markets. Such strategic moves increased the managerial complexity of large corporations in geometric fashion. New methods and technologies clearly were needed to help top management cope with an increasing array of strategic decisions. Formal, long-range planning seemed almost like a godsend to these top managers.

It has been estimated that three-quarters of all large corporations in the United States had some form of strategic planning in place by the end of the 1960s [3]. Eight basic approaches of corporate strategic planning have emerged over the past 35 years: (1) the Harvard policy model, (2) strategic planning systems, (3) stakeholder management approach, (4) business portfolio methods, (5) competitive analysis of key forces, (6) strategic issues management, (7) strategic negotiations, and (8) logical incrementalism [4].

A recent survey of 1500 companies worldwide indicated that more than two-thirds failed to integrate strategic planning with their financial and tactical planning processes [5]. One explanation for this disconnect is that all too often strategic planning is viewed as a senior management activity, causing executives to divorce it from planning activities at the operations level. According to the Hackett research, only 38% of management and less than 10% of the employees in the average company are given access to the strategic planning process. Many companies do not link incentives and rewards to strategic goals. Bonus pay is linked to financial plans for 97% of the companies, whereas only 58% of the same companies also tie incentives to strategic plans. As a consequence, many companies have failed to fully align their business goals with their strategic focus.

Based on their studies of planning in numerous corporations, Lorange and Vancil suggest five fundamental characteristics necessary to achieve effective strategic planning [6]:

1. Strategic planning is a line-management function. The corollary is that managers in the organization who will use a strategic planning system must design it.
2. An effective strategic planning system must help line managers make important decisions. Line managers are not interested in plans; they make decisions. They will devote time and effort to planning only if it assists in their decision-making process.
3. Effective strategic planning involves a process by which line managers work together to resolve strategic issues.

4. Strategic planning systems are unique to the organizational environments in which they reside. "The overriding design rule is that there is no general design."
5. An effective strategic planning system changes continually as a result of changes in the external environment of the organization as well as shifts in internal structure and power relationships.

According to the proponents of strategic planning as applied to the private sector, this approach:

1. Is oriented more toward actions, results, and implementation than is traditional public planning;
2. Promotes broader and more diverse participation in the planning process;
3. Places greater emphasis on understanding the organization (or community) in its external context through an environmental scan;
4. Encourages more competitive behavior; and
5. Assesses the strengths and weaknesses of the organization in the context of external opportunities and threats.

A key feature of corporate strategic planning is an assessment of strengths, weaknesses, opportunities, and threats (SWOT) as the basis for developing strategies and action programs to achieve goals and objectives. SWOT analyses (sometimes referred to as situational assessments) underscore the basic principle that the formulation of strategies must be predicated on a good fit between an organization's internal capability (its strengths and weaknesses) and its external situation (in part, reflected by its opportunities and threats). A SWOT analysis can help an organization determine its distinctive competencies which, in turn, will help determine what the mission of the organization should be.

A sound understanding of the values of customers/clientele is important for strategic planning in the private sector. While customers may be able to articulate what they want today or tomorrow, they cannot tell what will be exciting as a product or service three to five years from now. To define these products, the values that underlay today's customer requirements must be found. These underlying values must then be matched against what is possible to come up with the exciting quality of the future.

It also is important to prepare the organization to compete with products and services that will be brought to the market within the next three to five years. A key is to examine how technologies will evolve. Technological evolution often takes the form of an S-curve: at first, new products develop very quickly, then the number of changes slows, indicating the need for a major breakthrough in the product line. The monopoly cycle represents another line of evolution, in which products tend to diverge and then are grouped together. Under the concept of increasing dynamism, uneven development of parts shows where the weak links in the system are and where the next product breakthrough must come. Other lines of evolution have included the conversion from macro to micro entities and the development of automation.

1.2 Strategic Planning in the Public Sector

Efforts to apply strategic planning in the public sector began to surface in the late 1960s and early 1970s, in part as a response to criticisms of *comprehensive planning*—advocated in government (but seldom achieved) for over three decades. Catanese and Steiss described an alternative to the traditional planning approach in their 1970 book, *Systemic Planning: Theory and Applications*. This hybrid model, they suggested, focuses on probabilistic futures and combines the best features of more sophisticated analytical techniques with humanistic traditions of public planning [7]. Systemic planning was presented as a challenge to a new generation of planners to avoid technocratic determinism, while attaining a more systematic approach to public decision making.

The initial P in PPBS (Planning–Programming–Budgeting Systems) was a reflection of the same general concern for a longer-range perspective in formulating goals and objectives. It was assumed that such planning could provide a broader framework within which the more detailed functions of programming and budgeting could be undertaken. The PPBS approach was a top-down model in which goals and objectives were formulated in the upper echelons of the organization (similar to the corporate approach to strategic planning). These goals were then filtered down through a series of what Herbert Simon called *means–ends chains*. At the end of a lengthy process, specific programs were to be developed and implemented to achieve these goals and objectives. Under this approach, however, direction from the top often was poorly coordinated, contradictory, often counterproductive, or nonexistent. As a consequence, many public agencies operating under a PPBS mandate went through the motions of fulfilling the procedural requirements, using the appropriate buzzwords, but with little change in their traditional incremental approaches to the programming and budgeting of their assigned activities.

1.3 Long-Range Planning and Disjointed Incrementalism

It has been said, "If you don't know where you are going, any road will get you there." There is also truth in the notion that "If you don't know where you are going, no road will get you there." In short, planning is a prerequisite for effective management, whether in the private or public sector. Kast and Rosenzweig defined planning as

> the process of deciding in advance what is to be done and how. It involves determining overall missions, identifying key result areas, and setting specific objectives as well as developing policies, programs, and procedures for achieving them. Planning provides a framework for integrating complex systems of interrelated future decisions. Comprehensive planning is an integrative activity that seeks to maximize the total effectiveness of an organization as a system in accordance with its objectives [8].

Although the terms strategic planning and long-range planning often are used interchangeably, these two planning approaches differ in their emphasis regarding the *assumed environment* within which they are applied. Long-range planning generally involves the development of a plan for accomplishing a set of goals and objectives over a period of years, with the assumption that current knowledge about future conditions is sufficiently reliable to ensure the plan's validity over the duration of its implementation.

The common approach to public planning for many years has involved the formulation of a plan for some specific target date 10 to 20 years in the future. Under this approach, various demographic and economic factors are projected for a defined period of time, suggesting that by 2010 or 2020, the population of a particular jurisdiction will be of a greater magnitude (often expressed as a range). Based on these projections, it is then suggested that public services and facilities will need to be expanded accordingly, employment opportunities will be provided in a given quantity, land consumption will be of a given quantity (and perhaps quality), and so forth. As a rule, considerable attention is devoted to an identification of more immediate problems of growth (or lack of it) and to suggested solutions to these problems. Many public and nonprofit organizations outside of government have adopted a similar approach to planning.

Under such an approach, problem solving often takes precedence over the establishment of long-range goals and objectives. Program proposals frequently are based on anticipated demographic and economic conditions—a simple extrapolation of the status quo. When the overriding focus is on solutions to more immediate problems, the cumulative process becomes short-range planning, albeit applied to a relatively long time period. The results, benefits, and gains to be attained from such short-range plans cannot be ensured in the long run and, in fact, may be lost in the crisis of disjointed problem solving. A plan is of relatively little value if it does not look far enough into the future to provide a basis on which change can be logically anticipated and rationality accommodated.

The major assumption in strategic planning is that an organization must be responsive to a dynamic, changing environment (and not the relatively stable environment assumed for long-range planning). A general agreement has emerged in the public and nonprofit sectors that the broader environment is indeed changing in dynamic and often unpredictable ways. Thus, the emphasis in strategic planning is on understanding how the environment is evolving and on developing decisions that are responsive to these changes.

Charles Lindblom described public decision making as a process with little concern for goals and objectives. Lindblom asserted that public objectives are difficult to define and consensus rarely can be achieved. Therefore, the best course of action is *incrementalism* [9]. Democracies are composed of widely differing factions that compete for the public's interest (and resources). Even if these interests were not contradictory, our ability to foresee the full consequences of our actions (i.e., to plan) is so limited that, according to Lindblom, objectives must be approached in small, manageable steps, that is incrementally. The result is short-range programs rather than long-range policies.

Thus, Lindblom dismissed categorically any attempt to develop more synoptic or comprehensive approaches to public decision making on the grounds that such approaches do not conform to reality. Some writers have argued that disjointed incrementalism is a necessary—and desirable—consequence of the democratic process [10]. An extension of this assertion, some would argue, is that planning is contrary to, or at least inappropriate and difficult to achieve within a democracy.

The most significant flaw in the concept of disjointed incrementalism is that it fails to consider all of the incremental alternatives between existing approaches to decision making and the straw man extreme of synoptic planning. Lindblom and his followers oversimplified the alternatives and, thus, have stacked the argument in their favor. A planning approach that recognizes the need for inputs from the bottom up, that conforms to or adapts the ideals of the democratic process, and that, at the same time, secures a more rational basis for decision making, also is an option on this continuum that the "pragmatic incrementalists" seem to ignore.

1.4   From One-Shot Optimization to a Planning Process

Many traditional planning efforts, in both the public and private sectors, have tended to be "one-shot optimizations," drawn together periodically, often under conditions of stress. Once the "best plans" were laid, little attempt was made to test their continued efficacy against the realities of current conditions.

It has been said that: "Few plans survive contact with the enemy." And indeed, rarely are policies and programs executed exactly as initially conceived. Random events, environmental disturbances, competitive tactics, and unforeseen circumstances may all conspire to thwart the implementation of plans, policies, and programs. In short, the traditional planning process does not provide an adequate framework for more rational decisions about an uncertain future. Fixed targets, static plans, and repetitive programs are of relatively little value in a dynamic society.

What is required is a planning framework within which strategic decisions can be subjected to continuous testing, correction, and refinement. Through such an approach, alternative courses of action can be identified and analyzed, and a desirable range can be established within which choices can and should be made. The concept of strategic planning, as it has evolved over the past 35 years, offers an important response to this need for a more dynamic planning process. Bryson defined strategic planning as

> a disciplined effort to produce fundamental decisions and actions that shape and guide what an organization is, what it does, and why it does it. To deliver the best results, strategic planning requires broad yet effective information gathering, development and exploration of strategic alternatives, and an emphasis on future implications of present decisions [11].

1.5 A Planning Hierarchy

Another important component in the development of strategic planning was the recognition of a planning hierarchy in which the respective planning responsibilities at various levels within an organization are more clearly articulated. In private sector applications, Robert Anthony described this hierarchy as consisting of (1) strategic planning, (2) management planning, and (3) operational control [12]. Management planning is a pivotal ingredient in this approach, involving (1) the programming of approved goals into specific projects, programs, and activities, (2) the design of organizational units to carry out approved programs, and (3) the staffing of those units and the procurement of the necessary revenues to support the approved programs [13].

In the absence of a strategic planning framework, however, management planning can become disjointed and counterproductive. At the same time, without the consistent follow-through of management planning (programming and budgeting), strategic planning may be little more than a set of good intentions with little hope of realization. Thus, as emphasized in the discussion of strategic management, the linkages among the basic components are as important as the components themselves.

1.6 Strategic Planning Software

A number of software products are available to train and assist in strategic planning, to provide analytical tools and uniformity and integration of information, and to enhance participation [14]. Some strategic decision support systems, however, are too sophisticated, expensive, or restrictive to be used easily by managers. To be successful, strategic management must be a "people process." Strategic planning software should be simple and unsophisticated in order to allow wide participation among members of the organization, which is essential for effective implementation.

One software product that does offer a simple yet effective approach for developing organizational strategies is *CheckMATE*, which features a strategic planning process that is well tested and proven, both academically and in the business world. The software is simple to use and operates on any IBM-compatible computer system that runs Windows. (*CheckMATE* will not run on Apple computer products.) This software is a structured brainstorming tool that can be used to perform planning analyses to generate alternative strategies, and to enhance participation in strategic planning. It offers numerous help screens and examples throughout as well as clear printouts.

CheckMATE facilitates the development of an effective mission statement, goals, policies, and a budget to implement strategies recommended. The software includes strategic planning techniques, such as SWOT analysis, SPACE analysis, Grand Strategy Matrix analysis, and environmental analysis. No previous experience with computers or extensive knowledge of strategic planning is required.

One major strength of *CheckMATE* is its simplicity and participative approach. Users are asked appropriate questions, responses are recorded, information is assimilated, analyses are performed, and results are printed. Individuals can work through the software at their own pace, and then meet to develop joint recommendations for their organization. Thus, it promotes communication, understanding, creativity, and forward thinking among users.

2   A STRATEGIC PLANNING MODEL

From a systems perspective, strategic planning should be part of a continuous strategic management process that includes the allocation and management of resources, as well as performance evaluation and feedback. It should involve an examination of alternative courses of action and estimates of the impacts and consequences that are likely to result from their implementation. Explicit provision should be made for dealing with the uncertainties of probabilistic futures. The art of management is to reduce uncertainty and to bring risk within the bounds of tolerance. In this context, strategic planning can play an important role by assisting managers in organizing goals and objectives and in developing feasible action plans to achieve them. In so doing, major priorities can be ordered, the impacts of resource decisions can be assessed, and the activities and functions of the organization can be integrated into a more cohesive whole.

2.1   Basic Components of the Model

The Alliance for Nonprofit Management developed a five-step approach to strategic planning that is applicable to public as well as nonprofit organizations [15]. This generic model incorporates the basic components included in most approaches to strategic planning: (1) determine the organization's "readiness" for planning, (2) formulate mission and vision statements to guide the overall planning process, (3) carry out a situational (SWOT) assessment, (4) develop goals, objectives, and strategies, and (5) prepare a written plan.

Sorkin, Farris, and Hudak identified seven basic steps in strategic planning at the community level [16]:

1. Scan the environment
2. Select key issues
3. Set mission statements or broad goals
4. Undertake external and internal analyses
5. Develop goals, objectives, and strategies with respect to each key issue
6. Develop an implementation plan to carry out strategic actions
7. Monitor, update, and scan the environment.

In adopting a key feature of corporate strategic planning—a SWOT analysis—opportunities and threats are assessed in step 1 and used as the basis for action in steps 2 and 3. Strengths and weaknesses are identified in step 4 and are used to formulate strategies in steps 5 and 6. The process recycles with step 7.

The strategic planning model advocated here consists of five basic components:

1. Basic research and analysis to determine systems readiness.
    a. Collect basic data, prepare inventories, and conduct needs assessments.
    b. Identify issues, problems, or choices critical to the future well-being of the organization.
    c. Clarify roles and responsibilities, identify client groups to be served, and engage key stakeholders in the process.
    d. Develop an organizational profile and collect and analyze environmental information.
2. Statements of mission and vision, goals, and objectives.
    a. Formulate the organization's mission.
    b. Delineate significant structural changes required to realize the mission statement.
    c. Define the desired state of the system (vision statement).

      d. Identify program objectives to achieve the desired state:
          develop an objectives matrix; and
          redefine the desired state of the system in light of more detailed objectives.

3. SWOT analysis/situational assessment.
    a. Conduct internal and external environmental analyses.
    b. Diagnosis trends and needs:
        macro level trends and related considerations; and
        micro level technical and applied studies, including facilities analyses and specific needs assessments.
    c. Delineate a planning horizon.

4. Formulate strategies and analyze program alternatives.
    a. Identify strategies for organizational development.
    b. Prepare strategies that address how to develop, manage, and deliver programs.
    c. Develop strategies that focus on administrative and support needs and their impacts on the organization's efficiency and effectiveness.
    d. Delineate and analyze program alternatives to achieve desired strategies.

5. Policy alternatives and resource recommendations.
    a. Translate goals and objectives into general policies.
    b. Formulate explicit policy sets.
    c. Delineate effectiveness and efficiency measures:
        Establish decision guidelines for the allocation of financial resources.

Linkages among these basic components are shown in Figure 3.1.

This model of strategic planning assumes that a concentration of systemic data can provide the basis for theoretical constructs—preliminary goals and objectives—as to the desired future state of the organization or community. The emphasis is on an orderly evolution from a broad mission statement, to statements of more specific goals and objectives consistent with the organization's mission, to more explicit policies and implementing decisions. This emphasis seeks to establish or to re-inforce linkages that are missing in other planning approaches. The absence of consistency from the general to the specific is one of the major shortcomings of more traditional planning efforts.

The process for formulating goals and objectives also serves as a vehicle for avoiding the tendency to posit future plans merely on the basis of existing conditions. Policies (factual premises representing what can be done) can be tested against goals (value premises representing what should be done). Statements of goals and objectives play a vital role in the day-to-day process

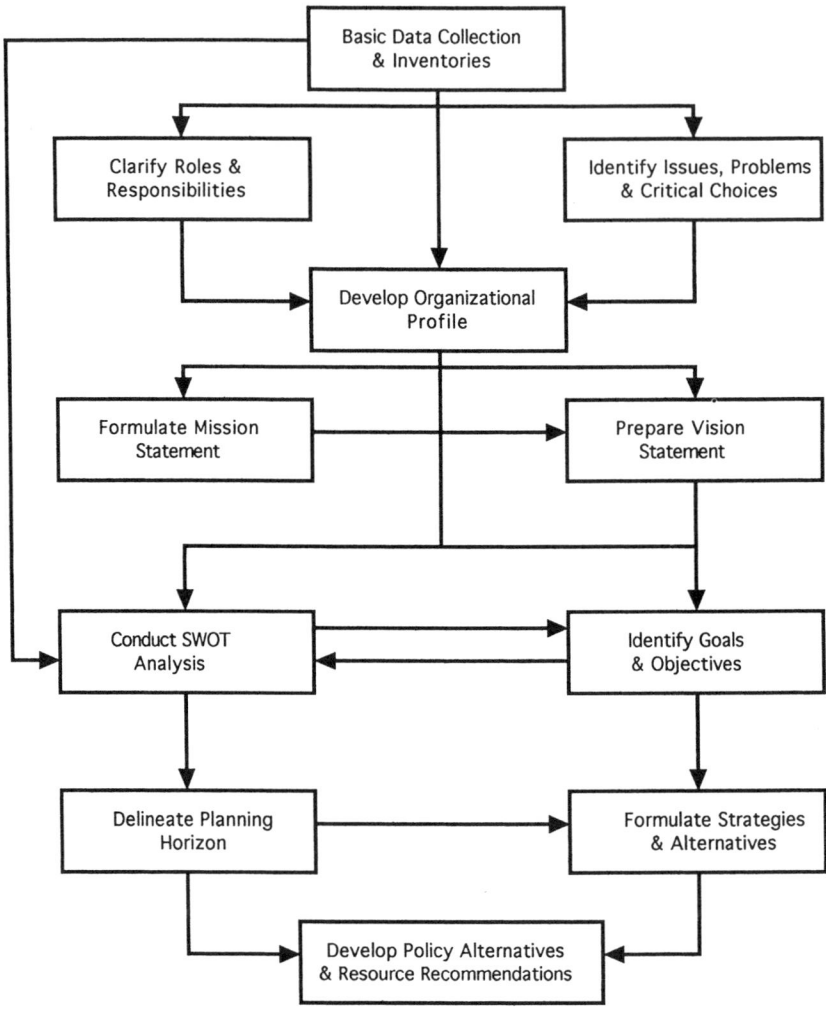

FIGURE 3.1 Schematic diagram of the strategic planning process.

of decision making. The application of this approach can go a long way toward circumventing the inherent danger of sacrificing the basic merits of the strategic plan to technical or politically expedient considerations. When compromises must be made—as they always will—decisions can be more clearly based on the optimal or normative conditions outlined in the statements of goals and objectives.

Several of the components outlined in this model are common to many strategic planning approaches. Others are unique to this model, however, and therefore merit further discussion. The unique elements include (1) the planning horizon, (2) the emphasis on program objectives, (3) the objectives matrix, (4) formulation of policy sets, and (5) the use of effectiveness measures. The balance of this chapter will focus on the first two components of the strategic planning process—determining the readiness for strategic planning, formulating mission and vision statements, and delineating appropriate goals and objectives. The other components of the process will be addressed in Chapter 4, which will include a discussion of some of the basic issues involved in the implementation of a strategic plan.

2.2 Systems Readiness

While many proponents of planning might suggest that "a little planning never hurts," many organizations initiate major planning efforts before they are ready to take on such a significant commitment. The subsequent results are almost always less than satisfactory. Therefore, a number of important issues must first be addressed in assessing the organization's readiness to undertake strategic planning.

> The organization's leadership must have an active commitment/involvement throughout the planning process.
>
> Major crises that may interfere with strategic thinking should be resolved before beginning the planning process.
>
> Management should have a clear understanding of the purpose of strategic planning and what it can and cannot accomplish, as well as a general consensus about expectations.
>
> Sufficient resources must be committed to adequately assess current programs and the organization's ability to meet current and future constituent/client needs.
>
> The organization's leaders must be willing to question the status quo and look for new approaches to perform and evaluate current and future processes for "doing business."

If these elements cannot be accommodated satisfactorily at the outset of the process, the organization may have to re-think its overall commitment to strategic planning. Too little planning can result in false expectations and recommendations that fall far short of meeting the organization's needs and/or fulfilling its true potential. Too much planning can consume excessive time and resources, and can fail to produce results that justify such commitments. "Enough planning" is when the organization's leadership understands and has achieved a consensus about a clear organizational direction.

Five tasks must be carried out to pave the way for an organized planning process:

1. Identify five to ten significant issues, fundamental problems, or choices critical to the future well-being of the organization that should be addressed during the strategic planning process.
2. Clarify roles (who does what in the process) and engage key stakeholders in the process.
3. Create a planning committee (five to seven individuals), involving both "visionaries" and "actionaries," to spearhead the process.
4. Prepare an organizational profile, and collect and analyze environmental information.
5. Identify the information that must be collected to help make sound decisions, including historical financial information, projected cash flows, and budgets.

The product of this initial phase is a *plan for planning*—an outline of the components necessary to demonstrate that the organization is ready to undertake strategic planning.

2.3 Mission and Vision Statements

It is important for the organization to articulate its overall mission in terms of what it is, what it is doing, and where it is going. A mission statement typically describes an organization in these terms:

Purpose: Why the organization exists and what it seeks to accomplish.
Business: The main methods or activities the organization undertakes to fulfill this purpose.
Values: Principles or beliefs that guide an organization's members as they pursue the organization's purpose.

The stated mission of the American Red Cross, for example, "is to improve the quality of human life, to enhance self-reliance and concern for others, and to help people avoid, prepare for, and cope with emergencies." The mission statement of the Internal Revenue Service is to "provide America's taxpayers top quality service by helping them understand and meet their tax responsibilities and by applying the tax law with integrity and fairness to all." A mission statement for a Child Development Center might read as follows: *Foster the social, ethical, and intellectual development of children (purpose) by developing, evaluating, and disseminating programs (business) that enhance their capacity to think critically and skillfully, while striving to deepen children's commitment to social values such as kindness, helpfulness, personal responsibility, and respect for others (values).*

In defining an organization's purpose, it is essential that the focus be on outcome and results rather than on methods. For example, the purpose of a mental health counseling agency would not be simply "to provide counseling services"—that describes a method or set of activities to be undertaken rather than an intended result. Rather, the purpose of the agency might be "to improve the quality of life" for its clients. Purpose statements usually identify the problem(s) or condition(s) that the organization will address and the change in the status of these problems/conditions that the organization hopes to bring about through its efforts.

Mark Moore offered the notion of a strategic triangle as a means of focusing attention on the three key questions that mangers must answer in testing the adequacy of their vision of organizational purpose:

> First, the strategy must be substantively valuable in the sense that the organization produces things of value to overseers, clients, and beneficiaries at low cost in terms of money and authority.
> Second, it must be legitimate and politically sustainable. That is, the enterprise must be able to continually attract both authority and money from the political authorizing environment to which it is ultimately accountable.
> Third, it must be operationally and administratively feasible in that the authorized, valuable activities can actually be accomplished by the existing organization with help from others who can be induced to contribute to the organization's goal [17].

Group discussions (through retreats, focus groups, and similar gatherings) of the elements and nuances of an organization's mission are important. However, one or two individuals should be assigned the follow-up task of committing the mission statement to paper.

A *vision statement* should present a guiding image of what success will look like, formulated in terms of an organization's anticipated contribution to the broader society. A vision statement is more encompassing than a mission statement in that it seeks to provide an image of success that will motivate people within the organization to work together. A vision statement should be appropriate to the organization's mission and consistent with the organization's values. It should be realistic and credible, yet ambitious and responsive to change. It should be well-articulated and easily understood. And it should challenge and inspire the group to achieve its mission. Bryson asserted that

> A vision statement should include the organization's mission, its basic philosophy and core values, its basic strategies, its performance criteria, its important decision-making rules, and its ethical standards. The statement should emphasize the important social purposes the organization serves and that justify its existence. In addition, the statement should be short and inspirational [18].

A tall order, indeed.

Many organizations combine their mission and vision into a single statement. However, the mission statement often focuses primarily on the organization's responses to current issues, problems, and challenges. A separate vision statement may be appropriate to provide some "stretch," to inspire its members to strive for a higher level of attainment, and to trigger the necessary changes in the organization's structure and processes to bring about the longer term improvements and broader contributions to society.

2.4 Formulating Goals and Objectives

In strategic planning, tentative sets of goals and objectives are formulated and then tested in the context of specific horizon alternatives, allowing new factors to emerge and be considered. In short, a deductive approach replaces the more traditional inductive technique of planning. Goal formulation should increase the awareness of the participants with respect to the changes that may be taking place within the organization. However, it also should allow these participants to react to these changes in accordance with their own values, norms, and expectations.

The phrase "goals and objectives" often is used in the literature of public and business administration as if these terms were linked like Siamese twins. This irrevocable coupling has the unfortunate effect of masking conceptual distinctions that are important to the formulation of effective planning mechanisms. As J. Brian McLoughlin observed:

> by their very nature goal-statements are somewhat vague and general— "political" people and the electorate which support them may find it very difficult to form a clear picture of what is involved in reaching a goal and planners may be disappointed, even disheartened at the lack of response. However, when a broad goal is translated into more detailed objectives or actions, politicians and their public are likely to show greater interest, response and desire to participate in discussions [19].

Most organizations operate, explicitly or implicitly, with a *hierarchy* of goals and objectives [20]. At the top of the hierarchy are the relatively durable goals—statements of desired results or outputs drawn from the broad purpose of the organization—its reason for existence, often framed in rather broad, immeasurable, and abstract terms as a mission statement. These goals, in turn, must be translated into more specific program objectives to give guidance to personnel at all levels within the organization. Program objectives provide the critical bridge between the broad goals of an organization and specific action commitments. As Anthony and Welsch noted:

> when a plan is prepared on the basis of any particular goal, there must be means of measuring the rate of progress toward the goal otherwise the whole planning process becomes arbitrary through lack of a measure of error to

guide implementation and controls; more detailed objectives provide such operational measures [21].

Herbert Simon described the relationship among goals and objectives as a means–ends chain, wherein lower level objectives (or processes) are intended to delineate the means for achieving higher level goals (or purposes).

> A "process" is an activity whose immediate purpose is at a low level in the hierarchy of means and ends, while a "purpose" is a collection of activities whose orienting value or aim is at a high level in the means–end hierarchy [22].

2.5 Three Levels of Objectives

The same goal may give rise to quite different objectives—either because they are framed by different groups or individuals from different perspectives or because they are deliberately varied in order to stimulate a "dialogue" from which mutual understanding and clarification may emerge or be enhanced [23]. By the same token, different objectives (or sets of objectives) may lead to the same goal but with varying costs and benefits. The action programs associated with each objective may involve different operating and capital costs. Approximations of these costs and benefits may assist in the discussions among various groups and the public in general in the further clarification of goals.

Strategic objectives define the expected change in conditions, welfare, or behavior as a consequence of the initiation of some program or activity (i.e., the justification for undertaking the program or activity). Such objectives relate to the impact of the programs or activities of an organization on its clientele or service groups (usually external).

The following statements, for example, might be considered an appropriate strategic objective for a City Planning Department: *Increase efficiency and ensure consistency in the administration of government activities by providing a full range of capital facilities planning to the service programs of the city.* This statement specifies the conditions that the application of strategic planning is intended to achieve (increased efficiency and consistency in the administration of government programs), and by implication, it identifies the community at large as the intended target group.

Strategic objectives should specify what the organization proposes to do and *why* it proposes to do so. The tendency, however, is to focus on the *how*. Thus, an appropriate strategic objective of a municipal fire department might be: "Reduce current response time to all fire and emergency vehicle calls by 25% during the next two years." A statement: "Build, equip, and staff a third fire station during the next two years" tells how the strategic objective might be accomplished and should be reserved for the next level in the delineation of specific program actions.

Management objectives should describe specific program actions in terms of *how* and *where* specific resources (project budgets) will be used. Management objectives identify the commitments required to translate a strategic objective into specific activities. Management objectives often reflect staffing requirements or other resource commitments required to achieve a *single key result*. Such objectives usually are *internal* to the organization and are often associated with and identified through such techniques as management by objectives (MBO). Management objectives may identify how an organization intends to carry out a particular program component.

Management objectives should be precise, measurable, and time bound. This degree of specificity is not easily achieved. The tendency often is to state objectives that simply describe current activities. In order to avoid this pitfall, objectives should be expressed in *words of change*—for example, to develop, to increase, to reduce, to eliminate, to prevent, to maintain, and so forth. Finz suggested the following criteria regarding the formulation of management objectives [24]:

1. Objectives should provide quantitative levels to be achieved.
2. Objectives that do not provide quantitative levels should at least provide a measure in terms of time and budget constraints.
3. Objectives can be expressed in terms of satisfaction or acceptance on the part of those affected by the services provided.
4. Objectives that cannot be expressed in the form of positive quantification nevertheless should be more specific than goals.

The so-called *rule of rigor* in the Social Sciences can be stated as: If you can count it, count it; if you can't count it, describe it; if you can't count it or describe it, forget it.

One management objective emerging from the previously cited strategic objective that the Planning Department might adopt is: *Conduct a series of public meetings and workshops to foster greater citizen involvement in identifying the community's long-range goals and objectives.* The specific actions by the planning staff involve the development and implementation of opportunities whereby the public could participate in discussions regarding the overall goals and objectives of the city. This statement implies that staff will be assigned to carry out or coordinate various tasks in the development and implementation of these public meetings and workshops.

Another management objective that the Planning Department might adopt would be: *Develop and disseminate information on public policies and procedures that affect the city's long-term economic development.* This management objective could be made more explicit by referring to the specific policies and procedures to be disseminated. These policies, in turn, would reflect an assessment of needs and issues current in the community.

Still another management objective might be: *Develop and implement communication mechanisms that will facilitate the further involvement of representative citizen groups in decisions that affect the allocation of public resources.* The specific actions by the planning staff involve the development and implementation of communication mechanisms. This statement implies that staff will be assigned to carry out or coordinate various tasks leading to this implementation. Such assignments could be made more explicit by incorporating them into the management objective.

Management objectives, in turn, should be related to *performance measures* and *measures of effectiveness*. These measures can be used to identify the service units, constituents or clients, and/or products associated with the activities of the organization. They provide mechanisms to determine the success (or lack thereof) of a program in achieving agreed-upon strategic objectives. Performance measures may be equated to costs or inputs. Efforts must be made, however, to go beyond the more common workload measures that tend to assess efficiency rather than measure effectiveness. Effectiveness measures examine the relationship of the program outputs to program objectives—the standards for the outputs.

Operational objectives most often are associated with the implementation and control of specific tasks, and the assignment of specific resources to achieve strategic and management objectives. Whereas the principal focus of strategic objectives is *effectiveness*, the keynote of operational objectives most often is *efficiency*. Operational objectives frequently reflect explicit performance measures that can be adopted by the organization to monitor its activities.

Examples of operational objectives derived from the previously cited management and strategic objectives might be: *Conduct a series of public meetings over the next three months to discuss the current criteria and procedures by which decisions are made in connection with the allocation of capital funds for major public facilities and improvements. Work with Financial Operations to develop new capital facilities planning mechanisms to assist service departments in the budgeting and management of their annual operating funds in response to identified program objectives.*

An operational objective often represents the best current statement of the most appropriate way to get the job done. Operational objectives should provide a basis for action. The primary purpose should be the detailed identification of activities and techniques that should be carried out in the implementation of a project or program. Operational objectives may involve the determination of specific resource requirements (personnel, equipment, materials, capital expenditures, etc.) and their appropriate order of commitment (project schedules) to ensure that specific tasks are carried out efficiently. Operational objectives often include references to relatively short-term completion dates (e.g., one to two years).

Operational objectives must be flexible enough to undergo revisions as the tasks and activities evolve. Detailed examination of the tasks required to complete a project may expose overly optimistic assumptions and can lead to more realistic project schedules. It may become apparent that the strategic and management objectives can not be met, either because they are too ambitious or because they have not been thought through sufficiently to ensure that necessary resources will be available when and where they are needed.

2.6   Objectives Matrix

Explicit recognition is given in this strategic planning model to the fact that value inputs (personal biases) are likely to occur at critical points, namely, in connection with the formulation of more explicit objectives. This tendency can never be completely eliminated. Therefore, objectives must be formulated within a concise framework that provides an opportunity to clearly identify conflicting positions, that is, statements of existing or potential value conflicts. An objectives matrix, as outlined in Figure 3.2, provides a basis for the identification of such conflict situations.

Conflicts can emerge on several different levels. The first dimension of potential conflict is between the overall objectives of the organization and

	Organizations			Individuals		
	Territorial Prerogatives			Territorial Prerogatives		
	Unit A	Unit B	Unit n	Unit n	Unit B	Unit A
Viewpoint/ Issue 1						
Viewpoint/ Issue 2						
Viewpoint/ Issue 3						
Viewpoint/ Issue n						

FIGURE 3.2   Illustrative format for objectives matrix.

the objectives of individuals or groups within the organization or served by the organization. A second level of possible conflict arises from territorial considerations, that is, the prerogatives of various units within the organization or community. A third level of conflict emerges with regard to explicit issues and the various viewpoints that can be brought to bear on their resolution.

The objectives matrix is built through a series of iterations, involving a broad cross-section of participants. First, an objective statement is posited for each identified issue area. These objectives are then categorized according to the three conflict levels. At the end of the first round, a number of cells in the matrix should be filled in and others likely will remain empty. The next iteration should focus on filling in the empty cells by identifying objectives that parallel (that is, complement or are in conflict with) those previously identified in the particular dimensions. This round may reveal additional issue areas, which produces yet another cycle. The end product of this phase of the analysis should be a fully articulated matrix, with each cell containing one or more objectives. Finally, those objectives should be identified that (1) are clearly in conflict with one another, (2) evidence potential conflict or consensus, and (3) are mutually reinforcing.

The purpose of this analysis within the strategic planning process is to more clearly identify both potential conflicts and areas of agreement and congruence. The objectives matrix merely provides a convenient scorecard for recording these points, so as to avoid the tendency to assume that objectives are mutually exclusive.

This approach has been successfully applied in small focus groups through the use of a modified Delphi technique and on a broader basis using a series of questionnaires and public meetings. The matrix can reveal different levels of understanding regarding the broader goals of the organization. Respondent conflict must be expected and analyzed. The general premise underlying this matrix approach is that information regarding conflicts among participants will be valuable in identifying levels of comprehension with respect to complex organizational issues. That is, it is better to know about these existing and potential conflicts at the outset than to get part way into a course of action and have it rapidly deteriorate when the conflicts surface.

2.7 An Iterative Process

While the delineation of objectives may be initiated sequentially, more often they are identified through a series of iterations (Figure 3.3). Strategic objectives, for example, may be further clarified through the establishment of appropriate management objectives and related programs and subprograms of an organization. This clarification, in turn, may assist in determining which activities should be placed within each subprogram. It may not be possible, however, to formulate

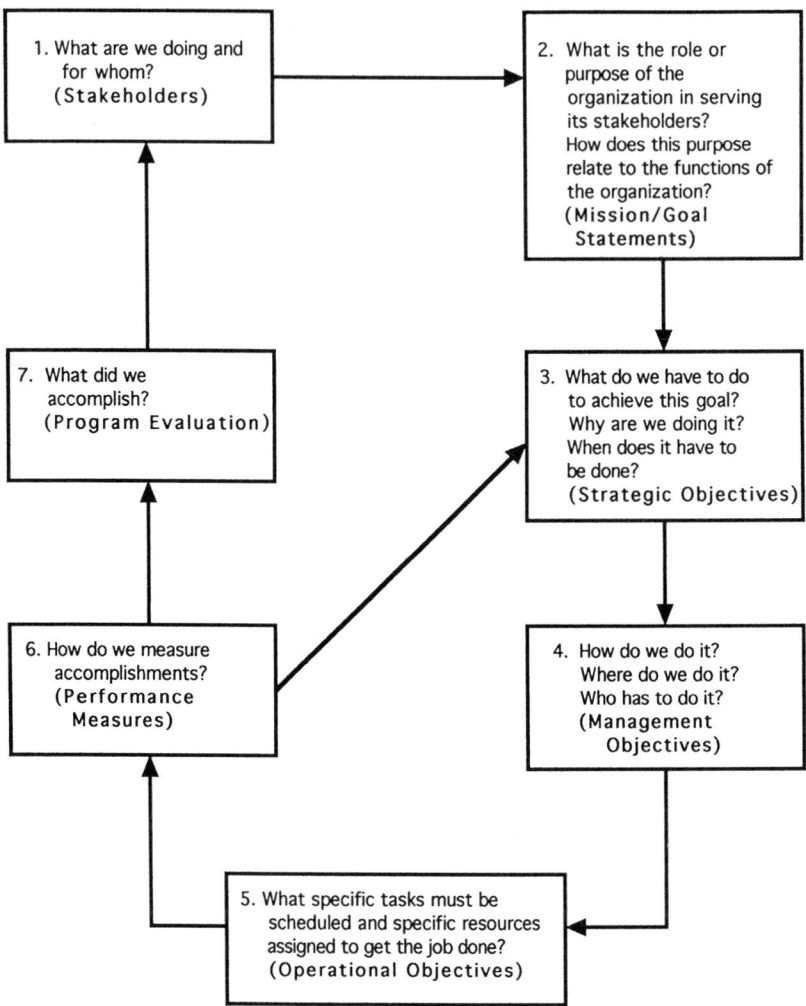

Figure 3.3 Iterative process for setting objectives.

precise statements of strategic and management objectives until operational objectives and their related activity schedules have been examined in some detail. The establishment of such schedules, in turn, may require careful examination of alternative strategies and associated measures of efficiency and effectiveness. Thus the process must be viewed from the top-down in terms of strategic objectives and from the bottom-up in terms of the organizational activities designed to carry out these objectives.

One of the advantages of this hierarchy is that, if someone begins by describing a management objective, the question can be raised as to the appropriate strategic objective to which it relates. Why is the organization making resource commitments to a particular project or set of activities? In what way will this commitment further the overall strategic objectives of the organization?

This approach can also be applied in the other direction. Those persons charged with the implementation of an agreed-upon strategic objective could begin to explore appropriate management and operational objectives in their respective areas of responsibility. As is usually the case, each strategic objective must be supported by several management objectives, and each management objective is likely to be tied to several operational objectives.

ENDNOTES

1. William R. King and David I. Cleland. Strategic Planning and Policy. New York: Van Nostrand Reinhold, 1978, p. 6.
2. B. W. Scott. Long-Range Planning in American Industry. New York: American Management Association, 1965, p. 63.
3. George Steiner. Top Management Planning. London: Macmillan, 1969.
4. See: John M. Bryson and William D. Roering. Applying private-sector strategic planning to the public sector. Journal of the American Planning Association. Vol. 53, No. 1, Winter 1987.
5. Hackett Benchmarking & Research, as reported on the Financial Executives Institute Website, November/December, 2000, at: www.fei.org.
6. Peter Lorange and Richard F. Vancil, Editors. Strategic Planning Systems. Englewood Cliffs, N.J.: Prentice-Hall, Inc., 1977, p. xiii.
7. Anthony J. Catanese and Alan Walter Steiss. Systemic Planning: Theory and Application. Lexington, MA.: Heath Lexington Books, 1970.
8. Fremont E. Kast and James E. Rosenzweig. Organization and Management. New York: McGraw-Hill, 1979, pp. 416–417.
9. Charles E. Lindblom. The science of 'muddling through.' Public Administration Review. Vol. 19, 1959, pp. 79–88; Charles E. Lindblom and David Braybrooke. A Strategy of Decision. New York: Free Press, 1964; Charles E. Lindblom. The Intelligence of Democracy: Decision Making through Mutual Adjustment. New York: Free Press, 1965.
10. Charles E. Lindblom. The Intelligence of Democracy: Decision Making through Mutual Adjustment. New York: Free Press, 1965; Aaron Wildavsky. The Politics of the Budgetary Process. Boston, Mass.: Little, Brown, 1964.
11. John M. Bryson. Strategic Planning for Public and Nonprofit Organizations. San Francisco, CA: Jossey-Bass Publishers, 1995, pp. 4–5.
12. Robert N. Anthony and Glenn W. Welsch. Fundamentals of Management Accounting. Homewood, Ill.: Richard D. Irwin, 1974, p. 303.
13. Alan Walter Steiss. Public Budgeting and Management. Lexington, Mass.: Lexington Books, 1972, p. 148.

14. For further discussion see: Robert Mockler. A catalog of commercially available software for strategic planning. Planning Review. Vol. 19, No. 3, May/June 1991; and John Sterling. Strategic management software review. Planning Review. January-February, 1992.

15. For a more detailed description of this model, consult the Alliance for Nonprofit Management website at: www.allianceonline.org/faqs/sp_main.html.

16. Donna L. Sorkin, Nancy B. Ferris, and James Hudak. Strategies for Cities and Counties: A Strategic Planning Guide. Washington, D.C.: Public Technology, Inc., 1984.

17. Mark H. Moore. Creating Public Value: Strategic Management in Government. Cambridge, MA: Harvard University Press, 1995, p. 71.

18. John M. Bryson. Strategic Planning for Public and Nonprofit Organizations. San Francisco, CA: Jossey-Bass Publishers, 1995, p. 165.

19. J. Brian McLoughlin. Urban and Regional Planning: A Systems Approach. New York: Praeger, 1969, p. 106.

20. For further discussion of this hierarchy see: Max D. Richards. Organizational Goal Structures. St. Paul, MN: West Publishing, 1978, pp. 1–35.

21. Robert N. Anthony and Glenn W. Welsch. Fundamentals of Management Accounting. Homewood, Ill.: Richard D. Irwin, 1974, p. 303.

22. Herbert A. Simon. The proverbs of administration. Reprinted in Jay M. Shafritz and Albert C. Hyde, eds., Classics of Public Administration. Chicago: Dorsey Press, 1987, p. 171.

23. For further discussion see: Charles L. Levin. Establishing goals for regional economic development. Journal of the American Institute Planners. Vol. 30, 1966, pp. 100–110.

24. Samuel A. Finz. A commentary on: 'The enlarged concept of productivity measurements in government—a review of some strategies.' Public Productivity Review. Vol. 2, Winter 1976, pp. 59–61.

4

Strategic Planning: SWOT Analysis, Strategies, Policies, and Implementation

Most approaches to strategic planning advocate the delineation of the organization's mission and vision, and the formation of goals and objectives as the initial steps in the process. However, many organizations become involved in strategic planning by first conducting an assessment of the challenges that confront them and their possible responses to these external conditions. A SWOT analysis is a relatively easy-to-use technique for getting a quick overview of an organization's strategic situation. This analysis, in turn, can precipitate a realization that a more systematic, long-range plan is essential for success (or perhaps, survival).

1 SWOT ANALYSIS

A SWOT analysis (sometimes referred to as a situational assessment) involves the compilation of current information about the organization's strengthens and weaknesses and performance information that highlights critical external issues (opportunities and threats) which should be addressed in the strategic plan.

1.1 Inputs, Throughputs, Outputs, Outcomes, and Impacts

A key component of a SWOT analysis is an evaluation of the efficiency and effectiveness of the organization's current programs and processes. This assessment should include process evaluations based on quantitative data (review of records, descriptive statistics related to various indices, formal performance evaluations) and qualitative data (constituents/clients opinions about the organization's programs). The effects of the organization's programs should be assessed in terms of:

Inputs: Resources required to operate the programs
Throughputs: Processes through which the programs are operated
Outputs: Immediate, observable results of the programs
Outcomes: How the programs affect constituents/clients
Impacts: Long-term benefits to clients and/or the broader society

Cost–benefit analysis might be applied in evaluating the inputs and outputs of an organization's programs. However, it may be difficult to apply cost–benefit techniques to many public and nonprofit programs. It any case, the results of such analyses should not be used as the sole criterion, but may provide a helpful tool when it comes to making difficult choices regarding the use of scarce resources. Management techniques for examining throughputs—such as process reengineering, benchmarking, and quality improvement (described in further detail in subsequent chapters)—can be applied as part of this basic assessment.

A SWOT analysis should include:

Internal and external stakeholders' perceptions about the organization, collected through brainstorming sessions, focus groups, in-person or telephone interviews, and questionnaires.

External trends that influence the organization, categorized into political, economic, social, technological, demographic, and legal forces, and including such circumstances as changing constituent/client needs, increased competition, changing governmental regulations, and so forth.

Senior management must respond to the following questions from their own perspectives and from the point of view of the people with whom they deal:

Strengths: What are the organization's advantages? What does it do well?

Weaknesses: In what areas could improvements be made? What is currently being done ineffectively and inefficiently? What should be avoided?

Opportunities: Where are the best chances for change and improvement? What are the interesting trends?

Threats: What obstacles does the organization face? What is the competition doing? Is changing technology threatening the "market position" of the organization? Does the organization have cash flow or bad debt problems? Are the specifications for the mission, products, or services of the organization changing?

In identifying strengths, it is important to be realistic, but not to be overly modest. Weaknesses should be considered from both an internal and an external perspective. It is best to be pragmatic and to face any unpleasant truths as soon as possible. Useful opportunities can come from changes in: (1) technology and markets on a broad and narrow scale, (2) government policy, and (3) social patterns, population profiles, lifestyle changes, and so forth. Carrying out a SWOT analysis often will be illuminating—both in terms of pointing out what needs to be done and in putting current problems into perspective.

Current strategies—patterns of operation and allocation of resources—should be analyzed to determine if they remain effective and should be continued in the future. Additional research may be needed to identify new opportunities that can be pursued (e.g., new products or services, new target markets, etc.) which may include an identification of start-up costs, competitor analyses, long-term financial projections, and break-even analyses. The products of a SWOT analysis include a database of quality information and a list of the most important issues the organization needs to address.

1.2 Analytical Tools

Weihrich suggested the use of a simple matrix to record the strengths and weaknesses, and the opportunities and threats confronting the organization [1]. The intersecting cells of the matrix provide a vehicle for identifying and recording initial strategies that might be adopted in response to the SWOT analysis (see Figure 4.1). For example, if an organization has recently upgraded its information technology to include e-commerce capabilities (strength), it may be well-positioned to take advantage of opportunities to accelerate financial and other transactions using the Internet.

Rowe, Mason, and Dickel developed the Strategic Position and Action Evaluation (SPACE) matrix as a means of determining whether aggressive, conservative, defensive, or competitive strategies are most appropriate for a given organization [2]. While the dimensions of the matrix are designed for private sector application, some parallels can be drawn for public and nonprofit organizations. As shown in Figure 4.2, the axes of the SPACE matrix represent two internal dimensions (financial strength and competitive advantage) and two external dimensions (environmental stability and industry strength). For public and nonprofit organizations, *financial strength* may include such factors as the elasticity of revenues and expenditures, the organization's cash flow position, liquidity and return on investments, and amount of working capital. *Competitive advantage* may include the level of constituent/end user satisfaction, use of technological know-how, and quality of service. *Environmental stability* may focus on factors such as the rate of inflation, regulatory impact, price elasticity, technological change, and competitive pressures. It is somewhat more difficult

	STRENGTHS List strengths	WEAKNESSES List weaknesses
OPPORTUNITIES List opportunities	Use strengths to take advantage of opportunities	Overcome weaknesses by taking advantage of opportunities
THREATS List threats	Use strengths to avoid threats	Minimize weaknesses and avoid threats

FIGURE 4.1   Weihrich's SWOT matrix.

to identify public sector counterparts in the area of *industry strength*, which in the SPACE matrix deals with such industry-wide indices as growth and profit potential, financial stability, productivity, and technological know-how. A possible surrogate would be the status of the organization in the broader economic environment in which it must function. For example, a suburban community that is largely residential with service-oriented businesses might "score" lower on this dimension than a city with a more diverse economy and a broader tax base.

The steps required to develop a SPACE matrix are as follows:

1. A numerical value ranging from $+1$ (worst) to $+6$ (best) is assigned to each of the variables selected to represent the financial strength and economic status dimensions.
2. A numerical value ranging from -1 (best) to -6 (worst) is assigned to each of the variables selected to represent the environmental stability and competitive advantage dimensions.
3. An average score is computed for each dimension by summing the values given to the variables, and dividing by the number of variables included in the respective dimension. For example, if the values assigned to the financial strength variables were $+1$, $+3$, $+4$, and $+5$, the average score would be $13/4 = +3.25$.

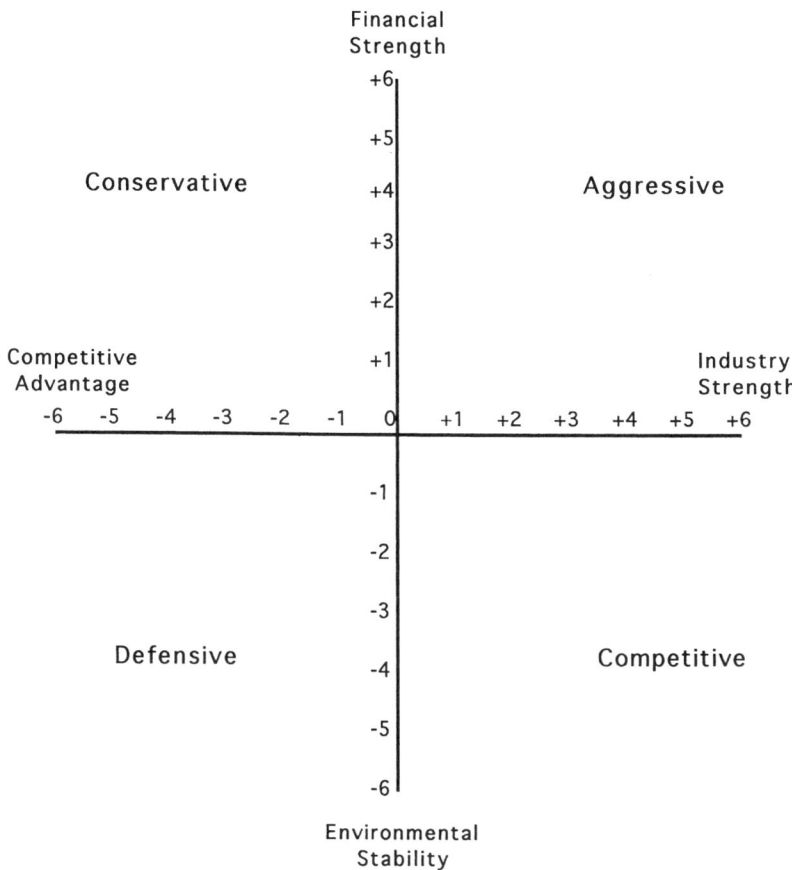

FIGURE 4.2 The SPACE matrix.

4. The two scores on the x axis are summed and the resultant point is plotted on X. The two scores on the y axis are summed and the resultant point is plotted on Y. The intersect of the new XY point then is plotted.

5. A directional vector is drawn from the origin of the matrix through the new intersection point. This vector reveals the type of strategies recommended for the organization.

If, for example, competitive advantages are low (e.g., -4) compared to economic status ($+2$), and financial strength ($+5$) outweighs environmental stability (-2), then the XY intercept would be (-2, $+3$). The vector would point to the conservative quadrant, indicating an organization that has achieved financial strength but without major competitive advantages.

Ian MacMillan developed a strategy grid to help public and nonprofit organizations assess their competitive status [10]. MacMillan's matrix examines four program dimensions that guide placement on the strategy grid and indicate implied strategies.

Alignment with mission statement: Degree to which a program "fits" or "belongs" within an organization.

Competitive position: Degree to which the organization has a stronger capability and the potential to deliver the program than other organizations.

Program attractiveness: Complexity associated with the management of a program.

Alternative coverage: Number of other organizations attempting to deliver or succeeding in delivering a similar program in the same region to similar constituents.

MacMillan suggested that an organization should divest itself of those services or programs that are not aligned with its mission, or that cannot draw on existing skills or knowledge within the organization. It should also jettison programs that are unable to share resources or for which activities can not be coordinated with other programs. On the other hand, programs that have a growing client base, stable financial resources, and a low client resistance are considered simple or "easy to manage" and should be built upon. Program attractiveness also includes the degree to which a program is appropriate from an economic perspective, for example, as an investment of current or future organizational resources.

The MacMillan matrix provides ten cells in which to place programs that have been reviewed in terms of these four dimensions (see Figure 4.3). Each cell is assigned a strategy that directs the future of the program listed in the cell (e.g., aggressive competition, joint venture, orderly divestment, etc.). One cell of the matrix, "Soul of the Agency," requires additional explanation. These are the difficult programs for which an organization is often the "last, best hope" for the constituents or clients. Management must find ways to use the programs in other cells to develop, piggyback, subsidize, leverage, promote, or otherwise support programs in this category.

1.3   Delineating a Planning Horizon

Basic to this approach to strategic planning is the identification of a planning horizon—the farthest point that can be anticipated based on an interpretation of what is known about existing conditions and emerging trends. A series of plans can be developed for given levels of service at the planning horizon. Just as with the natural horizon, as a specific service level is approached, the planning horizon

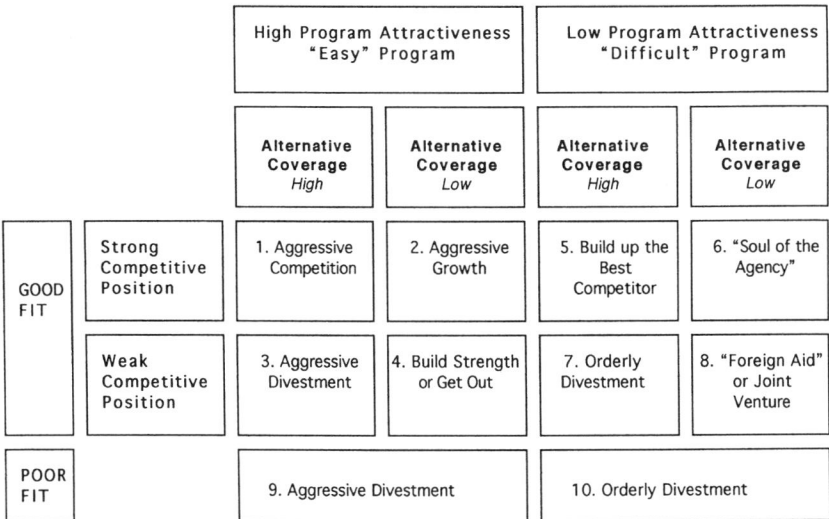

FIGURE 4.3   MacMillan matrix for competitive analysis of programs.

continues to recede, making adjustments in long-range goals and objectives both necessary and possible. Therefore, the horizon concept provides a more dynamic approach to strategic planning. The planning horizon can (and should) be changed, revised, or even dismissed as the body of information on which it is based is enlarged and clarified.

The planning horizon of any organization or community can be determined through the application of both objectives (measurable) and subjective criteria. The service capacity of the organization, for example, may represent one such criterion; optimal staff-client ratios might provide another criterion. In both of these examples, the criteria are closely tied to the availability of resources. And as resource availability changes, the criteria must also be adjusted. Some horizon criteria are products of the level of technology available at any given time. Other criteria are established on a somewhat more subjective basis, which may be altered (and should be re-evaluated) from time to time as changes occur in the organization's client profiles or the demographics of the community.

A strategic plan formulated on the horizon concept yields a series of policy alternatives to guide future organizational activities toward some desired state. The horizon concept offers the basis for a thesis rather than merely a synthesis (i.e., the more traditional cumulative approach to planning). This thesis emerges from a series of hypotheses or "what-if" studies, whereby various mixes of programs to serve the needs of the community (or client groups within the community) are explored within the overall parameters of the planning horizon.

Each plan alternative has different implications for the distribution and management of resource requirements. A number of combinations and permutations are possible based on a relatively well-defined set of pure alternatives. From these hypotheses, the mix that best fits the mission statement of the organization or community can be identified and set forth as the thesis of what should be (that is, the desired future state of the organization or community). Strategies, programs, and policies can then be developed to implement this chosen alternative.

2 FORMULATING STRATEGIES AND ANALYZING ALTERNATIVES

Goals and objectives identify the general and specific results desired, whereas strategies focus on the broad approaches to be taken. Goals and objectives should be sufficiently detailed to provide useful guidance for developing issues and strategies.

2.1 Hierarchy of Strategies

Ideally, an organization first establishes an agreed-up set of goals and objectives and then proceeds to identify issues that need to be addressed in order to achieve those goals and objectives. It may not be possible, however, to reach broad consensus on goals and objectives, in which case it may be necessary to move directly from a review of an organization's mission, mandate, and SWOT analyses, to the identification of strategic issues [4]. Bryson suggested that this direct approach may be necessary if there is no agreement on goals, or if the agreement is too abstract to be useful. It may also be necessary if developing a consensual-based vision is difficult or if there is no hierarchical authority that can impose goals on other stakeholders. In some situations, an organization may be confronted with considerable internal turbulence and external pressures so that development of goals or visions is considered unwise as it would only further "stir things up."

An organization's strategy typically is a blend of deliberate and purposeful actions, and reactions to unanticipated developments and external pressures. Since strategies are the "means" for achieving objectives, it follows that three different categories or levels of strategies can be identified:

1. *Organizational strategies* reflect strategic objectives and outline planned avenues for organizational development (e.g., new program initiatives, collaborations, acquisitions and mergers, expansions, etc.).
2. *Programmatic strategies* are designed to implement management objectives and address how to develop, manage, and deliver new and

existing programs (e.g., implement prenatal health care services for disadvantaged expectant mothers).

3. *Functional strategies* focus on administrative and support needs and their impacts on the organization's efficiency and effectiveness (e.g., adopt a program budget format, install a financial system based on an accrual method of accounting).

Formulating strategies involves a blending of rational, scientific examinations and educated intuitive best guesses. An effective method for generating strategies is to make separate lists of critical issues and organizational strengths, and to brainstorm on how those strengths or other skills can be applied to address the critical issues. An effort should be made to identify ways to synthesize opportunities and strengths. During this evaluation, it is important to ask several key questions: Does the proposed strategy meet or address the critical issue? Is it aligned with the organization's mission? Is this approach financially viable? Is this the best approach for the organization? Frequently at this stage, additional information will be required and/or the conclusions reached during the SWOT analysis may need to be re-evaluated.

Strategy making is a dynamic process, and rarely are strategies so well conceived and durable that an organization can avoid the periodic re-evaluation, refinement, and recasting of adopted strategies. Even the best-laid strategic plans must have the capacity to accommodate to shifting conditions, changing client needs and preferences, and emerging opportunities and challenges. Plans must be flexible enough to meet the maneuvering of other competing organizations, to adjust to the experience of what is and is not working, and to incorporate fresh thinking about how to improve the organization's performance. Frequent fine tuning and tweaking of strategies is quite normal. An organization's strategies are formed over a period of time and then reformed with changing conditions. Key elements of an organization's strategies often emerge in bits and pieces as a blend of holdover approaches, fresh actions and reactions, and potential responses (that may still be in the planning stage) to changes.

Occasionally, quantum changes in strategies are needed, especially in crisis situations, where adjustments often must be made quickly to produce a substantially new strategy almost overnight. However, such major changes can not be made too often without creating undue confusion and disruption to organizational performance. When strategies undergo frequent and fundamental changes so that the plan must be overhauled every few months, managers are almost certainly guilty of poor strategic analysis, erratic decision-making, and weak "strategizing" [5]. Well-crafted strategies normally should be good for at least several years, requiring only minor adjustments to keep them in tune with changing circumstances.

2.2 Program Alternatives

Program alternatives provide the fundamental building blocks for strategic planning. A program can be defined as a set of closely related, interdependent activities or services that contribute to a common objective. A program is concerned with a time-span of expenditures that often extends beyond the current fiscal period. The description of each program alternative should include all of the costs associated with its execution.

One such set of activities, cutting across several agencies or departments that focuses on problems of juvenile delinquency, can constitute a program. The establishment of a trauma unit in a hospital emergency room is another example of a program. The internal auditing process within the controller's office may be defined as a program. A university research center concentrating on the environmental sciences may be treated as a program, or may have a number of programs associated with its research mission.

Identifying program alternatives is perhaps the most critical part of the strategic planning process. While some program alternatives may focus on issues that are relevant to the organization as a whole, the majority of these alternatives will relate to management (programmatic or budgetary) concerns and operational or tactical activities. Program alternatives should be quantifiable—an effort should be made to specify a key result to be accomplished within a specific time period. While program alternatives should be realistic and attainable, they should also present a challenge to improve conditions consistent with existing organizational policies, practices, and procedures. They also should be consistent with the resources available (or anticipated) and should assign responsibility and accountability, even in joint efforts.

Under traditional management practices, decision-making frequently becomes *input-oriented*. That is to say, the analysis of objectives and alternative methods of achieving these objectives is based primarily on cost-related issues rather than being policy-based. Under this traditional approach, the effectiveness of these inputs seldom is assessed in terms of meeting identified constituent/client needs or the performance of services. As a consequence, there is no guarantee that the adopted strategies will be coherently responsive to comprehensive objectives.

The formulation of precise, qualitative statements that are *output-oriented*, however, is not an easy task. A common tendency is to describe what the organization does instead of addressing the question of why these activities are appropriate within its mandate. The objective of a public employment agency, for example, is not *to interview, test, counsel, and place unemployed persons in jobs*. This statement focuses on what the agency does—on a process—rather than on the strategic objectives of the agency. A more appropriate objective would be *to assist the unemployed and underemployed in securing satisfactory employment appropriate to their abilities so as to contribute to an increased standard of living for individuals and families within the community.* More specific management objectives might focus on accomplishing the principal purpose for specific target groups, such as the disadvantaged, handicapped, youths, residents of urban ghettos, and the rural unemployed.

Program alternatives describe *how* and *where* specific resources (personnel, equipment, materials, capital expenditures, and so on) will be used in the accomplishment of a strategic objective. Program alternatives often reflect or are drawn from management objectives. They specify the means for achieving a single key result based on the resources (fiscal and personnel) available or anticipated. These program alternatives, in turn, should be related to performance measures and measures of effectiveness that identify the products, service units, and the constituents/clients associated with the activities of the organization in carrying out the operations of the program. Appropriate measures of efficiency and effectiveness provide a base line against which to test the overall performance of the program. In the absence of such measures, the traditional "least cost" compromise is likely to prevail.

Assume, for example, that one of the strategic objectives adopted is *continue to provide for the overall welfare and prosperity of the City and its citizens by developing and enhancing the City's economic base.* Strategies formulated to achieve this objective may include to:

Further develop the City's infrastructure to accommodate future economic growth;
Seek to diversify the economic base;
Enhance the attractiveness of the area for "high tech" companies;
Identify prime areas that have the potential for future industrial and commercial development;
Improve the downtown commercial area; and
Further capitalize on the City's status as a regional trade center

Several program alternatives should be developed for each of these strategies. The strategy that pertains to the City's infrastructure, for example, may yield the following program alternatives:

Study the feasibility of expanding the City's water supply to accommodate the anticipated demands from growth and development anticipated through the year 2005.
Expand the service area and routes of the public transit system to meet the needs of new residential, commercial, and industrial development over the next five years.
Acquire and develop new sites to further expand the City's parks and recreation system in accordance with the recommendations of the strategic plan.

Most public programs extend beyond the period of the annual budget. Therefore, decisions regarding the allocation of resources can have significant implications well beyond the fiscal year under consideration. The extended time horizon of strategic planning makes explicit provision for this characteristic of public resource commitment by shifting the focus of decision from the traditional one-year cycle to a longer time frame. Multi-year program plans should be developed as inputs to each year's budget deliberations. These multi-year plans must be more than linear extrapolations of the current commitments and must reflect the complex shift in demands from increasing or decreasing client groups or constituencies.

Emphasis on program alternatives involves a shift in focus from traditional groupings of activities, based on organizational lines of responsibilities, to programs and subprograms directed toward the achievement of explicitly identified public objectives. The result is also a shift in the approach to resource allocation (budgeting). The traditional line-item/object of expenditure budget focuses on inputs, such as expenditures for personnel, material and supplies, travel, and equipment. The programmatic approach tends to emphasize the outputs of particular efforts that may involve more than one department or agency. These distinctions will be discussed in further detail in Chapter 8.

While these procedural steps may be initiated sequentially, more often they are carried out through a series of iterations. In identifying management objectives, for example, further clarification may be achieved as to the programs and subprograms of an organization. This amplification, in turn, may assist in determining which activities should be placed within each subprogram. Sometimes it will not be possible, however, to formulate precise statements of objectives until the schedule of activities have been examined in some detail. The establishment of such schedules, in turn, may require a further examination of alternative strategies and associated measures of efficiency, economy, and effectiveness.

3 EXPLICIT POLICY SETS

Policies include guidelines, rules, procedures, and administrative practices that are established to support the efforts to implement strategies and achieve objectives. Policies provide guides to decision making and facilitate solving repetitive or recurring problems. Policies are especially important in strategic implementation because they outline an organization's expectations of its employees and managers. They clarify what can and can not be done in pursuit of an organization's objectives. They set boundaries, constraints, and limits on the kind of administrative action that can be taken to reward and sanction behavior. Policies provide a basis for management control, promote consistency and coordination across organizational units, and reduce the amount of time and effort that managers must spend making decisions. Policies clarify what work is to be done by whom, and they promote the delegation of decision making to appropriate managerial levels where various problems usually arise.

3.1 Policy Matrix

In the context of strategic planning, policy statements are intended to cover the entire range of actions requires from the identification of goals to the point at which those goals are attained. The formulation of policy, therefore, embraces various points on a continuum of means, ranging from long-range, general, and educational objectives to more immediate, specific, and action-oriented programs. The number of points along this continuum, of course, will vary from situation to situation.

Five categories of policy may be suggested, spanning a range from norms and values, on the one hand, to relatively specific procedural guidelines on the other. General policies anchor one end of the continuum and control policies define the other end. Between these extremes are arrayed strategic policies, program policies, and implementation policies (see Figure 4.4).

The other dimension of this policy matrix is defined by (1) what is to be accomplished (objectives), (2) when it is to be accomplished (priorities), (3) where it is to be accomplished (locus), (4) how it is to be accomplished (means), and (5) standards for the evaluation of accomplishments. These five factors relate to and help to define the content of policy statements.

As shown in Figure 4.4, four quadrants in the policy matrix require the attention of various participants in the policy-making process. *Basic policy* is primarily of a strategic nature and focuses on objectives and priorities. *Executive policy* is required to establish operational means and standards within the framework of strategic planning. The objectives and priorities of implementation and control are part of the realm of *administrative policy*, whereas the means and standards of implementation and control, in most instances, involve *technical policy*. Each of these quadrants suggests a particular realm of responsibility for policy formulation and, furthermore, delimits the focus and emphasis appropriate to each of these realms. The notion of specific policy sets, therefore, underlines the importance of maintaining these parameters to ensure that one policy quadrant does not encroach unduly on the responsibilities of another quadrant.

The area formed by the demarcation between these four quadrants also is important to define. The vertical plane represents the trade-offs that must be made between executive and administrative policy, while the horizontal plane represents the overlap between strategic, managerial, and operational considerations. It is in these areas that potential conflicts between policies are inevitable.

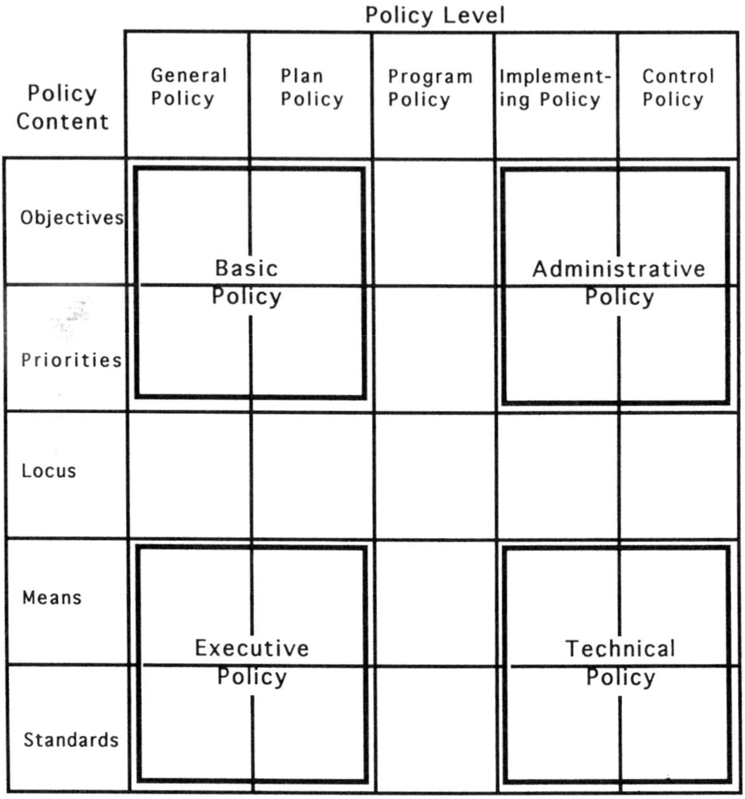

Policy Level

Policy Content	General Policy	Plan Policy	Program Policy	Implement-ing Policy	Control Policy
Objectives					
	Basic Policy			Administrative Policy	
Priorities					
Locus					
Means					
	Executive Policy			Technical Policy	
Standards					

FIGURE 4.4 Multiple-policy matrix.

Effectiveness measures must be formulated and applied to monitor the achievement of goals and objectives. Effectiveness measures involve a scoring technique for determining the status of an organization at certain points in time. They are indicators that measure both direct and indirect impacts of specific resource allocations in the pursuit of certain goals and objectives.

Effectiveness measures can be defined by (1) establishing current levels and types of performance in the organization in discrete categories, (2) estimating the current impacts of resources on this performance, and then (3) defining the desired levels and types of performance. The development of positive statements of performance provides a base from which change can be defined and evaluated.

Performance must be defined in output-oriented terms based on a vocabulary of understandable policy and program variables. Policy and program variables, in turn, must identify administrative and executive policies and those patterns of performance to be affected. An important assumption is that effectiveness measures can be derived or inferred from current conditions (but are not limited to those conditions). This means that current operations and their effects must be continually monitored (through the basic data collection component of the strategic planning model). This continuous evaluation is probably the most effective means available for initiating a goal-oriented planning and decision-making system within an existing organizational structure.

3.2 The Written Plan

The final step in the strategic planning process is to "put it down on paper"—to draft a final planning document and submit it for review by key decision-makers. The following sections are commonly included in a strategic plan.

Introduction or cover letter to give a "stamp of approval" to the plan by the chief executive of the organization.

Executive summary to provide the reader with an understanding as to what the organization aims to accomplish and what is most important about the strategic plan.

Mission and vision statements which should be capable of standing alone without any introductory text.

Organization profile and history to provide a context for the strategic plan.

Critical issues and strategies to make explicit the strategic thinking and assumptions behind the plan.

Program goals and objectives to serve as a guide for operational planning and a primary reference for evaluation.

Management goals and objectives to emphasize the distinction between organizational development goals and service goals.

Appendices to include any additional documentation that will enhance the reader's understanding of the plan.

Senior staff should be consulted to determine whether subsequent detailed action plans can be developed for accomplishing the goals and objectives proposed by the strategic plan. (The focus of annual operating plans will be discussed in further detail in Chapter 5 in conjunction with the concept of Hoshin planning.) Three important attributes of a good annual operating plan are:

1. An appropriate level of detail—enough to guide the work but not so much that it becomes overwhelming, confusing, or unnecessarily constrains creativity;

2. Format that allows for periodic reports on progress toward specific goals and objectives; and

3. Structure that coincides with the strategic plan—goal statements for both levels should be the same, while objective statements may differ with greater specificity evident in the operating plan.

TABLE **4.1**   Basic Components of the Strategic Planning Process

Process elements

Actively involve the organization's leadership to convey the importance and priority of
the strategic planning process;

Establish a list of expectations and provide training to achieve a common understanding;

Include in the planning process those individuals who will be called upon to carry out
the plan to ensure that the plan is realistic and capable of being implemented;

Focus on critical issues and priorities to ensure the credibility of the plan;

Agree on how the plan will be implemented and specify who will be responsible for
carrying it out; and

Schedule periodic evaluations to review progress.

Content elements

Focus on both internal and external issues and opportunities;

Articulate a broad framework—plans that are too detailed and specific become quickly
outdated and end up on the shelf;

Create a balance between the long-term vision and reality; and

Structure the plan to be "user friendly"—keep language, concepts, and format relatively
simple.

Usage elements

Actively use the strategic plan as a management tool;

Incorporate elements of the strategic plan in everyday management practices;

Organize the work of the organization by establishing operational objectives and
activities within the context of the strategic plan;

Design a system for controlling the process; and

Provide mechanisms to inform management on progress.

Source: Adapted from Alliance for Nonprofit Management, "How do we increase our chance of
implementing our strategic plan?"

The strategic plan should answer key questions about priorities and
directions in sufficient detail to serve as a guide for action plans. Real and
potential conflicts should be identified, because such conflicts, if left unresolved,
will inevitably undermine the potency of the strategic plan. The process, content,
and application components that should be included during the strategic planning
process to ensure the usefulness of the plan to the organization are summarized
in Table 4.1.

4 STRATEGIC PLAN IMPLEMENTATION

Webster's Dictionary states that "to implement" means "to provide for the
accomplishment or carrying into effect of a purpose." In the context of strategic
management, implementation is the process by which an organization moves
from the formulation of a strategic plan into the operations necessary to achieve
the specific objectives and strategies identified within the plan.

4.1 Implementation Feasibility Analysis

The objectives of a strategic plan are successfully implemented if actual operations correspond reasonably well to the planned operations and the actual outcomes correspond to the planned or anticipated outcomes. Organizations often are more accustomed to measuring activity levels in terms of inputs (dollars spent) rather than the outputs produced (objectives achieved). The same dollars spent on different objectives (or on alternative approaches to the same objective) may yield greatly varied results. Systematic analysis of program outputs is a cornerstone of more effective management. To undertake such analyses, explicit performance measures and measures of effectiveness must be identified and quantified.

The two basic approaches of program analysis are:

1. Fixed cost approach, where the objective is to maximize benefits for an established level of costs or predetermined budget allocation; and
2. Fixed benefits approach, where the objective is to determine the minimum level of expenditure necessary to achieve some agreed-upon level of benefits.

The first approach often characterizes cost–benefit analyses. The second is frequently followed in cost–effectiveness analysis.

Under the cost–benefit approach, an alternative is selected based on its marginal benefit/cost ratio; that is, the increase in benefits must be greater than the increase in costs for the alternative to be chosen. Cost–benefit analysis assumes that both costs and benefits are capable of being expressed in the same monetary units. Cost–effectiveness measures, on the other hand, help to determine the alternative that provides the greatest effectiveness for the least cost.

Many of the activities of government and nonprofit organizations cannot be sufficiently quantified for successful application of the techniques of cost–benefit analysis. As a consequence, rough surrogates often are developed to approximate the monetary measures of costs and benefits. It is important to recognize, however, that many decisions regarding the delivery of public services can not be predicated solely on a positive cost–benefit ratio (in which the measurable benefits exceed the costs). It may be necessary to commit public resources to the resolution of critical problems for which the benefits are long-term, intangible, and/or not measurable in specific monetary terms.

Ideally, an analysis of the feasibility of implementing a new strategy or program should be performed prior to making the final selection, since an alternative that is highly cost-effective may also be very difficult to implement. All too often, however, policy makers assume that if they can design it, someone else can implement and manage it. Many public policies are adopted with little thought to the particular actions that will be necessary to implement them and scant attention to the specifics of program management.

This reliance on "bureaucratic discretion" merely shifts the responsibility for authentic policy making to the administrative apparatus, where the relative difficulty of managing a program or project is likely to be a major deciding factor in making a choice from among the available alternatives. Therefore, programs chosen to implement broad public policy may take the path of least resistance, rather than the most appropriate course to an effective problem solution.

Even if an implementation feasibility analysis is not performed until after the decision of a specific strategy or program has been made, useful knowledge can be gained which, in turn, will likely increase the probability of successful implementation. Strategic planning must be an iterative process, involving continuous refinement and modification as dictated by changing circumstances in program delivery. The probability that program revisions will be required increases significantly as the time-span of the decision increases.

An analysis of implementation feasibility can be costly in terms of both financial and other resources. Therefore, a quick and direct approach for determining the need for such an assessment should involve an examination of each alternative in two areas: (1) the degree of consensus among the individuals and groups involved in or affected by the program, and (2) the magnitude of change that each program represents when measured against existing policies.

The degree of consensus should be based on an evaluation of the attitudes of at least five groups:

1. The target group—those who will benefit from the program and/or will be required to adapt to new patterns of action.
2. Political leadership, consisting of elected officials in legislative and executive positions, party leaders, and influential political actors.
3. Administrative and operating bureaucracies directly charged with policy execution and program management.
4. Elites in active constituencies—organized publics, interest groups, and community leaders.
5. Individuals and professional organizations that serve as "oversight groups," such as consultants, internal analysts, policy research contractors, and program evaluators.

Incremental changes, in which new programs depart only slightly from present programs, require the least change. New programs designed to foster sweeping developmental and social changes require much higher degrees of change and, therefore, are more difficult to implement.

4.2 Political, Social, and Organizational Constraints

Assessing the feasibility of implementation involves a projection of the political, social, and organizational constraints associated with the set of strategies and program options under consideration. Specifically, the following issues should be raised.

1. Whose ox is likely to be gored (political and economic climate)?
2. What quantitative and qualitative resources are required for successful implementation (resource climate)?
3. How well does the strategy/program option fit with the existing mission of the agency or organization (organizational climate)?
4. What factors of community or client disposition may affect implementation (social climate)?
5. How has the proposed implementation agency (or similar agencies) performed in the past and what difficulties are likely to be encountered in the future (climate of agency competency)?
6. What are the innovative aspects of the strategy/program option that may require major attitudinal shifts among the participants (climate of innovation)?

The ox-goring issue may seem obvious, but trade-offs between conflicting interest groups are seldom clear-cut. Someone is helped and someone else is hurt—even by a fairly innocuous program of system maintenance. Even when it appears that there are no losers, "relative deprivation" may produce the impression of a loss among certain groups. In essence, if a program makes one group better off, another group may feel worse off.

The political environment surrounding the implementation of a strategy or program may harbor potential problems that should not be overlooked. Therefore, it is important to examine some specific questions, such as:

1. Are there complicated legal questions and, if so, to what extent is new legislation required for successful implementation? Does existing legislation or legal precedent hinder implementation?
2. To what extent are private interest groups mobilized in support of or opposed to the strategy/program? What is the degree of cohesion or articulateness of opposing groups?
3. Will the interests of existing client (support) groups be adversely affected by the proposed strategy/program?
4. What is the partisan character of the implementing organization (or jurisdiction)?
5. To what extent does the proposed strategy/program threaten important officials with a reduction of power, prestige, or privilege?
6. Has a recent crisis lent support to the strategy/program? Could the strategy/program be more successful if implemented at a different time?

Future economic conditions are often difficult to predict, especially when dealing with a strategy that requires a long implementation period. Several questions must be asked about the economic implications of a proposed strategy or program:

1. To what extent will prevailing economic conditions be affected by the implementation of the strategy/program?
2. Will future economic resources be sufficient to support successful implementation?
3. To what extent can future political developments affect resource availability?

It is incumbent on the skillful manager to examine these questions before implementation and to assess potential disruptive effects on various interest groups. Standard forums for public involvement, such as public hearings, may not provide all the necessary clues. Citizen surveys and informal contacts with decision leaders may prove more useful in making this assessment. In either case, the strategic manager should strive to reduce the level of uncertainty regarding the impacts of the strategy or program, and to identify the option(s) that will require a lower level of entrepreneurship in terms of adjusting for competing claims.

While qualitative resource requirements for successful implementation often are implicit in the cost–benefit or other analysis of alternatives, an attempt should be made to make these resource issues more explicit. Qualitative resources might include highly specialized personnel, technological uncertainties (e.g., the availability of a particular computerized information system), or merely a certain level of required coordination between agencies. All these resources have intangible costs, and the strategic manager should try to calculate these costs, albeit crudely, and to identify the program option with the lowest qualitative costs.

All programs require quantitative resources—such as money, personnel, and time—for successful implementation. The following questions might be useful in examining these constraints.

1. What sources of funds are definitely available and how flexible are these funding sources in terms of allocations to different aspects of the strategy/program?
2. Does the strategy/program require additional funds in face of tight revenue constraints?
3. Will the strategy/program require space, facilities, and support services that may be difficult to obtain?
4. Are significant technological or procedural uncertainties involved in implementation?

5. To what extent are special personnel capabilities and/or training required?
6. Are significant organizational adjustments required to achieve effective implementation?

The organizational climate is a critical variable in assessing the feasibility of implementation. Strategies or program options that go against the grain of existing missions and/or organizational behavior patterns are likely to encounter difficulties in implementation.

The degree of influence exerted by a bureaucracy is dependent on (1) political support, (2) organizational vitality, (3) leadership, (4) the nature of the organization's task, and (5) the skills and expertise of the members of the organization. Several characteristics of the bureaucratic structure that also should be of interest include organizational history, traditional and legal bases, agency incentive systems, degree of decision-making autonomy, agency norms, and operation procedures.

Public officials often must rely on institutional mechanisms and procedures to increase the likelihood that agency staffs will act in a manner consistent with program standards and objectives. In addition to standard mechanisms of personnel control—recruitment and selection, assignment, advancement, and promotion—a wide variety of sanctions and symbolic or material rewards may be applied. Effective use of these mechanisms requires open and distinct lines of communication, both horizontally and vertically.

Community climate or client ethos is equally important to the choice of strategies or program options. While reflected to some degree in the assessment of interest groups, community climate is a broader and often more nebulous concept than interest group attitudes. Consideration of community climate involves a general assessment of recent events and trends that may impinge on the range of options under consideration. For example, a recent crisis may lead to support for one of the program choices. The manager, in turn, can use this support to aid in mobilizing resources. Exploring the horizon for catalytic social and economic events may aid in the implementation process.

The success of any new strategy or program rests ultimately on its acceptance by that portion of the community that it serves. Public opinion can be extremely influential in determining whether and how a strategic change is implemented. It is important to know the extent to which public opinion has been mobilized for or against the strategy or program and the degree to which community elites (such as business and social leaders), favor or oppose implementation.

Past performance of the designated agency is an obvious factor in determining the feasibility of implementation. Regular and systematic evaluations of performance are rare, however, and choice of the implementing agency or agencies may be predetermined. The following questions may be helpful in perceiving potential barriers to implementation, arising from the perceptions of those who will be called upon to implement the program.

1. Does the new strategy/program conflict with employees' values?
2. To what extent does the strategy/program require changes in the attitudes or behavior of government employees?
3. To what extent does the strategy/program threaten jobs?
4. What will the reaction of organized labor be to this new strategy/program?
5. What will be the difficulties associated with overcoming the natural resistance to change?

Characteristics that might either hinder or help a strategy/program become operational can be identified by asking the following questions.

1. Can the relative advantage be observed (that is, the degree to which the new strategy/program is perceived as better than the idea it is designed to replace)?
2. Is the innovation compatible with existing values, past experiences, and the needs of the client groups?
3. Is the innovation perceived as being too complex to understand and use?
4. Can the innovation be initiated on a limited, experimental, or pilot basis?
5. Are the results of the innovation observable to others?

Although the relative advantage of a new strategy or program may be measured in economic terms, factors of social prestige, convenience, and satisfaction are often of equal importance. A program that is not compatible with the prevailing values and norms of the community may experience considerable difficulty in achieving acceptance. Some innovations are readily understood by most members of the client groups. Others are not, and consequently, will be adopted more slowly. New ideas that can be tried on an "installment basis" will generally be adopted more quickly than those that must be accepted all at once. The easier it is for an individual to see the positive results of an innovation, the more likely they are to adopt it.

These dimensions of implementation are not always of equal importance. In some cases, one or more of these factors may have little significance for successful implementation. In other instances, one aspect—such as political support or technological uncertainty—may be so vital that an indication of difficulties in this dimension would be sufficient to eliminate an otherwise attractive strategy or program option.

4.3   Performance Measures

Once programs are implemented, measurement techniques should be applied to help in the determination of needed improvements and modifications. Program analysis tends to be prospective; program evaluation focuses on the actual performance of ongoing or recently completed activities. Program analysis and program evaluation represent an iterative cycle—analysis precedes program commitments and evaluation assesses the impacts and effectiveness of these decisions and commitments.

Performance measures should be formulated and applied to determine the level of achievement associated with agreed-upon goals and objectives. These measures involve a scoring technique for assessing the status of an organization at certain points. Performance must be defined in output-oriented terms, based on a vocabulary of understandable policy and program variables. An important assumption is that performance measures can be derived or inferred from current conditions (but are not limited to those conditions). Secondary measures of effectiveness—surrogates—often must be used to test alternative approaches and to evaluate costs.

Performance evaluation has been a watchword in both the private and public sectors for over four decades. Despite considerable fanfare, however, systematic evaluation of public programs remains more a promise than a practice. Public goals and objectives often are nebulous and ill-defined. Consequently, the measurement of program results is often elusive. Thus, in spite of the emphasis placed on evaluation in strategic planning, its application has largely been limited to postmortems of abandoned or drastically altered programs, or has focused on isolated components of larger program issues. Concepts and techniques of performance evaluation will be examined in further detail in Chapter 11.

5   A CONTINUOUS PROCESS, NOT A PANACEA

Strategic planning must be a continuous process performed in annual cycles and coupled with direct involvement of key management personnel. The cyclical nature of this process offers an opportunity to introduce the various components in a series of refinements rather than on a whole-cloth basis. Formalization of the process, however, is at the very root of successful strategic planning, as distinguished from forecasting and rather piecemeal analytical efforts of the past.

5.1   Information Requirements of Strategic Planning

Strategic planning can be characterized by (1) concern with the processes by which goals and objectives are formulated and policy decisions are made, (2) an extended time horizon on which to base decisions, (3) an emphasis on a more comprehensive program structure, (4) formal mechanisms for ongoing evaluation in terms of agreed-upon program objectives, and (5) application of quantitative techniques of analysis. Each of these elements has special information needs, as outlined below. An inability to provide for these needs can limit the successful application of the strategic planning process.

The concern with the decision-making process builds on the assumption that more rational decisions will be made if management is provided with well-organized, factual information at key points in its deliberations. Any decision, of course, is based on both fact and value. The principal contribution of the strategic planning approach is the strengthening of the factual basis for decision through the development of information management and program evaluation systems.

Such information systems, however, are highly dependent upon the storage and retrieval capacity of modern data processing hardware and software. These systems, in turn, are vulnerable to the problems of GIGO ("garbage in—garbage out") that accompany the use of computers in decision-making. Various standardized reporting formats and turnaround documents may be required in an effort to increase the consistency, reliability, and validity of information. Turnaround documents are periodic reports that provide data inputs to the information system and information back to the originating agency. Unfortunately, as more attention is devoted to the form of the reports and less to the content, there is an increased danger of the "medium becoming the message." These issues will be discussed in further detail in Chapter 12 on information management and decision-support systems.

5.2   Completing the Forward Pass

Bear Bryant once said that whenever you throw a forward pass, four things can happen, and three of them are bad. Unfortunately, the same thing can be said about attempts to implement a strategic plan. There are four possible consequences, three of which are relatively undesirable. First, a relatively poor plan can be developed; that is, the theory on which the plan is based is not very good and/or the analysis is not very sound. Even if this plan is successfully implemented, it is likely to end in failure. Such a plan will not meet the needs of the organization or community, since it is not an accurate reflection of these needs. The problem here is not in the implementation stage but in the planning stage.

Second, a relatively poor strategic plan that is poorly implemented will surely end in failure. And third, a plan that is poorly implemented is not likely to be successful in achieving the objectives envisioned in the original planning effort.

The final possible consequence is the desirable one—a good strategic plan is formulated (that is, one based on a reasonable theoretical basis, a comprehensive identification of objectives, and a sound analysis of the feasibility of implementation), and this plan is successfully implemented. The end result, therefore, is a successful program or project. The pivotal component in this formula for success is the careful and complete delineation of objectives.

As Dale McConkey observed,

> Even the most technically perfect strategic plan will serve little purpose if it is not implemented. Many organizations tend to spend an inordinate amount of time, money, and effort on developing the strategic plan, treating the means and circumstances under which it will be implemented as afterthoughts! Change comes through implementation and evaluation, not through the plan. A technically imperfect plan that is implemented well will achieve more than the perfect plan that never gets off the paper on which it is typed [6].

This overview of the rudiments of strategic planning runs the risk of generating an impression that the process is simple and relatively easy to implement. This is not the case, however. Organizations that have adopted this approach are well aware that it is not a panacea. Strategic planning will not immediately resolve all problems confronting an organization. Nor is its implementation easy to administer. To be successful, a firm commitment by those who will be involved to see the process through is essential.

ENDNOTES

1. Heinz Weilrich. The TOWS matrix: a tool for situational analysis. Long Range Planning. Vol. 15, No. 2, April 1982, p. 61.
2. Alan J. Rowe, Richard O. Mason, and Karl E. Dickel. Strategic Management and Business Policy: A methodological approach. Reading, MA.: Addison-Wesley Publishing Co., 1982, p. 155.
3. Ian C. MacMillan, Competitive strategies for not-for-profit agencies. Sol C. Snider Entrepreneurial Research Center, 1983. For more information on the MacMillan matrix, contact the Support Centers of America, (415) 974-5100.
4. John Bryson. Strategic Planning for Public and Nonprofit Organizations. San Francisco, CA: Jossey-Bass Publishers, 1995, p. 111.
5. Arthur A. Thompson, Jr. and A. J. Strickland III. Strategic Management: Concepts & Cases. Boston, MA.: Irwin/McGraw-Hill, 1996, p. 9.
6. Dale McConkey. Planning in a changing environment. Business Horizons. September-October 1988, p. 66.

5

Productivity and Quality Improvement

In the 1980s, leaders in both the private and public sectors became concerned by major declines in the nation's annual rate of growth in productivity and the apparent loss of competitive position relative to other nations. In 1989, the MIT Commission on Industrial Productivity concluded,

> First, American productivity is not growing as fast as it used to, and productivity is not growing as fast as it is elsewhere, most notable in Japan. Second, other indicators of industrial performance that are less easily quantified than productivity but no less important tell a disquieting story. In such areas as product development, American companies are no longer perceived as world leaders, even by American customers. There is also evidence that technological innovations are being incorporated into practice more quickly abroad, and the pace of invention and discovery in the United States may be slowing [1].

While everyone seemed to understand that the United States was facing significant "productivity problems," there was considerable disagreement about their causes and magnitude. Various factors were cited as causes of the decline in American productivity—from an erosion of the work ethic to the decline in S.A.T. scores tied to the number of hours of television watched, and from the decline in spending for research and development to the increase in divorce rates [2]. While it was obvious that the United States had not been keeping pace with its former rate of growth in terms of productivity and, in many areas, was lagging behind its major foreign competitors, economists and economic historians argued about whether that was bad, not so bad, or even meaningless.

1   NEW MANAGEMENT INITIATIVES

Concerns regarding productivity and quality have spawned a host of new management initiatives. Many of these approaches attempt to integrate more traditional measurement techniques with new forms of participative management and include team building, quality circles, quality of worklife, quality improvement, and gainsharing techniques. More recently, attention has focused on problems of performance and productivity as issues of quality of service. Polls have shown, for example, that the services of local government are rated extremely low in terms of quality, receiving ratings below even services that traditionally have registered widespread customer dissatisfaction.

1.1   Three Management Models

Management methods have continued to evolve to address changing organizational and societal needs. New methods have emerged either because changes in the broader environment made prior methods no longer as effective or because someone believed they had a new or better understanding of how to do something. Each new method, however, has been built on past experience and has attempted to improve upon previously established methods. Efforts to discover or confirm useful combinations of management methods applicable to different situations have also added to the mix. Thus, as in other fields of endeavor, management methods have evolved by redoing, sometimes discarding, and frequently building on previous methods.

Ackoff and Gharajedaghi have identified an evolution in management approaches—from mechanical to biological to social models—which provides a useful framework for examining established and emerging management methods [3]. These three models are not mutually exclusive. Things seldom are as clearcut in the real world as pure models would imply. As the evolution has occurred, some aspects of prior models often have been maintained and/or refined (see Table 5.1).

Organizations based on variations of the mechanical model were common around 1900. Such organizations are still frequently seen today. The Ford Motor Company, under Henry Ford, is a prime example of an organization built on the mechanical model. Once, while Ford was on a trip in Europe, some company employees made some design improvements that they felt could not be made while Ford was in Detroit. When Ford returned, the employees showed him their improved design. According to the story, Ford jumped on the redesigned car, smashing it, and said, "Your job is not to make improvements; your job is to do what I tell you to do."

TABLE 5.1   Three Management Models

Model	Characteristics	Role of manager
Mechanical	Draws an analogy between an organization and a machine. Each worker is assigned a particular procedure and taught to follow it rigorously. Assumes a static environment in which a machine can be built to carry out repetitive tasks.	To design the appropriate machine and control workers and inputs to minimize variations.
Biological	Draws parallels between an organization and a biological organism. Workers are the arms, legs, sensory, and other organs, ultimately serving the needs of the organism as a whole. Assumes that the parts do their job according to their own program (including communication among themselves).	To decide what the organism as a whole is to accomplish, observe the functioning of the parts, and provide feedback when outputs are not satisfactory.
Social	Uses an analogy between an organization and a society of individuals where each individual has the ability to think and learn for themselves. Much interaction among individuals who depend on each other for mutual adaptation and survival.	To design a desirable future and to find ways to achieve it by managing interactions among individuals and organizational components.

Source: Russell L. Ackoff and Jamshid Gharajedaghi. Mechanisms, Organisms and Social Systems. Strategic Management Journal. Vol 5, 1984.

The biological model is more appropriate for situations that require accommodations to change. If change is slow enough, the organization (organism) can evolve gradually to cope with it. If adapting to predictable change is within the organization's capabilities, the component parts of the organization can be trained to handle the new situations. However, the organism may become extinct if the required change exceeds its capabilities to adjust. Its ecological niche will be assumed by another organism better able to adapt to the new environment. In some cases, this new organism may have evolved from the original species.

The social model is well-suited to situations in which change is relatively unpredictable—and to situations in which it may be possible for the organization to create its own future. The social model is based on "learning from experience" and is applicable to situations that require the continual development of new capabilities. Management must foster a learning system through which a desirable future can be identified and means to achieve it can be planned and implemented.

Some interpretations of the social model assume that managers must forsake strong leadership in favor of empowering others. The absence of explicit leadership may work in some instances, such as in a small professional partnership. However, a complex organization trying to respond quickly and successfully to changing conditions requires both strong leadership and greater empowerment.

Individuals in an organization that has adopted the social model may have many different objectives, and, at times, these objectives may be in conflict with each other. The social model, however, makes possible a level of collective action that often can offset problems caused by a multiplicity of purposes.

1.2   Interpretations of the Social Model

Several interpretations of the social model seek to address issues of productivity, quality, and performance. While these models can be clustered in several broad categories, actual applications are rarely pure types—even when labeled as a productivity measurement system, a participative management process, or a quality management approach. Hybrid systems are generally the rule. Performance measurement and quality management approaches require employee acceptance and involvement. Participation and quality management approaches require some forms of measurement to focus efforts to solve problems and to evaluate results.

Most of the composite work measurement techniques developed by federal and state governments over the past 30 years have been incorporated in the *comprehensive productivity measurement* approach. While these methods have been around for some time, a more ambitious application of these techniques is involved in explicit efforts to incorporate measures of productivity into organizational processes for goal setting and budgeting. The composite approach goes well beyond the simple control and accountability systems applied in the public sector in the past (see Table 5.2).

The measurement concept has been taken a major step further by paradigms that attempt to combine multiple measures of performance with measures of productivity and resource usage. Participative management approaches that focus on correctional efforts usually result in a more integrated performance and productivity improvement model that includes more sophisticated measurement devices. These efforts attempt to link performance evaluation with the productivity capacity of the organization (see Table 5.3).

Major experiments to develop methods to analyze and evaluate knowledge-based, white collar organizations in terms of their resource and management requirements, and service and production capacity, are still in the initial stages of

TABLE 5.2 Comprehensive Productivity Measurement

I.   Document organizational goals and objectives.

II.   Identify specific organizational activities and programs to be measured.

III. Define work output measures. Methods include engineered work standards, time studies, average unit cost and workload measures, historical volume or output measures, supervisory estimations, and Delphi techniques.

IV.   Define input measures (usually in terms of cost or resource utilization).

V.   Determine requirements for data collection and productivity reporting systems. Determine feedback channels.

VI.   Integrate productivity measurements into organizational management practices through (a) performance appraisals, (b) monetary incentives, (c) performance targeting, (d) performance contracting, and (e) employee communication efforts.

Source: Adapted from U.S. Office of Personnel Management and U.S. General Accounting Office guidelines.

development (see Table 5.4). While early results are quite tentative, as methods for measuring white-collar productivity become more advanced, public and nonprofit organizations may be able to better understand their capacities for improved quality and productivity.

Team building involves a number of strategies designed to deal with intra- and inter-group competition and with unresponsiveness and structural rigidities within an organization. Employees are encouraged to address productivity and other operational problems by organizing flexible "semi-autonomous work groups"—operating teams, problem-oriented teams, or management teams

TABLE 5.3 Integrated Performance Productivity Measurement

I.   Define organizational goals and determine how performance management techniques can assist in achieving those goals.

II.   Hold orientation meetings between management and employee representatives.

III.   Determine productivity indicators.

IV.   Survey employee attitudes toward work environment and assignments.

V.   Survey client satisfaction with products and services of the organization.

VI.   Discuss productivity indicators, employee attitudes, and citizen satisfaction levels in organizational meetings.

VII.   Establish action plans to remedy identified problems.

VIII. Implement action plans and evaluate results.

IX.   Institute employee–management problem solving, communications, and team building and capacity building training efforts.

Source: Adapted from Total Performance Management System Report, City of San Diego, California, 1985.

TABLE 5.4 Experimental Productivity Measurement

I.   Analyze significant factors associated with tasks undertaken within the organization.
  1. Degree to which work assignments are structured and clearly defined.
  2. Degree of multiple dimensions to work aspects.
  3. Degrees of task ambiguity.
  4. Levels of judgment discretion required and permitted.
  5. Extent to which unforeseen events and results may impact work.
  6. Time lag between actions and outcomes.
  7. Subjectivity over value of outputs and inputs.
II. Develop an integrated approach to productivity measurement.
  1. Definitions and measurements of output must be tied to organizational strategies and goals.
  2. The analysis of productivity must focus on factors instinctively used by program managers.
  3. Output must be assessed in subjective terms for many knowledge work organizations.
  4. Reliability of data and relationship to performance must be stressed in productivity analysis.
III. Design conclusions.
  1. Managers are (or should be) concerned with broad concepts such as quality, innovation, and flexibility.
  2. Detailed indicators of effectiveness are needed that can be reliably assessed and correlated with each other.
  3. Systems must be flexible for different units of analysis.
IV. Experimental concept.
  1. Detailed indicators of effectiveness must be aggregated into clusters representing broad areas of output or effectiveness.
    a. Creativity, challenge, and teamwork.
    b. Standards and ease of work procedures.
    c. Pace and work intensity.
    d. Flexibility.
    e. Experimentation.
    f. Adequacy of resources for work.
  2. Use statistical methods to ensure reliability of results.
V.   System validation.

Source: Adapted from the work of Dr. Michael Packer, Laboratory on Manufacturing and Productivity, Massachusetts Institute of Technology, Cambridge, MA.

(see Table 5.5). A major emphasis is on building a framework for cooperation and communication.

Origins of the *quality control circle* are generally traced to experiences in Japanese industry where impressive productivity rates were attributed to highly goal-oriented, group activities within organizations. The underlying concept of

TABLE 5.5   Team Building

Objectives: improving organizational productivity.
  Job enrichment; increasing the variety of tasks to be performed and the skills of the employee.
  Encouraging greater worker participation and cooperation.
  Enhancing employee autonomy.
Major variations
  Operating teams: groups of employees who perform their normal day-to-day tasks as a team.
  Problem-oriented teams: groups of employees who are brought together to discuss and recommend solutions to specific problems.
  Management teams: groups of supervisory management personnel who work together regularly on operational problems and address problems with transcendental objectives.
Critical variables for success
  Teams must be assigned whole tasks with identifiable, meaningful, and significant objectives.
  Members of the team must have a number of different skills required for group completion of the tasks.
  Teams must be given autonomy to make decisions about methods by which work is completed.
  Evaluation of the team should be based on performance of the group as a whole rather than team contributions of individuals.

Source: Adapted from John Greinier. Productivity and Motivation. Washington, D.C.: The Urban Institute Press, 1981.

the quality circle is that small voluntary groups of key participants can do more than discuss problems—they can plan for and implement actual solutions (see Table 5.6). Three critical factors need to be considered in establishing such autonomous, voluntary groups: (1) management, employees, and the unions must be firmly committed to this cooperative approach, (2) a concept of measurement must be established to serve as the basis for the assessment of the work environment and productivity changes, and (3) some form of facilitative expertise must be provided to assist in organizing, focusing, and implementing the quality circle deliberations.

In the *quality of worklife* (QWL) approach, criteria for project evaluation can go beyond short-range performance and productivity measures to focus on broader measurements of the quality of life in the work environment. In the QWL approach, employees participate in all phases—research, planning, implementation of change, and evaluation—as part of a decision-making process based on obtaining consensus among all sectors of the organization (see Table 5.7).

TABLE 5.6 Quality Circles

 I. Initiation
    A. Obtain organizational commitment from management.
    B. Locate employee level interest and participation.
    C. Establish an organizational steering group and working group.
    D. Plan for facilitator and circle member training.
    E. Develop goals and objectives for the program.
 II. Development
    A. Train facilitators for quality circles in group dynamics, group leadership, and problem-solving techniques.
    B. Solicit names of employees interested in becoming circle members.
    C. Conduct circle member training (if desired, as necessary).
III. Implementation
    A. Establish circles and resolve mechanical issues: name, minutes, proceedings, rules, logistics, and communications.
    B. Conduct problem-solving techniques training within the quality circle process.
        1. Problem identification.
        2. Problem selection.
        3. Problem analysis and information collection.
        4. Develop solutions and make recommendations.
        5. Review process.
        6. Implementation by members of the circle.
IV. Evaluation
    A. Follow-up on circle activities.
    B. Assess impact of the circle's recommendations.
    C. Evaluate organizational impacts on circles.

Source: Adapted from NASA, Lewis Research Center, Report on Quality Circle Process. Cleveland, OH, 1985.

TABLE 5.7 Quality of Worklife

Objective: Jointly determine and implement organizational effectiveness by addressing explicit internal goals and objectives to include performance, behavior, and effective dimensions of work.

Project evaluation criteria: Go beyond both short-range measures of performance (e.g., productivity, efficiency, standards of performance) and long-range productivity measures (e.g., absenteeism, cooperation, grievances, and turnover) by focusing on specific measurements of quality of work life and work environment.

Participative management: Throughout all phases—research, planning, change, and evaluation. Organization and individual needs balanced in addressing productivity, performance, work environment, and quality of working life issues. Voluntary experiment to re-engage the "expertise" of the worker in dealing with organizational and individual problems.

---

2 TOTAL QUALITY MANAGEMENT

Total quality management (TQM) involves a series of techniques, formulated initially by W. Edward Deming, while working with the Japanese in the early 1950s. These techniques were elaborated upon by Joseph M. Juran (also working with the Japanese) and Philip Crosby in the 1970s. The writings of Deming, Juran, and Crosby have found more recent favor in the United States in such industrial entities as Ford, Xerox, Motorola, and Hewlett-Packard. TQM is "a structural system for creating organization-wide participation in planning and implementing a continuous improvement process that exceeds the expectations of the customer. It is built on the assumption that 90 percent of problems are process, not employee, problems [4]."

2.1 Total Delivery System

The basic premise underlying the *system of profound knowledge*, as espoused by W. Edward Deming, is that management must understand their processes at the grass roots level in order to successfully manage the implementation of major improvements [5]. The first among Deming's 14 points for management is to "Create constancy of purpose toward improvement of product and service, with the aim to become competitive and to stay in business and to provide jobs [6]." Deming's approach focuses on an organization as a total delivery system. This perspective builds on an understanding that performance is governed largely by the system within which an individual works. According to Deming, knowledge about performance variation is essential for the management of a system, including management of people. This knowledge must include an appreciation of what constitutes a stable system and some understanding of common and special causes of variation.

Deming's approach to understanding the causes of variation is highly statistical. It requires extensive charting of reliability and defects rates to ensure that workers incorporate work quality from the outset rather than relying on later inspections for defects. The third of Deming's 14 points is to "cease dependence on inspection to achieve quality. Eliminate the need for inspection on a mass basis by building quality into the product in the first place [6]." This zero defects and statistical reliability measurement approach, however, also is keyed to training workers to recognize and adhere to organizational policy with regard to quality. Crosby and Juran advocated the education and retraining of employees to increase their "quality awareness" and to develop attitudes that manifest strict adherence to product and service specifications—that is, "conformance to requirements."

2.2 Four Basic Concepts of TQM

TQM builds on four basic concepts: *continuous improvement, customer focus, total participation*, and *social networking*. Concepts and techniques for continuous improvement are fairly well developed. Customer focus is gaining acceptance. Total participation is somewhat underdeveloped, but many organizations still have not accepted the notion of social networking.

Continuous improvement is necessary for survival of organizations in a rapidly changing and highly competitive world. In contrast to the traditional approach of "if it ain't broke, don't fix it," continuous improvements advocates the continued search for ways to do things better, even when existing practices appear to be working reasonably well. As advocated by Deming and his followers, this approach subsumes the concepts of statistical process control, reactive improvement of existing products and processes, and proactive improvement of new products and processes. It uses the scientific method to determine which management methods really operate most effectively in given situations. Continuous improvement is the main avenue through which the other basic components of TQM were developed.

Customer focus contrasts with the more traditional notion that an organization knows best what its customers and service users need and want. Today, organizations must keep a constant eye on their customers and service users in order to respond quickly to new customer needs. Only in this way can they ensure that the finite resources of the organization are deployed as effectively as possible to provide customer satisfaction. A variety of techniques are applied to "take the pulse" of the organization's customers/service users in order to identify (and in some cases, direct) shifts in market requirements.

Total participation is in contrast to the more traditional view that some people in any organization do the work, while different people plan how the work is to be improved. Many feel that this traditional model does not adapt fast enough to change. In today's organizations, everyone needs to be involved in both *doing* and *improving* the work. Much of the current emphasis is on the creation of new knowledge, which often depends on the integration of insights and skills from people throughout the organization (and from people outside the organization, such as customers). Total participation fosters this kind of integration. Total participation embraces the ideas of quality circles, teamwork, cross-functional teams, and so forth. Total participation also includes procedures for developing and phasing in new management and quality methods. Included among these approaches are methods for developing necessary new skills and recognizing the importance of training, rewards and incentives, methods for alerting management to the need for change, and methods for aligning key activities to attain ultimate goals (e.g., Hoshin planning).

The traditional assumption has been that organizations must carefully guard their management and quality methods because these methods afford a competitive advantage. However, many organizations today do not have sufficient resources or insight to develop independently the new methods required to remain competitive. Rather, the most productive course is for organizations to participate in a mutual learning system or *social network*. Quality methods and "best practices" should be shared, and organizations should encourage each other to develop improved management methods. Two keys to *networking* are (1) exchange of real case studies, and (2) an explicit infrastructure for communications (for example, publications, national quality awards and certificates, quality societies, and reports on experiments with new methods).

Taken together, these four components of TQM form a rather comprehensive system of management. TQM makes a major break with many of the methods typically used in the mechanical and biological models. TQM's continuous improvement and customer focus have completed the move away from the mechanical model and toward the social model. And TQM's total participation and social networking move away from some aspects of the biological model and are more toward the social model. Tools and techniques most often applied in TQM are outlined in Table 5.8.

The concepts of TQM reinforce the social model of management by supporting a learning system.

Continuous improvement provides the basis for a learning system.
Customer focus provides a major source of feedback for the learning system.
Total participation enables the learning system to function in the organization (e.g., through voluntary quality circles, cross-functional teams, and so on).
Social networking supports the learning system from outside the organization.

While TQM is as applicable to public organizations as to private sector manufacturing and service industries, its application in public administration is somewhat more problematic. There are a number of reasons for this difficulty, including:

Public organizations tend to be bureaucratic and nonresponsive to service users needs;
Employees in public organizations often lack a sense of individual ownership, responsibility, client-care, and empowerment;

TABLE 5.8 Total Quality Management Tools

Tool	Definition	Purpose
Activity network diagram	Simplified version of a PERT or CPM diagram.	To map sequence in which activities will be undertaken.
		To identify activities that can be done simultaneously.
Affinity diagram	Similar ideas generated in brainstorming are grouped together with a header that captures the meaning of each group of ideas.	To organize facts, opinions, ideas, and issues into natural groupings to aid in diagnosis of complex problem.
Bar chart	Data points drawn as proportionally sized, side-by-side, or stacked bars.	To compare distinct (noncontinuous) items.
Cause and effect (fishbone) diagram	Pictorial representation of possible causes of an identified effect.	To show relationships between causes and subcauses and the consequences or effects.
Control charts	x bar R chart: Average values and ranges and their control limits. Used for continuous values, such as length, weight, or concentrations.	To determine whether process characteristics consistently approach extreme control limits.
		To determine whether a process is in or out of control.
	np, c, p, u charts: Discrete numbers of defects per unit or defective units for different types of samples.	To identify upward or downward trends in process characteristics.
		To separate variations due to assignable causes from those due to chance causes.
Datasheet	Data entries in a table of rows and columns, or on single cards	To organize, manage, and track data.
		To calculate relationships between data.
Histogram	Frequency distribution, drawn as proportionally sized bars.	To compare distributions.
	Shows distribution of variables.	To determine means and modes.
		To identify population control limits, mixtures, abnormality, or errors.
Interrelationship digraph	Causal relationships between items are shown by drawing arrows from ideas that are causes to ideas that are results.	To identify initial action items (ideas that are predominantly causes).
		To identify long-range targets (ideas that are predominantly results).

Tool	Description	Purpose
Ishikawa diagram	Graphic description of various process elements (same as fishbone diagram).	To analyze potential sources of variations or problems.
Matrix diagram	Relationships between two or more sets of items.	To facilitate analysis of the relationship of each item in one set to all items in the other set.
Pareto chart	Data points drawn as proportionally sized bars and ranked by relative size, with or without a line, indicating cumulative total with the addition of each item.	To break down broad causes into smaller categories. To identify the vital few and the trivial many for efficient problem-solving. To show where to put initial effort to get the most gain.
Pie chart	Shows the distribution of items and arranges them from most to least frequent. Percentages of a whole, depicted as proportionally sized slices of a round pie.	To visualize the proportions and relative importance of contributing items.
Prioritization matrices	Priority items selected by applying a set of criteria to each item.	To distinguish among multiple items in terms of their relative impacts.
Process decision program chart (PFPC)	Lists steps in a particular activity. Identifies what could go wrong at each step and lists counter measures	To identify appropriate responses to potential problems and issues in process-related activities.
Run chart	Data points in time sequences, connected by a line, with or without a filled area below the line.	To determine trends over time; shows history and pattern of variation
Scatter diagram	Multiple pairs of data plotted as points, with or without a regression line, that is the line of best fit for the data.	To analyze the correlation, if any, between two variables. To predict future relationships based upon past correlations.
Spider chart	Current state plotted on a circle that represents the desired or optimal state.	To visualize and compare the current state against the desired or optimal state.
Tree diagram	Breaks down a general purpose into more specific action items.	To answer the question "how accomplished?" (reading left to right). To answer the question "why?" (reading right to left).

Levels and extent of service tend to be determined by political as opposed to market considerations, especially for subsidized and zero-priced services;

Public employees often evident a lack of clarity about the multiple customers and stakeholders involved, even in single transactions; and

Problems of scale and complexity frequently are associated with large, centralized public organizations, and sometimes, with large-scale technological bases for their operations.

2.3 Hoshin Kanri

An approach to the implementation of total quality management is presented in Table 5.9. At the core of this approach is the concept of *hoshin kanri*. This system of planning and deployment evolved in Japan in the 1950s and 1960s, and is now being applied by many leading companies around the world. The literal translation of *hoshin* (from the Japanese) is *ho* meaning "direction" and *shin* meaning "needle" or the English equivalent of "compass." The word *kanri* can also be broken into two parts: *kan* translates as "channeling" or "control," and *ri* translates as "reason" or "logic." Taken together, *hoshin kanri* means *management and control of an organization's direction or focus.* It is a system of rules and forms that encourage employees to analyze situations, create plans for improvement, conduct performance checks, and take appropriate actions to correct deficiencies.

TABLE 5.9 Implementing Total Quality Management

I. Attain a "critical mass" of top management participants who understand TQM and are willing to initial pilot program to test its application.

II. Form pilot study team.

   1. Address specific, high-priority issues that (a) have a high probability of success, (b) management agrees are important, (c) issues one is presently working on, and (d) are very important to the customer.

   2. Document the results of the initial study in terms of (a) changes in process and procedures, (b) affects on worker attitudes and behaviors, and (c) levels of customer satisfaction.

III. Define customer needs through quality function deployment—an organized system to identify, prioritize, and translate customer needs into organizational priorities.

   1. Customers are placed into major groupings.

   2. Tools such as customer or user surveys, focus groups, complaints and feedback, etc., are used to identify customer needs.

   3. Customer needs are compared to the characteristics of the service system through a matrix.

(continued)

TABLE **5.9** (*Continued*)

IV. Initiate Hoshin planning.
  1. Identify the mission of the organization (including relevant goals and objectives to implement the mission).
  2. Clarify customer needs in light of the mission of the organization.
  3. Identify the critical processes involved in servicing the customers of the organization and establish the performance measures applicable to these processes.
  4. Formulate the "vision" of the organization (i.e., its long-range goal or target, built on the current mission of the organization and value statements of top management).
  5. Identify priority breakthrough items in key areas of service—items that must be initiated as a first critical step through achieving the organization's vision.
  6. Disseminate results of organizational breakthrough planning and initiate breakthrough planning efforts at the division and unit levels.
V. Form daily management teams.
  1. Daily management teams are composed of individuals who normally work together on the process under review. The roles of the team leader, facilitator, and team members must be clearly defined.
  2. A problem-solving process appropriate to the activities of the team should be identified and adopted to provide a common technique and language for process improvement.
  3. The discussions of the team in the application of the problem-solving process should be full documented to ensure replication of successful approaches.
VI. Establish cross-functional management teams.
  1. The purpose of cross-functional teams is to target team efforts on key projects that cross functional lines and to evaluate and improve the work of ongoing study teams.
  2. Cross-functional teams can integrate studies across divisional lines and improve systems at the policy level.
  3. Cross-functional teams can select projects aligned with priority breakthrough items.
VII. Reporting, recognition, and awards.
  1. A series of regular reports should be prepared by the teams and presented to top management.
  2. Prompt implementation of team recommendation provides tangible recognition of the efforts of the study teams.
  3. Awards should be provided for outstanding team or individual performance based on savings (time and money), uniqueness of solutions, and importance to the organization.

Source: Adapted from L. Edwin Coate. Implementing Total Quality Management in a University Setting. Oregon State University, Eugene, OR. July 1990.

Principles of *hoshin kanri* were first introduced as part of efforts to train Japanese managers and engineers in management techniques after World War II. This training included the work of Walter Shewhart and, in particular, the application of statistical quality control (SQC) techniques. Many members of the Japanese Union of Scientists and Engineers (JUSE) felt that SQC techniques were a major factor contributing to the United States' victory. In 1950, the JUSE invited Dr. Shewhart to participate in an eight-day management training course. He was unavailable, and W. Edward Deming, a Columbia University professor who had studied and applied Shewhart's methods, was recommended as the guest lecturer at this event. During a two-month period, Deming trained hundreds of managers, engineers, and scholars in Japan, focusing on three key areas: the use of the plan-do-check-act (PDCA) cycle, the importance of understanding the causes of variations between planned activities and actual performance, and process control through the use of control charts.

The idea of an integrated, organization-wide management system, bound together by a planning system, began to further develop in Japan during the 1950s and 1960s. These efforts were heavily influenced by

> The Deming Prize, established in Japan in 1951, which from the outset called for a system of planning.
>
> Widespread use of the PDCA cycle and the "seven QC tools" for management.
>
> The 1954 publication in Japanese of *The Practice of Management*, by Peter Drucker, which proposed the concept of management by objectives (MBO).
>
> JUSE-sponsored lectures by Joseph M. Juran on the role of management in promoting quality control activities.
>
> The divisional system of General Motors, which was a novel concept at that time.

In 1954, a visit by Joseph Juran led to a major shift in Japan's quality approach, from dealing primarily with technology to an overall concern for total quality management. Juran asserted that management must assume primary responsibility in leading quality improvement efforts by defining the organization's quality policy and assuring that everyone understood and supported it.

By the late 1960s, many Japanese companies had implemented MBO, and a number of leading companies—Bridgestone Tire, Toyota, Komatsu Manufacturing, and Matsushita—had developed their own innovative management approaches, going far beyond the original concept. These innovations, in turn, emerged from the significant expertise of these companies in statistical quality control, which at the time existed only in Japan.

The term *hoshin kanri*, referring to this new approach, became widely accepted in Japan in the mid-1970s. By the late 1970s, the first books on the subject began to appear, distilling the experiences accumulated in industry into a formalization of principles. The first symposium on *hoshin kanri* was held in Japan in 1981. In 1989, the Japanese Association of Standards published a series of works dealing with *hoshin kanri* practices.

A few leading companies in the United States began to implement their own versions of *hoshin kanri* during the late 1980s. Included among these companies were Hewlett-Packard, Procter & Gamble, Florida Power & Light, Intel, and Xerox. While many of these companies shared their experiences in the public domain, Western literature on this subject only started to become available in the early 1990s.

Various names have been used to describe this approach, such as policy deployment, management by planning, and hoshin planning. None of these terms captures the subtleties of the original meaning, however, and all are slightly misleading in some way. These terms are not in widespread use. Even in those organizations that have implemented *hoshin kanri* principles, most employees are simply aware of the workings of the system in use, and only a few specialists need to know more than this.

Hoshin kanri is one of the pillars of TQM and encompasses every part of an organization. It is involved in selecting and defining a small number of key targets for the organization to pursue and then in contributing to the accomplishment of these objectives. *Hoshin kanri* differs from other systems of planning in that its makes extensive use of quality management principles and techniques.

2.4   Hoshin Versus Strategic Planning

Hoshin often is defined as strategic planning. However, as applied in TQM, these two planning approaches are different. Strategic planning involves developing a *vision* for the organization and formulation of a *mission statement* as to how the vision is to be achieved within a certain time frame. Strategic planning must consider the interrelationships of mission, customer base requirements, and external environment with respect to the organization's potential performance. An improvement effort may be required to close the gap between the present and potential performance. The strategic plan identifies—in terms of breakthrough objectives—the dimensions of the improvement project, but not the means.

Broad goals and objectives of a strategic plan provide the basis for formulating an *integrated business/management plan* (see Table 5.10). The business/management plan identifies the more specific targets and the means for achieving agreed-upon objectives. These objectives are stated in terms of quality (including customer/service user satisfaction), cost, product and service delivery (including new product development and distribution), and morale (including satisfaction of stakeholders and the training and skills of

TABLE 5.10 Example of an Integrated Business Plan

Categories	Performance measures
Quality and customer satisfaction	Customer satisfaction index, defects, failures, number of customer complaints, and number of repeat customers.
Cost/finance	Sales, market share, labor costs, production costs, and profit margin.
Delivery response time	Development cycle and number of on-time deliveries.
Morale/human resources	Stakeholders satisfaction, employee satisfaction, number of appropriately educated employees, and amount of training.
Research & development	Number of new products or services, R & D costs, accuracy of research, and timeliness of research.
Strategies	Office location, headquarters location, business expansion, price strategies, and successful mergers and acquisitions.
TQM implementation	Number of problems solved and number of targets achieved.

employees). If properly executed, detailed, up-front planning will dramatically reduce project risks and the cost of conversion, will enhance the management of time and human resources, and will significantly improve the likelihood of success [7].

2.5 Hoshin Planning

Hoshin is an annual planning cycle for achieving the specific objectives developed in conjunction with management's choice of targets, and means, in terms of quality, cost, delivery, and morale. Each management area typically has six to eight targets. Half of these targets usually evolve from participation in a strategic planning effort, and half are related to the critical processes of the manager's regular job. All must be measurable with explicit target statements. A target statement can be established by combining at least one direction word (e.g., to increase or decrease), with a performance measure, target value, and time period. An example of a target statement may be "to decrease the budget preparation cycle from 6 to 4 months by December, 2003."

The next step is to determine the *means* for achieving the target. The means for achieving the target for the budget preparation cycle, for example, may include (1) establishing a more effective process for collecting basic data on revenues and expenditure patterns, (2) developing more appropriate documentation for the budget preparation process, and/or (3) implementing new budget models and training programs in their applications. Usually, a few means are identified for each target. The means may differ among organizations that share the same or similar targets.

Under the Hoshin or *plan-do-check-act paradigm*, planning must involve all levels of management in the organization. Hoshin plans are communicated and conflicts between plans are identified and resolved through a process known as "catchball." Consensus is reached among the various levels of the organization as to the targets and means by which they are to be achieved. Since targets and means are determined at different levels within the organization, it is important to identify the relationships between the targets and means at each level, and the targets between the different levels of the organization.

Hoshin plans must be clearly documented and monitored. They are not just once-a-year exercises that are put on a shelf to collect dust. Each manager is expected to monitor their plan on a monthly basis and to study successes and problems in order to make the necessary changes in behavior to ensure that the plan will be met and exceeded.

During the implementation of the Hoshin plan, each target should be assessed using performance measures drawn from the target statement. Ideally, the frequency of performance measure reviews should be determined prior to implementing the plan. Performance should be measured using charts and diagrams, such as run charts and Pareto charts (see Table 5.8). Each level of management should perform measurement. Thus, from top to bottom, all participants in the Hoshin planning process should be cognizant of the performance measure for each level. These periodic evaluations can provide guidelines for action to ensure continuous quality improvement and cost reduction. These monthly reviews, in turn, are consolidated in an annual review, which lists the successes and failures, and analyses from the various periodic reports. The annual review also focuses heavily on the planning process. What contributed to or detracted from effective planning? How can these problems or deficiencies be addressed? What adjustments in targets for the coming year are appropriate?

If the Hoshin target is achieved, the target value should be adjusted accordingly. Existing target values may have been too low, or the activities in pursuit of the means may have been more highly effective than anticipated. In both cases, it is significant to realize why and how the targets were achieved. The case may be that the target values do not require adjustment. Whether or not a target value needs adjustment should be decided based on the organizational situation.

2.6 Quality Function Deployment

The term quality function deployment (QFD) is a loose translation from the Japanese name for this method: *hin shitsu* (quality), *ki nou* (function), and *ten kai* (deployment). QFD is a systematic process for identifying the desires, wants, and needs of customers (the so-called "voice of the customer"). The data that are collected is then translated into the appropriate technical requirements that must be met at each stage of product development and production (i.e., planning, product design and engineering, prototype evaluation, production process development, production, marketing strategies, and sales) [8]. The result is a new set of target values for designers, production people, and even suppliers to strive to achieve in order to produce the output desired by customers.

The creation of QFD is generally attributed to Yoji Akao working in Mitsubishi's Kobe shipyard in Japan in 1966. The original approach was adopted and developed by other Japanese companies, notably Toyota and its suppliers [9]. By 1972, the power of the approach had been clearly demonstrated and in 1978, the first book on the subject was published in Japanese. In 1986, a study by JUSE revealed that of the 148 member companies surveyed, 54% were using QFD [10]. According to Akao, QFD "is a way to assure the design quality while the product is still in the design stage [11]." When appropriately applied, Akao suggested that QFD demonstrated the reduction of development time by one-half to one-third.

The first serious exponents of QFD in the United States were the "big three" automotive manufacturers in the 1980s, and a few leading companies in other sectors such as electronics. However, the uptake of QFD in the Western world appears to have been fairly slow. Users of QFD appear to be reluctant to publish and share information—much more so than with other quality-related methods. This reluctance may be because the data captured and the decisions made using QFD usually relate to future product plans, and therefore, are sensitive and proprietary.

QFD provides a visual language and makes use of a set of interlinked engineering and management charts, which include the so-called seven management tools [12]. Customer/user values are established and transformed into design, production, and manufacturing process characteristics. The result is a systems engineering process that ensures product quality as defined by the customer/user.

QFD is particularly valuable when design trade-offs are necessary to achieve the best overall solution, for example, because some requirements conflict with others. QFD also enables a great deal of information to be summarized in the form of one or more charts. These charts capture customer and product data gleaned from many sources, as well as the design parameters chosen for the new product. In this way, a solid foundation is provided for further improvement in subsequent design cycles. QFD is sometimes referred to as the "house of quality" from the characteristic house shape of a QFD chart (see Figure 5.1).

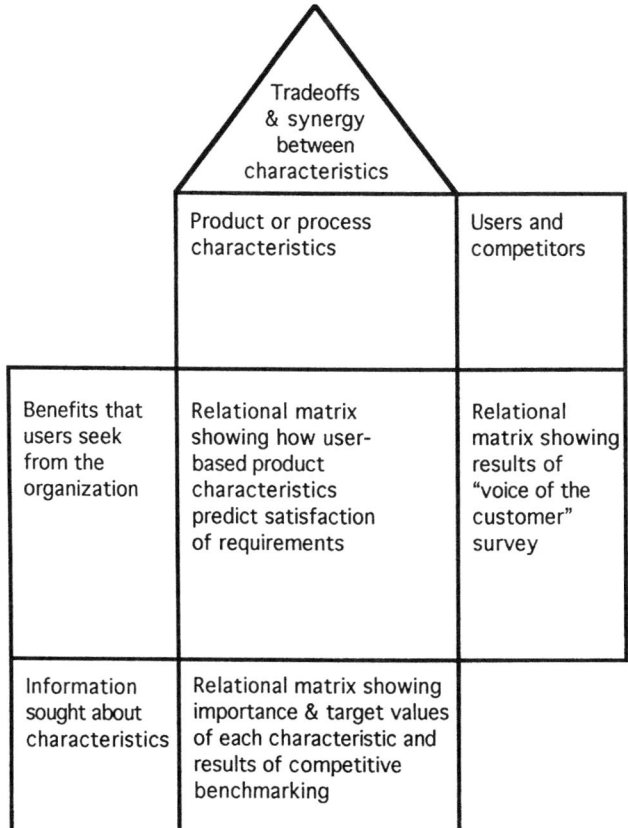

FIGURE 5.1   House of quality chart.

Achieving a technological breakthrough is key both to designing new products and to solving some of the most difficult problems in the production process. This area has seen the largest growth in the last few years with the discovery of the Russian theory of inventive problem solving (TRIZ) [13].

While quality function deployment (QFD) was conceived primarily for application in manufacturing and production processes, the four-phase QFD process could be adapted to public service programs as follows.

1.   Gather the voice of the customer. Put these data in words that are accurately understood by the public agency that is to deliver the service, and analyze this information in terms of the capability and strategic plans of the organization.

2. Identify the priority areas (or processes) where breakthroughs will likely result in dramatic improvements in the services (e.g., in terms of constituent/customer satisfaction).
3. Identify and design the improved process, including any new technology that may be required to achieve the breakthrough.
4. Deliver the improved service and new technology at the highest possible quality standards.

QFD has been applied by various federal and state agencies (most notably, NASA and the Navy), and has particular potential for customer-focused public and nonprofit organizations.

Among the main benefits of using QFD are improved communications and a sharing of information within a cross-functional team charged with developing a new product or service. This team typically will include people from a variety of functional groups. In the private sector, these cross-functional teams might include representatives from marketing, sales, service, distribution, product engineering, process engineering, procurement, and production. Comparable cross-functional teams could be established in the public sector. QFD also focuses on identifying "holes" in the current knowledge of the design team and on capturing and displaying a wide variety of important design information in one place in a compact form. It supports efforts to increase understanding, achieve consensus, and improve decision making, especially when complex relationships and trade-offs are involved. QFD creates an informational base that is valuable for repeated improvement cycles [14].

2.7   Systematic Innovation

A key focus of the theory of inventive problem solving (TRIZ) is the identification and solution of basic contradictions that are at the root of a problem. The basic TRIZ approach offered a systematic way of solving these contradictions, which, in turn, led to yet another "variation on the basic theme"—*systematic innovation* (SI). Systematic innovation starts with a thorough analysis of a problem or perceived opportunity by asking such questions as Why is it a problem or opportunity? For whom? Under what circumstances does the problem or opportunity exist? Is there a contradiction in the problem or opportunity?

Two major classes of contradictions are targeted in systematic innovation:

1. *Physical contradictions*—the requirement that something must have two opposite physical properties; and
2. *Technical contradictions*—when improving one parameter causes another to degrade.

The classic example of a physical contradiction is the requirement of airplanes to have wheels to maneuver on the ground, while not having wheels to be streamlined in the air. Separating the system's properties in time is recommended for this class of contradictions. In the case of airplanes, this separation leads to the idea of landing gear that can be present on the ground and absent in flight.

When a technical contradiction arises, conventional engineering frequently seeks a compromise. A trade-off is made based on how much good will result versus how much harm will be encountered. In SI, the contradiction serves as a springboard for identifying a breakthrough. The objective is to remove the contradiction, rather than to compromise the design by accepting the harm with the good.

The SI tools that are applied to facilitate this breakthrough include a contradiction matrix—a 39 × 39-cell matrix of characteristics that could be in conflict in any general technical system. Among the characteristics included in the classical contradiction matrix are such parameters as stability, durability, reliability, accuracy of measurement, convenience of use, adaptability, complexity of control, and level of automation. The rows of the matrix identify the characteristics to be improved. The columns are the characteristics that could be adversely affected. In other words, each of the 39 parameters might appear as a row heading and as a column heading. In a typical application, however, only certain parameters are included in the analysis (see Figure 5.2).

A contradiction might arise at the interface of any two parameters (e.g., stability versus adaptability). Up to five of the 40 principles of problem solving are shown in the cells of the matrix formed by the intersection of any two parameters. For example, suppose that the characteristic that the organization would like to improve relates to the stability of the product. How would increased stability impact adaptability, repairability, reliability, durability, and so forth? Each cell of the matrix can contain up to five of the 40 principles of problem solving and those represent possible solutions to the contradiction. The problem solving team reads the recommended principles, and the case studies that illustrate them, then uses advanced analogies to generate solutions to their problem.

One of the recommended principles, for example, is "localization of quality" which states that different parts of a system should be optimized to do specific functions. Application of this principle suggests that different perspectives on a given problem—at the level of the system, the supersystem, and any subsystems—may lead to an enriched set of solutions and the generation of better options.

SI also can be used to forecast technological change. The Air Force is an enthusiastic user of the technology forecasting methods of SI, applying them to create concepts of Air Force systems in the year 2025. It was reported that within two hours of first seeing examples of the SI methods, 13 cross-disciplinary teams had applied the techniques to four different technology areas and had developed scenarios that have accelerated their research.

Characteristic to be improved ↓ Characteristic affected →	12.	15.	27.	34.	35.	38.
12. Stability		8, 25, 33	9, 12, 34	5. 19, 33,38	11, 24, 33	13, 22, 35
15. Durability	1, 8, 32		10, 26, 33	11, 27, 35	22, 27, 39	2, 19, 27, 35
27. Reliability	6, 9, 10, 22	7, 10, 15, 26		9, 19, 29, 38	7, 12, 30, 40	16, 20, 35
34. Repairability	5, 8, 12	11, 20, 39	12, 23, 38		13, 20, 28, 35	6, 18, 27
35. Adaptability	7, 11, 24, 35	12, 22, 32	7, 19, 26	13, 23, 38		18, 21, 31
38. Level of automation	3, 5, 13, 36	2, 14, 18	16, 25, 33, 38	6, 13, 22, 29	12, 18, 24, 34	

FIGURE 5.2 Contradiction matrix (excerpt).

2.8 Six Sigma

The term "six sigma" was coined at the Motorola Corporation, where the original formulas were created in the 1980s. Following the adoption of this approach, Motorola experienced a period of unprecedented growth and in 1988, was recognized with the Malcolm Baldrige National Quality Award [15].

Sigma (a letter in the Greek alphabet) is used to denote the standard deviation or variability of a process. A classical measurement unit applied in manufacturing is defects per unit. A sigma quality level offers an indicator of how often defects are likely to occur—a higher sigma indicates a process that is less likely to result in defects. A six sigma quality level is said to equate to 3.4 defects per million opportunities (DPMO). It is estimated that companies operating at three to four sigma (the current average in the United States) lose 10–15% of their total revenue due to defects.

In practice, however, the term six sigma is used to denote more than simply counting defects. The concept goes beyond defect reduction to emphasize business process improvement in general, which includes cost reduction, cycle-time improvement, increased customer satisfaction, and any other metric important to the organization. Six sigma is now used to designate a whole set of strategies, tools, and statistical methodologies to improve the bottom line of companies (see Table 5.11). The objective is to achieve a high level of quality at reduced costs with a reduction in cycle time. Achieving this objective results in improved profitability and a competitive advantage for the organization.

When a company implements a six sigma business strategy, statistical tools are used in a structured fashion to eliminate waste and to create products or services that are improved, less expensive, and more timely. Repeated use of the tools on a project-by-project basis can significantly improve the bottom line [16]. However, if the techniques are not used appropriately, there is considerable danger that the effort will be counterproductive and frustrating.

At times, organizations can get too involved in determining how to count and report defects. They may lose sight of the real objective of six sigma—to orchestrate process improvement and reengineering through the wise implementation of statistical techniques. When an organization does not apply six sigma techniques appropriately, the tendency is to believe that the statistical techniques are not useful. However, the real problem may well be that the program was not implemented properly and/or the techniques were not effectively applied.

Often an organization does recognize that its problems are the result of current process conditions. Various key process output variables might be available—overall cycle time, defects per million opportunities metric, customer satisfaction, and so on. However, organizations often react to the

---

TABLE 5.11 What Is Six Sigma?

Six sigma is the structured application of statistical methods, tools, and techniques of total quality management to business processes to improve operating efficiencies and to achieve strategic business results. It includes:

A *Management Philosophy*: Six sigma is a customer-based approach that realizes that defects are expensive. Fewer defects mean lower costs and improved customer loyalty. The lowest-cost, high-value producer is the most competitive provider of goods and services. Six sigma is a way to achieve strategic business results.

A *Statistic*: Six sigma processes will produce less than 3.4 defects or mistakes per million opportunities. Many successful six sigma projects do not achieve the 3.4 ppm or less defect rate. That simply indicates that there is still opportunity for improvement.

A *Process*: To implement the six sigma management philosophy and achieve the six sigma level of 3.4 defects per million opportunities (or less), the six sigma process is: to define, measure, analyze, improve, and control.

up and down movements of these output variables in a "fire fighting" mode, seeking to "fix" the problems of the day. Management might even think that this type of "quick fix" activity is making improvements to the system. In reality, however, considerable resources often are spent without making any process improvements. Arbitrary tweaks made frequently in an attempt to control the variability in processes and to eliminate "noise" (e.g., material differences, operator-to-operator differences, machine-to-machine differences, and measurement imprecision) often can impact an output variable to such an extent that considerable nonconformance may result. This situation can be better appreciated when all the direct and indirect costs associated with an organization's current levels of nonconformance are considered. This point will be discussed in further detail in Chapter 7.

Organizations do not need to apply all the measurement units associated with six sigma. It is important to choose the best set of measurement tools for the particular situation and to focus on the wise integration of statistical and other improvement tools. Projects in critical areas of the business should be identified as part of an implementation. A road map, or visual description, is useful in developing a sound deployment of six sigma techniques [17].

To be successful, six sigma must have the commitment of top management and an infrastructure that supports this commitment. An executive management committee should be established to give direct support and champion the projects. The techniques are most effective when deployed through change agents (staff members) assigned to work full time on the implementation of projects selected on the basis of their likely beneficial return on investment. A good six sigma application involves the measurement of how well business processes meet their stated objectives and offers strategies to make needed improvements and to reduce variability.

2.9 Other Variations of the TQM Theme

The *quality improvement process* (QIP) is a variation on TQM developed in the mid-1980s by the Florida Power & Light Company, the first company outside of Japan to win the Deming Award. This approach builds on three basic elements:

1. Problem-solving teams established at various levels within the organization;
2. Formal mechanisms for the systematic identification and deployment of policy; and
3. Application of plan-do-check-act procedures to involve workers at all levels in quality improvement on a day-by-day basis (see Table 5.12.)

Like other quality improvement approaches, QIP requires a top-down commitment to the principles and techniques, and a willingness to permit manage-

TABLE 5.12   Quality Improvement Process

I.   Teams: various group dynamic and problem solving techniques used by lead teams, functional teams, cross-functional teams, and task teams to improve quality, develop employee skills, promote communications, and enhance the quality of work life.

II.   Quality improvement story identifies: (1) reason for improvement, (2) current situation, (3) situation analysis, (4) countermeasures—alternative approaches to improve the current situation, (5) results achieved, (6) mechanisms for standardization, and (7) future plans.

III.   Policy deployment.

   A.   Establish policy: (1) create the vision, (2) analyze present and future customer needs, (3) analyze the environment (benchmarking), (4) establish critical success factors, (5) analyze performance and year-end results, and (6) establish long-term and short-term plans.

   B.   Deploy policy: (1) select short-term plan co-ordinating executive, (2) announce short-term plan indicators and negotiated target, (3) develop business plans to achieve short-term plan, and (4) utilize teams and QIDW to achieve breakthrough.

   C.   Review policy: (1) line management reviews, (2) cross-functional committee reviews, and (3) presidential and executive reviews.

IV.   Quality in daily work (QIDW).

   A.   Application of plan-do-check-act (PDCA) to all activities necessary to meet customer needs and reasonable expectations on a daily basis.

      1.   Plan: identify (a) top priority job(s), (b) objectives, (c) customers, and (d) quality indicators.

      2.   Do: identify (a) targets or limits, and (b) control system.

      3.   Check: implement control system and check results.

      4.   Act: standardize and/or take countermeasures.

V.   Results.

   1.   Maintains gains achieved.

   2.   Promotes consistency in operations.

   3.   Clarifies individual contributions to meeting customer needs.

   4.   Improves daily operations.

   5.   Identifies and controls all critical accountabilities required to meet customers needs.

   6.   Can be used as a tool to teach employees.

Source: Adapted from a presentation by Bear Baila, Vice President, Division of Quality Services, QUALTEC, Inc., an FPL Group Company, at the University of Michigan, February, 1993.

ment personnel and field staff to devote extensive time and effort to its implementation.

The *language processing* (LP) *method* is another approach that facilitates the social model of management. The LP method consists of three phases [18]. In the first phase, each participant states their own views about a particular situation. Each participant is then asked to elaborate upon their views until each perspective is clear to the other participants, without anyone taking exception to the person's initial views. This second phase should be one of explanation and clarification, not argument. In the third phase, the participants work together to group similar views and to state what is common about them [19]. The LP method helps people to investigate complex situations collectively, to bring to bear the insights of all, and to prevent conclusions from being based on comparative positions in the organization's power hierarchy.

Concept engineering (CE) was developed by Gary Burchill in response to what he perceived as a lack of explicit methods within TQM for creating new products and services [20]. CE attempts to reveal, analyze, and draw conclusions based on the tacit knowledge that is available within the organization and across the marketplace regarding the need for new products or services. The CE process starts with team members asking open-ended questions and observing the technology that currently is being used in the marketplace. The team then develops a picture of potential marketplace needs stated in objective terms. These tentative market needs are then tested through market surveys. With the needs validated, the team develops a variety of product concepts and then selects the best available product solution (or hybrid concept).

Productivity gainsharing addresses a number of significant issues regarding traditional compensation systems by tying employee motivation directly to productivity efforts (see Table 5.13). "Shared savings plans" have been adopted by both private and public organizations, whereby a portion of the savings created by productivity improvements is returned to employees in the form of bonuses. Some critics have noted that these programs have relatively short life spans, especially if the participation of the workforce has not been firmly established.

It has been suggested that TQM could be strengthened through integration with other management methods [21]. A number of interesting management systems are available from which to choose. Situations involving complex, interlinked cause-and-effect relations are addressed through *systems thinking*, as formulated by Peter Senge. The *language/action perspective* of Fernando

---

TABLE 5.13 Productivity Gainsharing

Links a portion of the employee's pay to increased productivity and shares organizational savings with employees.

First used in the private sector in the 1890s by Henry Towne as part of his company's indirect incentive system.

Many variations on gainsharing have been adopted in the past ten years.

The Japanese compensation method pays nearly 25% of worker's wages in two yearly bonuses that are determined by the firm's current economic performance.

Flores provided a way to improve the day-to-day coordination of interactions among people. An approach for dealing with the individual and organizational defensive routines that prevent beneficial change was provided by the *action science* ideas of Chris Argyris. Both Argyris and Flores placed emphasis on language or conversation as a way of generating action—not just as a way of describing things. These approaches provide a foundation for the fundamental management functions of planning, operations, and change management with which all organizations must be concerned.

The *interactive management* approach of Russell Ackoff offered a method for creating the future rather than merely predicting it [22]. A key aspect of interactive management is the planning technique known as "idealized design," which seeks to make explicit all the weakness of the existing management system, including the concerns of all participants. Ackoff emphasized that a primary benefit of idealized design is the involvement of the participants' broad knowledge of the state of the organization which helps foster a feeling of ownership of both the problems and the new plans. This method enables the organization to design a new management system consistent with the principles of interactive management. Rather than attempting to predict and plan for a future environment, the ideal system is envisioned to deal with today's environment.

3 INTERNATIONAL QUALITY ASSURANCE SYSTEMS

The International Organization for Standardization (ISO) has promulgated a set of five universal standards for a quality assurance system that is accepted around the world. Currently 90 countries have adopted ISO 9000 as national standards. The standards apply uniformly to companies in any industry and of any size. When a company is registered to the appropriate ISO 9000 standard, the consumer has important assurances that the quality of the product or service purchased will be as expected. There is evidence of increasing interest in the development of public sector quality assurance systems that reflect ISO 9000 standards because of the need to control the quality of public services, to reduce the costs associated with poor quality, and to become more responsive to community needs and requirements.

3.1 What Is ISO?

The International Organization for Standardization is a nongovernmental federation of national standards bodies, with one representative from each of some 130 countries. Headquartered in Geneva, Switzerland, the Organization was established in 1947 with the mission to promote the development of standardization and related activities worldwide, to facilitate the international exchange of goods and services, and to develop co-operation in the spheres of intellectual, scientific, technological, and economic activity. Its work results in international agreements that are published as international standards.

ISO is not an acronym for the International Organization for Standardization. It is a Greek word meaning "equal," which is the root of the prefix "iso-" that occurs in a host of terms such as "isometric" (of equal measure or dimensions), "isosceles triangles" (meaning "equal sided"), and "isonomy" (equality of laws, or of people before the law). ISO is valid in English, French, and Russian, the three official languages of the International Organization for Standardization.

3.2 Why Are Standards Important?

The existence of nonharmonized standards for similar technologies in different countries or regions can contribute to so-called "technical barriers to trade." Export-oriented industries have long sensed the need to agree on world standards to help rationalize the international trading process [23]. International standardization is well established for many technologies in such diverse fields as information processing and communications, textiles, packaging, distribution of goods, shipbuilding, energy production and utilization, banking and financial services [24]. Such standardization will continue to grow in importance all sectors of industrial activity in the foreseeable future.

ISO 9000 registration is rapidly becoming a must for any company that does business in Europe and is rapidly becoming the most popular quality standard in the world. Thousands of organizations have already adopted this important standard, and many more are in the process of doing so. ISO 9000 can help both product-oriented and service-oriented organizations achieve standards of quality that are recognized and respected throughout the world.

ISO 9001 is the most comprehensive of the quality assurance standards and is applicable to industries involved in the design and development, manufacturing, installation and servicing of products or services. ISO 9001 focuses on the steps necessary to satisfy customers so that product nonconformities will be avoided. ISO 9002 deals with organizations that produce, install, and service products. ISO 9003 deals with situations in which product quality can be assured through final inspection and testing. ISO 9001, ISO 9002, and ISO 9003 present a quality assurance model that helps in the development of an appropriate quality system.

Many companies require their suppliers to become registered to ISO 9001, and because of this expectation, registered companies find that their market opportunities have increased. In addition, a company's compliance with ISO 9001 ensures that it has a sound quality assurance system, and that is good business. Registered companies have had dramatic reductions in customer complaints, significant reductions in operating costs, and increased demand for their products and services.

3.3 Achieving ISO 9000 Registration

An organization may decide that a quality assurance system should be developed that meets the ISO 9000 standards because of a need to control the quality of its products and services, the need to reduce the costs associated with poor quality, or the need to become more competitive. Or, an organization may choose this path simply because its customers expect it to do so, or because a regulatory body has made it mandatory. A quality system is then developed that meets the requirements specified by one of the three standards: ISO 9001, ISO 9002, or ISO 9003. In the course of doing so, many ISO guidelines may be considered (see Table 5.14).

Once a quality system has been developed and implemented, the organization must carry out an internal audit to make sure the system is working properly. Then an accredited external auditor (registrar) is invited to evaluate the effectiveness of the quality system. If the auditors like what they see, they will certify that the quality system has met all of the ISO's requirements. They

TABLE 5.14 ISO Guidelines

ISO 9000-1	Provides a "road map" for the ISO family of publications, clarifying concepts, and briefly explaining what each ISO publication is about.
ISO 9000-2	Provides help in implementing ISO 9001, ISO 9002, or ISO 9003.
ISO 9000-3	Directed to software businesses and describes how to use ISO 9001 to set up a quality system.
ISO 9000-4	Addresses issues of product dependability, meaning reliability, maintainability, and availability.
ISO 9004	Assists in the development of a quality system, provides focus on customer service, deals with organizations that process solids, liquids, or gases as part of their production process, and discusses concepts and methods for generating quality improvements.
ISO 10011	Assists in the development of an internal quality audit program and explains how to verify the existence of quality elements and how to verify that quality objectives are being met. Describes the qualifications that internal auditors should have. Describes how a quality system audit program should be managed.
ISO 10012-1	Ensures that the quality assurance measuring equipment meets all ISO requirements.

Source: Adapted from International Organization for Standardization website at: www.isho.ch.

will then issue an official certificate to the organization and they will record this achievement in their registry. The organization can then announce to the world that the quality of its products and services is managed, controlled, and assured by a registered ISO 9000 quality system.

ISO distinguishes between *quality system requirements* and *product quality requirements*. Quality system requirements are characteristics or properties that should be evident in systemic elements. Product quality requirements are characteristics or properties that products (or services) should have. ISO also distinguishes between four types of products: hardware, software, processed materials, and services (notice that a service is considered a product). The quality of a product depends on whether

> The product is routinely updated to meet changing market requirements and opportunities.
> Characteristics the marketplace needs and wants are designed into the product.
> Every instance of the product precisely conforms to the product design.
> Customer support is provided throughout the life cycle of the product.

An organization is viewed as a network of processes through which inputs are transformed into outputs. Organizations must identify, organize, and manage this network of processes. The link or interface between each process must be clearly defined and well-managed. Product quality depends on how well this network of processes works. Therefore, this network must be routinely monitored and analyzed, and the continuous improvement of this network must be a high priority. When evaluating a quality system process, the following questions must be examined.

> Have procedures been developed to control this process?
> Are the procedures that control this process documented and well-defined?
> Are the procedures that define this process completely deployed and implemented?
> Are the procedures that define this process able to generate the necessary results?

Quality systems are evaluated by executive managers, first party (internal) quality auditors, external quality auditors (independent bodies), and the organization's customers.

A quality system should be clearly documented by writing procedures, so that changes in quality are easier to detect and measure because they can be compared with the way things were done in the past. Documents provide objective evidence that a process has been defined, procedures have been approved, and procedural changes are under control.

4 SUMMARY

Many organizations, both in the public and private sectors, have adopted a management approach that builds on the four basic concepts of total quality management: (1) continuous improvement, (2) customer focus, (3) total participation, and (4) social networking. In contrast to more traditional management approaches that advocate "don't make waves" and "if it ain't broke, don't fix it," continuous improvement (CI) programs promote an ongoing search for ways to do things better, even when existing practices and procedures appear to be operating reasonably well. CI programs often originate from the "bottom-up" and tend to focus on incremental improvements in existing practices by applying detailed analyses to identify specific root causes of inefficiency and waste.

It has been suggested that TQM and related CI approaches have not been particularly effective in problem areas characterized by complex, interlocking causes and effects. And while broad participation and involvement is a cornerstone of TQM, strong, reliable methods for the day-to-day coordination of interactions among people within an organization have not yet been provided. TQM does not provide a viable alternative to the strategic planning model, where planners try to predict the future and then create a plan that addresses that future. However, various components from TQM/CI approaches can (and should) be effectively blended into an overall strategic management process.

Perhaps the most important lesson to learn from efforts in the 1980s and 1990s to improve productivity and to ensure the quality of services is the fact that it is relatively easy to establish a productivity and quality improvement program. The hard part is to sustain such efforts. The full potential of productivity and quality management techniques has not yet been realized in terms of their application to programs in the public sector. However, the increasing emphasis on efficiency, effectiveness, and accountability in the conduct of public programs provides additional incentives for administrators to undertake evaluations and apply the results in the improvement of program performance.

ENDNOTES

1. MIT Commission on Industrial Productivity. Made in America: Re-gaining the Productive Edge. Cambridge, MA.: MIT Press, 1989.
2. Mary Tenopyr. Trifling he stands. Personnel Psychology. Vol. 34, 1981.
3. Russell L. Ackoff and Jamshid Gharajedaghi. Mechanisms, organisms and social systems. Strategic Management Journal. Vol. 5, 1984, pp. 289–300.
4. L. Edwin Coate. TQM on campus: implementing total quality management in a university setting. Business Officer. Vol. 24, No. 5, November 1990.
5. W. Edwards Deming. The New Economics for Industry, Government, Education, second edition. Potomac, MD: W. Edwards Deming Institute, 1994, chapter 4.

6. W. Edwards Deming. Out of Crisis. Potomac, MD: W. Edwards Deming Institute, 1986, chapter 2.

7. Project Management Institute Standards Committee. A Guide to the Project Management Body of Knowledge. 1996. Covers a wide range of topics related to the management of projects and includes an extensive glossary to provide a common vocabulary for management planning.

8. L. P. Sullivan. Quality function deployment. Quality Progress. June 1986.

9. L. P. Sullivan. Quality function deployment. Quality Progress. June 1986. States that "The QFD system has been used by Toyota since 1977, following four years of training and preparation. Results have been impressive.... Between January 1977 and April 1984, Toyota Autobody introduced four new van-type vehicles. Using 1977 as a base, Toyota reported a 20% reduction in start-up costs on the launch of the new van in October 1979; a 38% reduction in November 1982; and a cumulative 61% reduction at April 1984. During this period, the product development cycle (time to market) was reduced by one-third with a corresponding improvement in quality because of a reduction in the number of engineering changes."

10. The sectors with the highest penetration of QFD were transportation (86%), construction (82%), electronics (63%), and precision machinery (66%). Many of the service companies surveyed (32%) were also using QFD. Specific design applications in Japan range from home appliances and clothing to retail outlets and apartment layout designs.

11. Yoji Akao, ed. Quality Function Deployment. Cambridge, MA.: Productivity Press, 1990.

12. After a worldwide search, the Japanese Society for Quality Control Technique Development proposed the following new tools for quality control in 1976: Relations Diagram, Affinity Diagram (KJ method), Systematic Diagram (Tree Diagram), Matrix Diagram, Matrix Data Analysis, Process Decision Program Chart (PDPC), and Arrow Diagram.

13. The Theory of Inventive Problem Solving (TRIZ) process was developed over a fifty year period from 1945 to 1995 under the leadership of Genrich Altshuller, based on his work in the Russian patent office. Altshuller began to classify patents from simple modifications to major innovations. As he studied the most innovative patents, Altshuller began to identify the principles that led to this innovation. He also began to develop a series of algorithms for solving the most difficult problems. One of the key focuses of TRIZ is identifying and solving the basic contradiction at the root of the problem—an approach different from trying to find a good trade-off. TRIZ is a systematic way of solving the contradiction. TRIZ is also useful in reducing unneeded functions in a product, and thus reducing its cost and improving its reliability.

14. The main "bottom line" benefits cited for QFD are (1) greater likelihood of product success in the marketplace (due to the precise targeting of key customer requirements), (2) reduced overall design cycle time (mainly due to a reduction in time-consuming design changes—an important benefit, since customer requirements are less likely to have changed since the beginning of the design project), (3) more frequent design cycles, which mean that products can be improved more rapidly than the competition, (4) reduced overall cost due to reducing design changes,

which are not only time consuming but very costly, especially those that occur at a later stage), and (5) reduced product cost by eliminating redundant features and over-design.

15. The Malcolm Baldrige National Quality Award, created in 1987, is given to business—manufacturing and service—and to education and health care organizations that are judged to be outstanding in seven areas: leadership, strategic planning, customer and market focus, information and analysis, human resource focus, process management, and business results. The award is named for Malcolm Baldrige, who served as Secretary of Commerce from 1981 until his death in a rodeo accident in 1987. His managerial excellence contributed to long-term improvement in the efficiency and effectiveness of government.

16. It is estimated that $500,000 to $1,000,000 bottom-line benefits can be achieved yearly (on average) for dedicated six sigma practitioners (often called six sigma black belts—a term originated by Motorola) through projects that can average $75,000 to $175,000 in value through the improvement of cycle time, reduction of defects, cost reduction, and so forth.

17. Forrest W. Breyfogle. Implementing Six Sigma: Smarter Solutions Using Statistical Methods. New York: John Wiley & Sons, 1999.

18. Language Processing Method. Center for Quality Management. Cambridge, Mass., 1995.

19. Ted Walls and David Walden. Understanding unclear situations and each other using the language processing method. Center for Quality Management Journal. Vol. 4, No. 4, Winter 1995, pp. 29–37.

20. Gary Burchill. Structure process improvement at the naval inventory control point. Center for Quality of Management Journal. Vol. 5, No. 1, Spring 1996, pp. 22–31.

21. Thomas Lee and David Walden. Designing integrated management systems. Center for Quality of Management Journal. Vol. 7, No. 1, Summer 1998, p. 14.

22. Russell Ackoff. Creating the Corporate Future. New York: John Wiley & Sons, 1981.

23. International standardization began in the electrotechnical field with the establishment of the International Electrotechnical Commission in 1906. Established in 1926, the International Federation of National Standardizing Associations (ISA) carried out pioneering work in a number of fields. The activities of ISA ceased in 1942, however, due to the Second World War. Following a 1946 meeting in London, delegates from 25 countries agreed to create a new international organization, "the object of which would be to facilitate the international coordination and unification of industrial standards." The International Organization for Standardization began to function officially on February 23, 1947.

24. The format of credit cards, phone cards, and "smart" cards, for example, is derived from an ISO international standard that defines such features as an optimal thickness (0.76 mm) that permits these cards to be used worldwide.

6

Resource Management: Process Reengineering

Both public and private organizations must satisfy the needs of their constituents or customers by effectively delivering the right services and products at the highest possible level of quality and the lowest possible level of cost—by no means an easy task. In many cases, significant "push-pull" conflicts occur between cost, the quality of service provided, product innovations, and employee involvement and morale. Today, it is no longer appropriate to compromise one objective for another. New management techniques have emerged in recent years to address the conflicts among these critical objectives. Unfortunately, in many cases, the massive volume of articles, books, newsletters, and consultant information about these new techniques has caused more confusion than enlightenment.

1 PROCESS REENGINEERING DEFINED

Hammer and Champy defined process reengineering as,

> the fundamental rethinking and radical redesign of business processes to achieve dramatic improvements in critical contemporary measures of performance such as cost, quality, service and speed [1].

Asking the fundamental questions—What are we doing and why?—forces an examination of current practices and processes, and an identification of those activities which may be inappropriate, erroneous, or obsolete. Radical redesign means getting to the root of things and not merely improving upon existing procedures and continuing to struggle with suboptimization. It often means disregarding existing structures and procedures and inventing new ways of accomplishing critical objectives. Hammer and Champy suggested that, in the broadest sense, reengineering is starting over, involving dramatic, holistic changes when an organization redesigns its business processes to achieve significant improvements in performance. The focus is on *processes* rather than people, structures, and tasks.

1.1 Processes Defined

Processes are the lifelines of any organization. A process can be defined as "a structured, measured set of activities designed to produce a specified output ... a specific ordering of work activities across time and place, with a beginning, an end, and clearly identified inputs and outputs [2]." Processes are the end-to-end work activities required to provide products and services to customers, end-users, or client groups. To be effective, an organization must optimize its processes in line with its mission and strategic priorities. For many organizations, achieving this optimization may require major changes in policies, procedures, organizational structure, management philosophy, and the use of technology. Organizations must be ready and willing to change. Albert Einstein's incisive definition of insanity, "Endlessly repeating the same process, hoping for a different result" applies equally well to organizations as it does to individuals.

According to Hammer and Champy, reengineered processes should be designed to be simpler than those they replace. Several functional operations might be combined, and the number of checks and controls reduced. Often, a new hybrid process is created, which combines centralized and decentralized operations. The result is that work is performed where it makes the most sense, and workers are able to make more decisions for themselves.

Successful organizations apply information technology to integrate processes that cut across functional boundaries rather than operating through organizational silos or functional hierarchies. Information technology has been used, in many cases, to achieve short-term improvements in existing and fragmented processes. However, as Guha et al. pointed out, this localized, incremental approach has often created extremely complex processes that contribute relatively little to the overall effectiveness of organizations operating in today's competitive environment [3].

Simply applying the latest information technology to existing processes does not ensure a valid solution to the problems of complex organizations. A further step must be taken to question current processes and to rethink fundamental activities. Unnecessary activities should be removed, and archaic processes should be replaced with cross-functional activities. Process reengineering focuses on the redesign of work processes to enhance productivity and competitiveness. In combination with the use of information technology as an enabler of change, process reengineering can lead to significant gains in productivity, efficiency, responsiveness, service, quality, and innovation.

1.2 Continuous Improvement Programs

Some authors have argued that *continuous improvement*—many small changes made by empowered teams of employees—is preferable to the more dramatic quantum changes often recommended through an enterprise-wide process reengineering initiative. Both approaches

> Focus on processes;
> Emphasize customer satisfaction;
> Use teams and teamwork;
> Work to decentralize decision making to the most appropriate levels within the organization;
> Apply performance improvement measures and problem-solving techniques;
> Require senior-level commitment and change management for success; and
> Bring about change in values and beliefs (when successful)

Continuous improvement (CI) programs however, often originate from the "bottom-up" and tend to focus on incremental improvements in existing practices by applying detailed analyses to identify specific root causes of inefficiency and waste. Process reengineering, on the other hand, must be driven from the very top by key leaders who believe that nothing is more important and, therefore, are willing to do whatever it takes to make process reengineering happen. Reengineering focuses on large, cross-functional processes and on entire systems.

It has been suggested that process reengineering and CI programs are analogous to what a driver and a putter are to a golfer—they are different yet complementary, and both are needed to win. Bold initiatives emerging from process reengineering should drive continuous improvements, which, in turn, should sustain periodic enterprise-wide efforts to re-evaluate basic processes that support the overall mission of the organization. As Thompson and Strickland observed,

> The two approaches to improved performance of value-chain activities are not mutually exclusive; it makes sense to use them in tandem. Reengineering can be used first to produce a good basic design that yields dramatic improvements in performing a business process. Total quality programs can then be used as a follow-on to work out bugs, perfect the process, and gradually improve both efficiency and effectiveness [4].

1.3   A Total Delivery System

Most managers are accustomed to dealing with functional units that can virtually stand alone. A much different perspective is needed for process reengineering. A vertical view of an organization is replaced by a horizontal view of many interlocking processes that cross the boundaries between subunits or functions and often organizational boundaries as well. Together, all of the processes in an organization form a *total delivery system* for services and products. Real value-added comes from the integration of activities across processes.

The significance of reengineering comes from the intense focus of satisfying end-user or customer requirements and expectations. A well-designed process focuses on activities that add value for the end-users or customers, while eliminating burdensome bureaucratic constraints. The primary objective is to deliver enhanced products and services to both the external and internal customers of the organization. The underlying principles of process reengineering are outlined in Table 6.1.

Process reengineering is normally used when there is a substantial gap between what customers and stakeholders expect and the actual performance of the organization. While perspectives vary, most experts assert that this approach will deliver major gains in performance. Gains of 40, 50 or 60% are frequently mentioned. Reengineering—with its radical changes in areas such as workflow, customer service, rules and regulations, job content, job skills, decision-making, organizational structure, and information systems—is a proven method for bringing about these levels of improvement.

1.4   Process Reengineering Body of Knowledge:
An Overview

For many years, an organization's success was considered secure if it was competitive in one of three areas: (1) cost/productivity, (2) quality/service, and (3) responsiveness/flexibility. More recently, however, many organizations are recognizing that to survive in a rapidly changing environment, it is essential to excel simultaneously in all three of these major areas. To accomplish this integrated performance, organizations must develop new processes to produce results that are important to their clients/customers. They must look for ways to become more flexible and responsive, while providing high quality products/services for a relatively low cost.

Michael Hammer is generally credited with coining the term "reengineering" in a 1990 article in the *Harvard Business Review*. He made the point that traditional methods of improving business performance to achieve this integration often did not produce the desired results. Information technology, for the most part, was not the solution either. He suggested that, in many cases, such technology has only caused inefficient processes to be performed more quickly.

TABLE **6.1** Underlying Principles of Process Reengineering

Focus on customer-driven results: Eliminate barriers that inhibit decision-making and the flow of work.

Compress time: Develop concurrent rather than sequential steps; utilize a standard methodology for consistency and efficiency; increase process velocity; and develop teams with customer or end-user focus.

Eliminate nonvalue-added activities: It has been estimated that 50% to 90% of the steps in any process are nonvalue-added (i.e., steps that customers would not feel good about paying for if they knew they were part of the process).

Define end-to-end solutions: Take a holistic view—processes should be examined across all functional and organizational boundaries (including customers, suppliers, and partners). Respect the "20/80 rule"—if you just do 80% of the job, you will only get 20% of the planned benefits.

Align to meet customer or end-user expectations: Determine what customers or end-users want and when they want it.

Empower people/distribute work: Align responsibility and accountability by giving employees the power to make decisions and incentives to utilize that authority. Drive decision-making into the organization so that those closest to the information are empowered to make the call. Provide the knowledge, tools, and authority needed to make decisions and execute processes effectively and thereby, foster a feeling of ownership at all levels of the organization.

Set far-reaching goals and measure improvements: Goals should be both aggressive and realistic and should directly support the organizational strategy. Employees must be challenged to beat the goals.

Quality at the source: Build in quality at the source by supplying timely performance feedback. Encourage self-inspection and peer assessments. Have the right people (well-trained, motivated, and organized), applying the right tools and systems, to carry out simplified processes, to produce products and services that have been designed for productivity, within the appropriate organizational infrastructure.

Implement continuous improvements: Aggressively question all procedures and practices in an ongoing basis to continually exploit opportunities.

Identify and communicate interdependencies: An organization is made up of a series of complex processes carried out by interdependent units. The linkages among these processes and units must be clearly understood by all participants.

Adapt cost-effective, leading-edge technology: State-of-the-art technology should empower employees to make decisions, increase flexibility, compress development time, and expand the capacity for positive change and improvement.

Do things once correctly: Enter data at the source that have been mutually agreed-upon as appropriate for effective decision-making; store and maintain these data centrally (replicated as necessary), and achieve one coherent view of administrative processes.

Process reengineering requires an organization to consider the final product of its efforts. Hammer believes that, used properly, information technology can be instrumental in redesigning the way organizations do business. However, information technology cannot serve as the "tail wagging the dog"—it must be the other way around. Management must lead the way with technology serving as an invaluable assistant.

When the environment was fairly stable, work was divided into simple, repetitive tasks to create efficiencies of scale. Layers of supervision and control were created to link these simple tasks together. As a consequence, the resulting processes became more and more complex.

Now, ever-increasing demands for flexibility and responsiveness are driving organizations to develop processes whereby people can perform relatively complex, multidisciplinary tasks with a minimum of "overhead." Too much time is required for a complex command structure to respond to changing conditions. Therefore, these new improved processes must be "governed" by a general understanding of an "organizational vision" and a consensus on appropriate procedures.

Following Hammer's 1990 article, numerous books were written on affecting dramatic and radical organizational changes, primarily focusing on applications in the private sector. H. James Harrington suggested that management devoted too much time correcting problems that should not have occurred in the first place if appropriate processes were in place [5]. The focus of management should be on preventing problem—on developing processes that work error-free. Harrington provided extensive lists of essential information that should be used in evaluating and improving processes.

Thomas Davenport covered the entire spectrum of topics essential to a successful reengineering effort, placing significant emphasis on how information technology can facilitate the overall reengineering effort [6]. Davenport made the point that marginal improvements in operating performance can not ensure long-term survival in a global economy and atmosphere of intense competition. A whole new view of how organizations do business must be explored, and that exploration must probe the very depths of the organization.

Michael Hammer and James Champy clearly identified the root cause of what is wrong with the way many American companies do business and then proceeded to outline, in concise and clear language, the steps organizations should take to reengineer their processes [7]. They suggested that many companies still adhere to the nearly two hundred year-old Adam Smith concept of work structure. In their opinion, these principles no longer apply in the dynamic, global-driven age in which companies compete in the 21st century. Many organizations lack the necessary focus on process (the logical way products and services are produced, or the way in which work is actually done) and, perhaps more importantly, they fail to give adequate attention and concern for those who pay the bills—the customer.

Hammer and Champy developed concepts and techniques that can be employed to turn organizations around. As evidenced throughout their book, the key to reengineering lies in the willingness to start afresh—that is, to proceed with no preconceived notions as to the best way to organize to do business, to the methods employed, or to the technology used in producing goods or services. It is a "clean slate" approach to problem solving. Emphasis is also on the customer and on the competition. The organization must be willing to set aside its old ways of doing things in the interest of making improvements. If that willingness is not there, Hammer and Champy strongly advise against attempting the reengineering effort.

Reengineering the Corporation spent many months on the nonfiction bestseller list of the *New York Times* [8]. Since its release, the concepts of reengineering outlined in this book have been put to the test by numerous organizations—from manufacturing concerns to nonprofit and governmental entities. Many of these organizations have documented significant increases in productivity, profits, customer satisfaction, and employee morale as a result.

On the downside, many reengineering efforts (by some estimates, 50% or more) do not succeed, or at best yield only marginal improvements. This lack of success could be due to any number of reasons, ranging from a lack of top management commitment to targeting the wrong processes or areas to reengineer. While reengineering may not be the ultimate answer to every organization's problems, a prudent executive would be wise to at least take a very hard look at its prospects (see Table 6.2 for a process reengineering glossary).

TABLE 6.2 Process Reengineering Glossary

Activity-based costing: Set of accounting methods used to identify and describe costs and required resources for activities within processes.

"As is" process: Description of the current flow of a process, including subprocesses and activities, showing how products and services are created.

Benchmarking: Comparison of the performance of organizational processes against an internal or external standard of recognized leaders. Most often the comparison is made against a similar process in another organization considered "world class."

Process: Collection of related, structured activities—a chain of events—that produces a specific service or product for a particular customer or customers.

Business process reengineering: Radical improvement approach that critically examines, rethinks, and redesigns mission-delivery processes and subprocesses, achieving dramatic mission performance gains from multiple customer and stakeholder perspectives.

Clean sheet: Concept popularized by reengineering experts which contends reengineering should totally abandon a current process and start from scratch in building and deploying a new process.

(continued)

TABLE **6.2**   (*Continued*)

Core or key process: Customer-facing, management, or support process considered vital to the organization's success and survival.

Customer: Groups or individuals who have a relationship with the organization, including direct recipients of products and services; internal customers who produce services and products for final recipients; and other organizations and entities which interact with an organization to produce products and services.

Cycle time: Time that elapses from the beginning to the end of a process or subprocess where inputs are converted into outputs.

Decomposition: Breaking down a process into subprocesses and activities.

Executive team or steering committee: Top management team responsible for developing and sustaining the process management approach in the organization, including selecting and evaluating reengineering projects.

Function: Set of related activities that are part of a process; often known as a subprocess within a process.

"Heroic" goal: Goal that requires a significant change in the performance (quality, quantity, time, or cost) of a process. Also called stretch goals, the targets are normally 50% or more.

Modeling or flowcharting: Graphic representation of the activities and subprocesses within a process and their interrelationships.

Performance gap: Gap between what customers and stakeholders expect and what each process and related subprocesses produces in terms of quality, quantity, time, and cost of services and products.

Process improvement approach: Approaches such as incremental process improvement, process redesign, and reengineering that can be used together or separately to improve processes and subprocesses.

Process owner: Individual held accountable and responsible for the workings and improvement of one of the organization's defined processes and its related subprocesses.

Stakeholders: Individuals or groups who influence programs, products, and services, such as legislative bodies and public interest groups.

Subprocess: Collection of activities and tasks within each process.

Timebox: A set, specified period of time during which specific tasks must be performed.

"To be" process: Description of the desired flow of a process, including subprocesses and activities, showing how products and services could be created under a new vision.

Value-added: Those activities or steps which add to or change a product or service as it goes through a process. These are the activities or steps that customers view as important and necessary.

World class organization: Organizations recognized as best for at least one critical process and held as models for other organizations.

Adapted from: National Academy of Public Administration Foundation, *Reengineering for Results*, Washington, D.C. (1994).

1.5   Process Reengineering in the Public Sector

The message that comes across most clearly with respect to the concept of process reengineering is that organizations must continually inquire as to why they do what they do. Many public organizations have become so inbred to the manner in which work is performed that it is hard to see any other way. Sharon Caudle notes that for decades, public officials have followed "the dogmas of the quiet past" in carrying out the work of government [9]. Legal mandates or internal tradition have resulted in a morass of processes that did little to serve the customers of government services. Seemingly trapped in a maze of outmoded ways of doing business, government managers simply requested more resources—more money and people—to keep current operations afloat. Little, if any, incentive existed to promote the rethinking of how government conducted its business. The result was an escalation of expenditures for services delivered at minimal and often declining performance levels.

Today, public resources are becoming increasingly scarce, and government performance no longer can be a hit or miss proposition. Operating with dwindling resources, government often must deal with a public that demands more and better services and is frustrated with efforts to deliver basic services. Outmoded operational practices that have been eliminated or replaced by more effective processes provide ample evidence of how government can truly work well. If reengineering of basic government processes does not occur, groups and individuals that rely on public services will remain as angry casualties of poor government performance.

Public managers have key roles to fill in process reengineering initiatives. First, they should be directly involved in making decisions on what projects should be initiated and how the resources for strategic planning and process improvement should be allocated. Second, they should run their own projects—planning, staffing, funding, designing, deploying, and monitoring results—and will have to integrate those efforts with other process improvement initiatives. Third, they should be called on to facilitate other groups' reengineering projects, serving as actual staff, providing special expertise for project teams, or serving on steering committees or advisory groups guiding those projects. To fulfill these responsibilities, public managers require a thorough understanding of the basic concepts and techniques of process reengineering (see Table 6.3 for six critical success factors in process reengineering).

2   AN OVERALL PROCESS REENGINEERING APPROACH

A standard methodology for carrying out process reengineering in public and nonprofit organizations has not yet been developed. However, existing methods

TABLE 6.3 Six Critical Success Factors for Reengineering

Understand Reengineering
  Understand process fundamentals.
  Know what reengineering is.
  Differentiate and integrate process improvement approaches.

Build a Business and Political Case
  Have necessary and sufficient business (mission delivery) reasons for reengineering.
  Have the organizational commitment and capacity to initiate and sustain reengineering.
  Secure and sustain political support for reengineering.

Adopt a Process Management Approach
  Understand the organizational mandate and set mission strategic directions and goals
    cascading to process specific goals and decision-making across and down the
    organization.
  Define, model, and prioritize processes important for mission performance.
  Practice "hands-on" senior management ownership of process improvement through
    personal responsibility, involvement, and decision-making.
  Adjust organizational structures to better support process management initiatives.
  Create an assessment program to evaluate process management.

Measure and Track Performance Continuously
  Create organizational understanding of the value of measurement and how it will be
    used.
  Tie performance management to customer and stakeholder current and future expec-
    tations.

Practice Change Management and Provide Central Support
  Develop human resources management strategies to support reengineering.
  Build information resources management strategies and a technology framework to
    support process change.
  Create a central support group to assist and integrate reengineering efforts and other
    improvement efforts across the organization.
  Create an overarching and project-specific internal and external communication and
    education program.

Manage Reengineering Project for Results
  Have clear criteria to select what should be reengineered.
  Place the project at the right level with a defined reengineering team purpose and
    goals.
  Use a well-trained, diversified, expert team and facilitate it working well.
  Follow a structured, disciplined approach for reengineering.

Adapted from: Sharon L. Caudle. *Reengineering for Results: Keys to Success from Government Experience*, Washington, D.C.: National Academy of Public Administration (1995).

developed by leading authorities and various consulting firms offering process reengineering assistance share several commonalties that can assist in the conduct of a process reengineering initiative.

2.1 Four Basic Components

Process reengineering involves four basic components central to the well-being of any organization: (1) defining strategic objectives, (2) improving processes, (3) applying technology, and (4) developing human resource capabilities. Strategic objectives and processes provide the foundation to enable the application of technologies and the redesign of human activities to achieve the overall mission of an organization. Strategic objectives must be relevant to internal and external constraints and must be defined in such a way as to motivate employees. Processes should be determined by customer or end-user requirements (tempered by organizational constraints). The shift from functional departments to interfunctional processes may include a redesign of the entire organizational structure and human resource system. This redesign should involve process optimization instead of task optimization. Information technology can be a major facilitator for spanning processes over functional and organizational boundaries and for supporting process-driven organizations. Such technology should be applied to enable innovative responses in a dynamic, changing environment and not merely to improve existing activities. The real challenge of any process reengineering initiative is to gain the support of middle management—the real change agents. These managers must identify and implement change opportunities, while facing perceived threats from process reengineering, which often is used to reduce hierarchies and downsize the work force.

These four components must be maintained in equilibrium with one another. Introducing new technology, for example, without fully developing the human resource capabilities necessary to utilize and maintain the technology is an invitation to disaster. Undertaking to improve practices and procedures on a fragmented, hit-and-miss basis without developing an overall strategic plan or vision is likely to result in considerable "wheel spinning," waste of critical resources, and often, counterproductive processes.

2.2 Defining Strategic Objectives

The first major component of process reengineering involves an identification of the strategic objectives of the organization. The focus of process reengineering is on the linkages between *strategy* and *process* rather than on the formulation of a comprehensive strategic plan. Nevertheless, the existence of an ongoing strategic planning process within the organization can be a major contributor to the overall success of any process reengineering initiative. The emphasis in strategic planning is on an orderly evolution—from a broad mission statement, to statements of more specific objectives consistent with the organization's mission, to more explicit policies and implementing decisions. This emphasis seeks to establish or reinforce linkages often missing in more disjointed, incremental approaches to decision-making.

Process reengineering is all about *change*. To facilitate change, it is essential that a *broad strategic vision* be shared across the organization. The involvement of senior management is critical during this phase of process reengineering because of the radical character of this undertaking. Responsible managers must be willing to devote sufficient time and effort to fully understand the general concepts and objectives of process reengineering. And they must be able to explain how these procedures will help the organization as a whole. They must set the example by demonstrating the willingness to take time away from other pressing problems to clearly articulate objectives and to discuss strategic needs and expectations. Top management's participation in these efforts should be designed to help to convince staff at the various operating levels to devote the necessary and appropriate time and effort to the task.

The formation of a strategic vision should begin with an examination as to how the organization should operate if there were no constraints whatsoever. This examination should not merely address the question of how current work can be improved, but what activities should be carried out to achieve maximum performance of all measures. This analysis involves the alignment of the process reengineering effort with the organization's overall strategic objectives. If existing strategic objectives appear to be obsolete or inappropriate, their re-definition might be necessary in order to adapt to new externalities. Convincing management of the necessity of abandoning existing procedures and methods and disregarding existing constraints is a critical success factor of this phase of process reengineering.

The values of all *stakeholders*—customers, constituents, end-users of services, policy-makers, employees, and so forth—must be reflected in the strategic objectives of an organization. It is particularly important to develop an understanding of the organization's "customers" so that processes can be reengineered to focus on providing superior value to these recipients of the products and services of the organization. In some cases, much of the information needed regarding customer values can be uncovered through existing efforts in strategic planning or market research. However, it often is appropriate to conduct a formal *customer analysis*.

2.3   Customer or End-User Analysis

Much of the literature on customer analysis falls into the area of for-profit business applications, placing great emphasis upon the goal of quality service. But what constitutes *quality service*, and how can it be measured and improved upon?

Traditionally, companies have relied upon internally defined customer service measures, which may continually indicate a high level of satisfaction. However, as the global aspirations of companies have developed, methods of measuring customer satisfaction have been subjected to more intense scrutiny. In 1993, Lochridge & Company surveyed some 60 major companies in an effort to identify the key elements of customer service. Lochridge's final report identified 19 high-level benefits fundamental to "the customer priority for consistent, problem-free service, a pro-active, responsive customer service organization, and global end-to-end coverage [10]." These values were distilled into five basic aspects of customer service:

Reliability	*Keeping promises to customers.*
Responsiveness	*Owning the problem.*
Assurance	*Inspiring trust and confidence.*
Tangibles	*The look-and-feel-good factor.*
Empathy	*Putting customers first.*

The notion of "customers" cannot be easily defined with all public sector applications. Citizens can certainly be considered customers of public services. However, the relationship between citizens and local government is much more complex than the somewhat casual contacts that occur in most customer or business interactions. Reliance of government departments upon central accounting and purchasing operations also constitutes a customer or service provider relationship. But here again, the relationship differs from the business world in that the "customer" usually cannot "shop around" if they are dissatisfied with the "service provider."

A more precise definition of customer analysis in the public sector would be *end-user analysis*. Simply defined, end-user analysis requires institutions, departments, and other organizational groups to clearly look at the end-users that are being served and the level of services being provided to these users. From this evaluation, the service organization should then modify and improve the services it provides to more fully meet the needs of its end-users.

Both citizens and departmental users of public resources generate direct or indirect costs within the local government when they access a service. But no one group directly profits from the other. This unique relationship requires customers to be viewed in a different light in the public sector. Emphasis must be placed on an examination of the quality of service provided and not on the potential or actual profit generated by the action.

All government agencies face a major challenge—they must find out what the users of their services really want—a major step that relatively few public agencies have taken. In order to accomplish this step, clear and specific *standards* for customer service must be established. Methods for achieving this objective vary from agency to agency.

Various techniques can be used to develop an end-user analysis. *Visioning* exercises often are implemented early in process reengineering to create agreement on purposes and values to assist in identifying users, issues, and strategies. An effective organizational vision includes (1) organizational performance criteria, and (2) ethical standards for employees and volunteers. In a similar fashion, *futuring* involves the identification of a "preferred future" and the formulation of specific ways to realize that image. This approach provides an organization the ability to determine what it wants to accomplish, what it should become in the future, and how to get to these points. These techniques will be discussed further in a subsequent section on the use of focus groups in process mapping.

Regardless of the source of data regarding customer/end-user satisfaction, the key areas to consider include:

1. *Value differentiation by various segments of the customer base.* Not all customers or end-users have the same needs or wants when accessing the services or products of the organization.
2. *Priority among values.* In all likelihood, it will not be possible to accommodate all of the values of all of the customers or end-users all of the time. Therefore, some criteria must be developed for establishing priorities among these different values.
3. *The organization's performance versus the "competition."* How well is the organization meeting customer or end-user needs in comparison to other organizations that are providing the same or similar services or products? And in what areas are improvements in performance most obviously needed?
4. *Process implications.* What does this assessment indicate with regard to the way in which the organization currently conducts its operations?

2.4   Identifying Core Competencies

Strategic objectives must also reflect the *core competencies* of the organization—what it does best, what it does well when compared to the "competition," and which areas need improvement in performance should be emphasized. As Thompson and Strickland observed,

> Typically, a core competence relates to a set of skills, expertise in performing particular activities, or a company's scope and depth of technological know-how; it resides in a company's people, not in assets on the balance sheet.
>
> The importance of a core competence to strategy-making rests with (1) the added capability it gives a company in going after a particular market opportunity, (2) the competitive edge it can yield in the marketplace, and (3) its potential for being a cornerstone of strategy [11].

An attempt should be made to match the resources of the organization with the opportunities and risks perceived in the broader environment.

This phase of process reengineering often begins with an examination of the organization's strengths, weaknesses, opportunities, and threats (SWOT)—a cornerstone of most strategic planning approaches. A SWOT analysis can help an organization determine its distinctive competencies which, in turn, will help determine what the mission of the organization should be. Carrying out a SWOT analysis will often be illuminating—both in terms of pointing out what needs to be done and in putting current problems into perspective.

The outcome of this phase of process reengineering should be a *shared strategic vision* of what the organization can and should strive to become in the future. This shared vision should reflect the core values of the organization as well as certain fundamental principles to which the organization is committed. Examples of the hierarchy of values, principles, and programs for human resources that should be recorded to document the shared strategic vision are provided in Table 6.4.

3   ESTABLISHING PRIORITIES

Determining more specific strategies necessary for the organization to achieve the shared strategic vision involves a shift in emphasis from the "why" and the "what" to the "how." Establishing priorities among the organization's strategic objectives provides a more specific focus for the process reengineering efforts.

3.1   Critical Success Factors

It is important to provide a barometer of the overall performance of an organization by identifying what needs to be done well. The pivotal focus of this approach is a determination of the set of factors that management considers critical for the organization's success. Success factors should specify how the major processes that have been identified are best measured. These factors, in turn, should be aligned with customer or end-user values and the shared vision of the organization. Once identified, these factors often are stated as management objectives, and the information required to monitor their performance should then be delineated.

Critical success factors (CSF) are not new. Ronald Daniel introduced the concept of "success factors" in 1961 [12]. However, the approach has been popularized by John Rockart and other researchers [13]. Rockart defined critical success factors as,

> ... the limited number of areas in which results, if they are satisfactory, will ensure successful competitive performance for the organization. They are the few key areas where 'things must go right' for business to flourish ... As a result, the critical success factors are areas of activity that should receive constant and careful attention from management [14].

TABLE 6.4 Core Human Resources Values and Principles

Core Values

Provide outstanding services to customers/end-users by recruiting and developing highly quality staff within the context of financial stewardship.

Highly value staff members for their knowledge, skills, talents, experience, service orientation, flexibility, creativity, and loyalty.

Treat staff members with fairness, respect, and dignity at all times.

Fundamental Principles

Develop and maintain policies and programs that support a creative, flexible, and high-performance staff.

Encourage staff members to generate creative ideas and innovative practices that enhance the ability of the organization to compete with its peers.

Develop and maintain an environment that promotes a cohesive, inclusive, and diverse workforce, affirming the inherent worth of all individuals.

Underscore the importance of teamwork, trust, and open communications.

Core Programs

Adopt and maintain a set of criteria for promotion and salary enhancement and reward staff members who meet and exceed these expectations.

Recognize staff members who demonstrate creativity and secure successful outcomes in support of the organization's objectives.

Provide a competitive salary schedule that adequately compensates staff members who support an efficient, high-quality organization.

Create pay-for-performance strategies that reward collaboration, team work, and superior results.

Provide staff with the tools and educational opportunities required to develop the new skills needed by the organization.

Develop career pathways and job transfer strategies that facilitate the advancement of high-performing staff.

Strive to retain staff members who have the needed skills, flexibility, ability to adapt to change, and demonstrated work performance.

Provide supervisors with the training necessary to enable them to manage staff effectively, especially during times of change.

Boynton and Zmud suggest that "CSFs provide a focal point for directing a computer-based information system development effort" by pinpointing key areas that require the attention of management [15]. KPMG Peat Marwick developed a CSF model for higher education, for example, that identified 67 critical success factors to be measured on an annual basis. Designed to be used by senior administrators, this model emphasizes the need to "compress information so that managers can focus their attention on high priorities in making and assessing decisions [16]."

The CSF approach provides a structured technique for identifying the information required to determine whether events are proceeding appropriately in each key area. By linking the perceived success factors to information development and reporting procedures, managers know what information is indispensable to their responsibilities. Critical success factors differ among individual organizations. For a given manager, CSFs can be expected to evidence some variation from year to year, but remain fairly constant for shorter periods of time. Primary sources of CSFs, as identified by the Rockart research team, are shown in Table 6.5.

Critical success factors can be identified through a series of interview sessions. In the first session, managers are asked to delineate their objectives and the CSFs underlying them. The interview is designed to explicitly extract those critical success factors that managers have been implicitly using. The second session attempts to identify a specific performance indicator for each CSF and the possible data and reports appropriate to monitor it. Additional sessions are held as necessary to achieve agreement on the CSFs, their performance measures, and the required reports for tracking them.

While the CSF approach paves the way for delivery of the "right" information to managers, by itself CSF does not ensure the consistency of a manager's perceptions with the overall strategic objectives. That concern remains part of the basic responsibility of top management for goal setting

---

TABLE 6.5 Sources of Critical Success Factors

1. *Industry-based factors*: Determined by the characteristics of the industry itself. For example, industry-based critical success factors of supermarkets include: (1) have the right product mix available at each store, (2) keep it on the shelves, (3) provide effective advertising to attract shoppers to the store, and (4) develop correct pricing.

2. *Competitive strategy, industry position, and geographic location*: Factors derived from whether an organization is a dominant or minor force among competitors; the niche it occupies or the basis of its competitive strategy (such as pursuing product differentiation or customer service advantages).

3. *Environmental factors*: Arising from areas that an organization has relatively little control but which affect performance, such as the cost and availability of energy, government regulations, changing customer demands, and the economy.

4. *Temporal factors*: Arising from issues that are critical for a time period, such as modernization of the physical plant, which when addressed will no longer determine success or failure.

5. *Managerial position*: Generic factors associated with each functional management position. For example, manufacturing managers would be typically concerned about product quality and inventory control.

6. *Managerial worldview*: Factors rooted in the perspectives brought by managers to their jobs, especially in regard to leadership.

Adapted from various working papers and publications of the Center for Information Systems Research, MIT Sloan School of Management.

and establishing performance standards that are valid, realistic, understandable, and measurable. Nevertheless, the use of critical success factors can help reconcile diverging individual views of the organization that may be present even if the organization's mission is clearly defined and its strategic objectives are explicitly stated. Once the CSFs of individual managers are identified, managerial agreement should be sought in a step that Rockart calls "alignment analysis" to arrive at the collective CSFs for that functional component of the organization.

3.2 Key Performance Indicators

Key performance indicators should be determined for each critical success factor. M.G. Dolence defined key performance indicators as a detailed list of measurements to monitor and evaluate management strategies—"numbers that can be used to indicate the effectiveness and efficiency of strategies and tactics [17]." Whereas critical success factors are preconditions for the success of a strategy, key performance indicators "help maintain a sharp focus on what must be measured." Establishing these performance indicators involves a review of current methods for measuring and reporting operational performance.

Critical success factors usually are limited to a relatively small number of factors and include "soft data" as well as external data. The key performance indicators are built on a much longer list, but are limited to data from internal sources. The development of a consistent format in which the data and analyses are presented is key to this approach. At the outset, the key users of these data should be interviewed to gather suggestions as to which indicators to include in the system and how they can best be monitored and reported. A list of topics and a presentation format should be agreed upon, but some flexibility should be provided during the initial iterations to add to or refine the indicators as new topics are suggested by the review of these data. Year-to-date figures often provide the most useful basis for comparisons, but monthly figures, comparisons with budgeted amounts, and year-end totals may also be important in monitoring certain activities. Targeted estimates, projections, and extrapolations of data to identify trends may also be appropriate.

Periodic meetings (e.g., monthly) to discuss the key indicators are an important feature of this approach. Data should be provided a few days before these meetings, with a summary of the key issues to be discussed. The participants can then focus on those items most pertinent to their areas of responsibility and should be prepared to comment on and discuss problems and trends that are evident from their perspective.

It is likely that some of the data that were deemed appropriate for inclusion as key indicators do not exist or are not readily available in the format desired. Where monthly data have not been collected in the past, it may be necessary to reconstruct such data or at least start collecting them in order to have the necessary data points from which to draw meaningful comparisons. When data are not consistent from one year to the next (for example, because of a change in data categories), it may be necessary to re-compute (or "crosswalk") the prior year's data to make them more comparable. In some cases, the units that provide the data may feel that the presentation format should be modified, and some negotiations may be necessary to arrive at an agreed-upon format that satisfies both user's needs and meets the perceptions of the source authorities.

Two or more units within an organization may track the same data and may provide different analyses and even conflicting information based on these data. In many instances, these different perspectives are useful, provided that the assumptions on which the data analyses are based are clearly identified and understood. In some cases, however, it may be necessary to agree upon one data set over another to avoid misunderstanding and confusion among the information users.

3.3   Benchmarking

Benchmarking often is performed within this phase of process reengineering to help set appropriate targets and metrics for the organization. The role of benchmarking must be seen in the context of the organization that is continuously examining itself, analyzing its performance and internal processes, and seeking to implement improvements. An organization that is planning improvements will set targets. For most organizations, it is most likely that these targets will yield some improvements early in the process relative to current performance. To sustain these early gains, however, usually requires the organization to "stretch further"—to set performance objectives that mirror the leading organizations in the particular field of endeavor.

Benchmarking practices vary dramatically in terms of the implementation or inquires undertaken. Some organizations look for consortia of partners to get together and exchange information. Other schedule visits to leading or comparable organizations to get a feel (often superficial) for their way of doing things. Others employ consultants, who interpret benchmarking as the collection and comparison of global measures (primarily financial data) of an organization's performance. In many cases, benchmarking takes the form of "best practices" research rather than collecting metrics to be used as "baseline data."

A crucial first step in benchmarking is to identify how well the organization currently is doing in terms of a set of key performance indicators. Once this initial assessment is accomplished, time-based targets can be established for improvements, and an *action plan* can be formulated to achieve these targets. However, if the improvement targets are established in isolation of any knowledge of what other organizations are doing or achieving, the targets may not be challenging enough to help the organization achieve the desired improvements in performance.

Key indicators are fundamental to an evaluation of performance—they show how much or how little is being achieved by the organization in comparison to competitors and to the world's best practices. These measures do not show the weaknesses or strengths in internal processes, however. They do not show how competitors and world leaders have secured their respective levels of achievement. They do not show what, if anything, is transferable to the organization's particular circumstances or how to make the transfer.

Benchmarking is not just about the comparison of measures, as it has often been mistaken to be. The benchmarking process does not stop when comparisons have been made and the organization has been found to be doing well or found wanting. This is merely the first step. The *how* and *why* need to be established, and methods of achievement must be evaluated for potential transfer, improvement, and implementation. In short, it is important to look for ideas to borrow from those organizations that are doing better, even perhaps in one very specific aspect. Thomas Edison once advised his colleagues: "Make it a habit to keep on the lookout for novel and interesting ideas that others have used successfully. Your idea has to be original only in its adaptation to the problems you are working on."

Setting quantitative targets, often called *metrics*, through benchmarking is arguably one of the best ways to establish strategic objectives. However, setting objectives comparable to or beyond those of the best-in-class without understanding the underlying processes that have enabled the best-in-class to achieve their results can be useless or worse. Understanding how those organizations achieve their results—the *how* and *why*—usually is more important and valuable than obtaining "hard data" during the study. This understanding will reduce the risk of losing sight of what an organization hopes to get from a benchmarking study: valuable learning.

3.4   Three Common Types of Benchmarking

Cooperative benchmarking is the most talked-about approach, because it is relatively easy to practice and makes interesting news copy. In cooperative benchmarking, an organization that desires to improve a particular process or set of activities contacts the "best-in-class" organizations and asks them if they will be willing to share knowledge with the benchmarking team. The knowledge usually flows in one direction—from the target organization to the benchmarking team.

Collaborative benchmarking involves a group of similar organizations sharing knowledge about a particular process or set of activities—all hoping to improve their individual practices based upon what they learn. For example, a group of university research administrators might collaborate on the identification of "best practices" for dealing with federal agencies that support sponsored research activities. Often, a third party serves as a coordinator, collector, and distributor of data.

Competitive benchmarking is the most difficult form of benchmarking because it targets other organizations that are not necessarily interested in helping the benchmarking team. In competitive benchmarking, current functions, process, activities, products, and/or services are measured against those of competitors. The ultimate objective is to improve elements to become the "best in class." But at a minimum, this approach seeks to improve elements so that they are better than those of the competition.

The primary value of benchmarking to process reengineering is its role in helping to identify and develop process innovations. Benchmarking is particularly valuable to process reengineering teams involved in projects designed to develop innovative processes and then to reverse engineer them into an existing environment. Benchmarking can also prove useful in forward engineering process innovations. And, it can be used to assist in either incremental change or quantum change. How benchmarking is done and how it is used depend largely on what problem the process reengineering team is committed to solve.

An essential purpose of benchmarking is to resolve a psychological predicament called "functional fixedness." This situation occurs when an organization is so embedded in a problem that it cannot find a novel solution. Current thinking is "fixed" by the problem. Benchmarking is intended to help organizations work through their functional fixedness by finding and applying appropriate analogies.

In trying to implement the processes of another organization, however, it also is necessary to accept that organization's paradigm. Otherwise the expected benefits from implementing the processes in the first place will not be fully realized. It is important to look inside the other organization to structure, compare, and analyze process analogies. An identification of stakeholders is a key aspect in the development of benchmarks for public and nonprofit organizations.

Benchmarking can be achieved by systematically examining a series of factors:

1. *Deciding what to benchmark.*
   Processes to be subjected to benchmarking should be important to the organization's stakeholders (e.g., constituents, customers, and end-users).
   Targeted processes should be consistent with the organization's mission, values, objectives, and milestones.

Processes should reflect important organizational needs.

Processes should be significant in terms of costs or key nonfinancial indicators.

Focus should be on areas where additional information could influence future plans and actions.

2. *Planning the benchmarking process.*

Scope of the study should be clearly delineated.

Constituents, customers or end-users for the study should be identified.

Characteristics that will be measured should be determined in some detail.

Information about the processes that is readily available should be collected and analyzed.

3. *Understanding the organization's own performance.*

Factors that influence the organization's current performance should be examined to learn which characteristics are most important and least important.

A baseline for comparison to benchmark organizations should be established.

4. *Studying others.*

Benchmark candidates should be identified.

The list should be narrowed to a few candidates.

General and specific questions should be prepared.

The best way to get those questions answered should be determined.

Benchmarking study should be performed.

5. *Learning from the data.*

Data collected should be analyzed and performance gaps identified and quantified.

Specific items of information that might be particularly useful for improving performance should be identified.

6. *Using the findings.*

A determination should be made as to how the benchmarking findings can best be used.

Other units within the organization that would benefit from these findings should be identified.

Benchmarking is not, in itself, a solution to a process improvement problem. Actually, once benchmarking helps a team find a good analogy, the team must determine a future state (i.e., define the "TO BE" paradigm or process). Then, and only then, can the team address the challenge of moving from the current state (the "AS IS") to the future state.

3.5   Developing an Operational Vision

The next major step in process reengineering is the formulation of an *operational vision* designed to translate the broader, more generic aspects of the strategic vision into specific applications within component processes and units of the organization. The good intentions of a strategic plan are likely to go unrealized unless the planning effort is further extended to include the development of an operational vision to organize and deploy the appropriate resources effectively and efficiently to accomplish the organization's strategic objectives.

An operational vision involves (1) programming approved strategic objectives into specific projects, programs, and activities, (2) identifying and budgeting the necessary resources to implement these programs over some specific time period, and (3) designing and staffing organizational units to carry out the approved programs. Ideally, the operational vision forms the link between strategic objectives and the actual performance of organizational activities. It is a mechanism for co-ordinating the sequence in which activities must be performed to complete a given program or achieve agreed-upon objectives.

An operational vision focuses on setting standards for the use of specific resources and on performance tactics to achieve overall objectives of the strategic plan. It is concerned with the development of a *work plan* and the *scheduling* of detailed program activities—determining the calendar dates or times that resources will be utilized according to the total resource capacity assigned to the organization. Resource availability, task or job sequence, resource requirements, and possible starting times for project or program activities must then be taken into account in order to produce an operational schedule. The forces that control a work plan are time, budget, and resources. If the work plan is not appropriate, one of these three forces has to "give." An effective and efficient operational vision can mean the difference between "on time" and "late" in the achievement of specific program objectives and ultimately, the difference between the effective utilization of scarce resources and waste.

Techniques for developing a work plan and for scheduling of operations will be discussed in further detail in Chapter 10, which deals with organizational control.

4   IMPROVING PROCESSES: GAP ANALYSIS

The next phase in process reengineering involves the documentation of *current processes* and the formulation of *future processes*, leading to a comprehensive analysis of the gaps between current and future processes. Gap analysis should

(1) provide an assessment of barriers to change, (2) identify "quick wins"—initiatives for the improvement of current processes that can be undertaken immediately, (3) establish the basis for major program or project initiatives, and (4) provide inputs for an analysis of the costs and benefits of undertaking required changes.

4.1 Process Mapping

The notion of process mapping was introduced in the early writings of Philip Crosby as part of his concept of "Systems Integrity" [18]. Process mapping enables managers to identify and assess the various processes that make up their organization and to develop a road map for performance improvement. In the private sector, every process that defines the customer-related activities of a business—the order taking process, product design process, production or delivery process, billing process, and so forth—can be viewed as the main customer "thoroughfares" of a process map. Also included at this first level are the major interchanges and management accountabilities. The "secondary roads" are those processes that do not directly produce results for the organization's customers, but are integral to the successful support of the primary processes—such as recruiting, hiring, and orienting new employees, ordering and receiving supplies, maintaining inventory, and so forth.

To improve a process, it is first necessary to understand, in some detail, what currently is being done—what activities are being carried out, what relationships between activities and information flows exist, and what is the "value added" of each activity. Understanding current processes facilitates the identification of issues and the ability to communicate these issues to top management. Determining future processes provides a "blueprint" for the policies, procedures, and organizational structure necessary to support the desired changes.

Existing processes must be described in sufficient detail to uncover any hidden pathologies, which may include high costs, inefficient work flows, inappropriate sequences of activities, insignificant value added for customers or end-users, and so forth. These inadequacies should be detected and documented using quantitative as well as qualitative methods, depending on the nature of the pathology.

In documenting current processes, the following factors are important to include:

Description of the entire process.
Identification of process elements and resources utilized.

Evaluation of the performance of the current process.

Analysis of processes to determine inconsistencies in application, unnecessary redundancies and wasted effort, missing linkages, and so on.

A number of basic questions should be asked about each process:

Why is this process undertaken?

What initiates the process?

What types of reviews or approvals are involved and when do they occur?

What are the nature, frequency, and cause of errors or problems?

How are problems and issues handled?

What is the output of the process and where does it go?

How long does the process take?

Process mapping (or event modeling) is a technique for documenting, from start to finish, the individual activities and key characteristics that define a process. Process mapping is the organizational equivalent of a financial audit, providing an accurate accounting of where an organization stands, process-wise. Two tools are generally applied:

1. Process flows: Visual depictions that show the order of activities and the movement of information into and out of a process (see Figures 6.1 and 6.2); and
2. Process profiles: Narrative descriptions that provide the detail behind the flow diagrams (see Table 6.6).

Both current and future processes should be mapped. Several key characteristics should be identified for each process:

Responsibilities: key participants and their roles in the process.

Individual activities or steps: sequence of events; linkages among events; and points at which responsibilities are delegated.

Inputs: information and data flows; tangible items; and activity triggers.

Outputs: key deliverables of each activity.

Customers/stakeholders: internal and external recipients of outputs.

Performance measures: time required to complete each activity; volume; frequency; and workload and productivity.

It is important to provide as much detail as possible about each process without compromising comprehension and readability.

Process maps usually are developed starting at a high level and progress to increasing levels of detail. The level of detail pursued depends upon the resources available, complexity of the processes, organization structure, magnitude of the

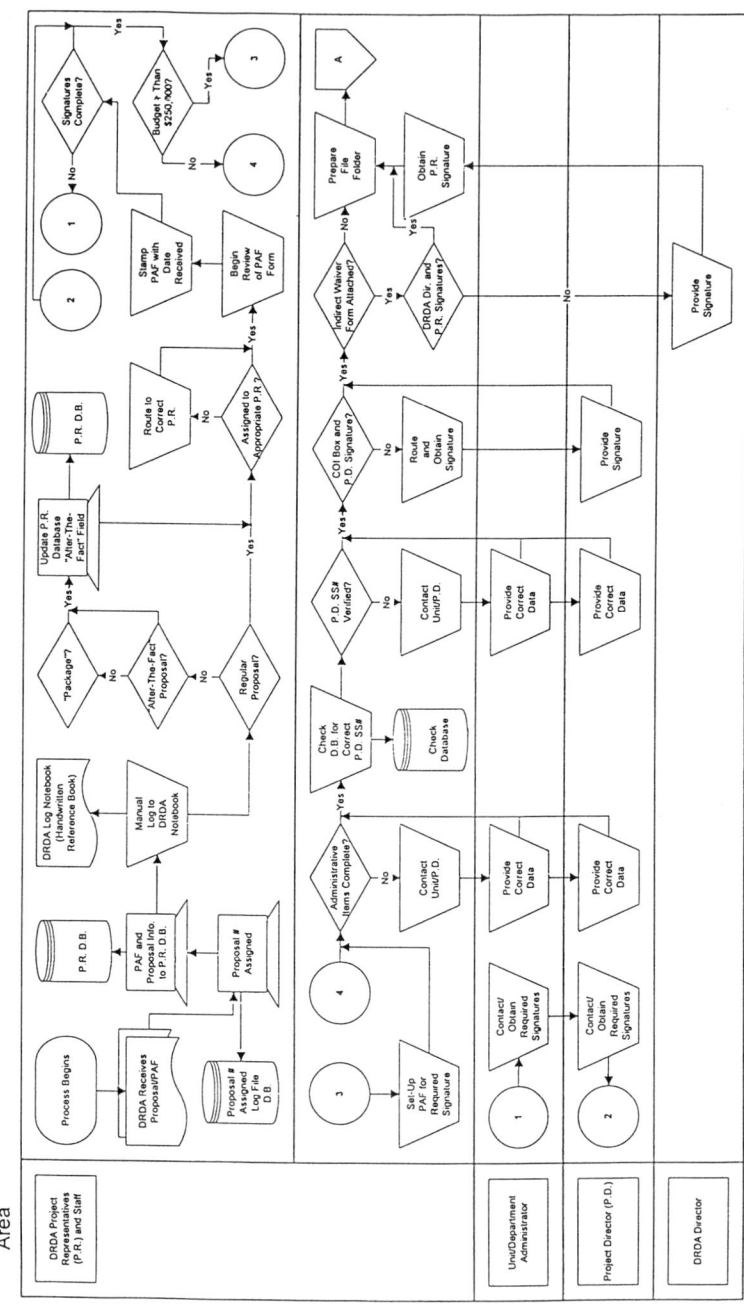

FIGURE 6.1 "As is" process flow: proposal processing and submission to sponsors.

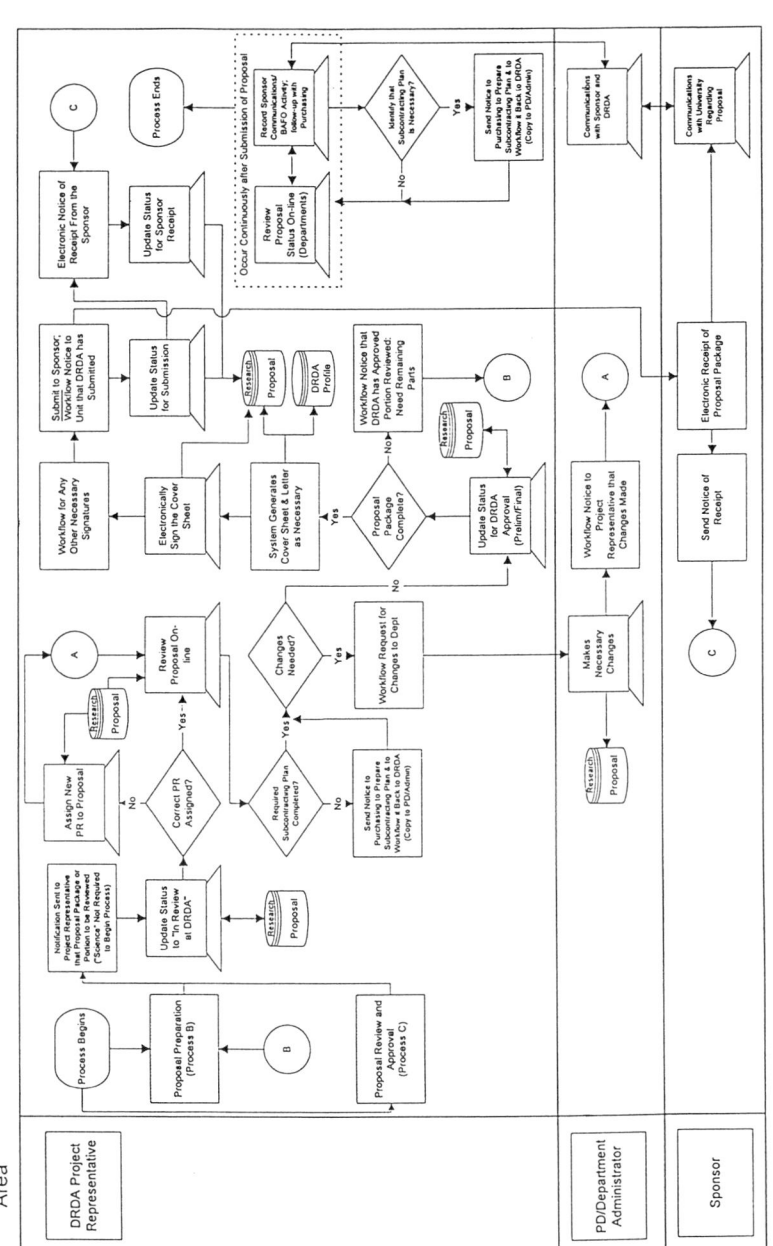

FIGURE 6.2 "Future" process flow: proposal processing and submission to sponsors.

improvements required, project objectives, and the overall "understandability" of the processes. In general the levels can be described as follows:

Level 1:   *Strategic processes*: Primary value-added building blocks of the organization.

Level 2:   *Process elements*: Major steps within each process; should be generic and not specific to a given unit within the organization.

Level 3:   *Functional activities*: Principal activities that constitute each process element, representing all of the inputs of a single functional group to a process element.

Level 4:   *Individual tasks*: Specific tasks within each activity, often performed by a single individual or small team.

Level 5:   *Work steps*: Lowest identifiable discreet form of work within each task.

In most applications, the focus of process mapping is on functional activities (Level 3).

The first task in constructing a process map is to identify the beginning and end of the process under study. It is important to establish the first step that must be taken and the first thing that must be accomplished, which is the initial activity that triggers the process. Then, the last thing that must be done should be defined. If an earlier step is subsequently identified, it can be added. The easiest way to identify the steps between the beginning and the end is to mentally "walk through" the process as it normally occurs. A new step begins when a new type of activity is required. The process description should include every operation, move, point of review or inspection, hand-off or transfer of information, and delay. It is important to list all the elements of the process regardless of how much time it takes to complete each one. Approaching the mapping of a process in this way helps to reduce the seemingly overwhelming nature of the task.

Once the process has been defined and all of the steps have been identified, the process map can be drawn. A process flow is created by using standard flow chart symbols. Software, such as *Visio*^{TM}, is available to facilitate the recording of process flows; activity network diagramming procedures, such as the critical path method (CPM) and program evaluation and review technique (PERT) can also be applied. An appropriate flow chart symbol should be chosen for each step and each step should be briefly identified, telling who, what, and/or where. The steps are connected with lines. The mapping continues in this manner until all the steps in the process are covered. Activities should flow from left to right. If possible, flows should be limited to one page. If a process requires more than one page, it may be best to divide it into subprocesses or to use an off-page connector. It is important to keep flow diagrams simple and to label flows to clearly distinguish between current and future processes.

Sometimes the process map may "branch." A common branch results from an "if," or conditional situation: "If a voucher is below a certain amount, it goes directly to the bursar for payment. If it above this amount, it goes to the controller for an additional signature." Branching can occur during a review step, as when errors are detected and returned for correction. Branching also occurs when several operations need to be carried out at the same time.

In order to improve the process flow, it is important to know the time required to complete each step. This information helps to determine where wasted time can be reduced or eliminated. If the time required to complete a step varies considerably, the circumstances contributing to this variation should be noted. The appropriate times should be recorded for each step in the process. It is important to record the time for delays and storage—these are good targets in the process flow for improvement.

It may be appropriate to assign a cost to each step in the process, but this is optional and will depend on the particular application of the process map. Cost information could provide incentives to eliminate unnecessary or duplicate steps.

In analyzing the current process map, it may be determined that many of the steps seem to be working reasonably well. For the time being, these steps should remain unchanged, but should be monitored or controlled so that change does not occur. The process map helps to identify the points in the process that are causing trouble. Once identified, a cause-and-effect diagram or other analytical tool might be used to examine the elements in the process step to find the cause of the problem. These analytical tools will be described in further detail in Section 4.4.

Improving the process means deliberately changing it in some way. Can any repeated operations be eliminated? Are there ways to shorten or eliminate moves and delays? Brainstorming, cause-and-effect diagrams, or storyboarding can be used to improve the process. Some other points to keep in mind are:

Is there a point in the process that slows or restricts the flow of work, information, or people, and if so, what can be done to improve this situation?

How can the sequence of operations be improved to increase effectiveness?

Can the way in which an operation or activity is carried out be improved?

Can the need for corrections, changes, additions, or recycling something in the process be reduced or eliminated?

Is there a better way to carry out this process?

A process map may show that the system is more complex than anyone realizes. There may be redundant or unnecessary steps which, once revealed, can likely be combined or eliminated. Simplifying the process that delivers the goods or service is the first critical step in improving quality, efficiency, and productivity. A process map also helps to identify the points in the process that need to be controlled—those activities that are most critical to providing the service in a timely and effective manner and those points in the process where trouble usually occurs.

Process mapping can help managers make the most effective use of both personnel and other resources. It encourages those individuals most closely involved in a work process to participate in determining how to use resources more efficiently. A good grasp of specific activities and their relationship to other groups helps managers make more effective decisions and leads to better relationships between units within the organization. Process mapping also provides an excellent basis for training packages for both management and employees. Ways to improve the flow of work can be determined by analyzing process mapping documents.

It may not always be possible or desirable at the outset to undertake the mapping of all processes. It may be more appropriate to concentrate on those processes that offer the greatest potential for major improvement in terms of quality, timeliness, service enhancements, and/or cost savings. Such improvements should have a visible impact on the overall performance of the organization—both in terms of the external customers and the staff members. Often these initial targets are processes for which the application of technology offers significant potential gains and enhancements. In other cases, the processes selected for a "pilot" program have significant potential for positive impact on the departmental and administrative culture of the organization and offer major opportunities for joint interunit problem solving and inter-action.

Processes that are selected for initial mapping should demonstrate results that are clearly measurable with objective criteria. These pilot processes should have a high likelihood of success in terms of demonstrated results within a reasonable scope and time period. They should also evidence a high degree of commitment from a "process owner" (i.e., the official within the organization with the authority to implement the process change).

In his book, Harrington advocated the formation of an executive improve-ment team (EIT) charged with identifying the critical processes and developing an appropriate change model [19]. A process improvement team (PIT), consist-ing of from 5 to 12 members representing all of the units involved the processes under analysis, should also be established. The PIT should (1) flowchart the pro-cess, (2) gather process cost and quality information, (3) establish measurement points and feedback loops, (4) qualify the process, (5) develop and implement improvement plans, (6) report efficiency, effectiveness, and change status, and (7) ensure process adaptability.

An early step in process mapping is to bring together those people who understand or are impacted by the process. *Focus groups*—five to fifteen people who are knowledgeable about a given process—may be organized to share ideas, discuss issues, and collaborate on defining activities and their relationships within processes. More complex issues should be broken down into manageable components for discussion in these focus groups. Reference materials should be distributed prior to the group's meetings to catalyze the discussion and to provide a common focal point for the participants.

Often, the same processes are performed differently by different segments within an organization. Therefore, it is important to consider all practices and to map the most representative process. Differences that may exist should be identified to highlight potential "best practices." Each process should be mapped at a level of detail appropriate to identify reengineering opportunities. Performance measures should be identified at this level of detail. Consistent names and labeling should be used to establish links between flows and profiles.

4.2 Process Profiles

Profiles should be recorded using a standard template that is applicable to both current and future processes (see Table 6.6). It may not be necessary to complete all fields for the current process; some fields may be applicable or important for the future only. As with the process flow diagrams, it is important to be as concise as possible, but to fully document the functional activities that make up the process. Profiles should be analyzed for redundancies, excessive paperwork, manual operations that could be automated, incidence of multiple authorizations (touches), delays and bottlenecks, nonvalue-added activities, and labor-intensive activities. The structure of the organization should be analyzed for (1) nonalignment with constituents (customers or end-users) needs, and (2) unclear or misplaced responsibilities.

Baseline performance measures should be established, and "quick wins" and longer-term recommendations for improvement should be identified. Benchmarking techniques may be applied to gather more detailed targets and metrics to compare information about a process that was generated through mapping. Possible performance measures include: (1) volume of transactions, (2) number of personnel involved in the process, (3) process time, (4) elapse or cycle time, (5) delay time, (6) touch time, (7) value added, and (8) customer or end-user satisfaction. Multiple measures should be applied to avoid suboptimization.

TABLE 6.6   Process Profile Template

Process Overview
1. Process objectives
2. Process description
3. Process owner(s)—responsible individual or office
4. Personnel impacted by process
5. Who and/or what initiates the process?
6. Cross reference to related processes/events (prerequisites and dependencies)

Process Requirements
1. Inputs to process (source and nature of input)
2. Processing requirements:
   Assumptions
   Process steps
   Frequency (daily, weekly, monthly, on request)
   Total organizational volume
   Edits and validation requirements (data validation checks)
   Exceptions in process
3. Output requirements:
   Interface to information system(s)
   Reports
   Additional information produced by the process
4. Related requirements:
   When is workflow routing required (future only)
   Required for approval or informational only
   Additional technology requirements (e.g., scanning/imaging, optical storage/
      retrieval)
   Security rules (include rationale)
   Forms (e.g., vouchers, warrants, letters, billings)
   Related external regulations, policies, contractual parameters, or existing
      procedures
5. Data conversion requirements (future only)
6. Unique training needs (future only)
7. Key performance indicators/metrics:
   Description
   Frequency
   Responsibility
8. Barriers to change: people/process/technology/infrastructure (future only)

Summary of Redesign Opportunities (current only)
1. Description
2. Benefits
3. Time frame (immediate, short-term, long-term)
4. Priority

Related Outstanding Questions/Issues

Adapted from process reengineering exercise for the Division of Research Development and
Administration, University of Michigan, 1997.

Process time is the total amount of time that a service or product is having something done to it (other than waiting). It is the sum of the *touch times* for activities that comprise the process and is measured by:

1. Defining the volumes and estimating the percentage of work on each path (sequence of activities).
2. Determining how much time is consumed at each step if the work goes down that path.
3. Multiplying the total path time by the percent of work on that path and summing the results for all paths.

Cycle time (also referred to as elapsed time) is the total amount of time taken from the point at which a service or product is requested until it is actually delivered or received. It includes process time and delay time and is measured by starting the clock the moment the service or product is requested (from the point of view of the customer) and stopping the clock when the service or product reaches the customer.

Value added analysis determines which activities in the process are most important to the customer or end-user and to the organization's strategy. Value-added steps are those considered essential to a process. Such activities usually meet the following criteria:

It relates to doing it right the first time.
It moves the organization one step closer to delivering the product or service to the customer.
It is something the customer is willing to pay for.

4.3 Designing Future Processes

Alternative designs and their possible implementations should be explored to determine the most appropriate process structure and enabling technologies. Designing new processes is a task of constantly questioning the necessity of performing certain activities and how, if at all, they should be performed. The following guidelines should be considered when beginning to map future processes.

Start with a clean slate and design the process as it should be performed; break patterns and disregard "common sense" solutions; and "think outside the box."
Align processes with strategic objectives and performance targets.
Consider redefining organizational boundaries; do not be bound by existing structure of the organization; and dismiss hierarchical structures.
Improve productivity by integrating fragmented work.

Eliminate pathologies and redundant activities.

Rethink roles and responsibilities to make the process work more effectively and efficiently, and assign people to processes instead to single tasks.

Use technology as an enabler of change.

In formulating future process models, some of the basic questions that should be raised about individual activities include:

Is this activity required by the customer or end-user and will they pay for it?

Could this activity be eliminated without affecting the final product or service (from the customer or end-user perspective)?

Could this activity be eliminated if some prior activity were done differently?

Does technology exist that would significantly change or eliminate this activity?

Focus groups that were organized to assist in documenting the current processes may become *vision groups* in formulating the future processes. Vision groups should be given license to be creative and to use divergent thinking so as to generate and evaluate new ideas, to challenge current assumptions, to break away from existing paradigms, and to throw out established rules. The current organization structure should be subject to re-evaluation. New options for the application of technology should be investigated. The underlying principle of process reengineering is paramount in the conduct of vision group discussions: adopt a "go-for-broke" approach, setting aside preconceived notions of how the organization currently views its structure and ways of doing business.

4.4 Tools and Techniques for Gap Analysis

The next step is to determine the "gap" between the current processes and the desired future processes and the reasons for the divergence. The primary objective is to establish the basis for major process initiatives—the necessary steps to "get from here to there." This analysis can also assist in delineating improvements of current processes that can be undertaken immediately ("quick wins"), identifying barriers to longer-term change, and can provide inputs for analyses of the benefits and costs involved in undertaking the required changes. Several common tools or techniques may be applied to assist in this gap analysis.

Brainstorming is a group problem-solving method that taps the creative ability of participants to identify problems and their causes by eliciting numerous ideas in a relatively short time. The leader of the brainstorming session should encourage participant's ideas and involvement, while exercising enough control to keep the group on track by walking a fine line between a free exchange and control. Brainstorming can be a key to team-building. Individual members are encouraged to contribute to the working of the group and to develop trust for the other members. The following guidelines can facilitate a productive brainstorming session.

> Be sure that everyone understands the topic or problem under discussion in the brainstorming session.
>
> Each person contributes one idea in turn; if someone thinks of an idea when it is not their turn, it should be written down to be used during their next turn.
>
> Every idea should be recorded (usually on flip charts), and the contributor should be satisfied with the way the idea is written down.
>
> Wild "off-the-wall" ideas should be encouraged; they may trigger someone else's thinking.
>
> Criticism should be held until after the session since it may block the free flow of ideas. The goal of brainstorming is creativity and quantity.
>
> Allow a few hours (or days) after the initial session for further thought—an incubation period that allows the mind to release more creative ideas and insights.

If a brainstorming session appears to be slowing down, the leader may suggest "piggybacking" by building on the ideas of others. Other techniques are to suggest opposites to ideas already recorded, to try quick associations, and to prod the brainstorming by tossing out ideas that lead the discussion in certain directions or explores possible issues or causes in greater depth.

Once a brainstorming session has run its course, it is likely that the list of ideas will be rather jumbled and in need of organization. An *affinity diagram* (also know as the *KJ method*, after its creator Kawakita Jiro) may be used to organize the various ideas generated through brainstorming into natural groupings of related thoughts. A header card identifies the common theme of each grouping of ideas. Stray ideas that do not fit any grouping may be explored further or assigned to a "parking lot" for subsequent discussion.

The *cause-and-effect* or *"fishbone"* diagram was developed in order to identify, explore, and display all the possible causes of a specific problem or condition [20]. Cause-and-effect diagrams are designed to focus on the cause of the problem instead of the problem itself. Like other tools, it may take a little while to become familiar with its application, but its ease of use makes this method a popular tool for process reengineering.

Cause-and-effect diagrams sort and segregate possible causes of problems into a logical order, identify areas for further data gathering activity, help to educate participants in problem-solving processes, serve as guides for discussion and help to keep meetings on target, and can be developed into a complete project management tool that displays actions taken and results achieved. In building a cause-and-effect diagram, it is important to define the characteristic (issue or problem) that is to be controlled or improved. This characteristic should be able to be quantified and measured.

The name "fishbone" comes from what the diagram looks like (see Figure 6.3). It is made up of a horizontal line (the spine) with a triangle or box at one end (the head), in which the problem is stated. Several angled lines come off the horizontal line forming the ribs or bones of the fish. A probable cause of the problem is listed at the end of each bone. Major cause categories that typically are used are shown in Figure 6.3. Contributors to the cause (or subcauses) are usually put on smaller bones off the rib. There is no perfect set or number of categories (causes and subcauses); they should fit the problems or processes under analysis.

A cause-and-effect diagram can be used to organize and sort ideas from brainstorming sessions into basic categories. Relationships between ideas are shown, and gaps from the brainstorming that need filling often can be identified. The diagram serves as a record of the brainstorm and helps to track the status of the group in the problem-solving process.

Cause-and-effect diagrams have two important limitations, however. Due to size limitations, the depth of search possible in the diagram cannot exceed two or three levels. Organizational problems often are very complex and, consequently, limited analytical success may result with this method. The diagram does not offer a quantitative mechanism with which to rank the critical variables. In other words, the fishbone does not help in identifying those variables that most significantly affect the quality of performance.

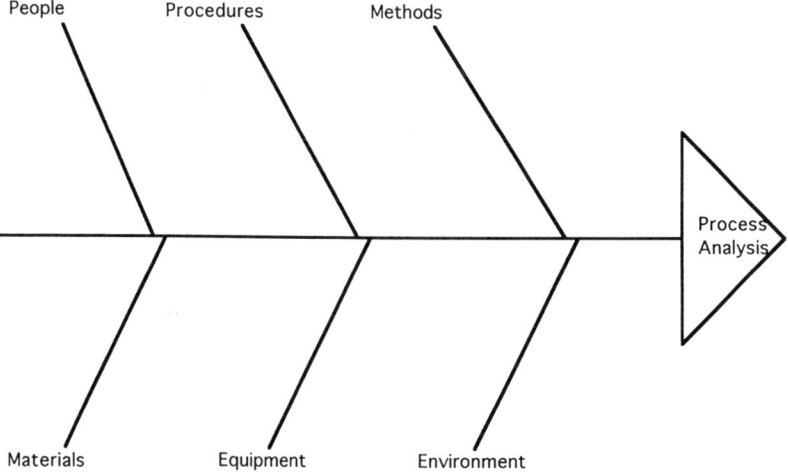

FIGURE 6.3 Cause-and-effect or fishbone diagram.

The best use of a cause-and-effect or fishbone diagram is when a specific problem area is known to need analysis, but there is some uncertainty as to which factors are creating the problem. For example, customer dissatisfaction with a financial process may be identified as the head of the fishbone, with some of the spines being communication problems, process inefficiencies, information reliability, lack of customer service, and issues of affordability. Using brainstorming techniques, each of these "spines" could be examined in greater detail (possibly even doing a fishbone diagram on each of them). A determination is made as to which areas were most instrumental in creating the dissatisfaction. The focus can then be on solutions that would have the most impact on the customers or end-users.

Storyboarding is a group process, like brainstorming, that encourages participation, creativity, and trust. A major difference is that, from the outset, storyboarding is more structured than brainstorming. Once the purpose of the storyboard session has been identified and understood by the participants, the main categories are selected that will serve as the focus of the exercise. Ideas are then generated and organized under these main headings, similar to the approach used in developing an affinity diagram. Participants write down their ideas on individual cards, which are then posted (pinned) on the storyboard under the appropriate heading (as selected by the participant). If an idea fits under more than one category, a duplicate card is prepared. If only a few cards are posted under a major category, the group's attention should be directed to this heading and additional ideas solicited or the heading re-assigned to another category. New headings also may be added during the storyboard session. During the follow-up evaluation, the most appropriate items are selected and prioritized by the group, and specific assignments are made.

Root cause analysis helps to describe *what* happened during a particular event, to determine *how* it happened, and to understand *why* it happened. The goal of root cause analysis is to find the real problem as opposed to simply treating symptoms. The most basic method to find a root cause is to ask "why" (at least) five times (see Figure 6.4). A decision diagram (root cause tree) may aid the investigator in identifying root causes. Once the root cause analysis has been completed, it is important to make sure all team members see the problem in the same manner to help direct the search for alternative recommendations. Each team member should prepare a brief description of the problem. Individual statements should be collated, and the team participants then should prepare a collective statement of the problem (consensus) for review and concurrence.

A *tree diagram* subdivides a process, event, or purpose into its component items (see Figure 6.5). The entries on the diagram, when read from top to bottom, progress from general purpose to specific actions, and answer the question "how is the purpose accomplished?" If read from bottom to top, the diagram answers the question "why?"—the logic or justification for certain actions being undertaken.

Step	Question	Answer
1	Why was the meeting unproductive?	Not every one was ready.
2	Why?	The meeting was called on short notice.
3	Why?	Another office needed a quick answer.
4	Why?	They didn't have sufficient information.
5	Why?	Previous meeting output was incomplete.
6	Why?	Nobody was ready. It was a short-notice meeting.

Root cause: The likely root cause is that people are not given enough time or direction to prepare for the meetings.

FIGURE **6.4**   Root cause analysis.

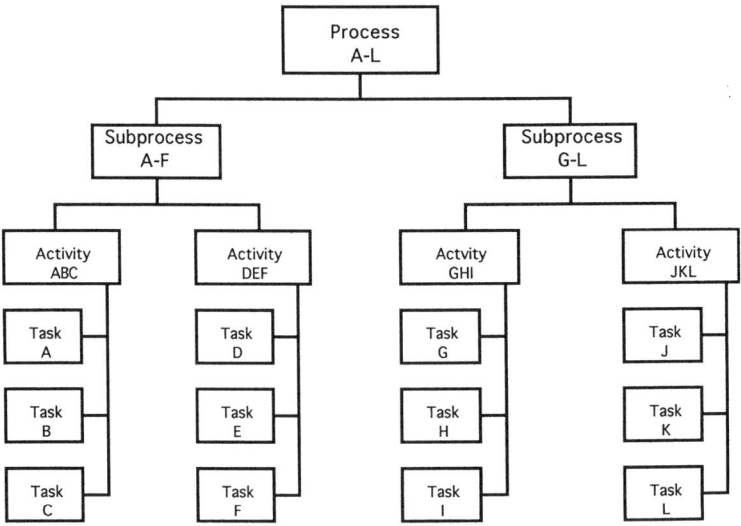

FIGURE **6.5**   Tree diagram.

A *matrix diagram* shows the relationships between two or more sets of items. The items are arranged in rows and columns on a chart that shows the presence or absence of linkages among collected pairs. The diagram facilitates an analysis of the relationship of each item in one set to all items in the other set(s). Thinking is often triggered that might not have occurred if this organized approach had not been used. The diagram is also helpful in identifying patterns of relationships: which items are major factors and which items do not relate to anything.

The *Pareto diagram* is a fundamental tool that can be extremely effective in determining which characteristic is causing problems in a given process. This technique is a deceptively simple, yet powerful, method for looking at the data to help find the root cause of a problem. It derives its name from the work of Vilfredo Pareto (1848–1923), an Italian economist who concluded that a fairly consistent minority (about 20%) of the people controlled the large majority (about 80%) of a society's wealth. Joseph M. Juran expanded on this notion to suggest that only 20% of the possible causes produce 80% of all effects—that is, a few root problems are responsible for the large majority of consequences. In practice, the percentages may not always be exactly 20:80, but there usually are "the vital few and the trivial many."

A Pareto diagram is constructed by categorizing and ranking data by frequency of occurrence or impact of problems. These data are then plotted in bar-chart form in descending order along the *x*-axis (see Figure 6.6). A cumulative sum line shows the percentage contribution of all preceding bars. This plot allows the analyst to determine the most important factor in a given process or situation. Sometimes it can be advantageous to plot dollars on the *y*-axis to emphasize the cost factor. After a Pareto diagram is plotted, the data will indicate what problem is most prevalent, and what kind of leverage can be gained from solving it. The diagram also provides strong clues as to what is the root cause of the difficulty. A Pareto diagram serves as a way to compare problems that existed before efforts were initiated to improve a process with those problems that still existed after the improvements were launched.

In some instances, however, the Pareto diagram will not appear to work—as when all categories are virtually equivalent and there is only a small gain to be made by solving the "worst" one. Not all Pareto analyses produce results leading to the detection of determinate causes and workable solutions. However, if the analysis does not produce a readily apparent cause at a reasonable leverage, it may be possible to sort the data using another characteristic to determine the true culprit variable.

Forecasting seeks answers to key questions about possible and/or probable futures: (1) What happens to object A in time B if the current course of activities is allowed to continue without change? and (2) What are the likely outcomes if change C is introduced? The most primitive method of forecasting is *guessing*.

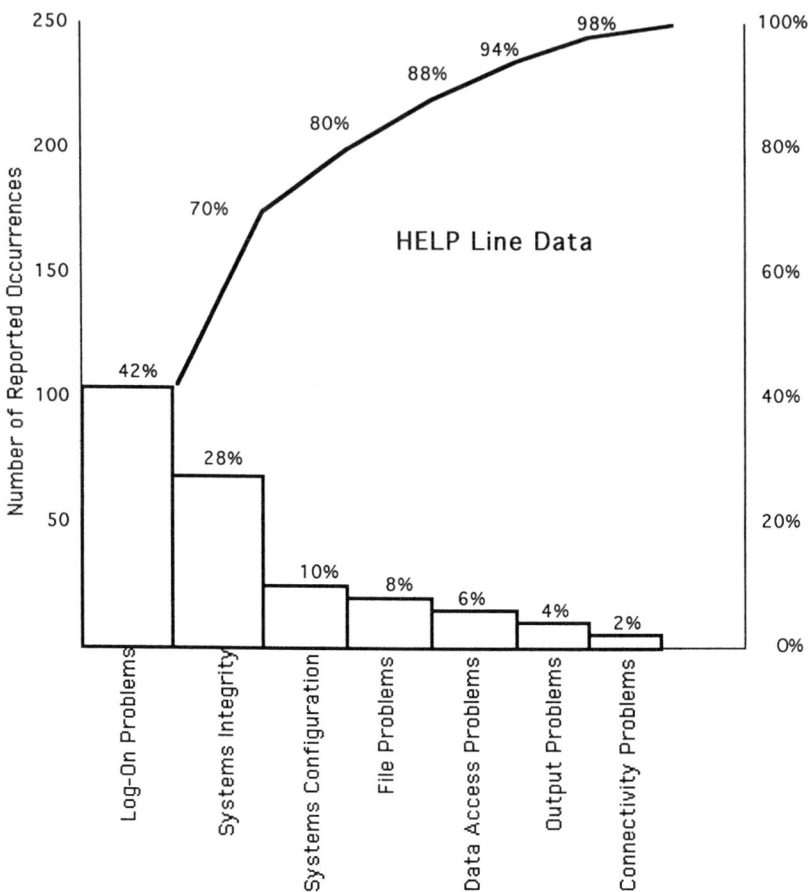

FIGURE 6.6 Pareto diagram.

The forecast may be more acceptable if the person making the guess is an expert in the matter. Guessing makes use of tacit knowledge that a specialist cannot express in exact words or numbers.

The best method for eliciting such an expert forecast is the unstructured interview that permits inquiry into the reasons and explanations for the presented forecast. Some things may be learned when interviewing an expert that later can be used to construct expanded forecasts through other methods. A questionnaire may be used instead of an interview when the number of experts to be consulted are numerous and/or at a distance.

In the *Delphi method*, identical questions are directed to a group of experts, asking for their opinions on the future development of a specific topic.

A summary is made of the replies received, and this summary is sent to the respondents, giving them the opportunity to revise their original responses. This procedure may be repeated several times until the responses approach some sort of consensus.

Extrapolation—the most usual method of forecasting—is based on the assumption that the course of events will continue in the same direction and with unvarying speed (or with steadily growing or diminishing speed, i.e., as a logarithmic extrapolation) until some major intervention occurs. The basis of an extrapolation is knowledge of the recent development of the phenomenon— sequential observations made at known points in time.

Statistical models, such as *linear correlation* and *regression analysis*, can be applied if the time series of observations is sufficiently large. Forecasting on the basis of statistical models often is feasible and successful even when the reason or explanation of the mathematical association found in the historical data is not known. Generally speaking, an effort should be made to determine the rational explanation behind a statistical association assumed as the basis of a forecast. It is always safer to forecast on the basis of a causal model than to forecast only on the basis of statistical association.

The *causal model* is the most accurate method of forecasting. This approach becomes possible when, through research, relationships are identified that show how the attributes and variables to be predicted depend on each other. In the best case, one of the variables in the causal model is *time*. When the correct time period is inserted, the model immediately becomes the desired forecast.

4.5 Process Redesign

It is important to explore alternative designs and their possible implementations to determine the most appropriate process structure and enabling technologies. In evaluating alternative designs, it is essential to establish quantitative and qualitative measures that identify what is to be *maximized* or *minimized*. Several dimensions are available as measures—time, cost, productivity, quality, and capital commitment. Multiple dimensions should be applied, since applying a single dimension in all likelihood would lead to the suboptimization of the process.

It may be useful to develop a prototype application to test the viability of a redesigned process. *Prototyping* provides opportunities for simulating and evaluating reengineering potentials within the organization, as well as the systems development area. It also provides important feedback on the progress and acceptance of the reengineering effort. Individuals who previously participated in focus or vision groups, or others who represent areas within the organization likely to be impacted by a redesigned process, may be brought together in a "hands-on" setting (sometimes referred to as *conference room pilots*) to test and critique the prototype design. During these sessions, participants are provided with the prototype applications to determine the "ease of handling and adaptability" of the new processes. User problems and issues that surface during the pilot sessions may cause the design team to "go back to the drawing board" or may result in "tweaking" various components of the proposed process. Continuous prototyping enables the reengineering team and management to make the necessary adjustments before a final process design is chosen.

The ability of the organization to adopt change (systems readiness) must be addressed in this phase of process reengineering. An inability to implement the necessary organizational change may result in costly project failure and potential lack of confidence of employees in future redesign proposals. Issues involved in the management of change will be examined in some detail in Chapter 9.

One of the steps in process redesign involves the use of information technology (IT) as an enabler for implementing change and supporting processes. Depending on the adaptability of the existing information technology, current information systems may need to be modified or replaced entirely. The first alternative involves software engineering without affecting the hardware. The second approach often involves a total overhaul of the current systems, including the installation of a new technical platform.

An IT platform (computer hardware) should be selected on the basis of its ability to support the redesigned processes. The adaptability of the IT platform to changing processes and new technologies also should be a major consideration. The architecture of the information system should be chosen with respect to actual and future information requirements. Several alternatives are likely to be available. And, in the spirit of reengineering, the choice of the IT platform should be performed without regard to constraints, whether they come from the "comfort level" of the computer department in terms of its familiarity with existing hardware, end-users within the organization, or any other interest group (constituents or customers).

4.6   Systems Integrity

Some organizations are beginning to seriously experiment with the concept of systems integrity, as envisioned by Philip Crosby [21]. Under this approach, all elements of an organization are viewed as components of a system with all parts interrelated and interdependent. Everyone within the organization must have access to a "system map" of their work processes and the interconnections among these processes. These "maps" become more detailed the deeper the analysis proceeds into the organization. This structured approach should lead to increased flexibility, since it is easier to move the component parts around if it is known where to find them in the first place. The increasingly more rapid changes necessary to respond to customers and the marketplace can be more quickly assessed, coordinated, and more successfully implemented. Every part of the organization impacted by change should be readily identifiable, and planned actions could be initiated to respond more effectively and efficiently. This systemic approach should minimize the time necessary to respond to needed change. In addition, the potential negative impacts of the change could be minimized or negated. Organizations should learn to design their changes rather than become victims of them.

A system map, however, is only a representation of a dynamic set of interconnecting activities and relationships that occur on a daily basis within an organization. The administration of this system map requires the creation of a new role in the organization to maintain the overall integrity of the system. To ensure systems integrity, someone must be given responsibility for maintaining the broadest view of the workings of the organization to be certain that appropriate stewardship for the total system is exercised. Two common organizational experiences—one an internally imposed force for change and the other an externally imposed change—can serve to illustrate the need for this stewardship role.

Many organizations operate as if a finite "window of opportunity" exists to develop new services or products. This "window" may become the singular focus of management, which proclaims that it must be met or "all is lost." As a consequence, compromises begin to be made regarding the future integrity of the service or product. Not all the appropriate tests are ordered or completed. The identification of problems usually leads to finger pointing and the placing of blame for the potential of missing the "window." When faced with a problem, the sole determining question often becomes: "How can we get past this issue and still meet the launch date?"

Under the concept of systems integrity, the scenario would play out quite differently. All of the work processes affected by the new service or product and their interconnections should be quite apparent in the system map. Therefore, the right people, including customers, can be part of the design team from the start of the project. By fostering this involvement, the plan for the new service or product can be effectively coordinated within the organization. In addition, it should be possible to implement the new service or product without unduly disturbing the smooth flow of current organizational activities.

An added advantage derived from a systems integrity approach is a well-defined and tested development process for the new service or product. This development process can then be incorporated into the organization's overall strategy and used to determine appropriate timing cycles for the release and subsequent evaluation of the new service or product. Consider a new service or product that has been launched where every affected process within the organization has been evaluated in the design and planning stage. All affected people should understand what they must do to successfully assist in the introduction of the new service or product.

A second example involves the enactment of a new government regulation that will impact the organization. The due date for compliance is externally imposed. In most cases, management mandates the new changes to the most obviously impacted parts of the organization. Others who might be affected are identified through a "ripple down" process. An inordinate amount of time and money may then be spent in policing actions necessary to ensure compliance. Unanticipated effects in other parts of the organization are then handled as they erupt.

Under the systems integrity approach, the new regulation would still be mandated and the compliance date set by external forces. However, the "system map" would clearly indicate the impacted portions of the organization's work processes, the underlying support processes, and all downstream activities. The communication of pertinent information and training of personnel in all affected parts of the organization could be planned and coordinated with a team of process experts—people who work in the areas affected by the new regulations. Before implementation, all affected processes would be systematically changed to reflect the new regulations. Implementation could occur without unnecessary disruptions, excessive policing, or finger pointing.

5 SUMMARY AND CONCLUSIONS

The National Academy of Public Administration defined process reengineering as,

> a radical improvement approach that critically examines, rethinks and re-designs mission, product and service processes within a political environment. It achieves dramatic mission performance gains from multiple customer and stakeholder perspectives. It is a key part of a process management approach for optimal performance that continually evaluates, adjusts, or removes processes [22].

Process reengineering includes a fundamental analysis of the overall organization and a redesign of (1) organizational structure, (2) workflows, (c) job definitions, (4) reward structures, and (5) control processes. In some cases, the organizational culture and philosophy must be re-evaluated to ensure the successful implementation of the proposed change.

Process reengineering involves four basic components that must be maintained in equilibrium: (1) defining strategic objectives, (2) improving processes, (3) applying technology, and (4) developing human resources. While the primary focus is on the linkages between *strategy* and *process*, the existence of an ongoing strategic planning process within the organization can contribute significantly to the overall success of any process reengineering initiative.

Constituent or customer values must be reflected in the strategic objectives of an organization so that processes can be reengineered to focus on providing superior value to the recipients of the organization's products and services. It may be appropriate to conduct a formal analysis to determine what constitutes *quality service* from the perspective of the constituent or customer, and how this service perspective can be measured and improved upon.

Strategic objectives must also reflect the core competencies of the organization—what it does best and those areas in which improvements should be initiated. An examination of an organization's strengths, weaknesses, opportunities, and threats (SWOT), can help determine its current competencies which, in turn, will help determine what its mission should be.

Critical success factors should specify how the major activities to be measured should be aligned with customer values and the shared vision of the organization. *Key performance indicators*—detailed measurements to monitor and evaluate management strategies—should be determined for each critical success factor.

Benchmarking helps to set appropriate targets and metrics for the organization by focusing on (1) using external standards to set targets, and (2) learning from others—learning *how much* and perhaps more important, learning *how* and *why* they succeed. Learning from others involves identify them, study them, and improving processes based upon what has been learned. Crucial internal processes need to be identified, and measures must be established. Comparisons in processes and performance must be made internally, as well as externally, and process improvements need to be put in place.

The formulation of an operational vision is designed to translate the more generic aspects of the strategic objectives into specific applications within the organization. An operational vision involves (1) programming approved objectives into specific projects, programs, and activities, (2) identifying and budgeting of necessary resources to implement these programs over some specific time period, and (3) designing and staffing organizational units to carry out approved programs.

Activities and characteristics that define a process can be documented through *process mapping*. Processes selected for mapping should yield results that can be measured with objective criteria. Each process should be mapped at a level of detail appropriate to identify reengineering opportunities and associated performance measures.

Gap analysis is a principal component of process reengineering. It establishes the framework for the comprehensive analysis of current processes, provides the basis for major program initiatives and the innovative design of new processes, identifies "quick wins," and assesses barriers to change. And it provides key parameters for the analysis of benefits and costs associated with the implementation of the new processes.

Adapting the organizational structure and human resources system to fit the newly defined processes is a crucial task. Employee empowerment, job rotation, and subunit reorganization often can be achieved without major disruptions. However, staff reduction, a frequent process reengineering recommendation, can cause major disruptions.

A new role must be created to maintain the overall integrity of the organization as a system. The broad view of the workings of the organization developed through process mapping must be maintained to be certain that appropriate stewardship for the system is exercised.

Reengineering requires that the organization recognizes its problems and seeks to dramatically overhaul the way it does business. According to Hammer, this is not something that can be accomplished in gradual steps (as espoused through the concepts of total quality management). Rather, a "go-for-broke" approach is required—one that entails setting aside any preconceived notions of how the organization views its structure and ways of doing business. If the leadership is unwilling to make this commitment, an organization is strongly advised against attempting any process reengineering effort.

Organizations must learn to question their beliefs concerning reality (i.e., their paradigms) in order to experiment and innovate. Paradigms can be helpful in ordering our world—in establishing clear boundaries between what is possible and what is not possible in an individual's universe. However, paradigms also can be hazardous to future success and can cause blindness within an organization. Innovation and creativity takes place, as a general rule, at the outer boundary of the current paradigm—at the point where the previously unreal becomes real and the unmanifest becomes manifest. Things that happen at the fringes of today's paradigms may well become mainstream tomorrow. Joel Barker asks the following paradigm-shifting question: "What is impossible to do in your business (field, discipline, department, division, technology, etc.), but if it could be done, would fundamentally change it [23]?"

Efforts to respond more effectively to customer or end-user requirements often result in higher costs to the organization. This cost differential is not always related to "hard" operating dollars, but may also be reflected in softer dollars—those costs associated with employee burn-out, managerial defections, and loss of customers.

Organizations often are confronted by challenging paradoxes. A fundamental survival strategy—becoming more responsive to the "marketplace"—can only be successfully accomplished by designing more effective work processes that produce a consistent output. Developing such processes, however, seems to go hand in hand with tighter structure and controls. How can an organization be flexible and better controlled at the same time? How can an organization better serve not only its customers or end-users, but also better serve the cadre of people who serve those customers?

ENDNOTES

1. Michael Hammer and James Champy. Reengineering the Corporation. New York: HarperCollins, 1993.
2. Thomas Davenport. Process Innovation. Boston, Mass.: Harvard Business School Press, 1993, p. 5.
3. S. Guha, W. J. Kettinger, and T. C. Teng. Business process reengineering: building a comprehensive methodology. Information Systems Management. Summer 1993.
4. Arthur A. Thompson, Jr. and A. J. Strickland III. Strategic Management: Concepts & Cases. Boston, MA: Irwin/McGraw-Hill, 1996, p. 280.
5. H. James Harrington. Business Process Improvement: The Breakthrough Strategy for Total Quality, Productivity, and Competitiveness. New York: McGraw Hill, 1991.
6. Thomas Davenport. Process Innovation: Reengineering Work through Information Technology. Cambridge: Harvard Business School Press, 1993.
7. Michael Hammer and James Champy. Reengineering the Corporation. New York: HarperCollins, 1993.
8. Other publications of note include: R. L. Manganelli and M. M. Klein. The Reengineering Handbook. New York: AMACON, 1994; David K. Carr and Henry J. Johansson. Best Practices in Reengineering. New York: McGraw-Hill, 1995; Michael Hammer and S. A. Stanton. The Reengineering Revolution: A Handbook. New York: HarperBusiness, 1995; Office of the Assistant Secretary of Defense for Command, Control, Communications, and Intelligence. A Benchmarking Report on Functional Process Improvement. November 1993.
9. Sharon L. Caudle. Reengineering for Results: Keys to Success from Government Experience. Washington, D.C.: National Academy of Public Administration, 1994.
10. Customer-Focused Process Improvement. Boston, MA: Lockridge & Company, 1995.
11. Arthur A. Thompson, Jr. and A. J. Strickland. Strategic Management: Concepts & Cases. Boston, MA: Irwin/McGraw-Hill, 1996, p. 94.
12. D. R. Daniel. Management information crisis. Harvard Business Review. September–October 1961, pp. 111–116.
13. For further discussion of these applications see: John F. Rockart. Chief executives define their own data needs. Harvard Business Review. March–April 1979, pp. 81–93; John F. Rockart. The changing role of the information systems executive: a critical success factors perspective. Sloan Management Review. Fall 1982, pp. 3–13; John F. Rockart. Current uses of the critical success factors process. Proceedings of the Fourteenth Annual Conference of the Society for Information Management. September 1982, pp. 17–21; G. B. Davis. Comments on the critical success factors method for obtaining management information requirements. MIS Quarterly. September 1979, pp. 57–58; P. V. Jenster. Firm performance and monitoring of critical success factors in different strategic contexts. Journal of Management Information Systems. Winter 1986, pp. 17–33.
14. John F. Rockart. Harvard Business Review. March–April, 1979, p. 82.
15. A. C. Boynton and R. W. Zmud. Sloan Management Review. Vol. 25, No. 4, Summer 1984.
16. Peat Marwick. Creating the "CIOs Dashboard" of Performance Measures. www.kpmgconsulting.com.

17. Michael G. Dolence. Key performance indicators. Planning for Higher Education. Vol. 17, Fall, 1989.
18. Philip R. Crosby. Quality Is Free: The Art of Making Quality Certain. New York: McGraw-Hill, 1979. For a hands-on guide see: V. Daniel Hunt. Process Mapping—How to Reengineer Your Business Processes. New York: John Wiley & Sons, 1996.
19. H. James Harrington. Business Process Improvement: The Breakthrough Strategy for Total Quality, Productivity, and Competitiveness. New York: McGraw Hill, 1991.
20. Kaoru Ishikawa, one of Japan's quality control pioneers, developed the cause-and-effect diagram in 1943 and published numerous books on quality control. In addition to his work at Kawasaki, Ishikawa was a long-standing member of the Union of Japanese Scientists and Engineers and a faculty member at the University of Tokyo.
21. Philip R. Crosby. Quality Is Free: The Art of Making Quality Certain. New York: McGraw-Hill, 1979.
22. Sharon L. Caudle. National Academy of Public Administration Foundation. Reengineering for Results. Washington, D.C., 1994.
23. Joel Barker. Future Edge: Discovering the New Paradigms of Success. New York: William Marrow and Company, 1992.

7

Resource Management: Cost Analysis

The most effective deployment of organizational resources is a primary focus of strategic management. A common denominator among organizational resources is the cost involved in their utilization. The consequences of past decisions form the basis for much of the cost analysis in complex organizations. Strategic management, however, demands analytical techniques that also can accommodate the risk and uncertainty inevitably associated with future decisions regarding the allocation of resources.

1 ANALYSIS OF COST DATA

Introducing a new strategy or process is analogous to rebuilding a ship while at sea. The current organization must be kept afloat and operating properly while at the same time processes and programs are introduced to move the organization in new directions. Managers often become so enamored with the potential opportunities of a new strategy that they fail to provide sufficient support to current operations. Therefore, in identifying appropriate sources of funds to implement a new strategy or process, it is critical that management also determine the fiscal needs of the current organization [1].

1.1 Strategic Funds

A fundamental approach to cost analysis considers the sources, flow, and uses of current organizational resources in an effort to identify discretionary funds that might be used to implement new strategies and processes. A future-oriented perspective regarding fiscal requirements and potential sources to meet those needs is provided through this approach. As such, it can be applied to both private and public organizations.

The first step is to conduct a *cash flow analysis* to determine how current fiscal resources are allocated and to show where potential adjustments might be made to yield discretionary funds. Generally speaking, an organization can generate new funds from three sources:

1. Regular operations and other internal sources (such as profits after taxes, depreciation, disposition of excess inventory or unused facilities or in the public sector, increased revenue through adjusted tax levies).
2. Expansion of short-term debt consistent with the fiscal structure of the organization (for example, having banks provide extended lines of credit, leasing rather than buying equipment, factoring accounts receivable).
3. Changes in the fiscal structure of the organization to permit the addition of new long-term debt or equity funds.

Funds accumulated from these sources generally comprise the total funds available for managing the organization's operations and fall into two categories: baseline funds and strategic funds.

Baseline funds support the current, ongoing operations of the organization. They are used to pay operating expenses, provide adequate working capital, and maintain the current plant and equipment. Baseline funds are used to (a) maintain the same level of production or services, (b) secure the organization's "market share," or (c) achieve a specified, ongoing rate of growth.

Strategic funds are invested in the new initiatives required to meet the organization's strategic objectives. They are used to purchase new assets, such as equipment, facilities, and inventory; to increase working capital; and to support direct expenses for research and development, marketing, advertising, and program promotions. In the private sector, strategic funds are also used for mergers, acquisitions, and market development. A market penetration strategy, for example, may call for a more intensive investment of funds in the current business. A market expansion strategy usually requires aggressive use of strategic funds for advertising and promotion. An organization must use strategic funds to produce more diverse products or services and to develop new markets for them.

The total amount of strategic funds available to the organization can be determined by subtracting baseline funds from total assets (revenue or appropriations). Once estimates have been made as to the funds required to carry out each strategy, they can be ranked according to their potential contribution to the achievement of the identified objectives. In undertaking this ranking, the kinds of strategic funds available and the level of risk involved must be taken into account.

Available strategic funds should be allocated to each program according to some set of priorities. Key decision points concerning risk and return are encountered (1) when funds available from internal sources have been fully consumed and (2) when readily available credit sources have been exhausted. At this point, proposed strategies must be evaluated in terms of changes required in the financial structure of the organization. The final step is to establish a management control system to monitor the generation and application of funds to achieve the desired results.

1.2 Basic Concepts of Cost

Cost can be defined as a release of value required to accomplish some goal, objective, or purpose. In the private sector, costs are incurred for the purposes of generating revenues in excess of the resources consumed. While this profit motive is not applicable to most public and nonprofit organizations, the test as to whether a cost is appropriate and reasonable is still the same: Did the commitment of resources advance the organization or program toward some agreed-upon objective?

It is important to distinguish between direct and indirect costs. A *direct cost* represents a cost incurred for a specific purpose that is uniquely associated with that purpose. Four direct cost components are involved in any process, project, or program: (1) labor or personal services (salaries, wages, and related employee benefits), (2) contractual services (services purchased from outside sources), (3) materials and supplies (consumables), and (4) equipment expenses (sometimes categorized as fixed asset expenses). In analyzing the overall operations of a day care center, for example, the salary of the center's manager would be considered a direct cost. However, the center might be divided into departments according to different age groups of children and a portion of the manager's salary may be allocated to each department. Then the manager's salary would be considered an indirect cost of each department. An *indirect cost* is generally considered to be any cost associated with more than one activity or program that cannot be traced directly to any of the individual activities. In the public sector, the terms indirect cost and overhead often are used interchangeably.

Costs can also be defined by how they change in relation to fluctuations in the quantity of some selected activity—for example, number of hours of labor required to complete some task, dollar volume of sales, number of orders processed, or some other index of volume (see Figure 7.1). *Variable costs* are more or less uniform per unit, but their total fluctuates in direct proportion to the total volume of activity. The cost for medical supplies in a public health clinic will increase in direct relation to the number of patients treated. *Fixed costs* do not change in total as the volume of activity increases, but become progressively smaller on a per unit basis. Utility costs involved in operating a public health clinic, for example, remain the same regardless of the number of patients treated by the clinic. However, the greater the number of patient visits, the lower the cost per patient for utilities.

Costs may also be *semi-variable*, whereby both fixed and variable components are included in the related costs, or *semi-fixed*, described as a step-function.

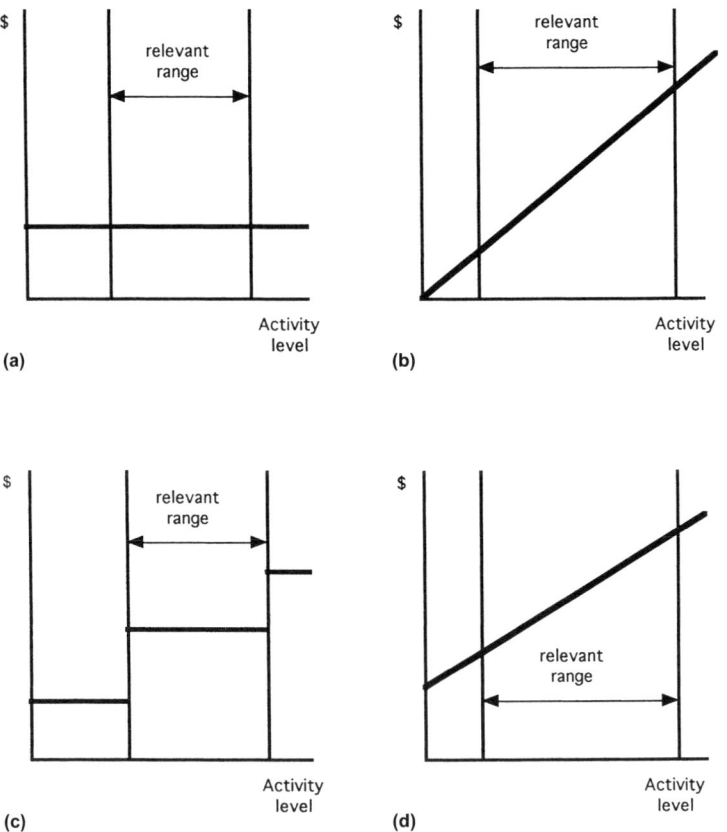

Figure 7.1   Graphic illustration of cost concepts. (a) Fixed cost; (b) variable cost; (c) semi-fixed cost; and (d) semi-variable cost.

Maintenance costs often exhibit the characteristics of semi-variable costs. A fixed level of cost is initially required, after which maintenance costs may increase with increases in the level of activity. Salaries of supervisory personnel might be described as semi-fixed costs; at some level of increased activity, additional supervisory personnel may be required. Since costs are usually classified as either fixed or variable, the incremental character of these mixed categories often is a determining factor. If the increments are relatively small, the costs are usually defined as variable; if the increments between levels of change are large, the costs may be classified as fixed.

1.3 Factors Influencing Future Costs

Any framework for resource management must include an examination of those factors that influence the future costs of the goods and services provided by an organization to its constituents, clientele, or customers. No program decision is free of cost, whether or not the decision leads to the actual commitment of organizational resources. Choices among alternative strategies for the accomplishment of the objectives of any organization are likely to involve many costs. Such choices include not only the expenditure of money, but also the employment of human resources, the consumption of physical resources, and the use of time—all critical commodities in any organization.

Often the tendency is to consider costs strictly in terms of dollar inputs—the financial resources required to support personnel, equipment, materials, and so on. Future costs that cannot be easily measured in dollar terms all-too-often are dismissed as noncost considerations. Such costs, however, may have important implications beyond their measurable monetary value.

Strategic managers must be cognizant of the following factors that influence future costs:

1. Scope and quality of the services or products to be delivered.
2. Volume of activity required to deliver these services or products.
3. Processes, methods, facilities, and organizational structure required to perform these activities.
4. Qualities and types of labor, materials, equipment, and other cost elements required by these programs.
5. Price levels of the various cost elements.

In addition, uncertainty in the economic, political, and social arenas—which might include exposure to risk—constitutes a major factor influencing the direction of future costs [2].

1.4 Monetary Costs and Economic Costs

Monetary costs are commonly reflected in financial accounts. They include research and development costs, investment costs, and the costs of operations, maintenance, and replacement. At times, it may be appropriate to look beyond these monetary costs to what economists call opportunity costs, associated costs, and social costs.

Research and development (R&D) involves front-end costs that may or may not figure into the actual expenses of a given program or project. R&D costs that are incurred explicitly for a given program or project should be included as a project expense. However, general R&D costs that eventually benefit more than one program or project must be considered as *sunk costs* and should not be included in the direct cost estimate for a specific program or project.

Investment costs are expenses incurred to obtain future benefits. Such investments may be classified as sunk costs or actual project outlays, depending on their timing. Consider the decision to develop a public recreational facility on land that was purchased some years earlier for another public purpose. Only those additional investment costs required to prepare the site for the recreational use should be considered as project outlays. The previous investment for the land purchase represents a sunk cost.

Sunk costs can become an *inheritable asset* if previous investments can be used to the particular advantage of one alternative over another. The decision regarding the site of the recreational facility should not be based solely on the past investment, however. If that location would be an inferior alternative in view of identified user needs, this decision would simply result in "throwing good money after bad."

Recurring costs include operating and maintenance costs that vary with both the size and duration of the program. Such recurring costs include salaries and wages, employee benefits, maintenance and repair of equipment, miscellaneous materials and supplies, transfer payments, insurance, and direct overhead costs. These recurring or operating costs do not add to the stock of capital. Rather, they are incurred to maintain the value of the existing stock. In preparing cost estimates, it is important that these recurring costs be considered over the life of the project or program, not just in the initial fiscal period.

It is also important to consider the *marginal* (or *incremental*) costs of increasing the size or scope of a program or project. Suppose, for example, that the decision is whether to build one or two public health clinics. It may be possible to get quantity discounts on materials and equipment that would reduce the cost of a second clinic. As a result, suppose the cost of building one clinic is $1,200,000, and the cost of building two clinics is $2,000,000. The *average cost* of each clinic would be $1,000,000; however, the *marginal cost* of the second clinic would be only $800,000.

If resources are committed to one program, the opportunity has been pre-empted to use these resources elsewhere. The concept of *opportunity costs* can be illustrated by returning to the health clinic example. Having determined the monetary cost of the proposed facility, it may be appropriate to describe some of the alternative uses of these resources. For example, for what other purposes could the land be used? What other use could be made of the required staff salaries? If bonds are to be issued, to what other programs might the funds required for interest and principal payments be allocated?

If these alternative uses are sufficiently important, an attempt should be made to estimate their value. This evaluation would consider the benefits that must be given up if the decision is made to go ahead with the proposed clinic. Keep in mind that a basic purpose of cost analysis is to estimate the value of alternatives foregone. Opportunity costs may be extremely important in making decisions among alternative program strategies.

Associated costs are "any costs involved in utilizing project services in the process of converting them into a form suitable for use or sale at the stage benefits are evaluated [3]." The beneficiaries of public programs and services often incur associated costs. The associated costs that must be borne by users of public recreational facilities, for example, include the incremental costs of travel, food, lodging, and so forth. If access to a recreational facility is improved, so that the users' travel costs are reduced, then these savings in associated costs may be considered as benefits arising from improved access.

Social costs can be defined as the subsidies that must be paid to compensate persons adversely affected by a project or program for their suffering or "disbenefits." Such compensation rarely is made (except perhaps when affected individuals enter into litigation and are awarded damages). Thus, social costs represent an analytical concept.

In making a cost analysis, social costs can be handled in one of two ways [4]. They may be treated as external costs and subtracted from the value of the output of the project to obtain a *net social value*. Alternatively, they may be treated as opportunity costs, by examining the *potential benefits* to those who are likely to be adversely affected if the project funds were spent on some other program. For example, the location of a sewage treatment facility may result in reduced property values in adjacent residential areas. These losses may be treated as "negative benefits" and subtracted from the overall benefits of the project to the larger community. Alternatively, the benefits that would accrue to these property owners from an alternative use of project funds (for example, development of a park site) might be calculated. The project with the larger "yield" would represent the better use of these resources.

Unfortunately, social costs, if included at all in a cost analysis, are seldom treated fairly. Such cost considerations are either underplayed by proponents of a project or overplayed by its opponents. Social costs often carry significant emotional overtones and, therefore, may be difficult to evaluate. Nevertheless, an evaluation of such costs may be a very important factor in the decision to invest organizational resources in a project or program.

2 ACTIVITY-BASED COSTING

Activity-based costing (ABC) is a method for measuring cost based on the activities that an organization uses in producing its output [5]. Activity-based costing identifies the cost pools, or activity centers, in an organization and assigns costs to products and services (cost drivers) based on the number of events or transactions involved in providing a product or service. ABC differs from traditional cost accounting techniques in that it accounts for all "fixed" and direct costs as variables, without allocating costs based upon a customer's unit volume, total days in production, or percentage of indirect costs. Information gathered through ABC can provide a cross-functional, integrated view of an organization, including its activities and its processes. Cost management and control can then focus on the sources of cost, rather than on where the costs are incurred or reported.

2.1 Traditional Methods for Recording Costs

Most accounting systems currently in use identify, record, and distribute costs by one of the following methods:

Organizational units or elements
Budgetary accounts
Traditional cost accounting with direct and indirect cost allocation.

Each of these methods has met the past needs of most organizations. Yet, each fails to meet the full requirements for strategic management.

Organization-based accounting systems assign identifiable direct costs to each of the elements of the traditional bureaucratic structure. Indirect costs—those costs that cannot be attributed to a specific unit or program—are usually captured in and paid through a central account with no attempt to further subdivide or distribute these costs. In many traditional organizations, only direct salary costs are allocated to the operating units. This approach was never intended to define output costs, either at the unit level or organization-wide. This model is inadequate for making decisions regarding variations in output or performance since costs are not applied to the process flows, activities, or ultimate outputs of the organization.

Budgetary accounts track costs in a manner similar to that of the organizational approach. Historically, public organizations have been most concerned with ensuring that total expenditures do not exceed the allocated budgetary resources. As a result, accounting systems became a safeguard mechanism to capture commitments, undelivered orders, and expenditures. To facilitate the monitoring of the budget's execution, direct cost data typically are divided by organizational units. A major objective is to fully use the resources allocated to each unit rather than to enhance productivity or to reduce expenses. Any attempt to conserve resources, in fact, may lead to a reduction in the level of future budget allocations. Like organizational accounting systems, no attempt is made to relate cost to output or, in many cases, to even define output.

The traditional *cost accounting* model has been the mainstay for over 100 years among those organizations that perform activities that require costs to be distributed to output. Most of these organizations are reimbursed by their customers based on sales of their goods and services. Hence, cost accounting operations were established to capture and distribute costs to the goods or services (outputs), using the classic model designed around the major factors of production: direct labor, direct materials, and overhead.

Traditional cost accounting methods track costs by functional area with functions tied to the end-items or outputs being produced. Direct costs can be identified relatively easily in this fashion, as can some, but not all, indirect or overhead costs. Indirect costs that cannot be attributed to specific functions typically are allocated across functional areas using a pro-rating formula. Thus, for example, if the identified indirect costs (central administration, accounting, purchasing, and so on) of an organization are $1 million and the total direct costs are $2 million, an indirect cost rate of 50% might be applied to distribute these indirect costs. If a particular service unit or product line accounted for $200,000 of the total direct costs, then the "burdened" cost (direct and indirect) of this unit/line would be $200,000 × 1.5 = $300,000.

2.2   Process-Oriented Approach

Cooper and Kaplan asserted that the traditional approach to cost accounting is flawed because certain cost behavior is a consequence of *activities* carried on in support departments and should not be driven by allocation factors related to the volume of production [6]. Activities describe what an organization does (see Table 7.1 for a glossary of ABC terms). The primary function of an activity is to convert resources (e.g., labor, material, and technology) into outputs (e.g., products and services). The total cost of all traceable activities is based on how much of each activity is consumed by the product or service, regardless of functional or organizational boundaries. A fundamental premise of ABC is that managers can learn how to identify and eliminate waste by focusing on the root cause of a cost rather than merely addressing the symptoms.

Activity-based costing recognizes that, while common processes or activities may be performed within each functional area, the pro-rating method of traditional cost accounting does not truly identify the usage variance in process costs that may exist in different units. The major difference between traditional cost accounting and activity-based costing is that ABC is a process-oriented method, based on the recognition that labor-intensive processes may represent the single largest contributor to the increasing cost of an organization's operations.

TABLE 7.1 The ABC Glossary

Activity
  Total cost of activity: The total amount of direct and overhead charges associated with or allocated to a single activity.
  Cost driver: A measurable factor that represents the amount of performance; and creates or affects the costs within a single defined activity (e.g., the number of iterations, amount of effort, square feet of floor space occupied, etc.).
  Elapsed time: The total amount of time (including the amount of time delay created while awaiting processing) consumed to complete the activity or an iteration of the cost driver.
  Cycle time: The amount of time to complete one cycle or iteration of the cost driver without including delay or wait times.

Process
  Total cost of the process: The total cost of all the activities in a process determined by the amount of the cost driver for each activity in relation to the output of the process.
  Cost of a single iteration: The total cost of a single incident or cost driver allocation for each of the activities in a process flow, which may be equal to the total cost when a single iteration occurs at each activity in the flow.

Output
  Cost of the output: The total cost of the activity model allocated by the applied activity drivers to the output of the activity model.

Identification of Change Opportunities
  Significant cost consumption: Activities identified that have an evidently larger consumption of inputs and mechanisms or the value of the output is less than the value of the inputs.
  Significant time use: Activities identified that have evidently larger time periods or use of time or large nonvalue delay periods.

Evaluation of Change Alternatives
  Cost comparison: Analysis of the allocated costs from the activity model to two or more alternative process methods.
  Time comparison: Analysis of the total time or cycle times of two or more alternative process methods.

ABC tracks the flow of activities in an organization by creating a causal link between the activity (resource consumption) and the cost object (e.g., products, services, customers, and market areas).

A commercial production line, for example, may consume more direct labor, material, and even space than the operations required for a small, high-precision, manufacturing contract undertaken as part of the NASA space shuttle program. However, the administrative overhead required to support the space shuttle contract is likely to be extraordinarily high, inflated by the additional (indirect) labor needed to perform such activities as the nonroutine handling of the small parts procurements, more stringent acceptance testing, and NASA contract reporting requirements. In similar fashion, a university research project involving engineering facilities is likely to require considerably higher indirect costs than research activities in the social sciences. In these situations, ABC can account for the significant variance in indirect costs and proportionately allocating those costs to the end item products that consume them.

Manufacturing firms gain the greatest benefit from ABC in the allocation of overhead costs. However, the approach also offers benefits to service industries in the tracking of both direct and indirect costs. The process orientation of ABC makes it valuable and applicable to all types of organizations, including government, nonprofit organizations, and colleges and universities.

2.3 Cost Drivers

The basic purpose of implementing ABC is to separate organizational activities into individual cost drivers. A *cost driver* is any event that causes a change in the total cost of an activity. *Inputs* are the resources that are consumed by activities (usually measured as costs). *Outputs* are the products (goods or services) that an activity supplies to its customers (internal or external). In addition to the obvious direct costs elements, such as salaries and wages and materials, cost drivers might include such activities as order processing, design time, employee training, application of special expertise, product or service delivery, securing credit, after-hour service, telephone expenses, and so on. When selecting cost drivers, it is important that they be relevant and easy to measure. Relevancy relates to the direct or indirect relationship the driver bears to the cost of doing business, and ease of measurement means that the costs must be attributable proportionally to the activities consumed.

Under the ABC approach, the focus of the analysis of costs shifts from the traditional cost accounting structure (which identifies *what* resources are being used) to the activities that the organization carries out (which relate *why* the resources are being consumed—*for what purpose*). Some costs can be directly associated with an activity (most labor costs, for example), whereas other costs must be allocated (such as utilities or rent). If costs must be allocated, the allocation basis is called a *first-stage driver*. An example of a first-stage driver is the square footage of floor space occupied by various activities. Costs of supporting departments (e.g., purchasing, accounting, personnel, and central administration) are initially accumulated in overhead cost pools and then are allocated to activities using appropriate cost drivers. Procurement costs, for example, might be allocated on the basis of the number of transactions involved in acquiring the materials and supplies required by each activity.

The next step is to quantify the volume of each activity's output, either as an actual (historical) volume or as a projected volume (defined as an *output measure*). The total cost of an activity is then divided by its total volume to determine the average cost per unit of output. The total costs of individual activities are allocated to a responsibility center or activity center (i.e., a unit having a common objective). If the costs of a responsibility/activity center are to be allocated to cost objectives, then the output measure (e.g., cost per unit of output) is a *second-stage driver*. Finally, *performance measures* are identified to determine the results achieved by an activity or activity center (e.g., average cost per patient treated for a particular ailment).

The ABC approach is likely to produce a more accurate representation of indirect costs attributable to final cost objectives than using surrogate measure such as direct labor hours or direct material dollars as a means for allocating costs to products. The two-stage ABC process identifies activities and focuses on the cost drivers that are the major causal factors behind cost behavior.

2.4   An Example of Activity-Based Cost Analysis

The Strigiformes Company produces two products: Output A and Output B. The production, market price, and product costs are shown below.

		Average	
	Production	Market price (\$)	Cost (\$)
Output A:	200 units	125	110
Output B:	800 units	18	20

Management has been concerned that the cost of Output B, which is above the average market price, makes it noncompetitive, and should be eliminated from the product line. The managerial analysis suggests that Output A is very competitive and is carrying the operation, while Output B costs too much and should be eliminated from production. Before the final decision is made, however, a request was made to provide more analysis using activity-based costing methods as a comparison to the current traditional system. The additional information gathered by the ABC analysis is shown in Table 7.2.

When the two sets of information were presented to management, the result was turmoil. The activity-based analysis yielded results that were entirely different from that of the managerial analysis. When costs were traced to the amount of activity actually used, rather than as a straight distribution based on output allocation, Output A was actually more expensive than originally thought and furthermore, was not competitive in the market. Output B was competitive and should be retained.

TABLE 7.2 Comparative Costing Example: Strigiformes Company

Direct Costs
Output A $100 per unit
Output B $ 10 per unit

Overhead Costs in Purchasing Department
Annual workload: 10,000 purchase orders
Annual cost: $10,000
Purchase orders required per unit of Output A: 30
Purchase orders required per unit of Output B: 5

Cost Distribution Table
Traditional cost accounting
Total output / Total overhead = Amount per unit of output
       1000 / $10,000 = $10
Activity-based accounting
Activity cost / Activity workload = Amount per unit of activity
       $10,000 / 10,000 = $1
Activity units × Amount per unit = Total output cost per unit of output
       Output A: 30 × $1 = $30
       Output B: 5 × $1 = $ 5

Total Cost per Unit Output
Traditional cost

	Direct cost	+	Overhead	=	Total cost
Output A:	$100	+	$10	=	$110
Output B:	$10	+	$10	=	$20

Activity-based cost

	Direct cost	+	Overhead	=	Total cost
Output A:	$100	+	$30	=	$130
Output B:	$10	+	$5	=	$15

Management became skeptical of both systems and complained about "voodoo" accounting practices. It was decided to ignore the new analysis and implement the decision to eliminate Output B. With Output B eliminated along with all associated costs, the output price for A immediately reverted to the remaining costs. Purchasing was unable to eliminate the costs as anticipated by management and the price for Output A rose to $130 per unit. This new price made Output A impossible to sell. The information below shows how the costs remaining after the elimination of Output B were allocated to the only remaining product.

Direct Material + Overhead = Total Cost / Production = Price
$20,000   + $6,000 = $26,000 /   200   = $130

If management had based their decision on the activity-based cost analysis, Output A would have been eliminated and the price for Output B would have been:

Direct Material + Overhead = Total Cost / Production = Price
$8,000   + $4,000   = $12,000   /   800   = $15

The elimination of Output A had no effect on the organization since the remaining costs were those associated with Output B and Output B always was competitive within the market.

This simplified example demonstrates that the traditional method of applying overhead directly to the output can overstate or understate the true cost, which can be determined when a full internal review is done of how the costs are incurred. Even though the example was simplified, it nonetheless is an accurate representation of how the activity-based methodology more fairly distributes costs with fewer arbitrary distributions normally associated with traditional cost accounting procedures.

The ABC method is more complex, however, and requires additional time and effort to determine the attribution of indirect costs. In many situations, it is uncertain whether marked difference results are obtained by using the ABC method instead of more traditional approaches. If the costing system is used to determine fees or prices or to measure performance of selected activity centers or indirect cost pools, then the more complex ABC method may be appropriate.

2.5   What Does ABC Provide to the Strategic ?lanager?

Strategic managers are always faced with difficult choices and multiple alternatives. Although decisions can be made based on feelings and intuition, this is not the preferred situation. Activity-based costing captures quantified costs and performance data and translates these data into decision information. ABC measures process and activity performance, determines the cost of process outputs, and identifies opportunities to improve process efficiency and effectiveness. These data assist in organizing variables into a format that makes the decision clearer and easier to make.

ABC supports process improvement initiatives. Collecting and translating existing cost data into the activity structure enhances the analysis of selected opportunities and alternatives. The various dimensions identified as activity costs are like a menu to be selected from, as deemed necessary, to support the process objectives. A vast amount of decision-support information can be provided to the process improvement team, depending on which items are selected for completion.

One major drawback to the adoption of ABC is that it is not readily supported by accounting systems currently in use by most organizations. Established charts of accounts focus on the tracking of costs by function rather than by process. ABC can only be fully implemented in organizations that have a clear understanding of the body of activities that are commonly performed in all functional areas. It is also necessary to have a means of identifying the time spent on these activities and an ability to relate them to charges against the general ledger accounts.

3 ANALYSIS OF COST AND BENEFITS

It has been suggested that: "One can view cost–benefit analysis as anything from an infallible means of reaching the new Utopia to a waste of resources in attempting to measure the unmeasurable [7]." Many of the criticisms of cost–benefit analysis are equally applicable to other analytical techniques. Since analysis can be difficult, costly, and troublesome, all too often, the assertion is made that more intuitive approaches should be applied. This is not a valid argument, however, for abandoning efforts to improve techniques for the analysis of benefits and costs.

3.1 Basic Components of Cost–Benefit Analysis

Given adequate estimates, the analysis of costs and benefit provides a relatively straightforward approach on which to base decisions regarding the allocation of available resources among economically desirable options. A comprehensive cost–benefit analysis requires that estimates be made of both the direct and indirect costs and the tangible and intangible benefits of a program or project. Benefits and costs must be translated into a common measure—usually (but not necessarily) a monetary unit. Benefits and costs are then compared by computing: (1) a benefit-to-cost ratio (benefits divided by costs), (2) net benefits (benefits minus costs), or (3) some other value that summarizes the results of the analysis (such as an internal rate of return).

The basic components of cost–benefit analysis, as first outlined by Otto Eckstein, included: (1) an objective function, (2) constraints, (3) externalities, (4) time dimensions, and (5) risk and uncertainty [8]. Selecting an *objective function* involves identifying and quantifying, in dollar terms to the extent possible, the costs and benefits associated with each alternative. Specifying benefits at times may be relatively straightforward, as in many technical and industrial projects. For many social programs, however, benefits often are diffuse, intangible, and difficult to define and measure. Costs are somewhat easier to identify. They are the direct and indirect inputs—the resources required to carry out the program or project. The evaluation of opportunity costs—the value of foregone opportunities—may be complex, however, even for programs for which extensive impact data are available.

Constraints are the "rules of the game"—that is, the limits within which an acceptable solution must be sought. Solutions that are otherwise optimal frequently must be discarded because they do not conform to these imposed rules. Constraints are incorporated into mathematical models as parameters or boundary conditions.

Projects may have spillover effects or unintended consequences that may be beneficial or detrimental. Since these *externalities* may be difficult to identify and measure, they often are excluded from the analysis initially in order to make the problem statement more manageable. The long-range effects of these phenomena must ultimately be considered, however, usually after the objective function and the analytical model have been tested and the range of feasible alternatives has been narrowed.

Benefits and costs occurring at different points in time must be made commensurable—that is, translated into a common unit of measurement. It is not sufficient merely to add the estimated benefits and subtract the estimated costs. The impact of deferred benefits and future costs must be taken into account. In so doing, the analyst encounters the problems of risk and uncertainty.

Benefits that accrue in the present usually are worth more to their recipients than benefits anticipated some time in the future. Similarly, resources invested today cost more than those invested in the future, since one option would be to invest the same funds at some rate of return that would increase their value. Therefore, the equivalent *present value* of future streams of benefits and costs must be determined by multiplying each stream by an appropriate *discount factor*.

Two common bases used for discounting reflect both local conditions and the marketplace for investments.

1. Cost of borrowing the capital necessary to finance a project or program, and
2. Rate of return that could be realized if an equivalent amount were invested for the same period of time.

Thus, if a project could be financed by borrowing the necessary capital at 8%, or if an investment of equivalent funds could be expected to yield 6%, either of these percentages might be used to discount future benefits and costs.

Although the choice of a particular discount rate may be difficult to justify, the procedures for discounting are quite simple. An appropriate discount factor can be expressed as:

$$1/(1 + i)^n$$

where i is the relevant interest rate per year, and n is the number of units of time into the future (e.g., years) that the benefits and costs will accrue. If i is

TABLE 7.3   Discounting $100,000 Annually Over Ten Years

	Discount factor @ 8%	Discounted value ($)	Discount factor @ 10%	Discounted value ($)
1	0.925926	92,593	0.909090	90,909
2	0.857339	85,734	0.826446	82,645
3	0.793832	79,383	0.751315	75,132
4	0.735030	73,503	0.683013	68,301
5	0.680583	68,058	0.620920	62,092
6	0.630170	63,017	0.564472	56,447
7	0.583490	58,349	0.513156	51,316
8	0.540269	54,027	0.466505	46,651
9	0.500249	50,025	0.424095	42,410
10	0.463193	46,319	0.385541	38,554
Total		$671,008		$614,455

positive (as is the usual case), the farther an event is in the future, the smaller is its present value.

Once an appropriate rate has been chosen, a table of discount factors can be consulted to determine the appropriate figure to apply to each year in the stream of costs and benefits. As the data in Table 7.3 illustrate, the selection of the discount rate can significantly affect the final decision. High discount rates mean that there is a significantly higher regard for present benefits than for equal future benefits and/or a willingness to trade some larger amount of future benefits for smaller current benefits.

3.2   Criteria for Analysis

Once an objective function has been identified, an indicator of "success" must be selected—that is, an index that will yield a higher value for more desirable alternatives. Conceptually, such an indicator involves the *maximization* of something. Businesses, for example, seek to maximize profits. Public officials are presumed to seek to maximize benefits for their constituencies. The frequent inability to quantify overall benefits, however, has led to the use of *cost minimization* as the objective function in many cost–benefit analyses.

It often is suggested that the goal of cost–benefit analysis should be to maximize benefits and minimize costs. In reality, however, both cannot be accomplished simultaneously. Costs can be minimized by spending nothing and doing nothing, but in that case, no benefits result. Benefits derived from a particular project or program can be maximized by committing organizational resources until marginal benefits are zero. But such action often may require far more resources than are available. Therefore, some composite criterion is needed. Three obvious choices are:

Maximize benefits for given costs.
Minimize costs while achieving a fixed level of benefits.
Maximize net benefits (benefits minus costs).

The *benefit/cost ratio*, introduced by the Flood Control Act of 1936, was the first cost–benefit criterion to be used. A benefit/cost ratio is defined as the present value of benefits divided by the present value of costs (or average annual benefits over average annual costs). Thus, for example, if the discounted stream of benefits over the expected duration of a program or project equals $800,000 and the discounted stream of costs equals $600,000, the benefit/cost ratio is 1.33.

Net benefits is the criterion recommended, if not used, most frequently in contemporary cost–benefit analysis. The net benefits in the previous example would be $800,000 minus $600,000, or $200,000. Net benefits measure *difference*, whereas benefit/cost calculations produce a *ratio*.

The results of these two techniques are not always interchangeable. The fact that the net benefits of Alternative A are greater than those of Alternative B does not imply that the benefit/cost ratio of A is greater than that of B. For example, suppose the benefits in Alternative A have a present value of $300,000, and the costs have a present value of $100,000. The net benefits of this alternative would be $300,000 minus $100,000, or $200,000; and the benefit/cost ratio would be $300,000 divided by $100,000, or 3.0. If the present value of benefits in Alternative B were $200,000 and that of costs $40,000, Alternative B would have lower net benefits ($200,000 minus $40,000 = $160,000), but a higher benefit/cost ratio ($200,000/$40,000 = 5.0). In addition to knowing the benefit/cost ratio for a given project or program, it is also necessary to know the size of the project or program.

3.3 Cost–Benefit Analysis: An Example

Costs and benefits seldom remain constant over the life of a project or program. Costs may increase due to inflation or increases in the numbers of units of service provided. Benefits may accrue more slowly at the outset of a project and then increase as additional "customers" are reached. In short, both benefits and costs may be a moving target during the course of the analysis. For this reason, benefits and costs must be discounted on a year-by-year basis, as shown in Table 7.4.

Assume that two alternative approaches have been identified for the implementation of an improved administrative information management system. Alternative A involves a substantial upgrade of the existing computer hardware and software at an estimated cost of $1,100,000. At the end of 10 years, it

TABLE 7.4 Comparison of Cost–Benefit Analyses

Alternative A

Year	Debt serv. costs	O&M costs @ 4%	Admin. costs @ 5%	Discounted costs	Discount factor	Benefits @ 4%	Discounted benefits
1	149,455	400,000	100,000	612,693	0.943396	650,000	613,208
2	149,455	416,000	105,000	596,703	0.889996	676,000	601,638
3	149,455	432,640	110,250	581,306	0.839619	703,040	590,286
4	149,455	449,946	115,763	566,476	0.792094	731,162	579,148
5	149,455	467,943	121,551	552,186	0.747258	760,408	568,221
6	149,455	486,661	127,628	538,410	0.704961	790,824	557,500
7	149,455	506,128	134,010	525,124	0.665057	822,457	546,981
8	149,455	526,373	140,710	512,306	0.627412	855,356	536,661
9	149,455	547,428	147,746	499,934	0.591898	889,570	526,535
10	149,455	569,325	155,133	487,988	0.558395	925,153	516,600
Totals	1,494,550	4,802,443	1,257,789	5,473,126		7,803,970	5,636,778
						Terminal value	279,197
Net present value (NPV)		442,850					
Benefit/cost ratio (B/C)		1.0809					

(continued)

TABLE 7.4 (*Continued*)

			Alternative B				
Year	Debt serv. costs	O&M costs @ 4%	Admin. costs @ 5%	Discounted costs	Discount factor	Benefits @ 4%	Discounted benefits
1	271,736	395,000	90,000	713,902	0.943396	720,000	679,245
2	271,736	410,800	94,500	691,559	0.889996	748,800	666,429
3	271,736	427,232	99,225	670,178	0.839619	778,752	653,855
4	271,736	444,321	104,186	649,710	0.792094	809,902	641,518
5	271,736	462,094	109,396	630,107	0.747258	842,298	629,414
6	271,736	480,578	114,865	611,327	0.704961	875,990	617,538
7	271,736	499,801	120,609	593,328	0.665057	911,030	605,887
8	271,736	519,793	126,639	576,070	0.627412	947,471	594,455
9	271,736	540,585	132,971	559,517	0.591898	985,370	583,239
10	271,736	562,208	139,620	543,633	0.558395	1,024,785	572,234
Totals	2,717,360	4,742,412	1,132,010	6,239,331		8,644,397	6,243,816
						Terminal value	502,555

Net present value (NPV) 507,040
Benefit/cost ratio (B/C) 1.0813

is estimated that the upgraded system will have a residual (or terminal) value of $500,000. Alternative B involves the installation of a new software system supported by a new platform at an estimated cost of $2,000,000 and a residual value 10 years hence of $900,000. The initial investments required by each of the alternatives are expressed in terms of the annual debt service payments to support 10-year annuity serial bonds, issued at 6% interest for $1,100,000 and $2,000,000, respectively. Annuity serial bonds have uniform annual debt service payments and, therefore, the discounted costs diminish over the 10-year period of analysis.

Estimated annual costs for the administration, operations, and maintenance of the two alternatives are shown in Table 7.4. Administrative, operations, and maintenance costs for the upgraded system (Alternative A) are estimated to be higher than for the new system (Alternative B). However, when the discounted costs and benefits for the first year are considered, Alternative A shows net benefits of $515 (i.e., $613,208 − $612,693), whereas Alternative B shows negative net benefits of −$34,657 ($679,245 − $713,902).

Administrative costs associated with each alternative are assumed to increase at an annual rate of 5%. Operation and maintenance (O&M) costs are projected to increase at a rate of 4%. Benefits (measured in terms of greater operating efficiency) for both alternatives are projected to increase at an annual rate of 4%, while the residual values ($500,000 for Alternative A and $900,000 for Alternative B) become a benefit in the 10th year of the analysis (and must be discounted accordingly). The discount rate applied to benefits and costs is 6% (to correspond to the rate of interest on the proposed bond issues). A range of other assumptions could be made about the annual rates of increases (or decreases) in the benefits and costs of these two alternatives. However, these fairly limited assumptions serve to illustrate why a more detailed cost–benefit analysis is necessary.

When the prospect of increases in costs and benefits are considered, Alternative B has a NPV of $507,040 and benefit/cost ratio 1.0813, whereas Alternative A shows a NPV of $442,850 and a benefit/cost ratio of 1.0809. These findings are in contrast with the calculations of the net benefits on a year-by-year basis, which favors Alternative A. The discounted benefits for Alternative A are greater than the discounted costs throughout the 10 years of the analysis. The discounted benefits for Alternative B are less than the discounted costs for the first five years of the analysis. However, a primary factor contributing to the higher NPV for Alternative B is the higher terminal value of the new system.

3.4   Limitations of Cost–Benefit Analysis

Application of cost–benefit technique does not solve all problems relating to the allocation of scarce organizational resources. Cost–benefit analysis provides only limited assistance in establishing priorities among various strategic objectives. Such analyses are of limited usefulness in evaluating programs that are relatively broad in scope, or for comparing projects with widely differing objectives.

The basic purpose of cost–benefit analysis is not simply to maximize the ratio of benefits to costs. At times, the "equalization" of benefit/cost ratios may serve as a necessary condition for achieving a desired objective. Equalization involves determining what adjustments can be made in the benefits and costs associated with a given alternative to achieve a more favorable benefit/cost ratio when compared with other alternatives. More often, however, other factors must be considered in selecting an appropriate or "best" decision. These factors include: (1) the time stream of costs and benefits and the time preference for present as opposed to future consumption of goods or services, (2) limitations imposed by revenue (budgetary) constraints, and (3) the question of whether objectives can be specified in sufficient detail to permit a fuller identification of direct and indirect costs and benefits.

4   COST-EFFECTIVENESS ANALYSIS

The effectiveness of a program can be measured by the extent to which, if implemented, some desired objective will be achieved. Since an objective usually can be achieved in more than one way, the analytical task is to determine the most effective approach from among several alternatives. The preferred alternative either produces a desired level of performance at the minimum cost, or achieves the maximum level of performance possible for a given level of cost. Costs can ordinarily be expressed in monetary terms. Measures of effectiveness or other nonmonetary indices usually represent levels of achievement—the direct and indirect effects resulting from the allocation of resources.

4.1   Output Orientation

Techniques of cost-effectiveness analysis originated in the early 1970s and initially were used in situations where benefits could not be measured in units that were commensurable with costs. In contemporary applications, the emphasis is on evaluating program strategies and on the use of measures of effectiveness to monitor progress toward agreed-upon objectives. The extended time horizon adopted in cost-effectiveness analysis leads to a fuller recognition of the need for life-cycle costing—that is, analysis of costs over the estimated duration of the program or project.

Cost-effectiveness analysis can be viewed as an application of the economic concept of *marginal analysis*. Some base level that represents existing capabilities and existing resource commitments provides the starting point for the analysis. The objective is then to determine what additional resources would be required to achieve some specified additional performance capability. Thus, the primary focus is on incremental costs.

Measures of effectiveness are applied to determine increments of output achieved relative to the investment of additional increments of cost. Effectiveness measures are often expressed in relative terms—for example, percentage increase in some measure of educational attainment, percentage reduction in the incidence of a disease, or percentage reduction in unemployment. These measures facilitate comparisons and rank ordering of alternatives in terms of the costs involved in achieving identified objectives [10].

Cost-effectiveness analysis often is applied in comparing the relative value of various strategies. In its most common form, a new strategy is compared with the current strategy/practice. The result might be considered as the "price" of the additional outcome purchased by switching from the current practice to the new strategy. If the price is low enough, the new strategy is considered "cost-effective." Labeling a strategy as "cost-effective" means that the new strategy is a good value. Being cost-effective does not mean that the strategy saves money. And just because a strategy saves money does not mean that it is cost-effective. Also note that the very notion of cost-effective requires a value judgment—what one analyst may think is a good price for an additional outcome, another may not.

4.2 Types of Analyses

Three supporting analyses are required under the cost-effectiveness approach.

1. *Cost–output studies* are concerned with the identification of feasible levels of achievement.
2. *Cost–effectiveness comparisons* assist in the identification of the most effective program alternative.
3. *Cost–constraint assessments* determine the cost of employing less than the most optimal program.

The focus of a cost–output study is on the development of a cost curve for each strategy or program alternative. This curve approximates the sensitivity of costs (inputs) to changes in the level of achievement (outputs). Costs may change in direct proportion to the level of achievement; that is, each additional increment of cost incurred may produce the same increase in output. However, if output increases more rapidly than costs, then the alternative is operating at a level of increasing return. This condition is represented by a positively sloped curve that rises at an accelerating rate, as illustrated by the initial segment of the cost curve B in Figure 7.2. If costs increase more rapidly than output, the alternative is operating in an area of diminishing returns (as in the upper segment of cost curve B in Figure 7.2).

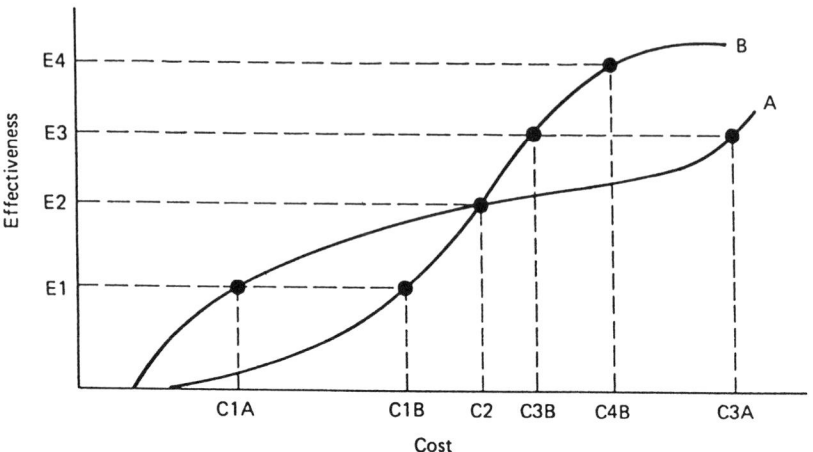

FIGURE 7.2 Cost–effectiveness comparison.

Practical models that relate incremental costs to increments of achievement can be developed with relative ease for some types of analysis. For other problems, cost curves can be approximated from historical data. Construction of cost curves and effectiveness scales should become increasingly more sophisticated as the input–output relationships associated with various strategies or program alternatives are better understood.

Assuming that the costs associated with different achievement levels can be determined for each alternative, the problem remains of how to choose among these alternatives. In principle, the rule of choice should be to select the alternative that yields the greatest excess of positive effects (attainment of objectives) over negative impacts (resources used, costs, and negative spillover effects). In practice, however, this ideal criterion is seldom applied, as there is no practical way to subtract dollars spent from the nonmonetary measures of effectiveness.

The best approach may be a cost–effectiveness comparison of alternatives, as illustrated in Figure 7.2. Alternative A achieves the first level of output (E1) at a relatively modest level of cost (C1A), whereas nearly twice the amount of resources (C1B) would be required to achieve the same level of effectiveness using Alternative B. Both alternatives achieve the second level of output (E2) at the same level of cost (C2). Alternative B requires a lower level of resources (C3B) to achieve the third level of output (E3). And only Alternative B achieves the fourth level of output (E4), since the cost curve of Alternative A is not projected to reach this level of effectiveness.

Which of these two alternatives is more desirable? To answer that question, it is necessary to define the *optimum envelope* formed by these two cost curves. If resources in excess of C2 are available, then Alternative B is clearly the better choice. However, if available resources are less than C2, then Alternative A provides greater effectiveness for the dollars expended.

In formulating program alternatives, significant shifts in the configuration of the cost curves frequently occur as additional levels of effectiveness are sought. Thus, one alternative may provide the most desirable ratio at one level of effectiveness (and cost), whereas some other alternative may provide the more desirable ratio at a higher level of effectiveness (and cost). It may not be possible to choose between two alternatives simply on the basis of cost-effectiveness unless one alternative dominates at all levels of achievement. Usually, either a desired level of performance must be specified and then costs minimized for that effectiveness level, or a cost limit must be specified and achievement maximized for that level of resource allocation [11].

In practice, organizations may adopt strategies or programs that are not the most effective available. Among the more obvious reasons for this are legal constraints, technical capacity, employee rights, union rules, and community attitudes. The purpose of a *cost–constraint assessment* is to examine the impact of these factors by comparing the cost of the alternative that might be adopted if no constraints were present with the cost of the constrained alternative.

This analysis, shown graphically in Figure 7.3, starts with the expressed objective O1 and two alternatives ($P_{\text{constrained}}$ and $P_{\text{not constrained}}$). $P_{\text{not constrained}}$ represents the most effective alternative as determined by cost–effectiveness analysis. The constrained alternative, however, may be the only program available. The cost of the constraints is the difference between the cost of $P_{\text{constrained}}$ and $P_{\text{not constrained}}$.

Once this cost differential has been identified, decisions can be made as to the feasibility of eliminating the constraints. This assessment provides decision makers with an estimate of how much would be saved by relaxing a given constraint. By the same token, the cost of the constraint suggests the amount of resources that might be committed to overcoming it. In some cases, however, maintaining a constraint may be more important for social or political reasons than implementing a more effective program.

5 RISK AND UNCERTAINTY

Strategic management often is concerned with future events that are inevitably characterized by uncertainty. It is important to recognize such uncertainty and to explicitly deal with it from the outset. Strategic decisions should involve an assessment of uncertainty and risk based on available estimates of alternative payoffs or gains. A risk is taken no matter what the decision. Even the decision to do nothing involves the risk of lost opportunity. An effective strategic manager, whether in the public or private sector, must be aware of how opportunity,

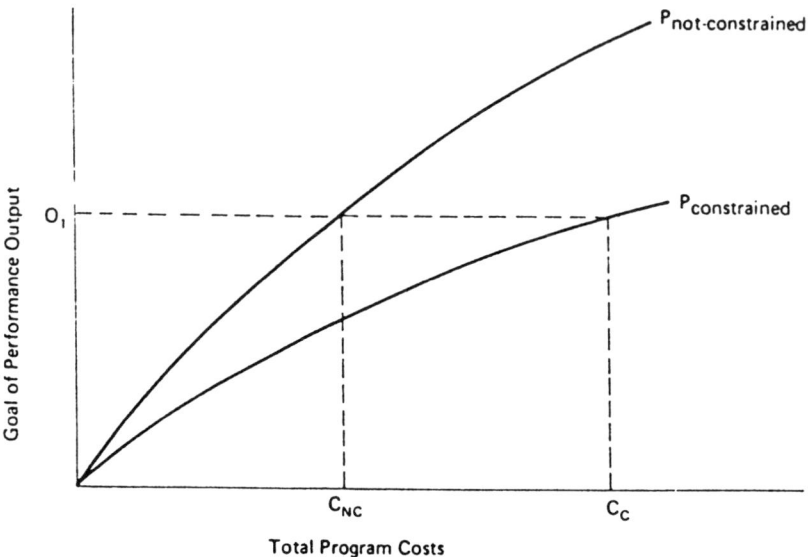

FIGURE 7.3 Cost–constraint assessment.

innovation, and risk are interrelated, and must be willing to take risks appropriate to their level of responsibility.

5.1 Converting Uncertainty to Risk

One manager's uncertainty may be another manager's acceptable risk. What one manager may interpret as an uncertain situation to be avoided, another may see as an opportunity, albeit involving some risk. Although the two terms often are mistakenly used interchangeably, the distinction between uncertainty and risk is important to understand.

Certainty can be defined as a state of knowledge in which the specific and invariable outcomes of each alternative course of action are known in advance. The key to certainty is the presence of only one state of nature (although under some circumstances, numerous strategies may be applied to achieve that state). This condition enables the manager to predict the outcome of a decision with 100% probability.

Uncertainty can be defined as a state of knowledge in which one or more courses of action *may* result in a set of possible specific outcomes. The probabilities of these outcomes, however, are neither known nor meaningful. As Archer observed, uncertainty involves a range of conditions in which probability distributions vary from a condition of relative confidence, based on objective probabilities, to a condition of extreme uncertainty, with little or no information as to the probable relative frequency of particular events [12].

If a strategic manager is willing to assign objective or subjective probabilities to the outcome of uncertain events, then such events may be said to involve risk. *Risk* is a state of knowledge in which each alternative leads to one of a set of specific outcomes, with each outcome occurring with a probability that is known to the decision maker. More succinctly, risk is reassurable uncertainty. Risk is measurable when decision expectations or outcomes can be based on statistical probabilities. The event of drawing a red card from a well-shuffled deck is an example of a risky outcome with a probability of 50%.

5.2 Sensitivity Analysis

Strategic managers must confront risk and uncertainty from two primary sources: (1) statistical uncertainty, and (2) uncertainty about the state of the real world in the future. The first type of uncertainty is usually less troublesome to handle. It arises from chance elements in the real world and would exist even if the second type of uncertainty were zero. Monte Carlo and related probability techniques can be used to deal with statistical uncertainty when it is encountered [13]. Uncertainty about the future state of the real world is more difficult to resolve. In such cases, the use of sophisticated statistical techniques may be little more than expensive window dressing.

It often is difficult to predict the exact cost of any given activity in a program or project. In such cases, it may be appropriate to provide a cost estimate that reflects the *most likely value* of an unknown distribution function. If the variation of this distribution is relatively small, then the most likely cost may provide a reasonably close approximation of the actual cost required to complete the activity. If the variance is large, however, the cost is said to be *uncertain*.

In most strategic decisions, a few key parameters exhibit considerable uncertainty, and a set of expected values must be determined for these parameters. *Sensitivity analysis* is designed to measure (often quite crudely) the possible effects that variations in uncertain decision elements (for example, costs) may have on the alternatives under analysis. Several values (optimistic, pessimistic, and most likely) may be applied in an attempt to ascertain how sensitive the results might be to variations in the uncertain parameters.

Sensitivity analysis can be used to determine the variations in rankings among alternatives based on anticipated costs. When some doubt exists as to the appropriate cost to be assigned to any project, the strategic manager should ask those who will be responsible for carrying out the project, "If everything goes right, what is the lowest cost you will require to complete this project?" Then the manager should ask, "If everything goes wrong—if the absolute worst happens—what is the highest cost required to complete this project?" Finally, assuming the range established by the answers to the first two questions, the manager should ask, "What is the most likely cost required to complete this project?" The optimistic cost estimate is based on the assumption that all of the uncertainty will be resolved favorably. The pessimistic cost represents the opposite assumption. The most likely cost figure falls somewhere in between these two extremes.

The data in Table 7.5 for the most likely costs are drawn from the previous cost–benefit analysis (as shown in Table 7.4). The optimistic cost data are based on an assumption of lower increases in operation and maintenance costs (3% annually) and administrative costs (4% annually). Higher terminal values ($550,000 for Alternative A and $1,000,000 for Alternative B) are also reflected in the discounted benefits. The pessimistic cost data are based on higher annual increases for operation and maintenance costs (5% for Alternative A and 6.5% for Alternative B) and for administration (6% annually for both alternatives). The expected values for the certain costs represent the debt service on the proposed bond issues discounted to present value—$1.1 million for Alternative A and $2 million for Alternative B.

Alternative A ranks first under all three levels of cost assumptions as a consequence of the substantially lower investment costs (certain costs). However, Alternative B ranks first in terms of net benefits when the most likely and optimistic cost estimates are considered. Which of these two alternatives is more desirable?

The *beta distribution formula* was developed to deal with situations in which the variance of the distribution of cost approximates a bell-shaped curve and can be expressed as the square of the standard deviation. This variance, in turn, can be estimated as roughly one-sixth of the range (i.e., the difference between the most optimistic and the most pessimistic cost estimate). The *beta distribution formula* can be expressed as follows:

$$\text{expected cost} = 1/6(a + 4b + c)$$

where

a = the most optimistic cost estimate,
b = the most likely cost estimate, and
c = the most pessimistic cost estimate.

Applying this approach to the data in Table 7.5, the estimated cost for Alternative A would be:

$$1/6[\$5,294,720 + 4(\$5,473,125) + \$5,660,745] = \$5,474,660$$

and the estimated cost for Alternative B would be:

$$1/6[\$6,070,565 + 4(\$6,239,330) + \$6,660,390] = \$6,281,379.$$

TABLE 7.5 Illustration of Sensitivity Analysis (in $)

Costs levels	Alternative A	Alternative B	Benefits A	Benefits B	NPV A	NPV B
Expected values of certain costs	1,100,000	2,000,000				
Optimistic expected values of uncertain costs	4,194,720	4,070,565				
Expected values of all costs	5,294,720	6,070,565	5,763,520	6,628,770	468,800	558,205
Ranking	1	2			2	1
Pessimistic expected values	4,560,745	4,660,390				
Expected values of all costs	5,660,745	6,660,390	5,513,390	6,269,880	(147,355)	(390,510)
Ranking	1	2			1	2
Most likely expected values	4,373,125	4,239,330				
Expected values of all costs	5,473,125	6,239,330	5,742,535	6,572,830	269,410	333,500
Ranking	1	2			2	1

Composite Expected Values ($)

$$\text{Alternative A} = [.30(-147,355) + .50(269,410) + .20(468,800)] = 184,259$$
$$\text{Alternative B} = [.30(-390,510) + .50(333,500) + .20(558,205)] = 161,238$$

The same approach can be used to determine the estimated benefits for these two alternatives.

Alternative A = 1/6[$35,294,215] = $5,882,369

Alternative B = 1/6[$40,223,945] = $6,703,991

Therefore the estimated net benefit of Alternative A is $407,709 and, for Alternative B, $422,612.

Probability theory also can be applied in connection with sensitivity analysis in situations in which the variance is not equally distributed. Assume, for example, that the probability of the most likely costs being realized is 50%; the most pessimistic costs, 30%; and the most optimistic costs, 20%. The composite expected values for all costs are shown at the bottom of Table 7.5. Given these assumptions, Alternative A would be the preferred alternative.

5.3 Social Preferences and Risk Aversion

Extensive research has been performed in the area of risk and uncertainty because the behavior of decision makers often appears to violate commonly accepted axioms of rational behavior. Although no exact probabilities may exist for the success or failure of a particular event, Kassouf observed that an individual with "clear-cut, consistent preferences over a specified set of strategies ... will act as if he has assigned probabilities to various outcomes [14]." The values for the probabilities will be unique for each individual and not unlike the values of utility that might be assigned to an individual through a study of their *social preferences*. The obverse of social preferences, of course, is *risk aversion*, a subject on which opinions vary [15].

There are numerous situations in which strategic managers must obtain a more careful reading of the various utility functions or preferences of their clientele and the organization as a whole. As Stokey and Zeckhauser explained, strategic choice under uncertainty is a threefold process [16]:

1. Alternatives must be assessed to determine what probabilities and payoffs are implied for individual members of the organization and its clientele.
2. Attitudes toward risk of these individuals must be evaluated to determine the certainty equivalents of these probabilities and payoffs.
3. Having estimated the equivalent benefits that each alternative offers to different members of the organization and its clientele, the decision maker must select the preferred outcome.

Although this process may sound simple, it often is very complex in application. Some basic tools have been developed to aid in unraveling these complexities [17]. These techniques can be brought into play, however, only after the strategic manager has a fairly good understanding of the preferences of the organization and/or clientele. The strategic manager will be better prepared to address uncertainties in a more systematic fashion once this groundwork has been laid.

A basic objective of strategic management is to reduce uncertainty by bringing to light information that will clarify relationships among elements in the decision process. This reduction of uncertainty may cause the risk associated with a particular decision: (1) to remain unchanged, (2) to decrease (as in the case where a reduction in uncertainty permits the assessment of more definitive probabilities), or (3) to increase (as happens when the additional information reveals risk factors that previously were unknown). Thus, although risk and uncertainty are interrelated, they must be treated independently in many decision situations.

6 SUMMARY

It is necessary to determining where discretionary funds may be available to implement new programs and strategies. Techniques used in programming strategic funds help to identify feasible options under various fiscal assumptions. The strategic manager, however, must still make an assessment of risks and payoffs before the "best" option is selected.

A thorough cost analysis must examine factors that influence future costs. Monetary costs—research and development costs, investment costs, and the costs of operations, maintenance, and replacement—are commonly reflected in financial accounts. It often is necessary to look beyond these monetary costs to opportunity costs, associated costs, and social costs. It is also important to distinguish among (1) fixed and variable costs, (2) recurring costs, and (3) marginal or incremental costs. These costs should be examined over the life of the strategy or program under analysis. The need to adopt an extended time dimension in such cost assessments has led to the development of cost–benefit analysis.

Activity-based costing can assist in the strategic management process by identifying and quantifying cost and performance data and translating these data into decision information. Through the application of the ABC approach, process and activity performance can be measured, the cost of process outputs can be determined, and opportunities to improve process efficiency and effectiveness can be identified. Significant variables can be organized into a format that makes the decision clearer and the choices easier to make.

Cost–benefit and cost–effectiveness analysis can be applied at two pivotal points in the evaluation of resource commitments. In the planning stage, cost–benefit analysis is based on anticipated costs and benefits. Such analyses are not necessarily empirically based. After a program or strategy has been implemented and shown to have a significant impact, cost–benefit and cost–effectiveness analyses can be used to assess whether the costs of the program were justified by the magnitude of net outcomes. Such after-the-fact analyses should be based on detailed studies of available empirical data.

Cost–benefit and cost–effectiveness models need not be adopted "whole cloth." A number of subroutines may be introduced into ongoing cost analysis procedures. Techniques of cost curve analysis can be applied to a variety of decision situations. An examination of expenditures in terms of strategic objectives and the evaluation of total benefits for alternative expenditures can be important derivatives of cost–benefit techniques. The extended time horizon adopted in these analytical methods leads to a fuller recognition of the need for life-cycle costing and benefits analysis. The importance of incremental costing, sunk costs, and inheritable assets also is underlined by this extended perspective. Cost–output and cost–constraint analyses add other important dimensions to the information available to the decision maker. As the complexity of the resource allocation problem becomes more evident, other subroutines may be adopted, depending on the availability of data and the capabilities of the analyst. Uncertainty can be reduced and risk can be brought within tolerable limits through the generation of management information that clarifies critical relationships among elements in the decision process.

ENDNOTES

1. Alan J. Rowe, Richard O. Mason, and Karl E. Dickel. Strategic Management and Business Policy: A Methodological Approach. Reading, MA: Addison-Wesley, 1982, p. 102.
2. For a further discussion of these factors, see: Alan Walter Steiss and Emeka O. Cyprian Nwagwu. Financial Planning and Management in Public Organizations. New York: Marcel Dekker, Inc., 2001, pp. 131–133.
3. U.S. Congress, House Subcommittee on Evaluation Standards, Report to the Interagency Committee on Water Resources. Proposed Practices for Economic Analysis of River Basin Projects. Washington, D.C.: U.S. Government Printing Office, May 1958, p. 9.
4. For a further discussion, see: Ronald H. Coase. The problem of social cost. Journal of Law and Economics, Vol. 3, October, 1960, pp. 1–44.
5. Processes are made up of sets of defined activities. Therefore, the ABC approach is directly applicable to the cost analysis requirements of process reengineering.
6. Robin Cooper and Robert Kaplan. Activity-based costing. Journal of Cost Management, Vol. 2, No. 2, Summer 1988, pp. 45–54.
7. A. R. Prest and R. Turvey. Cost benefit analysis: a survey. The Economic Journal, 1965, p. 583.
8. Otto Eckstein. Water Resource Development. Cambridge, MA: Harvard University Press, 1958.

9. Since benefits often are not converted to the same common denominator, the merit of any single project cannot be ascertained. It it also not possible to compare which of two or more projects with different objectives will produce the better returns on investment. It is only possible to compare the relative efficacy of program alternatives with the same or similar objectives.

10. For several examples of cost–effectiveness analysis, see: Alan Walter Steiss. Local Government Finance. Lexington, MA: Lexington Books—D.C. Heath and Company, 1975, pp. 240–258.

11. Stephen H. Archer. The structure of management decision theory. Academy of Management Journal, Vol. 8, December 1964, p. 283.

12. For a discussion of Monte Carlo techniques, see: E. S. Quade. Analysis for Public Decisions. New York: American Elsevier, 1975.

13. Sheen Kassouf. Normative Decision-Making. Englewood Cliffs, NJ: Prentice-Hall, 1970, p. 46

14. For a broader discussion, see Jack Hirshleifer and David L. Shapiro. The Treatment of Risk and Uncertainty, in Robert H. Haveman and Julius Margolis (eds.). Public Expenditures and Policy Analysis, 2nd ed. Chicago, Ill.: Rand McNally, 1977, pp. 180–203.

15. Edith Stokey and Richard Zeckhauser. A Primer for Policy Analysis. New York: Norton, 1978, p. 252.

16. Howard Raiffa. Decision Analysis. Reading, MA: Addison-Wesley, 1968. For an introductory discussion of Markov chains, see Stokey and Zeckhauser. A Primer for Policy Analysis. New York: Norton, 1978, Chap. 7.

8

Resource Management: Budgeting

A primary responsibility of strategic management involves the maintenance of fiscal stewardship through an effective budget process. Budgeting is a cyclical decision-making process through which limited financial resources are allocated among competing needs to achieve organizational objectives and priorities. It should involve a systematic evaluation of prior commitments in terms of anticipated outcomes or accomplishments.

> Fundamentally, financial budgeting is a method for specifying what must be done to complete strategy implementation successfully. Financial budgeting should not be thought of as a tool for limiting expenditures but rather as a method for obtaining the most productive and profitable use of an organization's resources [1].

Properly applied, budgeting can contribute significantly to greater efficiency, effectiveness, and accountability in managing an organization's resources.

1 BUDGETING: MAKING PRIORITY CHOICES

The budget is an important policy document for public and nonprofit organizations. "(B)udgets simultaneously record policy decision outcomes, cite policy priorities and program goals and objectives, delineate a government's total service efforts and measure its performance, impact and overall effectiveness [2]." The budget provides the link between political and economic choices. In the conflicts over available resources, the budget provides a scorecard of who won, who lost, or who stayed even.

1.1 Objectives of Budgeting

A budget can be defined as a strategic plan, expressed in financial terms, by which operating programs are effective for a given period of time. It includes estimates of (1) the services, activities, and projects to be carried out, (2) the resulting expenditure requirements, and (3) the usable resources for their support [3]. In the public sector, a budget provides the legal basis for spending and accountability. Through the budgeting/accounting process, revenue and expenditure information is structured to facilitate the continuous monitoring, evaluation, and control of financial resources. Financial authority and responsibility can be delegated, while appropriate strategic and management control is maintained.

An organization's total work program for the fiscal year is summarized in the budget. The annual cyclical nature of the budget process should not be misinterpreted as an inflexible routine, however. A budget must be more than a fixed document, presented annually for review and approval by a governing body. The needs of the organization, public interests, technology, and service delivery systems tend to change over time, and budgets must have the capacity to adapt to these environmental dynamics. Budgeting also involves decision making under conditions of uncertainty, where such decisions may have significant long-term consequences.

The budget provides a framework for making decisions about the size, allocation, and financing options appropriate to achieve program and policy objectives. The determination of objectives and the proportion of resources to be allocated for the accomplishment of these objectives "are the very real stuff of politics." Consequently, the attempt to allocate scarce resources among competing objectives often generates intense conflict among the participants in the budgetary process. And the smaller the available resources, the more intense will likely be the conflict.

1.2 Operating and Capital Budgets

The principal resource allocations to support the activities of an organization are reflected in its operating budget, which is subject to periodic review and authorization. The annual operating budget includes an estimate of expenditures in such areas as salaries, wages, contractual services, materials and supplies, and other "consumables" which, in turn, must be balanced against the recommended revenue program for the coming fiscal year. An operating budget:

1. Provides information for evaluating competing requests for limited financial resources.
2. Provides the basis for the adjustments to fiscal policy and adoption of revenue measures.
3. Facilitates the scheduling of work and the co-ordination of personnel and nonpersonnel service requirements.
4. Provides the basis for the adoption of a resolution or ordinance that authorizes agencies to incur obligations and to make payments with respect to these commitments.
5. Establishes the parameters for a fiscal audit and performance evaluation both during and after the close of the fiscal year.

Capital commitments for specific projects or programs that go beyond the current fiscal year may be included in an operating budget. These anticipated capital expenditures, in turn, should be reflected in a capital budget. A *capital budget* identifies the expenditures to be incurred to meet long-term improvements needs (capital facilities) and the means of financing these commitments for the current fiscal period. Different budgeting and accounting principles and procedures are associated with each of these basic budgets.

2   EVOLVING PERSPECTIVES ON THE BUDGET

Current perspectives on what constitutes prudent fiscal policy differ considerably from those of the past. These shifts in perspective have both emerged from and resulted in changing attitudes toward budgeting. As Charles Beard once observed, "Budget reform bears the imprint of the age in which it originated." These evolving perspectives have also impacted the budget formats that are most appropriate for strategic management.

2.1   Fiscal Control Mechanism: Objects of Expenditures

Historically, the fiscal control aspects of the budget have received the greatest emphasis both in practice and in the literature of public budgeting. The budget has been viewed primarily as an extension of the accounting and management control procedures, in which estimated expenditures for various programs are reviewed in monetary terms. Annual balancing of revenues and expenditures is regarded as a fundamental principle of sound fiscal policy.

Fiscal control is achieved primarily through an appropriation process and a line-item/object-of-expenditure budget. Funds may be appropriated to agencies on a lump-sum basis, leaving considerable discretion regarding the specific categories of expenditure that are permitted. Or appropriations may be made according to specific line-item categories—such as salaries, materials and supplies, travel, contractual services, and equipment. Under this latter approach, agencies often must receive legislative approval for any expenditure that exceeds the dollar amounts of the authorized appropriation.

Units may be authorized to shift funds from other operating (nonpersonnel) categories to salaries and wages, but not from salaries and wages to operations. In effect, appropriations for salaries and wages are encumbered, and any unexpended funds in this line item revert to central appropriations. This approach is used to prevent agencies holding positions vacant to generate more operating dollars (for example, for "windfall" equipment purchases). Such line itemization can also specify more detailed appropriations for various personnel categories (for example, professional staff, technical support personnel, and clerical personnel), or for specific object codes (for example, equipment or travel).

Budget requests are supported by detailed listings of the categories of expense required to operate each program—tabulations of the myriad items required to operate each program, including salaries and wages, employee benefits, rent, office supplies, travel, equipment, and other inputs. These more detailed *objects of expenditures* provide the critical linkage between the budget and the accounting system.

Object codes—three-digit or four-digit numbers—can be used to budget and record expenditures in considerable detail (see Table 8.1). These object codes (or class codes) represent cost items that are common to all government agencies and, therefore, provide across-the-board uniformity in the tracking of expenditures through financial accounting procedures. The validity of budget requests is judged primarily through comparisons with previous levels of expenditures.

Objects of expenditures, in turn, can be aggregated under broad expenditure characteristics such as for current operations, capital expenditures, and debt service. They can also be assigned to and recorded as the expenditures of a specific organizational unit, program or subprogram, activity classification, and/or basic function. For example, the following sixteen-digit code:

23-01-105-1245-45301

might be used to record a travel expenditure for meals and lodging (1245) of a staff member from the Police Department (105) under the public safety function (23) in conjunction with an out-of-town investigation on a specific case (45301). The code 01 might be used to designate the funding source (general funds) to which this expenditure is to be charged. The five-digit project code

TABLE 8.1 Line-Item Budget for Investigation Division

Budget Comments: As a result of the reorganization of the Police Department, it is requested that the staff of the Division be increased by three persons. The budget request shows an increase of 18.35% or $225,205 over the current budget period. Personnel Services show an increase of $142,165 (17.7%). This increase is the result of four new employees and a 5% salary increase for all city employees. Increased emphasis is placed on the purchase of drug information. The increase is shown under object code 1250. Additional data processing and laboratory equipment has been requested.

Object classification	Last fiscal year	Current budget	Next fiscal year
Personnel services			
1110 Salaries	737,223	802,975	945,140
1120 Wages	0	0	
1130 Special payments	0	0	
1140 Overtime payments	36,861	40,150	47,260
Subtotal: Personnel services	774,084	843,125	992,400
Contractual services			
1210 General repairs	398	440	505
1220 Utility services	996	1,100	1,265
1230 Motor vehicle repairs	2,520	2,750	3,165
1240 Travel	1,000	1,100	1,210
1250 Professional services	4,408	6,600	7,920
1260 Communications	795	880	1,010
1270 Printing	0	0	0
1280 Computing services	4,523	5,000	5,750
1290 Other contractual services	0	0	0
Subtotal: Contractual services	14,640	17,870	20,825
Supplies and materials			
1310 Office supplies	4,806	5,290	5,820
1320 Fuel supplies	6,540	7,195	7,915
1330 Operating supplies	2,667	2,935	3,230
1340 Maintenance supplies	1,988	2,190	2,410
1350 Drugs & chemicals	7,896	8,685	9,555
1360 Food supplies	0	0	0
1370 Clothing & linens	8,012	8,815	9,700
1380 Education & recreation supplies	0	0	0
1390 Other supplies	0	0	0
Subtotal: Supplies & materials	31,909	35,110	38,630

(continued)

TABLE 8.1 (*Continued*)

Object classification	Last fiscal year	Current budget	Next fiscal year
Equipment			
1410 Office equipment	0	1,500	3,000
1420 Electrical equipment	0	0	0
1430 Motor vehicles	30,000	45,000	40,000
1440 Highway equipment	0	0	0
1450 Medical & lab equipment	0	400	800
1480 Data processing equipment	0	5,000	8,500
1490 Other equipment	0	0	0
Subtotal: Equipment	30,000	51,900	52,300
Current obligations			
1530 Rental charges	0	0	0
1540 Insurance	3,700	4,000	4,500
1550 Dues & subscriptions	30	40	50
1560 Electrostatic reproduction	500	1,000	1,150
1590 Other obligations	0	0	0
Subtotal: Current obligations	4,230	5,040	5,700
Employee benefits			
1610 Retirement & pension benefits	73,722	88,325	118,141
1620 Social security contributions	50,500	55,005	67,576
1640 Group insurance	14,744	16,060	18,905
1650 Medical/hospital insurance	103,211	114,825	137,990
Subtotal: Employee benefits	242,178	274,215	342,610
TOTALS	1,097,040	1,227,260	1,452,465

might also be used to designate the program or subprogram (45xxx) and the activity classification (xx30x). The activity classification in this instance might represent a felony involving bodily harm to the victim. Using such multi-digit codes, accounting entries can be retrieved, sorted, and "crosswalked" to meet a variety of financial management, control, and reporting purposes.

Line-item/object-of-expenditure budgets have two distinct advantages over other budget formats:

1. *Accountability*: Object classifications establish a detailed pattern of accounts that can be controlled and audited. Each object of expenditure is subject to a separate documentation.
2. *Management control*: Personnel requirements are closely linked with other budgetary requirements. Control of authorized positions can be

used as leverage to control the whole budget. Projected expenditures may be backed up by a *personnel schedule*, which identifies the specific positions (i.e., by job titles) to be authorized and the anticipated salary commitments of each position (see Table 8.2).

Members of governing bodies and other public officials readily understand budgets based on objects of expenditure, which is one important reason why this budget format has survived for so long. It is relatively easy to grasp the fiscal significance of a proposed increase of 10% in printing or data processing or a salary reclassification for a specific position or salary class. Therefore, governing bodies can review the budget and alter the minutiae of proposed expenditures. Larger issues of efficiency and effectiveness, however, often remain buried in the detail of object classifications. Object classifications show in great detail *what* is intended to be purchased, but not *why* (i.e., the nature of organizational programs and accomplishments anticipated under those programs). Such classifications cannot provide a basis for measuring the progress made in the implementation of a particular set of strategic or management objectives or the performance of an agency or program.

Recent developments have emphasized the planning aspects of the resource allocation process. Unfortunately, some of these budget reforms have abandoned or have significantly altered the management control features of more traditional budget approaches. In part, this counter swing is a reaction to perceived shortcomings of the line-item/objective-of-expenditure budget. It also is a consequence of a more "top-down" approach to budgeting that seeks to improve the rationality of decision making through both structural and procedural changes. Techniques and procedures to increase the efficiency and effectiveness of resource allocation decisions should be incorporated in any strategic management approach that is responsive to these demands. By the same token, mechanisms of accountability and control must be retained in a balanced approach to budgeting.

2.2 Management Orientation: Performance Budgeting

As more reliable financial accounting systems were adopted, the budget was gradually freed from its primary role as fiscal watchdog. With the advent of Keynesian concepts in economics, it became evident that governmental spending could serve as a means to increase wealth, as well as to redistribute it, without displacing private investment. Adaptations of the budget process for the evaluation and improvement of administrative performance were also linked to the scientific management movement in the late 1920s and early 1930s. Government agencies sought to develop performance standards and rudimentary techniques of work measurement were introduced along with elements of cost accounting. If program accomplishments are examined in terms of benefits,

TABLE 8.2 Personnel Schedule for Investigation Division—City of Rurbania Police Department

Position title	Current authorized personnel	Requested personnel	Monthly salary range ($)	Current budget ($)	Next fiscal year ($)
Lieutenant	1	1	2,700–3,200	36,000	37,800
Laboratory supervisor	1	1	2,500–3,000	32,000	33,600
Sergeant	2	3	2,300–2,800	60,000	90,600
Inspector	3	4	2,200–2,700	86,750	117,500
Detective	15	17	2,000–2,500	425,000	494,250
Photographer	1	1	1,800–2,300	23,000	24,150
Property clerk	1	1	1,700–2,200	22,000	23,100
Laboratory technician	1	1	1,600–2,100	21,600	22,680
Photographer technician	1	1	1,400–1,900	18,500	19,425
Secretary	1	1	1,200–1,700	17,940	18,840
Clerk stenographer	4	4	1,100–1,600	60,185	63,195
Total	31	35		802,975	945,140

the task of budgeting must be redefined to include a more effective marshaling of fiscal and other organizational resources to achieve those benefits.

These efforts culminated in the concept of performance budgeting, which had its heyday in the late 1940s and early 1950s. In 1949, the Hoover Commission called for a budget approach that would

> focus attention upon the general character and relative importance of the work to be done, or upon the service to be rendered, rather than upon the things to be acquired, such as personal services, supplies, equipment, and so on. These latter objects are, after all, only the means to an end. The all-important thing in budgeting is the work or the service to be accomplished, and what that work or service will cost [4].

The principal objective of a performance budget was to help evaluate the *work efficiency* of operating units, by (1) casting budget categories in functional terms, and (2) providing work-cost measurements to encourage more efficient and economical performance of prescribed activities. A performance budget is built upon a series of work programs related to particular functions or activities carried out by public agencies or units within nonprofit organizations. Work programs are usually identified within the established organizational structure. Work–cost data are translated into discreet, measurable units to determine how efficiently prescribed activities are carried out by *performance units*—teams of staff members responsible for specific tasks.

Specific activities are linked to the responsibilities of distinct operating units through *activity classifications*. The term "activity" can be applied under various circumstances to mean a process, project, or purpose. A *process* approach would list as activities the various steps in carrying out the work program of a performance unit. A *project* approach might list the individual projects (often involving fixed assets and capital facilities) that go to make up the total activity areas of an agency. A *purpose* classification might group activities by clientele groups or according to broad functions (e.g., public safety, public health, or community development).

Unit cost measures aggregate all relevant costs associated with the delivery of a particular service and divide these costs by the total units of service provided. In the field of public health, for example, the unit cost for the administration of an immunization program for children would include the salary costs of the medical personnel involved as well as the cost of the vaccine, other supplies, and equipment. These costs may vary with the number of children inoculated and with the method of delivery (e.g., through public health clinics, in schools, or by private practitioners). Unit costs are likely to decrease as the size of the immunization program increases (through economies of scale). At some point, however, unit costs may again increase as hard-to-reach cases are encountered.

Workload measures reflect the volume of work performed during some time period. In a public welfare department, for example, it may be possible to determine the number of cases in various categories that can be handled by a caseworker on a daily, weekly, or annual basis. With this information and an estimate of the total number of cases to be processed, it is possible to calculate the number of personnel required during any fiscal period. Other common workload measures are number of customers served, tons of trash collected, number of children vaccinated, number of hospital patients served, number of inspections made, number of library books circulated, number of emergency calls responded to, and number of full-time equivalent students. Each of these measures also must include a time dimension—per day, week, month, or year. Workload measures provide basic budget-building information and, retrospectively, often indicate the adequacy of previous resource allocation decisions.

Unit cost measures are *input measures*—they indicate the resources used to operate a program. Workload measures, on the other hand, are *output measures*—in the aggregate, they indicate the volume of goods and/or services delivered by a program or agency. When workload (output) measures are related to unit costs (input) measures, the resulting index often is called a *performance measure*.

Performance measures often are used as indicators of operating efficiency—for example, the cost per patient-day of hospital service; the number of cases successfully prosecuted per law enforcement officer; or the response time involved in providing paramedical services. As may be seen from these examples, not all performance measures are expressed in cost terms. Performance measures provide basic information regarding program economics, that is, such measures can reveal important relationships between initial resource allocations (inputs) and the delivery of services (outputs).

Performance budgeting introduced a broader use of program information in the formulation of budget documents and the subsequent accounting of expenditures. Workload and unit cost measures and the concept of performance levels have been incorporated into many contemporary management applications that seek greater efficiency and economy in the allocation of limited financial resources. These measures have direct application to the implementation of strategic management.

2.3 Emphasis on Planning: Program Budgeting

The next major innovation in public budgeting was brought into the public spotlight in August, 1965, when President Lyndon B. Johnson announced that all federal departments would adopt the Planning-Programming-Budgeting System (PPBS) that had been used for years in the Department of Defense. PPBS was heralded by some as the holy grail of over one-half century of budget reform crusades. However, techniques that had been successfully applied in the evaluation of weaponry systems were soon found to have only limited applications to other public agencies. Much heat but relatively little light arose from the ensuing discussions of PPBS that took place in legislative chambers, agency conference rooms, and college classrooms.

As with many innovations introduced by dictum, inadequate groundwork was laid for the development of PPBS at the federal level, and even less at the state and local levels. Although PPBS received enthusiastic support from proponents of a more rational and comprehensive approach to financial management, it was met with corresponding skepticism by many who had experienced previous experiments with performance budgeting. The emphasis of PPBS on long-range planning to the near exclusion of the control functions proved to be disorienting to both operating agencies and policy-makers.

PPBS was an outgrowth of program-based budgeting techniques that had been developed earlier in business and industry [5]. The basic objective of *program budgeting* is to present budget requests in terms of program "packages" rather than the traditional object-of-expenditure format. A conscious effort is made (1) to state end objectives, (2) to seek a wide range of program alternatives, and (3) to link program and financial plans. In short, program budgeting recognizes that planning and budgeting are complementary processes.

> "The need for planning, programming, budgeting, and scheduling arises from the indissoluble connection between the allocation of resources and the formulation and conduct of governmental policy. When undertaken in the proper "mix," these processes constitute the means by which objectives and resources—and the interrelations among them—are taken into account to achieve a more coherent and comprehensive program of action... [6]."

The focus of program budgeting on aggregates of expenditures—broad programs that may cut across lines of responsibility—is intended to facilitate the evaluation of alternative courses of action in terms of costs and benefits (or effectiveness). Program budgeting departed from more basic models of cost–efficiency in which objectives were fixed and quantities of inputs and outputs were adjusted to secure an optimal relationship. In program budgeting, the emphasis is on organizing data into categories that facilitate comparisons among alternative mixes of expenditures to achieve defined policy and program objectives.

A *program crosswalk* provides a basis for translating object-of-expenditure budget data into program terms. Primary cost data are regrouped from the more traditional budget format into program and subprograms. Personnel costs— salaries, wages, and staff benefits—are the most significant elements of expense for most public activities. Therefore, personnel commitments serve as the focus for most program crosswalks, with other operating costs initially following the distribution of personnel costs. A crosswalk can also be used to convert program budget information into the more detailed object-of-expenditure format.

A program budget must be viewed from the top down in terms of strategic and management objectives and from the bottom up in terms of the specific activities necessary to carry out these objectives. The following aspects should be taken into account in identifying programs for budget-building purposes.

1. A program defines a series of activities within a larger process; some of the elements of a program are interdependent, while others may operate on a free-standing basis.
2. A program should facilitate the comparison of alternative methods of pursuing imperfectly determined objectives.
3. Each program should be delineated to permit at least partial quantification of its objectives.
4. Some programs may have overlapping structures that serve as the means to meet certain common objectives.
5. A program is concerned with a time span of expenditures beyond the current fiscal period, and every effort should be made to bring together all costs associated with its execution.
6. Program objectives must be consistent with the resources available (or anticipated) and should describe how and where specific resources (personnel, equipment, materials, capital expenditures, etc.) will be used.

It often is necessary to subdivide a program into its component parts—subprograms and program elements. More specific objectives and activities can then be associated with each component. Resources provided for subprograms often are interchangeable for maximum accomplishment. Given a budget target at the program level, a determination must be made as to how resources are to be distributed among the component subprograms to achieve the optimal output.

Systematic analysis of program alternatives is the cornerstone of strategic management. The same dollars spent on different program objectives (or on alternative approaches to the same program objective) may yield greatly varied results. In any organization, the best policy is to spend resources where they can produce the greatest net benefits. A systematic analysis of costs and benefits may be undertaken during the preparation of the budget, or on an ongoing basis, in an effort to determine optimal resource allocation and financial policy recommendations.

Program analysis and evaluation must be an iterative process, involving refinement and modification as dictated by changing circumstances in program delivery. *Program analysis* seeks (1) to determine whether a particular program or proposal is justified, (2) to rank various program alternatives appropriate to a given set of objectives, and (3) to ascertain the optimal course(s) of action to attain such objectives. *Program evaluations* may be carried out to (1) suggest changes in resource allocations, (2) improve current operations, or (3) plan future activities. The feedback from programs should be monitored on a continuous basis, as should any subsequent revisions to these programs. Program analysis is prospective; program evaluation focuses on the actual performance of ongoing or recently completed activities. Program analysis and evaluation operate within an extended time horizon and should include explicit consideration of both direct and indirect cost factors involved in the allocation of resources. The probability that program revisions will be required increases significantly as the time span of decisions increases.

Measures of efficiency and *effectiveness* provide the mechanisms for determining the success (or lack thereof) of a program (subprogram or element) in achieving agreed-upon objectives. Some measures may be expressed in terms of inputs, such as the number of worker-days, number of requests received, number of calls responded to, or number of cases per staff member. Such measures are appropriate in measuring agency or program efficiency. However, they do not provide a basis for assessing the effectiveness of programs or activities in relation to the costs incurred. Drucker has defined efficiency as "doing things right" and effectiveness as "doing the right things [7]." The output of many public programs may be difficult to define and measure in direct terms. As a consequence, secondary measures, called *surrogates*, often must be used to evaluate costs and to test alternative approaches. The direct benefits of a program that seeks to reduce the incidence of dropouts from high school, for example, may be difficult to measure. A surrogate measure might be derived by comparing the anticipated lifetime earnings of individuals who completed high school with those who dropped out. Such figures, available in terms of national averages, can be applied as rough measures (surrogates) of program benefits.

Program budgeting is particularly well-suited to strategic management. Under program budgeting, resources are allocated on the basis of goals, objectives, and strategies. These performance expectations, in turn, are translated into measures of effectiveness and efficiency. Program results (actual performance) are then evaluated on the basis of this planned performance. Data required to carry out such an evaluation include major elements derived from a cost-managerial accounting system. Other measures of effectiveness are based on the relative change in the situation that the program is meant to affect—for example, percentage decrease in the incidence of a problem following the introduction of the program. Meaningful cost–effectiveness or cost–benefit analyses can be developed by interrelating key indices from both of these measurement sets. Features of accountability and personnel management—distinct characteristics of the line-item/object-of-expenditure budget—can be retained through the application of a program crosswalk.

2.4 Zero-Base Budgeting and Service Level Analysis

For over 75 years, budget reformers have criticized the lack of coordination and the neglect of important values in traditional budget-building procedures. Such procedures, they argue, are arbitrary and irrational in that short-term results from previous allocation decisions are accepted as the primary criteria for future decisions. This approach produces only small, incremental changes in the status quo. Existing programs are continued into the future, often without intensive re-examination. A comprehensive analysis of previously allocated resources (the *budget base*) seldom is undertaken under this incremental approach. Other shortcomings of traditional budgetary procedures include:

1. *Insufficient information*: Traditional accounting and budgeting practices provide relatively little useful management information about: (a) the type and level of services provided, (b) the objectives and beneficiaries of the services, or (c) the special resources required in the provision of specific levels of service.
2. *Lack of choice mechanisms*: Traditional budgetary practices provide few mechanisms to help make choices or to identify the trade-offs among different services on anything approaching a cost–benefit basis.
3. *Impact of change*: No meaningful processes exist to (a) predict how significant changes in funding will affect service delivery, (b) determine the benefits in services afforded by increases in funding, or (c) identify the absolute minimum level of service that must be provided.

Incremental budgeting is suspect in terms of its ability to limit the growth of governmental appropriations or to allocate scarce fiscal resources in the most effective, efficient, and economical manner. As E. Hilton Young observed in 1924, "It must be a temptation to one drawing up an estimate to save himself trouble by taking last year's estimate for granted, adding something to any item for which an increased expenditure is foreseen. Nothing could be easier or more wasteful and extravagant [8]."

Advocates for reform assert that agencies should be required "to examine their budgets below the base; the base being their current level of expenditures. . . Zero-base budgeting requires each agency to specify—as part of its regular policy submission—possibilities for spending less money than the current year [9]." Although zero-base techniques have received the greatest publicity at the federal and state levels, they may have even more significant potential in application to the local level.

Current applications of zero-base budgeting (ZBB) have taken a somewhat more modest and more realistic approach in contrast with earlier efforts in the mid-1960s and early 1970s. Detailed examinations of programs "to the zero base" has been replaced by analyses focused on the resources required to deliver various levels of service. However, the basic objective remains the same—to circumvent the shortcomings of incremental budgeting.

The activities of local governments and of many nonprofit organizations can be readily identified and often measured in service delivery terms. Service level analysis is applicable to all *actionable* programs or activities—those in which some discretion can be exercised as to the courses of action to be pursued. While such programs make up only a portion of the total budget (less that 25%, according to some estimates), they often represent the more difficult activities to analyze and plan. All activities of local government that compete for general fund revenues (or the equivalent in other public organizations) should be included in a service-level analysis. Thus, more effective financial planning and control of these components through service-level analysis can greatly affect the entire financial commitments of the jurisdiction or organization.

Service-level analysis may have only limited application to programs for which the levels of expenditures are imposed by law or statute, formula-funded programs, intergovernmental commitments, or other legal or fiscal constraints. These special or restricted funds should be identified as part of a service-level analysis, however, in order to determine their importance to other organizational activities and to assist in identifying the costs of such imposed constraints.

One objective of service-level analysis is to identify essential service levels, so that an organization can maintain, deliver, and be held accountable for such programs in a more efficient and effective manner. Defining a service as *essential* is not the same as labeling its supporting expenditures as *fixed*. While local governments may have relatively little choice regarding the funding of essential service levels, such services often can be provided more efficiently (at less cost) or more effectively (with greater benefits).

For some essential services, continuation of the current approach at the current level of commitment may be the only feasible alternative. However, one of the underlying sources of waste and inefficiency in organizational operations is the maintenance of existing programs simply because "that's the way it has always been done."

Minimum service levels represent the highest priority services or the most critical needs of the government or nonprofit organization. By definition, the maintenance of an existing program or the initiation of a new program would not be feasible below this minimum level. A minimum service level also defines the minimum level of funding for each program or set of activities.

It often is difficult to identify a level of service or funding below the present level of support. In such cases, a percentage of the current level may be arbitrarily set as the minimum level (typically, 65 to 80% of the current appropriation). The budget unit manager is asked to identify the scope of services that could be provided at this reduced funding level and what current activities might have to be eliminated to accommodate this lower funding level.

Additional levels of service should then be identified. Each succeeding level should expand the services available until the level of service equals or exceeds current service standards. Each level of service must be analyzed in terms of the specific quantities and qualities of work to be performed (and services to be provided). Appropriate costs should be assigned to each level, and potential service impacts should be described.

The resources required to deliver each level of service should be summarized for each program (see Table 8.3). This summary should include detailed costs to be met from all funding sources with a listing of personnel, equipment, and other major resource requirements. The object-of-expenditure budget format can be reintroduced at this point. Once detailed cost data have been established for the minimum level of service, these data can be built upon in cumulative fashion for each successive level. Only in exceptional cases, where distinct service delivery alternatives have been identified, is it necessary to prepare separate object-of-expenditure budgets for each service level.

Once appropriate levels of service have been identified for all of the programs of a given agency, organization, or jurisdiction, they should be ranked to establish an order or priority among the various activities or programs [10]. Service levels are listed in descending order of importance until all levels have been included. Before ranking can begin, however, it is necessary to establish a set of criteria on which to base these decisions. Criteria should address a number of issues. Is the program or service legally required? Will the service delivery be cost-effective? Does the unit have the necessary technical skills to implement the planned activities? Does the proposed approach have a prior track record of success? Will lower-level management accept and execute the program?

In all likelihood, more service levels will be presented than can be funded from available resources. Three approaches can be used to bring proposed expenditures and projected revenue into balance.

1. Funds can be withheld from the lowest priority service levels.
2. Efforts can be made to reduce the cost of providing one or more levels of service.
3. Resources can be increased (for example, by increasing service fees, raising taxes, or liquidating assets).

Funds are allocated to the service levels in order of priority until the anticipated resources are exhausted. A funding "cutoff line" is drawn at this point, and those services below the line are not funded. Unfunded service levels should be re-examined, however, and if deemed necessary to the well being of the organization or community, efforts should be made to reduce costs or increase resources.

Without a ranking process, budgeting is little more than a juggling act. Decision-makers may try—often in a hit-or-miss fashion—to find the proper

TABLE 8.3 Service Level Analysis for Substance Abuse Prevention Program

Service level	Service level Total ($)	Positions	Cumulative Total ($)	Positions	Cumulative percentage Total (%)	Positions (%)
Volunteer service	9,550	0	9,550	0	7.44	0.00
5% Assignment	55,513	1.1	65,063	1.1	50.68	44.00
Substance abuse prevention team	63,308	1.4	128,371	2.5	100.00	100.00
Substance abuse prevention section	67,865	1.5	196,236	4	152.87	160.00
Add second team	86,540	2	282,776	6	220.28	240.00

	Service levels				
Object codes	1	2	3	4	5
Personal services					
1110 Salaries	0	31,988	31,013	37,800	49,200
1140 Overtime payments	0	1,599	1,551	1,890	2,460
Subtotal: Personal services	0	33,587	32,563	39,690	51,660
Contractual services	3,700	1,000	2,105	1,500	4,700
Supplies & materials	3,000	1,000	1,120	3,075	4,000
Equipment	1,000	9,000	8,400	6,900	10,000
Current obligations	1,850	50	200	2,045	1,900
Employee benefits	0	10,876	18,920	14,655	14,280
TOTALS	9,550	55,513	63,308	67,865	86,540

	Cumulative budgets				
Object codes	1	2	3	4	5
Personal services					
1110 Salaries	0	31,988	63,000	100,800	150,000
1140 Overtime payments	0	1,599	3,150	5,040	7,500
Subtotal: Personal services	0	33,587	66,150	105,840	157,500
Contractual services	3,700	4,700	6,805	8,305	13,005
Supplies & materials	3,000	4,000	5,120	8,195	12,195
Equipment	1,000	10,000	18,400	25,300	35,300
Current obligations	1,850	1,900	2,100	4,145	6,045
Employee benefits	0	10,876	29,796	44,451	58,731
TOTALS	9,550	65,063	128,371	196,236	282,776

pieces in a somewhat jumbled jigsaw puzzle that will add up to an acceptable whole. Unable to determine which programs or activities are of a lower priority, decision-makers often are forced to make across-the-board cuts. Service level analysis minimizes this need by creating an explicit priority listing.

Service level analysis can serve as an important mechanism of strategic management and control, helping to transform strategies and policies into plans, and plans into action. By seeking to eliminate unnecessary spending that may be the consequence of obsolete, inefficient programs or duplications of effort, service-level analysis can also drive accountability for budgeting and budget execution deeper into the organization. Funds are channeled to the more important demands, thereby increasing overall efficiency. Service-level analysis does not involve any radical departures from established management principles. It reflects the long-accepted practice of building a budget on a sound appraisal of needs matched against resource limitations.

2.5 Government Performance and Results Act

Congress enacted the Government Performance and Results Act (GRPA) in 1993 to improve the effectiveness, efficiency, and accountability of federal programs by requiring agencies to focus their management practices on program results. GPRA is based on the premise that the allocation of scarce resources among competing needs and priorities—that is, budget decisions—should be more clearly informed by expectations about program performance. In effect, GPRA represents a return to the basic objectives of performance budgeting—the more explicit application of performance information in budgetary deliberations, thereby changing the focus of the debate from simple inputs to expected and actual results [11]. Initiatives patterned after GPRA have been adopted by a number of state and local governments, either as the primary focus of their budget-building process or as a major addendum to an existing budget format.

GPRA requires that each federal agency develop a strategic plan covering a period of at least five years and updated at least every three years. Agencies' strategic plans must include the agency's mission statement; identify outcome-related goals and objectives; and describe how the agency intends to achieve these goals through its activities and through its human, capital, information, and other resources. Strategic plans must include a description of how long-term general goals relate to annual performance objectives, how program performance in achieving those goals will be measured, and a description of the program evaluations that were used in establishing goals. As part of the strategic planning process, agencies are required to consult with Congress as well as solicit the views of other stakeholders.

GPRA also requires that each agency prepare an annual performance plan to include performance indicators that will be used to measure "the relevant outputs, service levels, and outcomes of each program activity" in an agency's budget. The annual performance plan is to provide the direct link between strategic goals outlined in the agency's strategic plan and what managers and employees do on a day-to-day basis. When an agency believes it is not possible to express a measurable goal for a program activity, the agency may ask for authorization from the Office of Management and Budget to use a nonquantifiable goal. In addition, GPRA allows agencies to aggregate, disaggregate, or consolidate program activities for purposes of performance planning.

GPRA requires agencies to plan and measure performance using the same structures (program activities) that form the basis for the agency's budget request. This critical design element of GPRA aims at assuring appropriate links among plans, budgets, and performance information and the related congressional oversight and resource allocation processes. However, the suitability of agencies' current program activity structures for GPRA purposes is likely to vary widely and require modification or the use of crosswalks.

Past initiatives demonstrate that any link between performance information and resource allocation decisions is unlikely to be straightforward. The implicit presumptions of PPBS and ZBB—that systematic analysis of options could substitute for political judgement—ultimately proved unsustainable. GPRA recognizes that decision-makers, rather than budget systems, must provide judgements needed within a public sector context. In a political process, performance information can change the terms of the debate, but not necessarily the ultimate decision.

As a recent report of the General Accounting Office suggested, the budget process has and will likely continue to evolve.

> Past initiatives illustrate a progression from the straightforward, efficiency notion implicit in the Hoover Commission recommendations, through increasingly complex and mechanistic processes of PPBS and ZBB. Budgeting is the process of making choices, and all of these initiatives sought to improve the rationality of budget choices by focusing on the results of activities—however those results might be defined. [12].

2.6 Variations on the Basic Performance Theme

The State of Texas adopted a new budget format in 1991. This new approach, which was labeled *strategic budgeting*, provided an integrated set of decision-making tools and accountability elements and, included strategic planning at the agency level and on a statewide basis, outcome-focused performance measurement, performance-based budgeting and legislative appropriations reform, and performance reporting, monitoring, evaluation, and auditing. Recent refinements have focused on improving the use of performance data in legislative and gubernatorial decision-making, the reporting of performance data for accountability purposes, the use of performance information in management decisions, and various system enhancements, including performance benchmarking, customer satisfaction assessments, investment budgeting, and service type categorization [13].

Outcome-based or *results-based* budgeting offers another variation on the performance theme. Under this approach, the budget is explicitly focused on the achievement of outcomes agreed upon by public officials and citizens. Public agencies are required to establish budget processes that link resource allocations to intended results, re-allocating resources to the highest-priority results and demonstrating how public investments affect the achievement of agreed-upon objectives. Spending plans are established according to the likelihood that they will result in improved outcomes. Such a budgeting process provides information on proposed spending by function and result, in addition to the more standard array by agency and program. Long-term cost trends are presented in an effort to identify why programs have failed to achieve more positive outcomes. Outcome-based budgeting provides a framework within which to consider the long-term costs and benefits of improving outcomes. And it provides a tangible audit trail between spending plans and the outcomes they are intended to improve.

Friedman suggested that "Performance budgeting is a necessary and useful part of an outcomes-based budgeting system, but it is not the same thing [14]." Performance budgeting is an essential component of a complete outcome-based budgeting system. However, it is a supplement to, not a substitute for, an outcome-based approach.

Performance budgeting is concerned with ensuring that the program components designed to implement an adopted strategy are properly carried out. A primary focus of performance budgeting is on the use of performance measures to make decisions regarding the management of agency funding programs. Performance measures can be used to identify program performance that is improving or declining. Performance measures can also be used to provide incentives to agencies. Outcome-based budgeting does not replace these important management functions. Rather, outcome-based budgeting focuses on using performance measures and other indices to assist in choosing the best cross-agency strategies to improve outcomes.

3 RESPONSIBILITY CENTER BUDGETING

The basic concepts of responsibility center budgeting are particularly appropriate in implementing the objectives of strategic management. Responsibility center budgeting seeks to assign greater accountability to those managers who can exercise significant influence over cost on a day-to-day basis [15]. All pertinent direct and indirect costs and the funds necessary to support these costs are assigned to various organizational units—departments, divisions, agencies, bureaus, programs—designated as responsibility centers [16]. Each responsibility center is then held accountable for the specific outcomes that have occurred as a result of the total allocation of resources in support of the unit's activities.

3.1 Organizational Design

The design of an organization under responsibility center budgeting should be governed by two basic rules.

1. The structure should be determined by the pattern of strategies (i.e., policies and purposes) that defines the organization and its mission, and that positions the organization relative to its environment.
2. The organization should be as decentralized as possible. Most management authorities believe that the effectiveness of large, complex organizations improves when authority and responsibility are delegated within the organization.

Authority and responsibility should not be delegated arbitrarily or capriciously, however. Decentralization requires that the purpose or function of each administrative unit and responsibility center be fully clarified, that procedures be established for identifying objectives and for monitoring and rewarding performance, and that an accounting structure links each responsibility center to the goals of the organization as a whole.

Thompson and Jones suggested that responsibility center budgeting should be concerned with (1) administrative structure, (2) responsibility structure, and (3) accounting or control structure [17]. Under responsibility center budgeting, administrative units and responsibility centers should be coterminous and fully aligned with the organization's accounting structure. Work activities should be allocated according to mission, function, and/or purpose; authority and responsibility must be unambiguously assigned. The information on inputs, costs, and outputs that the accounting structure provides should be used to coordinate unit activities, as well as to influence the decisions of responsibility center managers.

In responsibility center budgeting, an organization's strategies and policies are converted into financial targets that correspond to the spheres of activities that have be assigned to responsibility centers and their managers [18]. Delegation of authority means giving managers the maximum feasible authority needed to make their units productive—or, in the alternative, subjecting them to a minimum of constraints [19]. Therefore, delegation of authority requires that operating budgets be structured to motivate and inspire subordinates. Under responsibility center budgeting, the ideal operating budget would be relatively sparse in terms of details but would reflect a number of financial targets for each administrative unit or responsibility center. Alfred Sloan of General Motors, one of the fathers of responsibility budgeting, believed it was inappropriate for corporate managers to be concerned with the details of responsibility center operations. During budget execution, operating performance is monitored based on the financial targets, and program managers are evaluated and rewarded accordingly. Expressing operating performance targets in financial terms facilitates comparisons across unlike responsibility centers, thereby permitting the relative performance of managers to be evaluated and increasing the motivational efficacy of internal competition.

3.2   Controllable and Noncontrollable Costs

Under traditional approaches to public budgeting, operating units often are only held responsible for managing their *direct costs*—that is, those costs incurred by a unit that are uniquely associated with a specific purpose. Salaries and wages, materials and supplies, travel, equipment acquisition, and maintenance are generally considered to be direct costs that can be controlled by a given operating unit or program.

Direct costs can be narrowly or broadly defined; the more narrow the definition, the larger the aggregate amount of indirect costs. *Indirect costs* are costs associated with more than one unit, activity, or program which cannot be traced directly to any of the individual activities of the organization. Costs associated with various administrative units (e.g., purchasing or accounting) often are considered to be indirect costs.

In theory, given a long enough time, all costs are controllable by someone within an organization. For purposes of budgeting, however, *controllable costs* often are defined as those costs subject to the direct influence of a given manager of a given program or unit during a given time period. An emergency room supervisor, for example, might exercise significant control over the assigned nursing staff, the use of supplies (and therefore, their costs), and maintenance of the facility. However, the ER supervisor may have little or no control over the cost of the doctors working in the emergency room, or the utility costs that support the running of the emergency room, or the insurance premium costs allocated to this aspect of the hospital's operations.

Noncontrollable costs include all costs that do not meet this test of "significant influence" by a given manager. Thus, costs assigned to the manager of any department may contain both controllable and noncontrollable elements. Although clear distinctions often are difficult to make, every effort should be made to separate these basic cost components for purposes of performance evaluation.

3.3 Increased Responsibility for Indirect Costs

The ability to control costs is a matter of degree. Responsibility center budgeting places increased emphasis on the full allocation of costs in relation to well-defined areas of responsibility. When all costs are fully allocated, the illusion of free goods and services disappears. Under traditional budgeting approaches, for example, space and utilities appear to operating units to be "free commodities," since space costs seldom are charged to these units (e.g., in the form of rent). However, more than 10% of an organization's general expenditures typically are allocated for the operation and maintenance of facilities. Goods and services that may appear to be free to operating units are not free to the total organization [20].

Operating units may be able to exercise considerable control on a day-to-day basis over such traditional indirect costs as utilities (the use of heat, light, air conditioning), facility maintenance (e.g., custodial services, maintenance of buildings and grounds), and even insurance premiums (e.g., through safety programs). Managers of responsibility centers are encouraged to adopt policies and practices that specifically address the monitoring and control of these indirect cost categories. In turn, funds necessary to support these indirect costs are included in the budget allocations of the responsibility centers. Concerted efforts to conserve electricity and other utilities, to maintain good housekeeping practices in work areas, and to adopt other programs to increase efficiency are "rewarded" by allowing the responsibility center to retain the cost savings from these initiatives.

In some cases, responsibility centers are authorized to purchase on a "least-cost basis" certain supporting services that traditionally have been provided by central administrative units (e.g., central stores, data processing, motor pool vehicles, travel services). Thus, if it can be demonstrated that certain supporting services can be obtained from external sources on a contract basis for less cost than from an internal service unit, responsibility centers may receive budget allocations to pursue these options.

Not all indirect costs are controllable at the responsibility center level. Long-term effects of such costs as depreciation, long-term lease arrangements, and the like, seldom qualify as controllable costs on the performance report of a specific manager. Therefore, these expenses should be further broken down between those that are controllable and those that are noncontrollable at the responsibility center level.

To illustrate these points, consider the costs of nursing services in a hospital. The extent to which these costs are controllable at the responsibility center level will depend on the policies of top management regarding intensive care, the lead time available for planning the number of nurses in relation to patient load, the availability of short-term or part-time help, and so on. Some managers may have relatively little control over such cost-influencing factors.

Clearly, an item such as depreciation on the hospital building is outside the realm of controllable costs at the responsibility center level.

Sources of financial support (revenue or income) are also attributed to the responsibility centers on some equitable and consistent basis. Fees generated by building inspections, for example, should be "credited" to the responsibility center (e.g., Public Works Department) that carries out these inspections. Fees from public recreational facilities should be attributed to the Parks and Recreation Department. Grant-in-aid programs and other intergovernmental revenues that are earmarked for specific programs should be recorded as part of the budget allocations to the centers designated to carry out these responsibilities. Costs associated with internal service units (that is, units that do not receive revenue or income from external sources) are either charged to the responsibility centers on a *fee for service* basis or are recovered from the responsibility centers through some form of *assessment*. A distinction often is made between a service center—which is assigned only the direct portion of overhead—and a cost center—which is fully burdened with indirect costs.

Once all income or revenue and costs have been fully allocated to the responsibility centers, in all likelihood, there will be some "surpluses" and some "deficits." Responsibility centers should be permitted to retain all or a major portion of their "surpluses." On the other hand, the deficits or shortfalls between total costs and revenues/income must be covered through some form of *subvention*—a central allocation to ensure the continued operation of programs existing at the time the new allocation model is implemented.

What is the source of the funds for the subvention? One approach would be to "take funds off the top," that is, to hold back some portion of the general funds to cover these costs. Another approach is to initiate a surcharge or "assessment" on the expenditure of the resources that have been fully allocated. The revenue collected through this levy can then be reallocated to responsibility centers, both as subvention to provide a level playing field for those units faced with deficits and to "seed" additional activities that may have organization-wide benefits. A portion of the assessment could also be used to support internal service units.

The biggest difference between traditional budgets and responsibility center budgets is that traditional budgets tend to be highly detailed plans for acquiring and spending resources. To be successful, traditional budgets must be scrupulously executed just as they were approved [21]. A responsibility center budget contains far less detail in terms of objects of expenditures and provides greater flexibility in terms of the discretion that can be exercised by the managers of the center. Cost savings resulting from good stewardship of resource allocations remain with the responsibility center rather than reverting back to the central coffers. The ability to retain and re-allocate such cost savings is a major component of the incentive system that serves as a foundation for responsibility center budgeting.

4   NEED TO INTEGRATE PLANNING AND CONTROL OBJECTIVES

The traditional role of budgeting since the turn of the 20th century has been fiscal control. The *line-item/object-of-expenditure* budget serves well the purposes of internal fiscal control. It offers two distinct advantages over other budget formats: (1) a detailed set of accounts through which expenditures can be recorded, controlled, and audited, and (2) the close linkage between personnel and other budgetary requirements permitting the use of position controls to control the entire budget. However, object classifications merely show *what* is purchased, but not *why*, that is, the nature of organization's programs and anticipated accomplishments under those programs.

Performance budgeting strengthens the management aspects of the budget process by focusing on operating economies and performance efficiencies. Three components distinguish performance budgeting from other approaches: (1) identification of work programs, (2) delineation of performance units, and (3) measurement of performance costs. A *performance unit* is a team of workers responsible for carrying out a specific task (i.e., a work program). *Performance costs* are those costs directly associated with carrying out these activities. *Workload* and *unit cost measures* provide detailed information useful to operating managers in assessing the efficiency of their programs and organizational units.

Program budgeting combines a planning framework with the basic functions of management and control. A *program* is a distinct organization of resources directed toward a specific objective. *Program objectives* describe how and where specific resources (personnel, equipment, materials, capital expenditures, etc.) will be used. *Multi-year program plans* often are developed to identify the anticipated outputs of services and facilities according to the program objectives. The extended time horizon of the program budget shifts the decision focus from the one-year budget cycle to a multi-year time frame, thus providing a more comprehensive basis for annual budget deliberations. The focus of program budgeting is on policy analysis and planning. Resources are allocated on the basis of goals, objectives, and strategies. Measures of effectiveness and efficiency are used to evaluate program results (actual performance) in terms of planned performance. It may be possible to carry out meaningful cost–benefit or cost–effectiveness analyses by interrelating key indices from these sets of measurements.

The basic objective of zero-base analysis is to circumvent the shortcomings of incremental budgeting. Under current applications, detailed analyses of programs "to the zero base" have been replaced by the concept of *service-level analysis*. The identification of budget units and decision packages provide a rough parallel to programs and subprograms in the program budget format. By arranging levels of service in descending order of importance and determining a funding cutoff point, the analyst can rank alternative approaches according to their capacity to meet program objectives.

The Government Performance and Results Act (GPRA) represents a return to the basic objectives of performance budgeting. Under GPRA, budget decisions should be based on explicit information regarding expectations about program performance. However, since the process of budgeting is inherently an exercise in political choice, performance information can be one, but not the only, factor underlying budget decisions.

Outcome-based or *results-based budgeting* focuses on the achievement of specific outcomes agreed upon by public officials and citizens. Budget processes link resource allocations to intended results and spending plans are established and approved according to the likelihood that improved outcomes will result.

Responsibility center budgeting places emphasis on pertinent costs in relation to well-defined areas of responsibility. Responsibility center managers are encouraged to adopt policies and practices to control the direct and indirect costs involved in their center's operations. Sources of support (revenue or income) are attributed to the responsibility centers on an equitable and consistent basis. Cost savings are retained and can be re-allocated to enhance the center's performance in pursuit of its strategic objectives.

Each of the budget formats outlined in the preceding discussion arose from the financial management needs at a particular point in time; each reflects varying decision-making capacities; and each has varying management information needs and output capacities (see Table 8.4). The past 35 years have been a period of considerable experimentation in the processes of public budgeting.

An evident shortcoming of these new budgetary approaches, however, has been the failure to fully integrate these more systematic procedures with the other basic components of strategic management. In particular, more recently developed budgeting techniques—such as program budgeting and zero-base budgeting—have not been well-aligned with appropriate management control procedures. These new budgetary formats tend to emphasize the planning function. Far less attention is given to the equally important techniques and procedures for financial control. As a result, these new approaches, in many cases, have failed to produce the desired improvements in terms of more efficient, economical, and effective governmental operations.

A hybrid approach to budgeting is necessary to meet the needs of strategic management—one that combines the best features of each of the basic budget formats. The program structure and longer time horizon that serve as the foundation for the program budget is particularly applicable to the framework of strategic management. The focus on activity classifications, workload and unit cost measures, and building of the budget as a series of work programs related to particular functions, derived from performance budgeting, also serve the

TABLE 8.4 Basic Differences Among Budget Orientations

Characteristics	Objects of expenditure	Performance budget	Program budget	Zero-base budget/service level analysis	Outcomes-based budget	Responsibility center budget
Control	Central	Operating	Operating	Operating	Central	Operating
Management	Dispersed	Central	Supervisory	Dispersed	Central	Decentralized
Planning	Dispersed	Dispersed	Central	Central	Dispersed	Dispersed
Role of budget agency	Fiduciary	Efficiency	Policy	Effectiveness	Analysis	Performance
Information decision flow	Bottom-up aggregative	Bottom-up aggregative	Top-down Disaggregative	Iterative	Iterative	Bottom-up aggregative
Information focus	Objects of cost	Activities	Programs	Decision packages	Outcomes	Controllable costs
Decision basis	Incremental	Incremental	Programmatic	Programmatic	Outcome improvements	Programmatic
Key budget stage	Execution	Preparation	Analysis	Analysis	Execution	Execution
Personnel skills	Accounting	Administration	Economics	Management	Evaluation	Management
Appropriation/organization's linkages	Direct	Activity-based	Across-the-board	Budget units	Cross-function cross-agency	Resposibility centers

Adapted from: Allan Schick. The Road to PPB: The Stages of Budget Reform, in Planning Programming Budgeting: A Systems Approach to Management. Fremont J. Lyden and Ernest G. Miller, eds. Chicago, Ill.: Markham Publishers, 1968, p. 50.

objectives of strategic management. Service-level analysis can provide important financial information, especially in connection with the development and analysis of new strategic initiatives. And the traditional focus on accountability and management control provided by the line-item/object-of-expenditure format completes the budget hybrid and serves as a critical link to the control and evaluation components of strategic management.

ENDNOTES

1. Fred R. David. Strategic Management. 4th edition. New York: Macmillan Publishing Company, 1993, p. 306.
2. Albert C. Hyde. The development of budgeting and budget theory: the threads of budget reform. Government Budgeting, Theory, Process, Politics. Pacific Grove, CA.: Brooks/Cole Publishing, 1992, p. 1.
3. Committee on Budgeting of the Government Finance Officers Association, Chicago, IL. (www.gfoa.org/services/nacslb)
4. U.S. Commission on Organization of the Executive Branch of the Government. Budgeting and Accounting. Washington, D.C.: U.S. Government Printing Office, 1949, p. 8.
5. David Novick, often credited for the formulation of PPBS, observed that the concepts of program budgeting "have rather ancient and hoary origins." Large corporations, such as du Pont de Nemours & Co. and General Motors, were applying program budget techniques in the early 1920s. For a further discussion of the roots of PPBS, see: David Novick, ed. Program Budgeting: Program Analysis and the Federal Budget. Cambridge, MA: Harvard University Press, 1967.
6. Alan Walter Steiss. Public Budgeting and Management. Lexington, MA: Lexington Books-D.C. Heath Co., 1972, pp. 154–155.
7. Peter F. Drucker. The effective decision. Harvard Business Review. Vol. 45, January-February 1967, p. 95.
8. Cited in Aaron Wildavsky and Arthur Hammann. Comprehensive versus incremental budgeting in the Department of Agriculture. Administrative Science Quarterly. Vol. 7, December, 1965, p. 321.
9. Allan Schick. Putting it all together. Sunset, Zero-Base Budgeting and Program Evaluation, Proceedings of a Conference on Legislative Oversight. Richmond, VA.: Joint Legislative Audit and Review Commission, 1977, p. 41.
10. In some applications of service-level analysis, the selected levels of service are first ranked within an agency as part of its budget request. Service levels within the budget requests are then ranked to form a composite priority listing for the organization or jurisdiction.
11. U.S. General Accounting Office. Performance Budgeting: Past Initiatives Offer Insights for GPRA Implementation. Washington, D.C.: Government Printing Office, March 1997, p. 4.
12. U.S. General Accounting Office. Performance Budgeting: Past Initiatives Offer Insights for GPRA Implementation. Washington, D.C.: Government Printing Office, March 1997, p. 7.

13. Jeffrey Epstein. Strategic budgeting in Texas: A systems approach to planning, budgeting, and performance measurement. ASPA Task Force on Government Accomplishment and Accountability Case Studies. Washington, D.C.: American Society for Public Administration, 1996.

14. Mark Friedman. From Outcomes to Budgets: An Approach to Outcome-Based Budgeting for Family and Children's Services. Washington, D.C.: Center for the Study of Social Policy, 1995.

15. Charles T. Horngren. Introduction to Management Accounting. Englewood Cliffs, NJ: Prentice-Hall, 1978, p. 252.

16. For a discussion regarding the definition of responsibility centers, see: Edward L. Whalen. Responsibility Center Budgeting: An Approach to Decentralized Management for Institutions of Higher Education. Bloomington, IN: Indiana University Press, 1991, Chapter 3.

17. Fred Thompson and L. R. Jones. Responsibility budgeting. International Public Management Journal, 2000, vol. 3, no. ER2, pp. 205–207.

18. Robert N. Anthony and David W. Young. Management Control in Nonprofit Organizations, Fifth ed. Homewood, IL: Richard D. Irwin, 1994, p. 19.

19. OECD. Budgeting for Results: Perspectives on Public Expenditure Management. Paris: Organisation for Economic Co-operation and Development, 1995.

20. Whalen (see Ref. 16, p. 51) suggested that if charges are not levied for such services, aggressive managers will seek to secure more "free" inputs until the additional contributions to the productivity of their units from these additional "free" inputs diminishes to zero. However, since these inputs are not free to the total organization, its overall performance is not optimized by such practices.

21. Fred Thompson and L. R. Jones. Reinventing the Pentagon: How the New Public Management Can Promote Institutional Renewal. San Francisco: Jossey-Bass Publishers, 1994.

9

Change Management

An ancient Chinese proverb states, "The greatest opportunities are created out of crisis. Crisis forces people to change and change often brings new opportunity." People typically resist change, however, and employees within any organization can significantly delay (or even stop) change from happening. As Hussey and Langham observed,

> Resistance to change is often emotionally based and not easily overcome by rational argument. Resistance may be based on such feelings as loss of status, implied criticism of present competence, fear of failure in the new situation, annoyance at not being consulted, lack of understanding of the need for change, or insecurity in changing from well-known and fixed methods. It is necessary, therefore, to overcome such resistance by creating situations of participation and full explanation when changes are envisioned [1].

Managing change is by far the most difficult aspect of strategic management and the least receptive to mechanical approaches.

1 BARRIERS TO CHANGE

Barriers to change can arise from four major sources: people, technology, infrastructure, and process. While these four areas often reinforce one another, it is useful to examine each in turn before discussing their potential interactions.

1.1 People Barriers

No organization is better than the people who work in it. As a consequence, one of the most critical tasks within the strategic management process is the design and implementation of a human resources system appropriate to proposed changes that result from the application of performance improvement techniques.

People barriers are the most difficult to fully identify and overcome. Often such obstacles to change are not overt but exist just below the surface as skepticism and lack of confidence in the proposed direction for change. People barriers can stem from a *lack of shared vision.* A more thorough effort may be required to involve and educate those members of the organization who will be called upon to implement the proposed changes or who will be most directly impacted by these changes. It may be necessary to recycle the earlier phase of the strategic management process in which strategic objectives were formulated to ensure that members of the organization have the opportunity to provide inputs to the process through focus groups and other awareness raising activities.

Reducing or "flattening" hierarchies within an organization often implies that employees will be empowered to make decisions appropriate to their areas of responsibility. This change requires training and education, as well as motivation on the part of those given this expanded decision-making role. It also requires the trust of top management that people are willing and able to take responsibility. This tenant of strategic management stands in stark contrast to the more traditional approach to management that asserts "trust is good, but control is better."

Sacred cows and *fiefdoms* also are major sources of barriers to change. When asked, "Why is this particular task carried out in that fashion?" the all-too-frequent answer is, "That's the way its always been done!" Traditional ways of doing things and cultural beliefs that are frozen in time are the basis for "sacred cows" that can be challenged only with great care and the laying of appropriate groundwork. Similarly, the existence of turf issues between different units (fiefdoms) within an organization can be major obstacles to change. Perceived ownership of data is often a source of these turf issues. "Our unit must initiate this process by entering these data, because we are held accountable for the end results (in terms of information or other outputs)."

In an organization that is highly decentralized in its decision-making authority, the various units are likely to have their own set of procedures (and related "shadow systems") for handling data. Attempting to accommodate this diversity in perceived data needs can be a monumental undertaking— assuming that all participates share the same vision regarding the objectives of the project—which in all likelihood they do not.

Insufficient "buy-in" by top management and the lack of a champion for a particular new activity can serve as significant barriers to change. Top management must be the driving force behind the introduction of new strategies and processes. As Anthony and Herzlinger suggested, "... it is unlikely that a majority of operating managers will voluntarily embrace a new system in advance of its installation, let alone be enthusiastic advocates of it [2]." Sufficient time and effort must be devoted by the leadership of the organization to fully understand the general concepts and objectives of the proposed changes. In turn, they must be able to explain how these new procedures will help the organization achieve its strategic objectives.

At times in the implementation of new strategies and processes, the top leadership of the organization may undergo significant turnover. While the new executive officers may continue to support the basic objectives, they were not involved in the overall development of the project. And each of the new officers is likely to have their own agenda (which, from time-to-time, may come into conflict with one another and with the proposed changes). In such circumstances, it is especially important to brief the new leadership to get them "up to speed" as quickly as possible as to the reasons for and organizational benefits stemming from the proposed changes.

Operating managers are more likely to support a proposed change if they can be convinced that, on balance, it will benefit them in carrying out their assigned responsibilities. Managers at all levels must be convinced that the new strategies and processes, in fact, are going to be used and that their implementation will assist them do a better job. The best way to "pass the word" is for top management to discuss the new strategies and processes with their subordinates, who then carry the message to their subordinates, and so on. This approach results in "champions for change" and aids in the education of all those involved.

General *inertia* and the *inability to implement* recommend strategies and processes are fundamental people-based barriers to change. The familiar definition of inertia—"a body at rest tends to remain at rest"—is applicable to many processes in complex organizations. The extended definition—"a body in motion tends to remain in motion until acted upon by some external force"— is also applicable. Overcoming either form of inertia—the start-up of a new process from "at rest" or the redirecting of an existing process that is already "in motion"—can be a major challenge in implementing strategic management recommendations.

Failure to successfully implement a recommended change can be a major set back to the overall strategic management process, as it re-enforces the "I told you so" resistance to change. Often the inability to implement is tied to an incomplete (or incorrect) analysis of the problem or issue. As Rapoport noted, the first step in solving any problem is to state it with clarity [3]. If the problem cannot be stated specifically—preferable in one sentence, including one or more objectives—the analysis has been inadequate or of insufficient depth. The more a given problem can be extended through the examination of timely information about the situation, the greater the promise of a successful solution.

Emotional bias, habitual or traditional behavior, and the human tendency to seek the path of least resistance may contribute to a superficial analysis, followed by a statement of an *apparent* problem rather than the *real* problem. An excellent solution to an apparent problem will not work in practice, because it is the solution to a problem that does not exist in fact. Short-circuiting this phase in the process may actually result in more time spent later to get at the real problem when it becomes painfully evident that further analysis is required before a successful solution can be implemented.

1.2 Technological Barriers

Barriers to change related to information technology usually are assumed to stem from the lack of the latest available equipment and related software. However, "technology overload"—the inability to utilize the technology that is available within an organization—may be equally to blame for delaying change. Preparing end-users to apply the available technology through carefully constructed *transition workshops* and training programs is a critical component of change management. The introduction of new technology often raises the level of anxiety among end-users. Therefore, it is important to clearly identify those groups and individuals within the organization that will be affected by the introduction of the new technology. Its also critical to ensure an adequate lead-time for training before the "change over" occurs. In fact, in most cases, it is advisable to run the old and the new technology in parallel for some period of time, if possible. This approach will ensure a smoother transition and provide a "back up" in case some component of the new technology "fails" in its initial roll-out (which is an almost inevitable occurrence when new complex systems are introduced).

A major technological issue that often must be confronted in the implementation of new processes relates to data access. Most units want "real time" access to data, especially financial and personnel data. However, providing all users direct access to the database in which actual transactions are recorded potentially could cause significant processing delays. It may be necessary to establish a replica of the on-line database that can be refreshed periodically (e.g., hourly) and a data warehouse to contain historic data for comparisons with current information. Therefore, rather than maintaining one central database, it may be necessary to construct and maintain (synchronize) three databases with appropriate access controls to each. Implementation of multiple databases adds significantly to the training requirements of the change management process.

It may not be possible (or desirable) to introduce new information technology "whole cloth" or across-the-board within an organization. However, a phased implementation will mean that some portions of the organization and/or some portions of the technology will continue to operate on so-called *legacy systems*—that is, the existing technology. Building bridges between legacy systems and the new technology may be more time consuming and resource demanding than the implementation of the new systems. However, most organizations have no other choice—to change all of the legacy systems at one time would be to invite the worse form of "technology overload," assuring across-the-board systems failure.

At times, some components of the current version of the software package that have been adopted are not sufficiently robust to meet the organization's needs. Therefore, while waiting for an upgrade of these software components, it may be necessary to develop considerable "patches" between the new systems that are implemented and the legacy system.

1.3   Infrastructure Barriers

Barriers to change emerging from the infrastructure of an organization may be tied to organizational structure or to physical facilities. An organization may be functionally decentralized with key roles and responsibilities distributed throughout the organizations often resulting in duplication of effort and redundancy. Or it may be spatially decentralized—located in various parts of a city, region, or even the nation. In either case, the organization is likely to encounter problems of communications that can represent significant barriers to change. At the other extreme, an organization that is centralized, but with many layers in its hierarchy (physically or functionally) may also suffer from communication breakdowns that will result in barriers to change.

Adapting the organizational structure to fit the newly defined strategies and processes is a crucial task. Changes in the human resources system must be carefully implemented in a new organizational structure to ensure that no more than marginal disturbances occur in the motivation of the individuals being affected. Subunit reorganization, job rotation, and employee empowerment often can be achieved without major disruptions. However, organizational restructuring that results in the reduction of staff—which often emerges as a principal reengineering recommendation—can cause major disruptions.

1.4   Process Barriers

A primary objective of strategic management is to address barriers to change that are associated with or emerge from current processes. In practice, organizations may adopt processes that are not the most effective approaches available. Some processes may be dictated by external factors (for example, governmental regulations, legal constraints, employee rights, union rules, and community attitudes). These external factors, in turn, must be accommodated within the overall recommendations of strategic management. A *cost–constraint assessment* may be undertaken to examine the impact of these factors by comparing the cost of the process that might be adopted if no constraints were present with the cost of the constrained process. Once this cost differential has been identified, decisions can be made as to the feasibility of eliminating the constraints. This assessment gives decision makers an estimate of how much would be saved by relaxing a given constraint. By the same token, the cost of the constraint suggests the amount of resources that might be committed to overcoming it. In some cases, however, maintaining a constraint may be more important for social or political reasons than implementing a more effective process.

Process monitoring must be continuous in order to scan the performance and contribution of the implemented changes to quality improvement. The performance of the new processes must be measured and compared to the processes being replaced in order to determine the overall success (or failure) of the change efforts. This measurement should include the following aspects.

Process performance: Cycle times, value added for customers, quality of services provided.
Information technology performance: Rates at which data and information are accessed and the system is use.
Productivity: Output of employees, production process, and service operations.

This evaluation is made possible by an iterative process, in which the new processes become inputs to the diagnostic phase of process reengineering and then are "looped." In short, process reengineering projects are not simply initiated, performed, and finished, but rather should become an ongoing effort of continuous improvement.

2 MANAGING CHANGE

The term "managing change" has at least two meanings. One meaning refers to initiating change in a planned or systematic fashion. The aim is to implement new processes and strategies more effectively in an ongoing organization. The changes to be managed are within the organization and are controlled by the organization. These internal changes often have been triggered by events outside the organization, however, in what often is referred to as "the broader environment." Therefore, a second meaning of managing change encompasses the response to changes over which the organization can exercise little or no control (for example, shifting economic conditions, new legislation or government regulations, social or political upheaval, actions of competitors, and so on). Responses to such external changes can be either after-the-fact and reactive or anticipated and proactive.

2.1 Hard Stuff and Soft Stuff

Many organizations focus their primary change management efforts on identifying and implementing innovations, especially in terms of the introduction of new technology. They mistakenly assume "technological determinism"—that the effects of technology are independent of the organizational structure and processes of which it is an integral part. As Tom Melone, President of Milliken & Company, observed, "The hard stuff is easy, the soft stuff is hard, and the soft stuff is more important that the hard stuff [4]." Research has shown that, while investments in information technology (the "hard stuff") often are associated with higher productivity, complementary changes in organizational processes and practices (the "soft stuff") are at least as important, if not more so [5].

Many organizations have encountered difficulties in implementing change, in large part, because of an inadequate recognition of the critical linkages among technology, strategic objectives, and day-to-day practices—the inability to coordinate the right technology with dozens of appropriate strategic and structural issues all of the same time. Regardless of how beneficial a new technology may appear in isolation, the acid test is how it interacts with numerous other aspects of the organization. These interactions sometimes can make it impossible to successfully implement a new, complex system in a decentralized, uncoordinated (or under-coordinated) fashion [6]. Often, the problem is not that the proposed system is unworkable, but that the transition proves more difficult than people had anticipated [7].

Although the rate and intensity of change has escalated over the years, human nature has stayed the same. People do not change because they are told to do so or because of the advent of new technology. Rather, people change when they feel that their anxieties about loss of competence, territory, and control are understood—that is human nature.

2.2 Pitfalls of Change Intervention

In reality, each time anyone undertakes a change intervention, they are standing at the edge overlooking an abyss. Rarely are the dangers of taking the first important steps recognized, however.

There is another old proverb that states, "You cannot cross an abyss in two steps." The same wisdom applies to many efforts to implement organizational change. All too often, managers proceed with change in a hit-or-miss fashion, attempting to deal with the most visible elements of a complex problem, unaware of critical linkages that may be revealed only through more thorough analysis. Some types of organizational change are much riskier if undertaken incrementally or on a piecemeal basis. However, existing tools for managing change often are inadequate when enterprise-wide change is contemplated [8].

One of the reasons why change often is difficult is because managers bring their old perceptions with them; they cannot get rid of them. They simply charge ahead without adequate planning or taking into consideration the fundamentals of human behavior. Before they know it, too much time and money has been spent, and the tangible results are not sufficient to justify continuing with the project. When the project is terminated, they then wonder, "Where did the project go wrong?"

Organizational change sets into motion profoundly complex actions and reactions that must first be understood and then managed. All too often, management may not come close to understanding what they are dealing with during the critical process of transformation. They may look at current situations with a mindset conditioned by past experiences. They often feel disoriented and confused. Rather than using this state of uncertainty as one in which to explore and discover, they may jump to incredibly simple-minded explanations. While this response may return the organization to a state of equilibrium, it does so without providing any new insight.

During the "good times" of economic growth, for example, public officials often are reluctant to increase taxes to enable the government to "share in the wealth," which was created, in part, by investments in public facilities and services. In fact, they may propose tax cuts since the economic growth has generated a revenue "windfall." However, when there is a downturn in the economy, public officials again may be reluctant to increase taxes and, instead, may reduce services (often some of the services that would help the economy to turn around).

Management frequently assumes that the models that have been developed for a given "reality" can be generalized to other situations. For example, change facilitators may believe that what they learned working for the Department of Commerce is equally applicable to the U.S. Postal Service; or what was done at General Electric is transferable to General Motors. They may assume that specific solutions, which worked successfully in the private sector, will be equally successful in public organizations. Their assumptions usually are wrong. Perceptions as to how the universe is (or should be) vary significantly based on the individual focal point of participants in different types of organizations.

Advances in information technology adopted in response to rising competition and the need to "work smarter" have led to new modes of organizing work. Many of these new approaches depart significantly from past practices instead of simply improving upon them in an incremental fashion. As operations become more tightly coupled through the application of these new organizational paradigms, the buffers of time and space often are eliminated. The key question is how to simultaneously achieve significant improvements in quality, service, cost, and efficiency, while overcoming the inertia of "business as usual." Ignoring such interdependencies is becoming increasingly "risky business."

2.3 People and Process Issues

Managers must take into account and coordinate the interactions among all the components of the organization. In the ideal situation, these interactions should create a cycle of positive feedback that amplifies even small steps in the right direction. Relatively few organizations have the luxury of re-designing their structure or processes from a "clean slate." People, prior operational knowledge, and existing equipment and facilities cannot be easily scrapped. Organizational change is a learning process in which unanticipated opportunities and unforeseen impediments may emerge. Movements like TQM have recognized these characteristics of changes and have developed processes for continuous improvement through incremental learning. When the costs of change are considered, however, it may not be clear whether the best course is to strive for incremental change, radical change, or no change at all [9]. This dilemma may exist even if a strategic objective is precisely envisioned and represents a clear-cut improvement.

It is generally recognized that change management must be involved with *people* (human or behavioral issues) and *processes* (nonhuman issues, such as new information technologies, accounting procedures, marketing methods, statistical analyses, and so on). Until recently, however, much of the emphasis in new management techniques had been on process issues. Organizations often implement new technology and new processes without modifying their human resource practices.

There is increasing awareness that much more emphasis must be placed on people issues, however. Two reasons for this growing awareness are:

1. Basic methods of TQM and process reengineering require more involvement of the people who will be called upon to implement change or will be impacted by change (for example, knowledge-creation activities require insights from people throughout the organization), and
2. Recognition that human issues determine whether the rest of the methods (human or otherwise) are used effectively or are rejected.

Thomas Powell wrote that the successful result of new management systems most often are correlated with intangibles of human behavior, such as executive commitment, an open and trusting culture, and employee empowerment [10]. All of these factors are beneficial in their own right and enable quality procedures to have the desired effect.

2.4 Skill Requirements for Change Management

Managing the changes encountered by and instituted within an organization requires a finely honed set of skills. Chief among these are people skills, analytical skills, system skills, organizational skills, and an understanding of the political processes within the organization.

Organizations are first and foremost social systems. Without people, there can be no organization. Moreover, people come in all shapes and sizes, intelligence and ability levels, attitudes toward work and life, personalities, religious beliefs, priorities, and many other dimensions along which people vary. And any would-be manager of change must be capable of dealing with *all* of these dimensions.

The skills most needed in this area are those that typically fall under the heading of *communication* or *interpersonal skills*. Managers of change must be able to listen, restate, reflect, clarify, draw out participants, lead or channel discussions, plant ideas, and develop them. Change managers must learn to see things through the eyes of others within the organization. A situation viewed from a service delivery perspective, for example, may be entirely different when seen through the eyes of an information systems person. A major part of the job of a change manager is to recognize and resolve conflicts between and among disparate points of view.

To be successful, managers of change must be skilled at carrying out *complex analyses* of problem situations confronting the organization. Insight and intuition often can yield useful perspectives, and sometimes they may bring about brilliant breakthroughs. But such insights are very difficult to sell and almost impossible to defend. While decision-makers can ignore, or even suppress, a rational, well-argued analysis, such analyses are seldom successfully contested. And, in most cases, rational analyses, if properly communicated, will have some measurable impact on the final decision.

Two sets of analytical skills are particularly important: (1) analysis of workflow or operations and (2) financial analysis. Managers of change must be able to disassemble operations and processes and then re-assemble them in novel ways. They also must be able to determine the financial impacts of what has been done. Conversely, managers of change must be able to start with some financial objective, measure, or indicator and quickly determine which operations and processes would have the desired financial impact when reconfigured in a certain way. Those who master these two analytical skills (known in the trade as "solution engineering") have learned techniques that will be in demand for the foreseeable future.

As noted earlier, an organization is a system—an arrangement of resources and processes intended to produce specified results. To organize is to arrange, and a system reflects organization. Therefore, managers of change need to master two sets of *systems skills*.

The first is the set of skills most people associate with computers and information technology. This set of skills actually pre-dates the computer, however, and is known in the aerospace industry and elsewhere as "systems engineering." This skill set, for the most part, is most concerned with understanding "closed" systems, that is, mechanistic or contrived systems that have no purpose of their own and are incapable of altering their own structure. In other words, closed systems cannot "learn" and cannot change on their own volition.

The second set of system skills is associated with a body of knowledge generally referred to as "general systems theory." General systems theory is not so much a rigorous explanatory theory as it is a way of isolating certain important aspects of reality. It is a shorthand way of looking at the world, providing a framework within which apparently distinct sets of phenomena can be united [11]. As a cognitive window on reality, general systems theory focuses not only on root causes but also on the complex interrelationships that may constrain the development of effective solutions. Such a systemic perspective is a necessary, although not sufficient, condition of strategic management.

Complex organizations survive as open systems in a continuous inflow and outflow with their environment. And in so doing, they can create conditions that permit them to attain new structural and functional configurations, that is, to survive at a new level. Unlike closed systems, organizations never exist in a state of equilibrium, in the chemical or thermodynamic sense, but are maintained in a so-called steady state. Such systems seek stability rather than equilibrium.

Managers of change must acquire a set of skills that deals with "open" systems—people, organizations, industries, economies, and so forth—that operate as purposeful, socio-technical entities. Open systems are capable of carrying out transactions with other systems and are focused on survival, continuance, prosperity, dominance, and a host of other strategic objectives.

A change manager must understand how an organization works, particularly, the organization in which and on which they are working. This entails an understanding of the organization's resources—where they come from, where they go, how to get them, and how to keep them. It also requires knowledge of the basic components that are of importance to the survival of the organization.

Organizations are intensely *political entities*. And, as one wag has pointed out, organizational politics often are so intense because so little is at stake. In an era of fiscal austerity, in particular, the competition for limited organizational resources can be fairly intense. Change managers must not join in the political game, but they must understand it. This area is one in which managers of change must make their own judgments and keep their own counsel—no one can do it for them.

2.5 Basic Strategies for Managing Change

Bennis, Benne, and Chin suggested three basic strategies for initiating and managing change [12]. Nickols has added a fourth approach to this set [13]. Under a *rational–empirical* approach, it is assumed that people are rational and will follow what is in their best self-interest—once it has been clearly revealed to them. Change is based primarily on the successful communication of information and on the extension of incentives. The *normative–re-educative* approach assumes that people are social beings and will adhere to cultural norms and values. Change is based on the re-definition and re-interpretation of existing norms and values, and on the development of commitments to new ones. The *power–coercive* approach is based on the assumption that people are basically compliant and will generally do what they are told, or can be made to do so. Change is based on the exercise of authority and the imposition of sanctions. Nickols suggested an *environmental–adaptive* approach to change, which assumes that people are opposed to disruption and loss of things familiar, but can adapt readily to new circumstances. Change is based on building a new organizational structure and gradually transferring people from the old to the new structure.

According to Duncan, a rational, self-interest change strategy consists of four steps [14].

1. Invite employees to participate in the process of change—to give their opinions, to feel a part of the change process, and to identify their own self-interest regarding the proposed change.
2. Provide some motivation or incentive to change; self-interest can be an important motivator.
3. Develop an open communication system so that people can understand the purpose for the changes.
4. Encourage feedback both from and to the employees; everyone enjoys knowing how things are going and how much progress is being made.

Generally speaking, no single change strategy will work in all situations. For any given initiative, some mix of strategies will likely best serve the overall needs of the organization. Which of the preceding strategies to use is affected by a number of factors. If the proposed change is likely to meet with strong resistance, a coupling of the power–coercive and environmental–adaptive strategies may be most appropriate. A combination of the rational–empirical and normative–re-educative strategies may be most appropriate in situations of weak resistance or concurrence. If the time frame for change is relatively short, a power-coercive strategy may be required; longer time frames suggest the need for a mix of the other three strategies.

A mix of all four strategies is appropriate when the stakes are high and nothing can be left to chance or when the population affected by the change is large. Management's ability to command or demand may be relatively limited if the organization is highly dependent on its people (staff and/or clientele). Conversely, if people are dependent upon the organization, their ability to oppose or resist change is limited. Having adequate expertise available to assist in making change argues for some mix of the strategies outlined above. Not having such expertise available argues for reliance on the power–coercive strategy.

3 STRUCTURAL AND CULTURAL CHANGE

Any significant change is likely to be disruptive to the structure and culture of an organization. Organizations that have attempted initiate improvements while ignoring this syllogism have invariably failed.

3.1 Structural Change Management

The management of structural change is concerned with the ways in which functional units are organized to carry out their work responsibilities. It has to do with things or facilities and the rules and regulations that relate to them. The primary focus includes facilities and equipment, management and staffing, human resource policies and practices, and other procedures and regulations that relate to these structural elements. The focus of strategic management must include the design of the organization's structure, decisions about what needs to be done to implement structural change, and how to accomplish it. One size does not fit all, and therefore, it is not appropriate only to follow a recipe book. The design of the management system must be tailored to the particular organization and its environment, including making certain that the chosen set of management components fit well together.

Peter Drucker offered a comprehensive description of what needs to be done regarding the planning, operation, and management of structural change as part of a modern management system [15]. He suggested that "organization structure will not just 'evolve.' The only things that evolve in an organization are disorder, friction, malperformance [15]." The first step, according to Drucker, is to identify and organize the *building blocks* of an organization—those activities that must be included in the final structure and that will carry the "structural load" of the final edifice. Building on the work of Alfred D. Chandler, Drucker asserted that to be effective and sound, *structure must follow strategy*.

> Structure is a means for attaining the objectives and goals of an institution. Any work on structure must therefore start with objectives and strategy...
>
> Strategy, i.e., the answers to the questions 'What is our business, what should it be, what will it be?', determines the purpose of structure. It

thereby determines what the key activities are in a given business or service institution. Effective structure is the design that makes these key activities capable of functioning and of performance. And in turn the key activities are the 'load bearing elements' of a functioning structure. Organization design is, or should be, primarily concerned with the key activities; the rest are secondary [16].

Drucker suggested that four questions must be dealt with in designing (or re-designing) the building blocks of the organization:

1. What should the units of the organization be?
2. What components should join together and what components should be kept apart?
3. What size and shape pertain to different components?
4. What is the appropriate placement and relationship of different units?

More recently, Drucker has placed increased emphasis on recognizing the interactions among various parts of a system [17]. In some sense, all of the components of an organization interact. Depending on the intended change, however, interactions among some components may be strong, while interactions among other components may be relatively weak. When interactions among components are strong, one component cannot be changed without taking into account the other closely linked components. For example, every organization needs to consider its strategies, its product and market mix, its day-to-day operations and processes, and its organizational structure. Typically, strong interactions exist between the strategies and the product and market mix. However, the interactions between these two and others components within the organization often are weaker. It may be appropriate to treat those components (among which only weak interactions are apparent) as if they are independent, and thus work on them independently of other components.

3.2 Cultural Change Management

Cultural change management is concerned with the ways in which people interact with each other, both in superior/subordinate relationships and in peer relationships. People and culture—the human dimensions of an organization—are what can make or break any change initiative.

A desired organizational change must be enforced and the participants motivated until the benefits of the change can be understood and the change becomes habitual. This basic notion is illustrated in the causal loop of behavior and culture. *Culture* may be defined as the ways in which people habitually think and do things. People *behave* in ways that are consistent with the culture of the society, community, or organization of which they are a part. In turn, by continuing to behave in the same way, people reinforce and perpetuate their culture. To change the culture, it is necessary to start by changing the behavior of participants. To accomplish this change in behavior, an appropriate management system must be designed and a strategy must be developed for phasing in this system. The design of a management system—like the design of any system—requires a give and take between what needs to be done and how to do it.

Employees often are skeptical, since cultural change is based on an organizational perspective, not on individual needs—each of which is different. Fear and concern center around issues of compensation, job security, sense of worth, perceptions by others, position and social patterns. Employees may not be confident that the organization will properly manage the transition. They may also be concerned about a lack of support while moving to a new job—if they have one at all.

Resistance to change can be overt or covert. Individuals may have the courage to voice their concerns about impending changes, and such "speaking out" should be encouraged. Covert resistance is far more dangerous, since it is impossible to manage because it cannot be confronted. We have all been in meetings where everyone appears to agree with a proposed change and even congratulate each other on the group's collective wisdom. Then the participants go back to their offices to tell their colleagues what a dumb idea they have just been wasting time discussing.

Reactions to change often are governed by perceived loss of control. However, people rarely are comfortable in expressing honest emotions in an organizational setting, so what they say may not be what they mean. An individual may object to a proposed change on the basis of a specific omission of some report or data element for which they may have primary responsibility. They may really be saying: "I knew how to play by the old rules and I'm concerned that I may not be as successful under the new process." Even if the issue is accommodated as stated, the real cause of the resistance may not be addressed.

Ansoff observed that resistance to change "if left unmanaged ... becomes conflict-laden, prolonged, and costly in both human and financial terms [18]." He suggested the following basic steps to deal with such resistance.

> Management of resistance involves anticipating the focus of resistance and its intensity. Second, it involves eliminating unnecessary resistance caused by misperceptions and insecurities. Third, it involves mustering the power base necessary to assure support for the change. Fourth, it involves planning the process of change. Finally, it involves monitoring and controlling resistance during the process of change... [18].

Bryson noted that the implementation process must be explicitly considered prior to its initiation to minimize difficulties [19]. It also must be continually reconsidered during the actual implementation. In short, the implementation of change must be carefully thought out and the likely impediments must be identified before the actual change process is initiated. The roll-out of major organizational change cannot be something that is "flown by the seat of the pants."

Staff members must know what is happening, when it will happen, and how they will be impacted. Employees must believe that they will get the necessary training, knowledge, information, and authority to manage the performance that affects the products and services they deliver.

In implementing a new financial management system for a local government, a decision was made (in spite of warnings to the contrary) to shut down the legacy systems concurrent with the new systems "going live." A major problem developed in the area of purchasing, where it soon became evident that insufficient training in the use of the new software had taken place in the various units to handle the changeover to the new procedures. No fallback alternative was available since the legacy system had been abandoned. Purchase orders and requisition were backed up for months and many vendors were not paid on a timely basis. Many smaller suppliers refused to do business with the local government because they could not "carry" the charges incurred.

Change must have strong, credible leadership. Sufficient time and resources must be provided for high levels of communications, information gathering, participation, collaboration, education, training, and appropriate incentive and reward systems. Employees may require support groups to help members deal with change, one person at a time. They also need time to adapt. Therefore, change activities should begin in the initial phases of strategic management and continue through to implementation. The management of change cannot be just an afterthought.

3.3   Organizing for Change Management

Senior management often envisions change as being handled by broad-based initiatives through a series of clearly defined steps. This perception arises because senior managers usually are steeped in the realities of organizational pressures and fully recognize the changes that must occur. They think of change initiatives in broad terms: "We are redesigning our cost accounting process." The vision and objectives are so clear in their own minds that they assume staff members will understand that change is necessary and will support the initiatives in every way. In so doing, they fail to recognize (or lose sight of) a critical principle of change management: *organizations don't change; people do.*

Employees seldom perceive change with the same clarity and determination as does senior management. Employees tend to think of change in terms of their own specific responsibilities: "With the new cost accounting procedures, do I keep producing this spreadsheet or not?" To successfully implement and sustain change, initiatives must be presented (translated) to show implications for each individual who will be affected by the change. This is a key reason why change programs usually take longer than initially planned.

Marshall and Connor suggested that people may resist change even when they view it as a good idea, likening this response to change to the early stages of a marriage [20]. Initially, the introduction of change may be met with naive enthusiasm based on insufficient data—this stage is akin to the honeymoon period of a marriage. This period of "uninformed optimism" may be followed by "informed pessimism," when the real price of the change is discovered—the honeymoon is over. While the overall decision may have been a good one, there are significant costs that initially were unexpected or unknown. This point is critical in the management of change. Individuals who at the outset were in support of the change may publicly reverse their position, or what may be more disruptive in the long run, they may harbor undisclosed resentment and conflict.

If the organization can get past this turning point, then a stage of "hopeful realism" may be achieved—a view of the light at the end of the tunnel based on a more complete understanding of both the costs and the benefits of the change. This stage gives way to "informed optimism"—a sense that the change is achievable and that a great deal has already been accomplished.

An appropriate strategy may be to assign the responsibility for managing change to a separate team, chartered to support all change initiatives. A primary role of the change management team is to ensure that the new strategies and improved processes will be successfully assimilated into the organization's structure and culture. This team must accomplish four general objectives:

1. Understand the organizational changes that are needed as a consequence of strategic management initiatives.
2. Design the necessary structural changes within the organization needed to support the new initiatives.
3. Design a program that will begin the cultural transformation of the organization to one aligned with the principles behind the proposed improvements.
4. Anticipate, recognize, and resolve the barriers to change that will surface in reaction to the change management plan.

One of the most difficult tasks is to determine how to phase in the improved processes that constitute the new system. Some people inside the organization will try to create an all-or-nothing situation. For a variety of reasons, they will assume that there are the only two choices: (1) make comprehensive changes from which there can be no deviance, or (2) make no changes. Experts in various management system components may reinforce this assumption. And even if the experts do not encourage this attitude, people at all levels within the organization may adopt it.

A first step to phasing in new strategies or processes is to increase the level of commitment by finding ways to produce quick results that are representative of the benefits of the proposed change, while also giving a flavor of the effort involved in implementing the total system. It may be appropriate to initiate change in sub-systems (or units) that are representative of the larger system or method. Another approach is to find a balance between the degree of challenge given to employees and their ability or energy to deal with the challenge. Staff members can get turned off quickly when they are directed to work on trivial tasks. However, the challenge should not be so aggressive that employees feel they have no chance of success—this situation will also be a major turn-off.

It may be important to link new initiatives with ongoing operations, since in an era of resource constraints, new initiatives often must compete directly with ongoing programs, products, services, and operations. New procedures must be blended with ongoing operations in such a way that internal support is generated from those persons charged with maintaining these ongoing activities.

An important but tractable problem, for example, should be selected as the initial focus of change to allow individuals to gain skill with the new methods or procedures before they attack crucial but less tractable problems. In installing a new procurement system, for example, the initial focus might be on relatively routine purchases (e.g., office supplies, travel arrangements, etc.) before undertaking more elaborate acquisitions requiring vendor bidding, encumbrances, set-up and maintenance costs, and so forth. Problems rooted in behavioral issues should be avoided until after staff members have gained some initial skill with the new method or procedure. Similarly, the first applications may involve situations in which there is an assumption of cause and effect. In such cases, it may be appropriate to analyze the networks of cause and effects (e.g., by using relations diagrams or causal loop diagrams).

As Bryson observed, implementation will flow more smoothly and quickly if the proposed changes are conceptually clear and are based on well-understood cause-and-effect relationships [21]. To the extent possible, they should fit with the values of key participants. Proposed changes should be demonstrated and made "real" prior to implementation. Pilot studies and other opportunities should be provided for those who will implement the new strategies and processes to get "hands-on" experience. They should be operationally, as well as conceptually, clear and relatively simple to grasp in practice. A start-up period should be provided in which people can learn about the pending changes and can engage in necessary training/retraining and development of new norms and operating routines. And perhaps most importantly, adequate attention must be given to payoffs and rewards. There must be clear incentives for those who will be called upon to adopt the new strategies and procedures.

4 ROLE OF COMMUNICATIONS IN CHANGE MANAGEMENT

Open communication is the key to the successful management of change. The content of messages should be carefully planned for every phase of the change management process; the messenger or managers of change should be thoroughly trained; the medium (or media) of communication should be determined from the outset. But most important is that the communication should be honest, flexible, and empathetic.

4.1 Expectations and Communication

Expectations play an important role in organizational communication. Patterns of interaction develop among communication nodes when messages are systematically sent and received. Habitual use of particular communication channels generate expectations that, over time, have the force of custom. Message often must be carefully worded according to a certain set of expectations shared by the recipients. Any message that does not conform to such shared expectations is likely to be ignored or produce a negative response on the part of the recipient.

Communications are accompanied by the implicit expectation that, if the meaning is apprehended (and within the set of expectations of the recipient), responses will be forthcoming within a given range of possibilities. If an appropriate response is not produced, the communicator has three courses of action.

1. Ignore (or fail to notice) the discrepancy between expectations and responses and proceed as if there were no discrepancy.
2. Take note of the discrepancy and try again, perhaps by modifying the mode or content of the communication.
3. Take note of the discrepancy and revise their expectations to conform to the responses that have been observed.

As a rule, the usual outcome of such situations is either 2 or 3, or a combination of these. These operations, in which the communicator modified their behavior (either internally or externally) on the basis of observation, are examples of *feedback* in human interaction.

As a person experiences their external and internal environment, expectations are built up, reinforced, or modified by the operation of feedback. The interaction of expectations and the resulting feedback makes communication possible by acting as standards by which each person can gauge the extent to which they understand the other and, in turn, is understood. Feedback permits self-correction or behavior adjustment in light of comparisons between responses and expectations. The relationship between expectations of the initiator and the respondent(s) in a decision-making system are reciprocal or complementary. Interaction takes place within the framework of these complementary expectations and both influence and is influenced by the other.

Four conditions must be met in order for a communication, or any portion of it, to be informative.

1. A communication is informative to the extent that the recipient learns something from it—an idea, concept, a point of view, or a relationship among these.
2. The information must be acceptable to the recipient according to their own ideas, beliefs, needs, and attitudes. People are most likely to accept information that (1) they are looking for, (2) they can see some possible use for in the immediate future, or (3) they fancy because of the physical or contextual conditions under which it occurs.
3. The content of the communication must be clear. If the message, or any portion of it, seems ambiguous to the recipient, to that extent it will be either noninformative or misinformative.
4. The message must be meaningful to the recipient. The content of the message must be such that it can be readily assigned to any appropriate place in the recipient's knowledge of the subject and the relationship between ideas as the recipient sees them.

Often the communication network through which information is transmitted has an important bearing on its acceptance by individuals within an organization.

4.2 Communication Networks

Organizational communications consist of a number of superimposed networks. These networks often can be separated for empirical analysis. At times, however, the sorting of messages into different networks lacks refinement because of the tendency of individuals to use rewarding communication channels again and again, even though such usage goes beyond the intent for which a particular channel was established.

Analysts have given considerable attention to communications involved in the exercise of *authority relations*. Channels in this network are defined in terms of the legitimacy that one individual or group has vis-a-vis others with respect to the issuance of directives, commands, and decisions. Such networks have *directionality*—orders usually flow vertically within an organization, from a relatively few individuals at the top to many in the lower echelons of the authority structure.

The *information exchange* network is sometimes thought of as an inversion of the authority communication flow. Messages in this network usually are concerned with internal operations and with the broader external environment. The flow is generally from the operational level to the top of the organization. This network also can be used to supply information for operational decisions—to establish guidelines or parameters with which such decisions can be made.

The *task expertise network* provides technical know-how regarding the performance of organizational activities. An important feature of this network is its fragmentation. Relatively unrelated islands of expertise are created throughout an organization. Occupational groups and professions use specialized jargon in handling the tools and techniques of their trade. Such groups also provide norms concerning work standards and appropriate levels of performance.

Informal lateral networks sometime develop when regularized channels fail to function adequately. Unlike formal channels, highly specialized, informal communication networks often are not directly subject to management control. Such networks frequently are the result of natural social groupings. These informal communication networks, sometimes called the "grapevine," can reinforce formal information flows or can work contrary to these channels.

Networks carrying messages about *status* may be less well-defined. Such networks have many occasional and fleeting connections that cut across almost all other networks. Status often is attached to nodes within a network, as well as the network overall. Perceptions of one's own position within the status system also influences the extent to which certain communication channels are utilized.

When communication networks are undifferentiated and overlap extensively, one set of messages may be submerged by another set. Perhaps the most evident situation arises from an overlap of the networks of authority and friendship. In such cases, orders and commands may not carry sufficient force to be implemented effectively. By the same token, an undue overlap between the status and information exchange networks may result in information input receiving greater weight than it merits, simply because of the status enjoyed by the source.

4.3   Selective Filtering: Omissions and Distortions

As information is transmitted within an organization, the omission of detail may provide one means of reducing *communication overload*, which is a major problem in any large organization. When such omissions are systematic with respect to certain categories of information, the process may be labeled *selective filtering*. In complex situations, such selective filtering often is crucial to effective communication.

Communication systems become more effective when the languages employed carry larger amounts of meaning with relatively fewer symbols. Organizations find such communication devices as occupational jargons, coding and classification systems, charts, diagrams, and other "visuals" helpful in increasing the efficiency of communications. The degree to which knowledge relevant to a given problem may be transmitted within an organization, however, depends on the extent to which details may be summarized and condensed in an efficient, shared language. Very often, technical jargon loses its meaning as it is transmitted upward in the organization.

Selective filtering may lead to the deletion of important aspects of communications or may introduce message distortions. It is often difficult to provide meaningful information about intangible and nonstandard objects or concepts. Therefore, conscious efforts must be made to develop the means by which less objective communication contents can be handled more effectively. As Cyert and March observed,

> Any decision-making system develops codes for communication about the environment. Such a code partitions all possible states of the world into a relatively small number of classes of states. . . Thus, if a decision rule is designed to choose between two alternatives, the information code will tend to reduce all possible states of the world to two classes [22].

Such rules for the codification of information inputs, however, frequently introduce additional distortions.

Subordinates often shield "the truth" from top management. This systematic biasing of information may be designed to "keep the boss happy" by only passing along the "good news." As a consequence of this selective filtering, top management may be oblivious to critical problems and issues and may not have the information necessary to make effective decisions.

Systematic biasing of the content of messages may not always be dysfunctional, however. In experimental situations, Allport and Postman found that transmitted messages ". . . tended to grow shorter, more concise, and more easily grasped and told," and that there were ". . . selective perceptions, retention, and reporting of a limited number of details from a larger context [23]." In other words, the messages often were sharpened.

Omissions and inaccuracies may increase the ambiguity of messages. However, since ambiguous messages are open to multiple interpretations, the recipients may attach more agreeable meanings to them. Thus, while ambiguity may result in slippage between the sender and recipient, such slippage may also promote consensus and agreement at least at one level of understanding. This consensus, in turn, may establish a working basis for further elaboration. However, unless this issue is pursued to ensure that a true consensus is reached, the eventual consequences of the ambiguity and multiple interpretations may become an obstacle to the successful implementation of change.

4.4 Communicating About Pending Change

It is appropriate for initial communications regarding anticipated or pending changes in an organization's processes or structure to be issued by the upper levels of management and be transmitted through the authority network. This approach provides an important endorsement to the new initiatives and to the overall change management effort. Unfortunately, many organizations limit the communication about change to this initial pronouncement, usually with negative consequences. Depending on the nature of the forthcoming change, these consequences may include widespread resistance to the proposed strategies and processes.

The initial communication (announcement) should be followed up with a series of informative exchanges (transition workshops) and more directed communications using the task expertise network (e.g., hands-on sessions through demonstrations and conference room pilots). Transition workshops are designed to provide structured presentations to fairly sizable audiences (25 to 100 participants), with ample provision for question and answer sessions and audience comments and reactions. The participants should "take something away" from the workshop (e.g., handouts) and should be encouraged to follow-up with further questions and comments. A web site or email address can be used to record these follow-up responses. Demonstrations and conference room pilots are directed to a smaller (15 to 20), more specialized audience. Participants in transition workshops might be grouped according to their knowledge and expertise (or lack of same), regarding the proposed changes. A series of demonstrations or pilot sessions should then be scheduled to provide participants with differing levels of expertise a hands-on opportunity to deal with (and react to) various aspects of the proposed change. These demonstrations and pilot sessions should simulate the proposed new systems, providing the participants with the opportunity to "try their hand" at initiating and following through with the new processes and procedures.

When communication networks are highly differentiated, isolation may be very costly. Duplicate channels may need to be maintained for certain communication functions, and the content of messages may be lost due to high friction of transmission between channels. This situation arises when an organization is highly structured along functional hierarchies (often referred to as "silos"). The development of cross-functional communication networks may be required to ensure that "everyone is on the same page" when it comes to learning about and understanding the proposed changes in organizational processes and structure. The change management team should have cross-functional representation.

Such conditions also frequently occur in situations that require inputs from both members of the organization and the broader public. External interest groups may develop their own communication networks and gain access to the parallel networks of the organization at a variety of points. Informal points of contact may supersede formal channels, with the result that the more normative patterns of communications are circumvented or blurred. The demands of various interest groups may become distorted in transmission through the group's communication channel and may be further distorted when transmitted from one communication system to another.

4.5   Consistent Presentation Formats

A *communications coordinator* may be assigned the task of organizing a consistent flow of information regarding the proposed changes in an organization's processes and structure. Periodic progress reports, newsletters, and outreach visitations are among the tools that the communication coordinator might draw upon to orchestrate a campaign to inform and educate members of the organization. If the organization has an established e-communications network, a web site devoted to the new initiatives should be developed. A logo can be created to increase the visibility of the proposed changes. A "help desk" should be established to answer questions and provide assistance regarding the implementation of new procedures and related software. Personnel serving at the "help desk" should be familiar with the functional areas affected by the procedural changes as well as the new technology that may be implemented to facilitate these new processes.

It is important that a timeline for the implementation of the proposed changes be established. This timeline should be realistic and should provide a sufficient level of detail to allow groups within the organization to see "where they fit" within the implementation schedule. Progress reports should include references to the timeline. Any adjustments required in the implementation schedule should be made promptly and notification should be distributed throughout the organization.

A key factor in effective communications is the development of a consistent format in which information, data, and analyses are presented. At the outset, key participants within the organization should be interviewed to gather suggestions as to which data to include and how best to communicate this information. A list of topics and presentation formats should be agreed upon, but some flexibility should be afforded during the initial iterations to add to or refine the format as new topics are suggested by the review of the data and indices. Time spent up-front in the design of the format to facilitate data entry and analysis, to communicate information regarding progress toward implementation, and to ensure quick turnaround in accessing and printing reports is effort well invested.

Information is likely to be drawn from a number of sources within the organization, and some manipulation of the data may be necessary to ensure that comparisons will be valid and consistent. A preprinted data-collection form may assist in the gathering of these data. This form should include the data previously reported over several time periods. Space should be provided for comments regarding any notable changes in the latest data entries when compared to the entries for the previous time periods. When the changes are deemed to be significant, representatives from the areas of the organization responsible for the activities may be called upon to make a further presentation to explain these data.

Periodic meetings (e.g., monthly) to discuss the implementation process are an important feature of this approach. Data on progress to date should be provided a few days before these meetings, with an executive summary of the key issues to be discussed. Participants can then focus on those items most pertinent to their areas of responsibility and should be prepared to comment on and discuss problems and trends that are evident from their perspective.

It is likely that some of the data deemed appropriate for inclusion in these discussions do not exist or are not readily available in the format desired. Where data have not been collected in the past, it may be necessary to reconstruct such data or, at least, start collecting them in order to have the necessary data points from which to draw comparisons. When data are not consistent from one year to the next (for example, because of a change in data categories), it may be necessary to re-compute (or "crosswalk") the prior year's data to make them more comparable. In some cases, the units that provide the data may feel that the presentation format should be modified. Some negotiations may be necessary to arrive at an agreed upon format that both satisfies user's needs and meets the perceptions of the source authorities.

Two or more units within an organization may track the same data and may provide different analyses and even conflicting information based on these data. In many instances, these different perspectives are useful, provided that the assumptions on which the data analyses are based are clearly identified and understood. In some cases, however, it may be necessary to agree upon one data set over another to avoid misunderstanding and confusion among the information users.

Particular effort should be made from the outset to maintain the accuracy of the data to ensure the credibility of reports. Presentations of the data should be focused and to the point in order to maintain everyone's attention. The objective is to raise questions at an early stage before problems get "out of control" and to alert senior management to significant trends that need to be factored into future decision-making. Major changes in an index should prompt questions and may lead to changes in policies or procedures.

The information management system (IMS) should encourage officials to focus on the same information and should help to educate senior managers concerning areas of the organization outside their direct responsibility. Those attending the periodic meetings should become more attuned to areas of concern for the overall organization. Offices providing data should become more aware of their accountability. They should develop a sense of participation by providing not only data but also answers to important questions in areas for which they have responsibilities. As with many of these management techniques, the process of developing the information management system (IMS) may provide valuable contributions to the overall well-being of the organization. The development of an appropriate IMS in support of strategic management will be discussed in further detail in Chapter 12.

5   REACTIONS TO CHANGE

All changes within organizations are not the same. Nor do all participants in the change process perceive the consequences in the same manner. Some people ignore minor changes; others are very upset by them. Big changes may not bother many employees if these changes are perceived to "affect central administration" or to be "at the corporate level." It is important to understand the different possible reactions to change and to adopt appropriate responses in the change management plan.

5.1   Stages of Change

Eileen Wolfe identified three behavior patterns, or reactions, that are exhibited in stressful change management situations: victims, survivors, and navigators [24]. *Victims* perceive themselves as independent of the facts and feel threatened with hostile situations they cannot handle. They may panic and react with a "fight or flight" response. Or they may become fatalistic. Victims tend to oversimplify the world into good or bad, and thereby limit their alternatives. They are never happy and complain about everything. They become pessimistic and cynical about the intentions of management. And they may react by simply waiting to be overtaken by the impending change.

Survivors believe they are at the mercy of circumstances they cannot change. However, they feel that they can survive the change if they simply "hold on" or become competitive with other employees. They often convince themselves that "grasping" and "clinging" are necessary for self-protection. They anticipate whatever is coming and behave accordingly by responding defensively.

Navigators face the inevitability of change and take a proactive approach. They create a vision of the desired future, gather pertinent information, and assertively pursue their vision. They manage the stress of change by developing a belief in their own ability to deal competently with the situation—by being part of the cause and influence of events rather than being merely the victim. As the label suggests, a navigator has greater control—has a hand on the tiller—and can help to steer the necessary changes in a direction that benefits both themselves as well as the overall organization.

Individuals and groups may experience four stages of change during the implementation of strategic management recommendations: uncertainty, frustration, examination, and accommodation. In the stage of *uncertainty*, the initial reaction to change may be shock and disbelief. The proposed change may appear to be so unreal and chimerical that some individuals cannot fully comprehended it. For many, change is seen as a threat—they are afraid and react accordingly. People tend to focus on things as they were and deny the change. It is important that management be very clear that change will happen and allow ample time for the news to sink in. The strategic vision and objectives that underlie the proposed change must be repeated again and again. It is for this reason that the change management process must begin early on, rather than being relegated to an "end-game" event.

In the *frustration* stage, letting go of the past is extremely difficult. Individuals hold on to and defend the old ways of doing things. When long held beliefs are challenged by new information, perceptions and attitudes may become destabilized. The attitude of many people may be: "If I ignore it, maybe it will go away." People turn inward, preoccupied about what will become of them. They may dig in their heels and resist the efforts to implement change. Frustration may turn to anger which, in turn, may be misdirected at other employees. During this stage, management must be willing to listen, acknowledge feelings, and deal with these festering concerns.

When the *examination* stage is reached, people are willing to consider the pros and cons of the pending changes. The need for change has been made clear and feelings and concerns have been acknowledged. A transformation begins when employees begin to recognize things could be changed to their advantage. They begin to see the value of change, begin to explore what is new, and to consider how they might deal with it. There is a release of energy—things might not be so bad under the new approaches. Efforts are made to seek and test ways to feel more comfortable about accepting change. Individuals may seek to negotiate ways to minimize the impact of the change (including requests for deadline extensions, modifications to the change initiatives, or even reassignment). Not everyone in the organization reaches this stage at the same time (if at all) and therefore, this period often is chaotic. Management must seize the opportunity to engage members of the organization in brainstorming sessions, to set short-term objectives, and to train end-users regarding the new processes. Continuous assurance must be provided that adequate resources will be available to successfully implement the proposed changes.

Finally, at the *accommodation* stage, people are ready to commit. They feel comfortable with the change and are ready to adapt the new processes and procedures. Perceptions, attitudes, and behavior begin to stabilize again when most employees believe the organizational benefits warrant the perceived risks attached to the proposed changes. Longer-term objectives can be agreed upon, and the organization can look ahead. It is important at this stage to celebrate innovation and to reward accomplishment. Successful change management requires an understanding that change is difficult and that people affected by the change must be treated with consideration, allowing time for them to turn the corner. It also is important to replace top-down control with individual self-direction and ingenuity.

Unfortunately, not all participants in the change process move successfully through these four stages. During the examination stage, for example, if bargaining efforts to minimize the impact of change fail, individuals may become so depressed at the realization that the change is real and permanent that they "want out." Management must detect those who cannot change; they may be the casualties of the change process. The challenge for management is to recognize the stage of change within each employee and to respond accordingly. A significant amount of individual attention and communication is required during this transition, since everyone will be in different stages at different times.

5.2   Matrix of Change

Brynjolfsson, Renshaw, and van Alstyne developed a "matrix of change" (actually involving three matrices—see Figure 9.1), designed to help managers deal with such issues as how quickly change should proceed, the order in which changes should take place, and whether proposed processes are sufficiently stable and coherent [25]. Construction of the matrices involves four steps.

1. *Identify critical processes*: List existing objectives, processes, and ways of creating value for the constituents/clientele of the organization. Current processes are then broken into component practices, suggesting how they are accomplished. This analysis is then repeated for new or target processes, resulting in two parallel matrices.

2. *Identify system interactions*: Processes and practices that are complementary (reinforcing) or are competing (working at cross-purposes) are identified through the use of a grid that connects each process/practice in an interference matrix. Plus (complementary) and minus (competing) signs are used at the junction of each grid to designate the relationship between processes. A plus sign does not indicate that an interaction is "good," only that it is reinforcing.

3. *Identify transition interactions*: Existing and target processes are combined in a transition matrix to help determine the degree of difficulty in shifting from current to future processes.

4. *Stakeholder survey*: Stakeholder evaluations provide an opportunity for individuals and groups to state the importance of the processes to their current activities or interactions with the organization. A determination is made as to where various internal and external stakeholders stand with respect to the retention of current processes and the implementation of target processes.

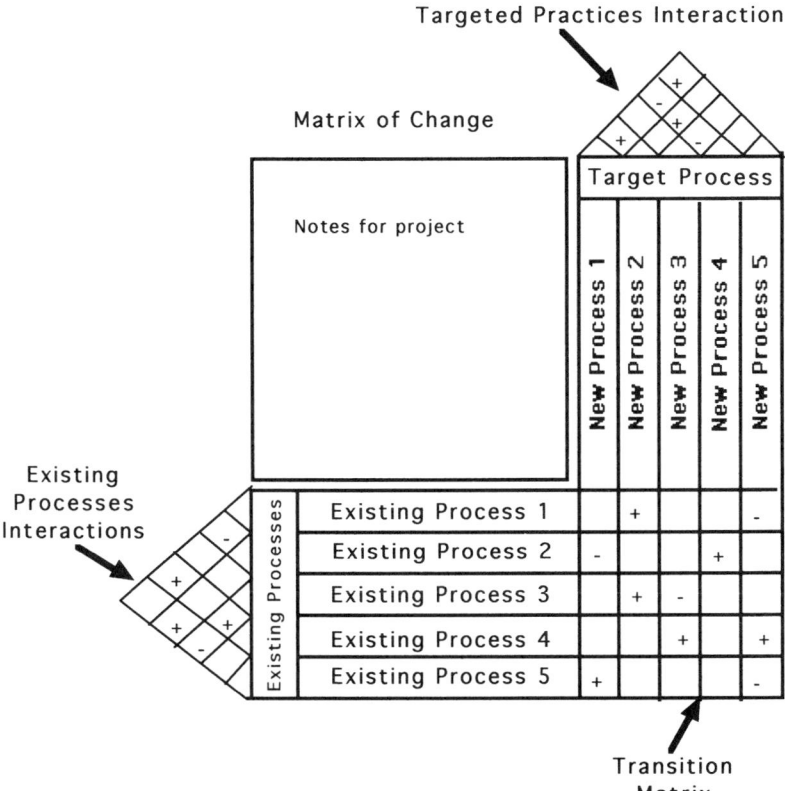

Figure 9.1 Major components of the matrix of change.

The sign (plus or minus), strength, and density of interactions indicate the coherence and stability of processes. Processes with numerous reinforcing relationships are coherent and, therefore, inherently stable. Processes with numerous competing relationships, on the other hand, are inherently unstable. These relationships are especially critical in the transitional state. When faced with a new process that conflicts with current operations, well-intentioned managers will seek to optimize their segment of the organization. Consciously or unconsciously they may undermine change by pushing the organization back toward a prior state that they view as being stable. From a local perspective, each manager's resistance appears logical and even efficient. However, from an overall organizational perspective, change may become almost impossible to achieve under these circumstances.

It may be tempting to eliminate existing processes or practices that clearly are contrary to proposed strategies and processes. However, this approach can be dangerous in that the remaining system may become even more entrenched and difficult to change. New processes that complement existing ways of doing business are the easiest to implement. However, caution must be exercised where new processes or practices strengthen old habits in ways that make dismantling the old system even more difficult. "Linchpin" processes that support a large number of other processes must be handled with great care.

In the transition matrix, the density of interfering relationships indicates how disruptive the proposed changes will likely be [25]. Increasing interference indicates a greater need for isolation. At times, a new process needs to be protected from old bad habits. As long as contrary practices remain, the natural tendency is toward local optimization, which eventually will likely push the organization toward a prior stable state. In such situations, it may be better to introduce the desired change in a completely new venue rather than in an existing location.

The notion of "venues" relates not only to location, but also attitudes. Radical change requires significant adjustments in mental as well as operational perspectives. The use of an outside change agent may be necessary in the case of radical change to help organizational personnel see the processes differently. It may also be necessary to replace current program managers because they are too closely tied to the former operating procedures. Groups may perceive they have been disadvantaged by the change—in terms of their responsibilities, influence, access to "perks," and so forth. This issue is best addressed early on because members will seek to re-assert their former roles.

5.3 Nature and Pace of Change

In preparing for the implementation of change, it is important to distinguish between the *nature* (incremental or radical) and the *pace* (gradual or rapid) of the proposed changes [26]. Radical change may best be staged over several steps, especially if available resources have already been allocated and initial conditions are likely to result in resistance to change. Organizations have established procedures and routines that must be followed. Advocates of change must understand these procedures and "go by the book" in introducing new strategies and processes. Implementing radical change in a single step may be too disruptive, too expensive, or too confusing and result in discontinuity in the organization's operations. In other situations, change may need to be an all-or-nothing proposition, where halfway solutions may lead to wasted resources, dysfunctional organizational exposure, or even failure.

Three factors help to determine the appropriate pace of change: organizational receptiveness to change, task interdependence, and external pressure [25].

An organization's culture provides some important clues as to its *receptiveness to change*. If an organization is reasonably comfortable with risk-taking, it is more likely to be receptive to change. Under such circumstances, a direct, single-step approach to implementation may be more viable. A staged implementation, on the other hand, can promote experimentation and learning. Therefore, if change needs to be distributed through several areas of an organization, late adopters can gain access to the know-how and know-why of early adopters without repeating their mistakes [27]. However, if the culture of the organization punishes failed experiments, a staged implementation that encourages "learning-as-you-go" is unlikely.

Evaluations prepared by employees can make expectations and preferences more explicit, thereby clarifying the organization's receptiveness to change. The very act of asking workers for their opinions and values and then taking these viewpoints seriously can have a positive effect on the change process by giving employees a sense of ownership and responsibility. If employees give existing practices low marks, they are more likely to support change. Conversely, if they give existing practices high marks, it is unlikely that they will support change. High variance among employee evaluations indicates different priorities and a fragmented strategic vision.

Task interdependence concerns the extent to which the essential steps of change can be divided or modularized. Bryson recommended breaking proposed changes into clusters or programs, consisting of specific projects that can be implemented in a manageable fashion [28]. By organizing tasks into modules, the scope of change is reduced and the coordination problem is more manageable. The pace of change within each module may be fairly rapid, while the pace of change between modules may be much slower.

If *external pressure* is low, the organization may have sufficient time for a gradually paced adoption. However, the option of a staged change may be precluded if the organization faces a crisis. With extreme external pressure, a concern for survival and the absence of slack resources may force an extremely rapid pace. Transition times should be minimized if there is a history of opposition to change or a pattern of regressive change.

Bryson suggested that direct, single-step implementation should be considered when immediate action is necessary for the organization to survived in a crisis (i.e., when faced with external pressure) [28]. This approach may also be viable when the situation is technically and politically simple. And when the proposed changes entail some "lumpiness" (i.e., when the component tasks cannot be divided but must be implemented "whole cloth"), a single-step implementation may be the only available choice. Implementing a new accounting system, for example, may need to be carried out on a direct or "whole cloth" basis because the component parts of the system are so interrelated (lumpy) that they cannot be divided into workable modules. A new procurement system, however, may involve different processes and procedures for different levels (thresholds) of purchases and may be amenable to a staged or modular approach.

Bryson suggested that the staged approach should be considered in difficult situations. He further advocated the design and application of pilot projects when faced with technical difficulties and the use demonstration projects as a means of overcoming political difficulties [28]. When the implementation process is staged, particular attention must be given to those individuals within the organization who will be called upon to implement the changes in the early stages. It is important to involve people with sufficient skills, experience, and desire to make the changes work.

6   CONCLUSION: SUCCESSFUL CHANGE MANAGEMENT

Barriers to change can arise from four major sources: people, technology, infrastructure, and process. People barriers are the most difficult to fully identify and overcome, since they often exist just below the surface as skepticism or lack of confidence in the proposed direction for change. Barriers related to information technology may stem from the lack of the latest available equipment and software or from the inability to use the technology that is available within an organization. Infrastructure barriers may arise from functional or spatial decentralization. While the primary objective is to address barriers to change associated with current processes, in practice, it may not be feasible to adopt the most effective programs available.

The basic phases of change management are *awareness*, *understanding*, and finally, *acceptance*. These phases have direct correlation to commitment. If each phase is handled well, the level of commitment to change generally increases. An effective change management process requires individual consideration, as demonstrated by the following steps.

1. Describe change and the reasons for its initiation.
2. Explain the impact of change on employees, encourage questions, and allow for expression of concerns.
3. Respond to any questions and concerns.
4. Restate or re-emphasize alternative behaviors.
5. Gain commitment to change, seek input on implementation plans, and establish a follow-through process.

In the early stages of change, when enthusiasm is relatively high, a true accounting of the likely costs of the change should be provided to minimize the impact of uninformed optimism. While this "full disclosure" may result in many change projects "never getting off the drawing board," that is a better outcome than having the project fail in implementation.

Major issues regarding resistance to change should be addressed through open communication:

Recognize the inevitability of resistance to change and address it honestly and consistently.

Acknowledge that resistance will be experienced differently based on positive or negative reactions to change.

Encourage overt expressions of concern to get problems out in the open.

Create an atmosphere that facilitates honest communication, recognizing that people may not be comfortable expressing their true reasons for resistance.

Open communication will go a long way to ensure that employees understand what the change entails and feel comfortable expressing honest resistance openly. This level of communication will also enable managers to understand whether employees are having a positive or negative reaction to change. Open communication means that throughout the change process, management is consistently working with employees to help them understand the individual implications of the change initiatives so that resistance can be recognized, surfaced, managed, and overcome.

Navigating through the basic steps of change requires solid commitment from the organization's top management. It requires a clear vision, shared throughout the organization, repeatedly communicated, and widely circulated. Successful change management maintains a connection with what was done well in the past. It focuses on the process, not the people, and it uses the past as stepping stones to guide future activities. Change management means caring, listening, and responding to individual needs and concerns: It is people management. It also means helping people to use their insight, skills, and sense of values to move forward through team efforts and joint diagnosis. Most importantly, successful change management means openly valuing personal contributions to the process.

As Wolfe observed, "Effective human change management is a long journey and in many respects we have just begun. Each change we face presents new circumstances, challenges and opportunities. As change leaders, we have not only the responsibility, but the privilege of encouraging and guiding others through change journeys. As we learn to initiate and embrace change, we will do much to forward our organizations and the people within them [24]."

ENDNOTES

1. David E. Hussey and M. J. Langham. Corporate Planning: The Human Factor. Oxford, England: Pergamon Press, 1979, p. 138.

2. Robert N. Anthony and Regina Herzlinger. Management Control in Non-Profit Organizations. Homewood, Ill.: Richard D. Irwin, 1975, p. 316.

3. Anatol Rapoport. What is information? ETC: A Review of General Semantics. Vol. 10, Summer, 1953, p. 252.

4. Straford Sherman. How tomorrow's best leaders are learning their stuff. Fortune, November 27, 1995, pp. 90–102.

5. Erik Brynjolfsson and Lorin Hitt. Paradox lost? Firm-level evidence of the returns to information systems spending. Management Science, Vol. 42, 1996.

6. Paul Milgrom and John Roberts. The economics of modern manufacturing: Technology, strategy, and organization. American Economic Review. Vol. 80, No. 3,1990, pp. 511–528.

7. James Champy. Reengineering Management. New York: Harper Business, 1995.

8. Thomas Davenport and Donna Stoddard. Reengineering: Business change of mythic proportions? MIS Quarterly, Vol. 18, 1994, pp. 121–127.

9. Erik Brynjolfsson, Amy Austin Renshaw, and Marshall van Alstyne. The Matrix of Change: A Tool for Business Process Reengineering. Cambridge, Mass: MIT Sloan School of Management, 1997.

10. Thomas C. Powell. When lemmings learn to sail: Turning TQM to competitive advantage. 1995 Handbook of Business Strategy. B. Voss and D. Willey (eds.). London: Faulkner & Gray, 1995, pp. 42–54.

11. For a comprehensive examination of this approach see: Ludwig von Bertalanffy. General Systems Theory. New York: George Braziller, 1968. For an exploration of the application of General Systems Theory in the context of strategic management, see: Alan Walter Steiss. Strategic Management and Organizational Decision Making. Lexington, MA: D.C. Heath and Company, 1985, Chapter 2.

12. Warren G. Bennis, Kenneth D. Benne, and Robert Chin (eds.). The Planning of Change. New York: Holt, Rinehart and Winston, 1969.

13. Fred Nickols. Change Management 101: A Primer. (www.home.att.net/~nickols/change.net)

14. Jack Duncan. Management. New York: Random House, 1983, pp. 381–390.

15. Peter F. Drucker. Management: Tasks, Responsibilities, Practices. New York: Harper & Row, 1974.

16. Alfred D. Chandler in his book, Strategy and Structure, Cambridge: MIT Press, 1962, provided the fundamental work on this relationship through his in-depth study of modern organization in pioneering American companies.

17. Peter F. Drucker. The information executives truly need. Harvard Business Review. January-February 1995, pp. 54–62.

18. H. Igor Ansoff. Strategic management of technology. Journal of Business Strategy. Vol. 7, No. 3, Winter 1987, p. 38.

19. John M. Bryson. Strategic Planning for Public and Nonprofit Organizations. San Francisco, CA.: Jossey-Bass Publishers, 1995, p. 175.

20. Jay Marshall and Daryl R. Conner. Another reason why companies resist change. Strategy & Business Briefs. New York: Booz-Allen & Hamilton, 1999.

21. John M. Bryson. Strategic Planning for Public and Nonprofit Organizations. San Francisco, CA.: Jossey-Bass Publishers, 1995, p. 177.

22. Richard M. Cyert and James G. March. A Behavioral Theory of the Firm. Englewood Cliffs, N.J.: Prentice-Hall, 1963, pp. 124–125.

23. Gordon W. Allport and L. Postman. The basic psychology of rumor. In The Process and Effects of Mass Communication, edited by W. Schramm. Urbana: University of Illinois Press, 1954, pp. 146–148.

24. Eileen Wolfe. Human management: The achilles heel of business process reengineering. Enterprise Reengineering. September, 1995.

25. Erik Brynjolfsson, Amy Austin Renshaw, and Marshall van Alstyne. The Matrix of Change: A Tool for Business Process Reengineering. Cambridge, MA: MIT Sloan School of Management, 1997.

26. Michael Gallivan, J. Debrah Hofman, and Wanda Orlikowski. Implementing Radical Change: Gradual versus rapid pace. Vancouver, B.C.: Association of Computing Machinery, 1994.

27. D. Leonard-Barton. Implementation characteristics of organizational innovation: Limits and opportunities for management strategies. Communication Research, Vol. 15, 1988.

28. John M. Bryson. Strategic Planning for Public and Nonprofit Organizations. San Francisco, CA.: Jossey-Bass Publishers, 1995, pp. 177, 183–185.

10

Organization Control

Some form of control has been exercised for as long as formal organizations have existed. However, increased emphasis on accountability, efficiency, and effectiveness in both the public and private sectors has made the adoption of more effective control techniques even more imperative.

1 ORGANIZATION CONTROL DEFINED

As Peter Drucker so clearly articulated, the terms "controls" and "control" have altogether different meanings in the context of social institutions.

> The synonyms for controls are measurement and information. The synonym for control is direction. Controls pertain to means, control to an end. Controls deal with facts, that is, with events of the past. Control deals with expectations, that is, with the future. Controls are analytical, concerned with what was and is. Control is normative and concerned with what ought to be [1].

A system of controls should provide tools for determining whether an organization is proceeding toward established objectives and should alert decision makers when actual performance deviates from the planned performance. These procedures should also help to measure the magnitude of the deviations and to

283

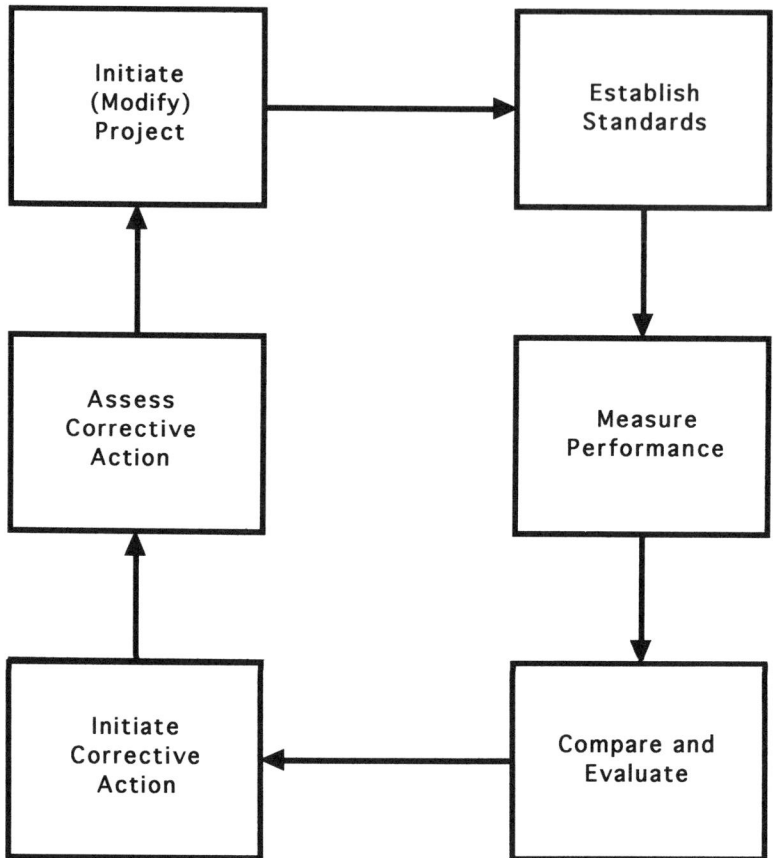

FIGURE 10.1   Organization control cycle.

identify appropriate corrective actions to bring the activities back on course. A system of controls involves six interrelated activities, as shown in Figure 10.1.

1.1   A Hierarchy of Controls

Drucker asserted that, since organizational controls involve the measurement and analysis of events, they can neither be objective nor neutral. Events selected to be measured (that is, to be "controlled") are considered to be of importance to the organization and, therefore, they acquire value. Controls "endow events not only with meaning but with value. And this means that the basic question is not 'How do we control?' but 'What do we measure in our control system [2]?'"

Thus, the controls that an organization develops and applies should be linked in some fashion to its mission, purpose, goals, and objectives—that is, should be an integral part of the organization's strategic thinking and management.

Organizational controls must focus on results—on the consequences of processes and program activities. Many of these results occur outside of the organization in the broader environment in which it operates. Measuring these results often is concerned with the *effectiveness* of the organization's strategies, processes, and programs. It may be relatively easy to record and therefore to quantify the *efficiency* with which an organization operates (in relation to the costs incurred). It is much more difficult, however, to measure effects. As a consequence, control systems tend to be built on internal measures of efficiency. The increased data processing capacity of contemporary information systems introduces a very real danger that large quantities of data regarding measures of efficiency will be generated to the point where more critical issues of effectiveness are completely overlooked.

Organizational controls must also deal with nonmeasurable events. Measurable events, for the most part, are things that have happened in the past. Events that are not amendable to measurement often are those which have not yet occurred and for which it is only possible to make assumptions. Assumptions establish parameters within which results will be deemed appropriate and acceptable as the events unfold. Therefore, a critical ingredient of any system of organizational controls is the clear and comprehensive identification of the assumptions upon which strategic decisions are based.

Drucker identified seven specifications that an organizational control system must satisfy (see Table 10.1). These characteristics, coupled with the need to focus on both measurable and nonmeasurable results, suggest that a hierarchy of controls must exist within an organization to parallel and compliment the hierarchy of objectives outlined in Chapter 1.

1.2 Strategic Controls

Strategic controls are used to evaluate the overall performance of an organization or a significant component of that performance. In the private sector, standards such as profitability, ratio of assets to liabilities, sales growth, and return on investment provide a broad basis on which to assess the overall performance of an organization. In recent years, standards applicable to public sector activities have been detailed in terms of *measures of effectiveness*.

When organizations fail to meet such broad strategic control standards, the remedies may need to be equally broad. They may include the recasting of goals and objectives, reformulating plans and programs, changes in organizational structure, improved internal and external communications, and so on. Strategic controls should assist decision makers in identifying when unanticipated changes

TABLE 10.1   Specifications for Controls

1. *Control is a principle of economy.* The fewer the controls, the more effective they will be. Adding more controls does not give better control. All it does is create confusion.

2. *Controls must be meaningful.* Events to be measured must be significant either in themselves or must be symptoms of at least potentially significant developments. Controls should always be related to key objectives and priorities.

3. *Controls must be appropriate to the character and nature of the phenomena measured.* The measures selected must have formal validity and statistical reliability. But more importantly, they must be measuring the right things.

4. *Measurements must be congruent with the events measured.* It is important to avoid the trap of false precision: to know when an approximation is more accurate than a precise-looking figure worked out in great detail. Qualitative descriptions of phenomena often are more accurate (and more rigorous) than any specific figures.

5. *Controls must be timely.* The time dimension of controls should correspond to the time span of the event being measured. Frequent measurement and rapid "feedback" do not necessarily give better control. "Real time" often is the wrong time span for real control.

6. *Controls need to be simple.* Complicated controls tend to confuse and to misdirect attention from what is to be controlled toward the mechanics and methods of control. Controls that are overly complex and contain ambiguities and subtleties seldom work.

7. *Controls must be operational.* Controls must focus on action and must fall within the realm of responsibility of those individuals who are capable of taking the controlling action.

Source: Peter F. Drucker. Management: Tasks, Responsibilities, Practices. New York: Harper & Row, 1974, pp. 498–504.

occur in the broader environment and in determining appropriate corrective actions.

In addition to monitoring the results of past decisions (through financial measures), strategic controls should include measures of the organization's ability to build competitive advantages in terms of efficiency, quality of service, innovation, and responsiveness to customers (measures of future performance). As Hill and Jones observed,

> Strategic control is not just monitoring how well an organization and its members are achieving current goals or about how well the firm is utilizing its existing resources. It is also about keeping employees motivated, focused on the important problems confronting an organization now and in the future, and working together to find solutions that can help an organization perform better over time [3].

A system of strategic controls should provide a basis by which goals and objectives can be modified and the methods of control can be enhanced to achieve increased productivity and overall effectiveness.

1.3 Management Controls

Large amounts of data may be required to achieve effective strategic control. Therefore, the application of management controls to continuously monitor activities may be more appropriate to ensure that corrective action is taken on a timely basis. Management controls involve the measurement and evaluation of program activities to determine if policies and objectives are being accomplished as efficiently and effectively as possible. Management controls provides the basic structure for coordinating the day-to-day activities of an organization, encompassing all those activities involved in ensuring that the organization's resources are appropriately used in the pursuit of its goals and objectives.

Accounting and finance departments traditionally have served as the primary locus of the management control functions in most organizations. An accounting system is designed primarily to serve the requirements for external financial reporting as well as the needs of internal fiscal decision making. Accounting data can also provide a significant component in a contemporary control system to monitor performance. Output from the accounting system, for example, can provide managers with important measures to assist in determining if the decisions made and actions taken have led to the desired results.

Management controls are often designed to anticipate and identify problems before they happen. An obvious approach is to attempt to anticipate possible deviations from some established standards or criteria of performance—the basic objective of statistical quality controls. This "feed forward" approach also can be applied as a budgetary control. The possibility that a major expenditure might exceed the budget allocation, for example, should be ascertained before-the-fact rather than after the funds have been spent. Such controls involve various forecasting and projection techniques.

1.4 Operational Controls

Operational controls seek to ensure that specific tasks or activities are carried out efficiently and in compliance with established policies. These controls involve a determination of program resource requirements and the order of commitment necessary to achieve specific program objectives. It sometimes is difficult to distinguish between management controls and operational controls. Techniques used initially for management control may become even more significant when converted to operational control purposes.

Operational controls focus on specific responsibilities for carrying out those tasks identified at the strategic and management control levels. These controls must provide management with the ability to consider the costs of other program alternatives in dollars and time, and to establish criteria for resource allocation and scheduling. They also provide a basis for evaluating the accuracy of estimates and the effects of change. Data regarding program activities can be assimilated and revised or updated operational plans can be communicated.

Operational controls often are very specific and situation-oriented. They measure day-to-day performance by providing comparisons with various criteria to determine areas that require more immediate corrective actions. Productivity ratios, workload measures, and unit costs are examples of such performance measures. Such measures are concerned most frequently with issues of efficiency and economy.

The balance of this chapter will be devoted to a discussion of the origins and applications of management and operational controls. The development and exercise of strategic controls will be discussed in further detail in Chapter 11.

2 ACCOUNTING SYSTEMS: BASIS FOR MANAGEMENT CONTROLS

The role of accounting in the public sector is expanding as a consequence of the increased attention in recent years to the need for greater economy, efficiency, and effectiveness in the operations of government. There is growing recognition that, in addition to the functions of financial record keeping and external reporting, accounting can and should serve as a tool for planning, decision making, and control.

2.1 Financial Accounting

Accounting data form the basis for much of the financial analysis conducted in complex organizations. Although accounting data may be used as a basis for future plans (e.g., for budget building), financial accounts are concerned primarily with the historical results of fiscal transactions and the financial position of the organizational entity.

Numbers connote precision, and precision is often assumed to have its own virtue. However, it is important to bear in mind that the numbers provided in balance sheets and income statements are condensed from many detailed accounting records and reports. Therefore, any further analyses based on these data must be undertaken with full awareness of the abstractions that have already been made. While accounting data reflect important fiscal dimensions, other important factors that impinge on the overall performance of the organization must also be considered. Accounting data do not reflect factors that are more difficult to measure, such as the quality of the services being delivered or the overall performance of the service delivery agents. Measures of performance—

such as customer satisfaction or accommodation of client needs—can only be indirectly reflected in balance sheet and other financial statements.

The basic financial accounting equation can be expressed as follows:

$$\text{Assets} = \text{Liabilities} + \text{Fund Equity} + \text{Revenue} - \text{Expense}$$

For-profit entities seek to generate net income. Public and nonprofit organizations strive to "break even"—that is, to balance revenues and expenses.

In dealing with public organizations, the basic accounting equation must be changed to show expenditures instead of expense. An *expense* is a resource consumed during the accounting period—once written off as an expense, the resource has expired as an asset. An *expenditure*, on the other hand, is an amount of cash spent (or to be spent) during the accounting period. Since government funds usually do not include long-term assets or liabilities, expenditures (and not expense) are measured in these accounts. In addition, there is no owner's equity as such in governmental funds. Instead, the residual portion of the equation would be the *fund equity* or *fund balance*. Thus, the equation for governmental funds would read:

$$\text{Current Assets} = \text{Current Liabilities} + \text{Fund Balance}$$
$$+ \text{Revenue} - \text{Expenditures}$$

Key concepts in financial accounting for public and nonprofit organizations are defined in Table 10.2.

2.2 Fund Accounting

Fund accounting provides the primary mechanisms for the control of governmental activities. In the private sector, the accounting entity often is related to the legal organization—the corporation, partnership, or individual proprietorship. Within public and nonprofit organizations, other accounting entities, called funds, are established for the purposes of maintaining records and preparing financial statements. A *fund* is an independent accounting and fiscal entity to which resources are assigned, together with all related liabilities, obligations, reserves, and equities. Financial transactions are made between funds. Separate financial statements are prepared for each of the major funds, and combined statements of funds with similar purposes often are distributed. Standard fund designations frequently applied in local governments are shown in Table 10.3.

Revenues are controlled through an appropriation process, whereby public agencies are authorized to incur financial commitments based on the estimated revenues to be collected. Proposed expenditures are controlled through line items in the budget. Expenditures for any line item (such as salaries, supplies and

TABLE **10.2**   Basic Accounting Vocabulary

Accounting entity is an independent fiscal, accounting, and often legal entity to which all resources and related liabilities, obligations, reserves, and equities are assigned.

Financial statements are prepared for each of the major government funds, which represent the accounting entities of public organizations, and combined statements of funds with similar purposes often are distributed.

An *income statement* reflects the profit performance of an entity for some specific period of time.

Revenue represents an inflow of money and/or other representations of value in return for selling goods or providing some type of service. In the public sector, revenue is the equity in resources (other than proceeds from bond issues or transfers from other funds) that is received during the fiscal period and is available to be spent in that fiscal period.

Expense represents an outflow of resources, or incurring of obligations, for goods and services required to generate revenues.

Expenditures are the resources that are expended during the fiscal year; management must make certain that the funds appropriated/allocated to an agency or program are not overspent, or over committed for expenditure, during that fiscal period.

Net income is the excess of revenue over expense.

Assets represent the amount of resources available to the entity and may be in the form of actual cash on hand, amounts owed to the entity by others, equipment and facilities, or other things of value owned by the entity. Only those assets that can be converted into cash in a relatively short period of time—no more than one year—are included in governmental funds.

Liabilities represent obligations and debts. In governmental funds, liabilities include only those commitments that would be paid in cash in a relatively short period of time.

A *balance sheet* shows the financial position of an entity at a particular time—resources available (assets) and liabilities outstanding (obligations and debts).

Equity is equal to the assets minus the liabilities of an entity. Claims for amounts due to creditors and employees (such as salaries payable) have legal priority.

Owner's equity (sometimes called net worth, capital, or proprietorship) represents the residual interest in the entity after various obligations have been deducted. In governmental accounting, the concept of fund equity is substituted for owner's equity.

Fund balance is the difference between assets and liabilities and is determined by the excess of revenue over expenditures during the current or prior fiscal year.

A *trial balance* offers proof that a ledger is in balance, but it does not verify that transactions have been correctly analyzed and recorded in the proper accounts.

Source: Alan Walter Steiss, Financial Management in Public Organizations. Belmont, CA: Brooks/Cole Publishing Company, 1989, Chapter 2.

TABLE **10.3**   Standard Fund Designations

General fund is used to account for all financial resources, and activities financed by them, that are not accounted for in some special fund.

Special revenue funds are used to account for taxes and other revenues (except special assessments) that are legally restricted for a particular purpose.

Debt service funds account for the financing of interest and the retirement of principal of general long-term debt.

Capital project funds account for those capital projects that are financed either on a "pay-as-you-go" basis or out of capital reserves, grants-in-aid, or transfers from other funds.

Special assessment funds are established to account for special assessments levied to finance improvements or services deemed to benefit properties or individuals against which the assessments are levied.

Enterprise funds are established to account for the financing of services rendered primarily to the general public for compensation.

Internal service funds (working capital funds) are established to account for the financing of activities or services carried on by one department for other departments of the same governmental unit.

Trust and agency funds account for cash and other assets held by a governmental unit as trustee or agent (for example, employee pension funds).

Source: Alan Walter Steiss and Emeka O. Cyprian Nwagwu. Financial Planning and Management in Public Organizations. New York: Marcel Dekker, Inc. 2001, p. 27.

materials, equipment, contractual services, or travel), cannot exceed the dollar amount that has been appropriated or allocated to that particular expenditure category.

A new "model" for state and local government financial reporting has been developed by the Governmental Accounting Standards Board (GASB) in an effort to make annual financial statements easier to understand and more useful to those who rely on this information to make decisions. The new GASB guidelines, released in June, 1999, change the way financial information is communicated to legislative oversight bodies, creditors, citizens, bond rating organizations, the media, and anyone else interested in how a government is doing financially. Annual financial statements must include an analysis, in narrative form, of the jurisdiction's financial activities during the fiscal year, including information about the full cost of providing government services and supporting public buildings, bridges and roads. The guidelines require that *full accrual accounting* be used to prepare financial statements for all government activities—not just those for which costs are covered by charging a fee for services, as was previously required. Accrual accounting also reports all of the revenues and costs of providing services each year, not just those received or paid in the current year. This new approach to financial reporting provides much more useful information to those interested in the "big picture" of public finances [4].

2.3 Budgetary Accounting

The emphasis on budgetary control is a major distinction between governmental accounting and for-profit accounting. The adoption of a budget by the governing body represents the legal authority to spend. In most cases, actual expenditures should closely coincide with budgetary appropriations—the budget should serve as both a mandate for and a limitation on spending. Appropriations may be subdivided according to agencies, programs, and classes of expenditures. These subdivisions, known as *allocations*, become the first accounting entries for the new fiscal period. Allocations may be made to specific line items or object codes, and specific limitations may be imposed as to the deviations permitted within these expenditure categories.

Provision also may be made for an *allotment system*, through which allocations are further subdivided into time elements—for example, monthly allotments for personal services (salaries, wages, and fringe benefits). Allotments are particularly useful where expenditures are contingent on future events, such as the availability of state or federal grants, or the initiation of a new program or the anticipated opening of a new facility. Allotment procedures that require monthly approvals by the governing body, however, can become cumbersome, generate operational uncertainties, and may result in false economies.

Good budgetary accounting provides for *encumbrances* to record the placement of purchase orders or the letting of contracts as an obligation against the agency's allocation. By reserving a part of the allocation (or appropriation), the agency is prevented from overspending funds available during any fiscal period. In some cases, specific allocations are encumbered and liquidated on an "as-billed" basis.

For budgetary accounting, four new items must be added to the accounting equation. *Estimated revenue* is the amount of revenue anticipated above current assets that can be used as expendable resources for the fiscal period. *Appropriations* are the amounts of estimated resources provided by the governing body for expenditure during the period and should be included on the liability and fund balance side of the equation. *Encumbrances* are used to obligate amounts for goods and services ordered but not yet received. Encumbrances are subtracted (shown as a minus figure) from the liability and fund balance side of the equation, just as are expenditures. The *reserve for encumbrances* is used to allocate a portion of the appropriations for the goods and services ordered but not yet received, and is shown as an addition to the fund balance side of the equation. Thus, the expanded equation is:

$$\text{Assets} + \text{Estimated Revenue} = \text{Liabilities} + \text{Fund Balance} + \text{Revenue}$$
$$- \text{Expenditures} + \text{Appropriations}$$
$$+ \text{Reserve for Encumbrances}$$
$$- \text{Encumbrances}$$

Financial accounting is concerned primarily with the accurate and objective recording of fiscal transactions and with the preparation of financial reports largely for external distribution. Although these traditional outputs of financial accounting may be used to guide certain types of internal decisions, many management decisions must be based on other types of information. In recent years, the techniques of managerial and cost accounting have been developed and refined to fulfill this need. Linkages among these accounting systems and other critical components of the strategic management process are illustrated in Figure 10.2.

3 COST ACCOUNTING

Cost accounting involves the assembly and recording of elements of expense incurred to attain a purpose, to carry out an activity, operation, or program, to complete a project or other unit of work, or to do a specific job. As such, its supports the objectives of both financial accounting and managerial accounting. Cost accounting systems can be found in both profit and nonprofit organizations and in both product- and service-oriented entities. Cost allocation methods provide a means for accumulating and determining the necessary costs of the service or product. The expense of obtaining cost data must be maintained at a reasonable level, and cost allocations should not go beyond the point of practical application for more efficient and effective operations.

3.1 Measurement of Costs

A basic objective of cost accounting is to identify and measure costs incurred in achieving some program goal or objective. Several approaches to the measurement of costs may be relevant, however, depending on the informational needs of management (see Table 10.4).

Full costing, for example, attempts to delineate all costs associated with some operation or activity. In the governmental and nonprofit areas, full costs often are called *program costs*. Patient care costs, for instance, involve hospital room costs, meals, laundry, drugs, surgery, therapy, and other items that are more or less directly attributable to the patient. But what about admission and

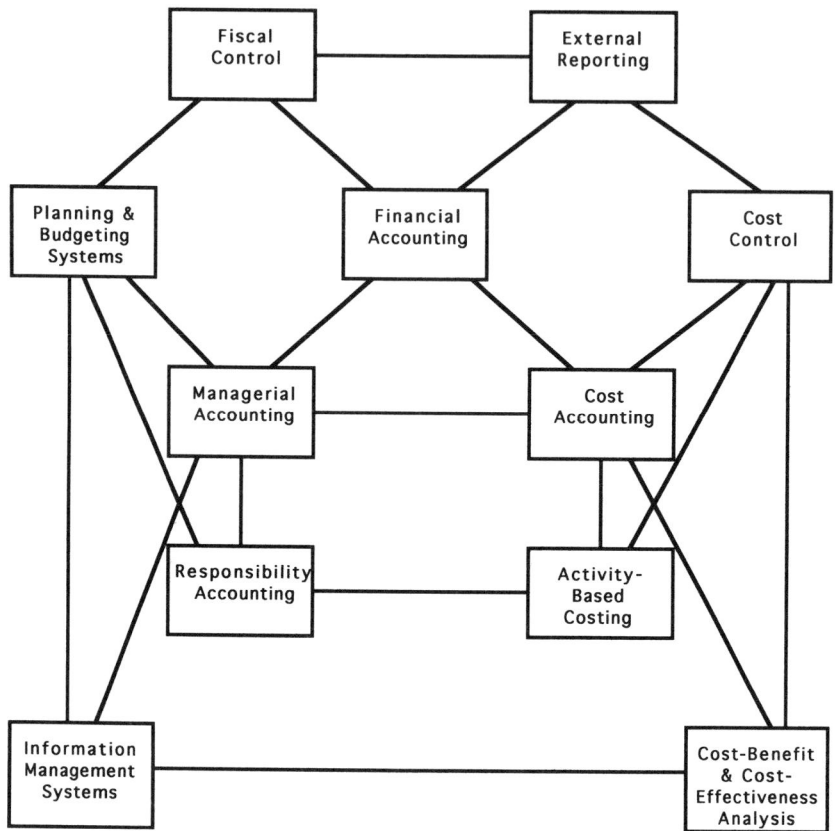

FIGURE 10.2   Accounting system linkages.

discharge costs, nursery care, or heat, light, and other utilities? Several problems may be encountered in considering all the fixed and variable costs associated with particular activities unless an accrual accounting system has been adopted to track these costs over several fiscal periods [5].

One of the more controversial aspects of the full-costing approach is the method of assigning overhead or indirect costs to operating departments. Overhead includes the cost of various items that cannot conveniently be charged directly to those activities or operations that are benefited. General administrative expenses illustrate this concept of overhead or indirect costs. It can be argued, for example, that the cost of a personnel department, an accounting department, and other service or auxiliary units should be assigned in some fashion to an organization's operating departments. By the same logic, utility costs, building

TABLE 10.4 Cost Accounting Terminology

Absorption or full costing: Considers all fixed and variable costs associated with the provision of the goods or services in question.

Actual overhead costs: Typically are recorded by means of an overhead clearing account and some type of subsidiary record, such as a departmental expense analysis or overhead cost sheet.

Allocated or applied overhead (indirect costs): Distributed through the use of predetermined rates.

Average unit costs: Determined by dividing accumulated costs by the quantities produced during the period; can then be multiplied by the number of units transferred to obtain applicable total costs.

Direct costing: Considers only the variable or incremental costs of a particular operation.

Job order costing: Used by companies in which products are readily identifiable by individual units or batches.

Overhead: Includes the cost of various items that cannot conveniently be charged directly to those jobs or operations that are benefited.

Process costing: Often found in industries characterized by the mass production of like units, which usually pass in continuous fashion through a series of uniform production steps called operations or processes.

Responsibility costing: Assigns to an operating department only those costs that its managers can control or at least influence.

Standard costs: Relate the cost of production to some predetermined indices of operational efficiency to provide a means of cost control through the application of variance analysis.

Unit costs: Often determined simply by dividing the current budget allocation for a given activity by the number of performance units.

Workload measures: Focus on time-and-effort indices such as number of persons served per hour, yards of dirt moved per day, or more generally, volume of activity per unit of time.

Source: Alan Walter Steiss. Financial Management in Public Organizations. Belmont, CA: Brooks/Cole Publishing Company, 1989, Chapter 3.

maintenance costs, depreciation, and so on should also be assigned to specific operating units. These indirect costs are often distributed (pro-rated) on a formula basis, as determined by the number of personnel hours, labor costs, or total direct costs associated to each activity or operation. The allocation of some of these indirect costs may appear to be fairly arbitrary because they cannot be traced directly to the individual organizational units.

Assume, for example, that the total annual cost of a public health clinic is $3 million, of which $2 million can be identified as direct cost. The ratio of direct to indirect cost, therefore, is 2 to 1, or for every $1 of direct costs incurred, the clinic records $0.50 of indirect costs. If the direct cost associated with the prenatal health care program of the clinic were $250,000, then prorated indirect cost would be $125,000 and the full cost of this program would be $375,000.

Many indirect costs are clearly beyond the control of the managers of the operating programs or departments, however. In recognition of this fact, *responsibility costing* assigns to an operating unit only those costs that its managers can control, or at least influence. Many argue that this approach is the only appropriate measure of the financial stewardship of an operating manager.

A useful approach to cost accounting is to consider only the variable or *incremental costs* of a particular activity or operation. For example, a city manager might want to know how much it would cost to increase the frequency of trash collection from once to twice a week, or how much extra it would cost to keep the community's public swimming pools open evenings. The management of any organization that delivers a service on some regularly scheduled basis might raise the same type of questions. This approach, called *direct costing*, is relatively easy to associate with an organization's budget. Direct costing can be very helpful in making incremental commitments of resources.

Process costing is most often found in organizations characterized by the production of like units, which usually pass in continuous fashion through a series of uniform production steps called operations or processes. Departments (often identified by the operations or processes for which they are responsible) accumulate costs, with attention focused on the total costs for a given period in relation to the number of units processed. *Average unit costs* may be determined by dividing accumulated department costs by the quantities produced during the period. The unit costs for various operations can then be multiplied by the number of units produced or transferred to obtain total costs. Process costing creates relatively few accounting problems in those instances where this approach can be applied to various types of service organizations, including public agencies and nonprofit organizations. However, this method cannot be used to determine cost differences in individual products or outputs.

Unit costs often can be determined for many activities simply by dividing total program costs for a given period by the number of persons served (or tons of trash collected, number of inspections made, miles of road patrolled, or some other applicable measure of the volume of activity during some fiscal period). It is important to reduce unit costs to some measure that can be applied consistently over a variety of situations, however. Remember the eight grade algebra problem: "If a farmer and a half can plow a field and a half in a day and a half at a cost of $75, how much will it cost to plow 200 acres, assuming that the farmer's field is 10 acres?" First it is necessary to determine how much it costs to plow one acre. The farmer can plow a ten-acre field in one day at a cost of $50. Therefore, it costs $5 an acre, and to plow 200 acres would cost $1,000.

This classic problem illustrates one of the dilemmas frequently encountered in developing unit costs: Is it important to consider the number of persons carrying out the task or delivering the service? If it takes two people three hours to paint a flagpole, should unit costs be expressed in terms of both individuals? Or should the costs be translated into an hourly cost, since some flagpoles may be higher than others and, consequently, may take more time to paint? This question must be considered and carefully resolved for each situation for which unit costs are being developed. There are no hard-and-fast rules by which this determination can be made other than the logic of consistency.

In some public programs, unit costs are often determined simply by dividing the current budget allocation for a given activity by the number of performance units. If the annual budget of the welfare department is $2 million and the caseload is 5,000, then the "unit cost" is $400 per case. This approach may produce rather misleading results, however, since important variables that may influence the cost of providing agency services may be masked by such an aggregate method. Therefore, it may be appropriate to further subdivide the case load into more detailed categories—for example, by various client groups, by the relative ease (or difficulty) various services are delivered, by the level of staff skills or other resources required to handle the cases, and so on.

Budgetary appropriations may not always be a good measure of current expenses, since encumbrances for items not yet received may be included in such allocations. At the same time, expenditures to cover outstanding encumbrances from the preceding fiscal period may be excluded. Even if costs are limited to expenditures, current unit costs may be over stated if new capital equipment is included in the expenditures or if there is a large increase in inventories. Conversely, in many organizations, unit costs may be understated because of a failure to account for the drawing down of inventories or for depreciation (or user costs) of equipment.

Each activity should be examined in terms of the cost components that go to make up the total cost. In some cases, it may be appropriate to determine a unit cost for each component—personnel, materials and supplies, equipment, and so forth. These costs are then summed in the appropriate mix to determine an aggregate unit cost for the particular activity or task.

3.2 Cost Allocation

Cost allocation is necessary whenever the full cost of a service or product must be determined. The variable, fixed, direct, and indirect cost components must be considered in making these allocations. Examples of this requirement in the public sector include the costing of governmental grants and contracts, the establishment of equitable public utility rates, or the setting of user rates for internal service units expected to operate on a "break-even" basis (that is, recover full costs). This approach also may be appropriate in determining service fees (such as for inspections, processing of licenses and permits, use of public recreational facilities, and so forth). Many public agencies do not fully recover the actual costs of providing a service through the fees charged. Often the fee structure is not updated frequently enough to reflect the actual costs incurred.

Variable costs directly associated with a given service or activity usually do not present an allocation problem. As a rule, such costs can be measured and assigned to appropriate programs or activities that generate such expenses. As additional units of work are undertaken, variable costs usually increase in some predictable and measurable fashion.

A given organizational unit may also experience direct fixed costs (such as rent or utility costs). The allocation of such costs to specific services or projects can be more problematic, however, since these direct costs do not vary with the activities being measured. They might be allocated by assuming some level of operation, such as number of persons to be served. The total annual cost can then be divided by the estimated level of activity to arrive at a unit rate. In other instances, direct fixed costs may have to be allocated on the basis of some arbitrary physical measure, such as the floor space occupied by various activities. In either case, it is important that costs are allocated on a fully accrued basis to avoid the problem of encumbrances.

In determining full unit costs, it is important to allocate to the various departments or programs those costs that are identified as direct to the total organization. This cost allocation represents a major problem, however. The salaries of various administrative and support personnel in a hospital, for example, are direct costs to the hospital as a whole. When allocated to various separate departments or service functions—such as the intensive care unit, nursery, surgery, cafeteria, laboratories, and other components of the hospital—these administrative and support salaries become indirect costs to these operating units. Although often arbitrary, the basis for such allocations should be reasonable and should be based on services provided to these related units.

3.3 Indirect Cost Pools

One approach to the allocation of indirect costs involves the identification of a number of indirect cost pools. Each pool represents the full costs associated with some specific administrative or support function that cannot be allocated directly to individual projects or activities. Examples of these indirect cost pools include the operation and maintenance of the physical plant (including utility costs); general building and equipment usage (depreciation); central stores, motor pool, computing center, or other internal service units; and central administrative functions (financial management, purchasing, personnel, and so forth). Some costs associated with internal service units often can be assigned directly as operating units draw upon these services (e.g., when materials and supplies are drawn from central stores). Indirect costs often represent the "fixed" costs of these service units (that is, the basic cost of having the services available).

Once the indirect cost pools have been identified, they can be arrayed from the most general to the most specific with regard to the particular programs or activities for which indirect cost rates are to be established. Costs from the more general pools are allocated (or stepped down) to the more specific pools and, finally, to the primary functions or activities of the organization.

Of the eight indirect cost pools shown in Table 10.5, the equipment use allowance (depreciation) and operation, and maintenance pool are "stepped down" to each of the other pools, as well as having distributions to the four primary functions of the organization. The computing center and general administration pools include distributions to the remaining four pools as well as to the primary functions. An indirect cost rate is determined by dividing the total direct costs associated with a given program or activity into the total indirect costs allocated to that primary function. Of the total indirect costs of $525,539, for example, $136,638 is attributed to primary function #3, which, in turn, accounted for $267,800 in direct costs. Therefore, the indirect cost rate for this function of the organization is 51% (i.e., $136,638 divided by $267,800). It is possible through this method to determine the impact of changes in these indirect costs on the full costs of individual programs, projects, or activities.

Under- or over-application of indirect costs may develop when predetermined rates are used, and significant differences may arise from month to month. However, if the cost allocation methods have produced reliable estimates, these accumulated differences should become relatively insignificant by the end of the fiscal year.

3.4 Posting to Cost Accounts

Procedural steps for summarizing and posting data to cost accounts are outlined in Figure 10.3. Field reports provide the primary record of work performed and expenses incurred. The particular design and maintenance of such reports often depends on local circumstances. A job ordering system may be installed, for example, to monitor and record the costs for street maintenance. A crew foreman or project supervisor may prepare the field report. Or it may be desirable to have each employee prepare a daily or weekly "time and effort report," indicating specific work assignments and the time spent on each operation. Supervisory personnel provide separate bills of materials used and statements of equipment used for each job or operation. Field reports should be summarized before posting to job cost sheets or work and cost ledgers.

TABLE 10.5   Step-Down Method for Determining Indirect Costs

Indirect cost pool	Operations & maintenance	Computing center	General administration	Personnel	Financial management
Use allowance (depreciation)	5,255	7,883	788	158	263
Operations & maintenance	145,992	19,970	5,255	4,204	4,887
Computing center		69,895	263	5,255	7,883
General administration			56,494	2,628	3,153
Personnel				60,751	158
Financial management					58,597
Other internal service units					
Commuity relations	————	————	————	————	————
TOTAL	151,248	97,749	62,801	72,996	74,941
Direct costs					
Indirect cost rate					

The information gathered through these field reports serves several purposes. Reports used to determine the cost of labor entering into each operation or job can provide a basis for payroll preparation (a general accounting function). Daily reports by equipment operators provide summaries of the pro-rated costs (equipment rental charges) to be distributed to the various jobs on the cost ledger. These reports can also be used to post individual equipment records (showing, for each piece of equipment, the expenses for labor, gasoline, oil, and other supplies, repair costs, overhead, and depreciation). Materials and supplies reports indicate stores withdrawn from stockrooms, providing credit to central stores accounts, as well as charges to operating costs accounts.

Many indirect costs can be reported in substantially the same manner as direct costs—from time reports, store records, and so forth. Certain indirect costs can also be determined from invoices on such items as travel expenses, utility services, and general office expenses. These indirect costs are initially posted to an overhead cost sheet and then allocated to jobs and activities on some predetermined basis.

The job cost sheet is the final assemblage of the information with respect to all work performed and all costs incurred. Accounts in the work and cost ledger are generally posted monthly and closed upon completion of a specific job or at the end of the regular accounting period, when unit costs on an activity or program are recorded.

Monthly summary statements of work completed, expenses, unit costs, and employee-hour production can readily be compiled from data on the job cost sheets. Other statements may be prepared periodically, according to management needs, on such subjects as total labor costs, employee productivity, equipment

Other service units	Community relations	Primary function #1	Primary function #2	Primary function #3	Primary function #4	TOTAL
4,204	53	8,987	14,379	11,683	9,885	44,933
10,511	1,314	21,021	33,634	27,328	23,123	105,106
5,255	1,577	15,503	24,805	20,154	17,053	77,516
10,511	1,051	9,092	14,547	11,819	10,001	45,458
1,051	53	14,347	22,955	18,651	15,782	71,735
10,511	53	12,875	20,601	16,738	14,163	64,377
50,766	53	18,551	29,682	24,117	20,406	92,756
	19,699	4,730	7,568	6,149	5,203	23,649
92,809	23,851	105,106	168,170	136,638	115,617	525,530
		250,200	317,330	267,800	240,850	1,076,180
		42.01%	53.00%	51.02%	48.00%	48.83%

rental costs, noneffective time and idle equipment, and loss of supplies through waste or spoilage.

3.5 Standard Costs and Variance Analysis

Standard cost systems have been widely used in the private sector, but have been relatively limited in their government and other nonprofit applications. Nevertheless, such standards have relevance in a number of organizational environments.

Standard costs relate service delivery costs or production to some predetermined indices of operational efficiency. If actual costs vary from these standards, management must determine the reasons for the deviation and whether the costs are controllable or noncontrollable with respect to the responsible unit. Misdirected efforts, inadequate equipment, defective materials, or any one of a number of other factors can be identified and eliminated through a standard cost system. In short, standard costs provide a means of cost control through the application of methods of variance analysis.

In setting up standards, optimal or desired (planned) unit costs and related workload measures are established for each job or activity. After these measures have been established, total variances can be determined by comparing actual results with planned performance. Differences between standard costs and actual costs should then be examined in terms of price, rate, or spending variances. Quantity or efficiency variances can be developed for measured differences between the anticipated and actual volume of activity. Knowledge of differences in terms of cost (price) and volume (efficiency) enables the manager to identify

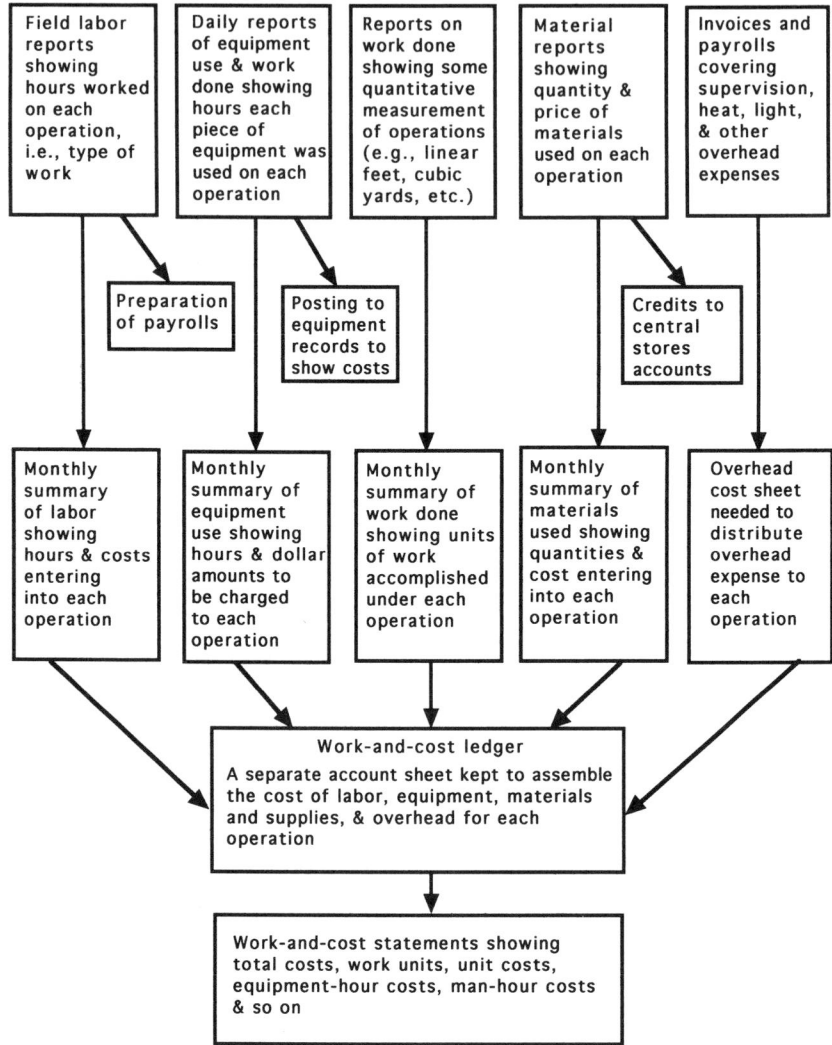

FIGURE 10.3 Posting data to cost accounts.

more clearly the cause and responsibility for significant deviations from planned performance.

There are no hard-and-fast methods for establishing cost standards. Workload and unit cost data from prior years serve as a logical starting point. More detailed studies may be required to determine the quantity and cost of personal services, materials, equipment, and indirect costs associated with particular kinds of effort or volumes of activity. Unit costs can be estimated for each cost element by adjusting trend data for expected changes during the next fiscal period (e.g., anticipated increase in personnel costs as a result of salary increases). Standards should be established for each cost element entering into a given job or operation. These standards can be combined to establish an overall cost standard for the particular type of work, activity category, or program element.

Standard costs should be systematically reviewed and revised when found to be out of line with the prevailing cost conditions. Changes in these standards may be required when new methods are introduced, policies are changed, wage rates or material costs increase, or significant changes occur in the efficiency of operations. Furthermore, standard costs are "local" in their application. Such standards often differ from organization to organization, reflecting different labor conditions, wage rates, service delivery problems, and operation methods. It may be inappropriate, for example, to evaluate regional offices of a state health department using a single standard cost for delivery of key services. Program costs in more rural areas may be higher because of transportation distances, or may be higher in urban areas because of "hard-to-reach" cases.

4 MANAGERIAL ACCOUNTING

A basic objective of managerial accounting is to improve the effectiveness of the management planning and control functions. Management planning depends on the same reporting and control mechanisms that make central oversight possible and decentralized management feasible [5]. Building the planning process on one data base (program analysis) and the mechanism of control on another (financial accounting) places too great a burden on the management system as the intermediary. Managerial accounting involves the formulation of financial estimates of future performance (the planning and budgeting processes) and, subsequently, the analysis of actual performance in relation to those estimates (performance evaluation and control).

4.1 Functions of Managerial Accounting

Managerial accounting is concerned primarily with four basic functions: management planning, cost determination, cost control, and performance evaluation. Significant features of managerial accounting are summarized in Table 10.6.

Managerial accounting provides interpretations of financial data to assist in the planning and control of current and future operations, and in the formulation of policies and decisions. The informational boundaries of managerial accounting are not rigid or predetermined by standards of "generally accepted accounting practices." Financial information often is collected and presented in formats that are completely different from those followed for external report-

TABLE 10.6   Components of Managerial Accounting

Experimentation and innovation are encouraged in the types of management information provided.

Information generated for *planning* and *programming* purposes to establish a better balance with the control function of accounting.

Cost consciousness is increased among operating units through the identification of cost and responsibility centers and the use of performance standards.

Cost analyses facilitate the linkages among management control, program budgeting, and performance auditing.

Emphasis is on *cost estimation* for planning or control purposes, rather than on financial reporting.

Costs are monitored to determine if they are reasonable for the activities performed.

Performance standards (workload and unit cost data) are added to traditional accounting control mechanisms, by which legal compliance and fiscal accountability are evaluated.

Crosswalks of financial data are made to accommodate various external and internal reporting needs.

Source: Alan Walter Steiss and Emeka O. Cyprian Nwagwu. Financial Planning and Management in Public Organizations. New York: Marcel Dekker, Inc., 2001, p. 352.

ing purposes [6]. There is little point in collecting data, however, unless their management value exceeds the cost of data collection.

Strategic managers often need information on a *real-time basis*, that is, as problems occur and opportunities arise. They may be willing to sacrifice some precision to gain currency of data. Therefore, in managerial accounting, approximations often are as useful as (or even more useful than) numbers that are calculated to the last penny. Financial accounting cannot be absolutely precise in spite of the mystique that often surrounds its data. Thus, the difference is actually one of degree.

Although managerial accounting reports contain financial data, much of the information in these reports is nonmonetary (for example, number of employees, number of hours worked, quantities of materials used, and purpose of travel). Managerial accounting also includes estimates and plans for the future of cost centers and responsibility centers, as well as information about the past.

Managerial accounting provides information to program managers to assist in making decisions about the allocation of resources and the exploitation of program opportunities. The success of a decentralized management system depends on an understanding of the rules of the game by managers at the department level, as well as the incentives and expectations that govern the planning and budgeting functions. An important task of managerial accounting is to enlarge the circle of those familiar with the processes of planning, budgeting, and control through the communication of pertinent management information as well as financial data.

Public organizations often must operate under an accounting system developed to satisfy externally imposed legal requirements, rather than to meet their own management needs. A state university, for example, may have to operate under an accounting system that meets the financial reporting requirements of state government. Such an accounting system may track revenue and expenditures on a cash basis and require account closeouts at the end of the fiscal year. Externally funded, sponsored research projects within the university, however, do not operate on a cash basis and do not conveniently match the fiscal year cycle anticipated by the state accounting system. These sponsored programs may produce as much as one-third of the university's total financial resources and may have a multiplicity of reporting requirements not easily served by the state accounting system. Managerial accounting techniques make it possible to "crosswalk" data from the accounting system mandated by the state to formats more applicable to sponsor requirements. Local governments may face similar requirements to crosswalk data when programs are funded by federal grants or from private sources and/or when projects are initiated at times other than the beginning of a fiscal year.

A major focus of managerial accounting is the determination of *component costs*. These costs should be identified before decisions are made regarding the commitment of resources in support of particular objectives or programs. Costs must be evaluated, both in the immediate future and in the long run, and must be weighed against anticipated benefits. Once commitments have been made, costs must be monitored and controlled to ensure that they are appropriate and reasonable for the process and activities performed. And the overall performance of a process, program, activity, or subunit must be evaluated to improve future decisions regarding resource allocations.

The cost categories frequently encountered in managerial accounting are listed and defined in Table 10.7. Many of these cost categories operate in opposing pairs (for example, product and period costs, investment and recurring costs, out-of-pocket and sunk costs).

4.2 Cost Approximation Methods

Cost approximation, or cost estimation, involves efforts to find predictable relationships between a dependent variable (cost) and an independent variable (some relevant activity), so that costs can be estimated over time based on the behavior of the independent variable. This cost function is often represented by the basic equation:

$$y = a + bx$$

TABLE 10.7 Cost Categories Used in Managerial Accounting

Engineered costs are any costs that have an explicit, specified physical relationship with a selected measure of activity. Most variable costs fit this classification. Direct labor and direct material costs are prime examples.

Discretionary costs are fixed costs decided upon by management at the beginning of a budget period as to the maximum amounts to be incurred. Examples include research and development, advertising, employee training programs, and day-care services for employees' children.

Committed costs consist of those fixed costs associated with the physical plant and equipment of the organization. Examples include depreciation, rent, property taxes, and insurance. Salaries of key personnel may also be considered committed costs. Such costs often cannot be reduced without adversely affecting the ability to meet long-range goals.

Product costs are initially identified as part of the inventory on hand. They become expenses only when the inventory is sold.

Period costs are deducted as expenses during a given fiscal period without having been previously classified as product costs (for example, general administrative expenses).

Out-of-pocket costs involve current or upcoming outlays of funds as a result of some decision.

Sunk costs have already been incurred and, therefore, are irrelevant to the current decision-making process. Allocation of costs based on depreciation and amortization schedules are examples of sunk costs.

Marginal costs represent the cost of providing one additional unit of service (or product) over some previous level of activity. An example would be the cost of keeping the library open an extra hour each evening.

Differential costs (or incremental costs) represent the difference in total costs between alternative approaches to providing some product or service.

Opportunity costs involve the maximum return that might have been realized if resources had been committed to an alternative investment; that is, the impact of having to give up one opportunity to select another.

Associated costs are incurred by beneficiaries in using programs or services. An example is the cost incurred by individuals in traveling to a public recreational facility.

Investment costs vary primarily with the size of a particular program or project but not with its duration.

Recurring costs are operating, maintenance, and repair costs that vary with both the size and the duration of a program. Recurring costs may include salaries and wages, equipment maintenance and repair, and materials and supplies.

Life-cycle costs are incurred over the useful life of a facility or duration of a program, including investment costs, research and development costs, operating costs, and maintenance and repair costs.

Source: Alan Walter Steiss and Emeka O. Cyprian Nwagwu. Financial Planning and Management in Public Organizations. New York: Marcel Dekker, Inc. 2001, p. 353.

where y is the dependent variable (cost), x is the independent variable, and a and b are approximations of true (but unknown) parameters. For example, if the cost of inoculating 20 children is \$50, and the cost of inoculating 50 children is \$80, then the fixed costs (a) are \$30 (\$80 − \$50), and the variable costs (b) can be calculated as \$1 per child (\$50 − \$30 = \$20/20 children or \$80 − \$30 = \$50/50 children).

In practice, cost approximations typically are based on three major assumptions.

1. Linear cost functions can be used to approximate nonlinear situations.
2. All costs can be categorized as either fixed or variable within a relevant range.
3. The true cost behavior can be sufficiently explained by one independent variable instead of more than one variable.

Problems of changing price levels, productivity, and technological changes also are assumed away under this approach. The analytical task is to approximate an appropriate slope coefficient (b)—defined as the amount of increase in y for each unit increase in x—and a constant or intercept (a)—defined as the value of y when x is zero. The analyst may use goodness-of-fit tests, ranging from simple scatter diagrams to full-fledged regression analysis, to ensure that the cost function is plausible and that the relationship is credible. The five most commonly applied methods for approximating cost functions are listed in Table 10.8. These methods are not mutually exclusive and frequently are used in tandem to provide cross-checks on assumptions.

Whatever method is used to formulate cost approximations, it is important in managerial accounting to have reasonably accurate and reliable cost predictions. Such cost estimates usually have an important bearing on a number of operational decisions and can be used for planning, budgeting, and control purposes. The division of costs into fixed and variable components (and into engineered, discretionary, and committed categories) highlight major factors that influence costs. Although cost functions usually represent simplifications of underlying true relationships, the use of these methods depends on how sensitive management decisions are to the errors that may be introduced by these simplifications. In some situations, additional accuracy may make little difference in the decision. In other situations, such accuracy may be very significant. Selection of a cost function is often a trade-off between the cost and the value of the information obtained [7].

4.3 Performance Evaluation under Managerial Accounting

Under managerial accounting procedures, performance is often measured by comparing actual costs incurred against a budget allocation. The difference

TABLE **10.8**   Methods for Approximating Cost Functions

Analytic or industrial engineering methods entail a systematic examination of labor, materials, supplies, support services, and facilities—sometimes using time-and-motion studies—to determine physically observable input–output relationships.

Account analysis involves a classification of all relevant accounts into variable or fixed cost categories by observing how total costs behave over several fiscal periods.

High-low methods call for estimations of total costs at two different activity levels, usually at a low point and a high point within the relevant range. The difference in the dependent variable is divided by the difference in the independent variable to estimate the slope of the line represented by *b*.

Visual-fit method is applied by drawing a straight line through the cost points on a scatter diagram, which consists of a plot of various costs experienced at various levels of activity.

Regression methods refer to the measurement of the average amount of change in one variable that is associated with unit increases in the amounts of one or more other variables.

---

between the amount budgeted for a particular activity and the actual cost of carrying out that activity during a given period is defined as a *variance*. Variances may be positive (under budget) or negative (over budget).

Performance data can also be developed for management purposes independent of the budget and control accounts. This kind of performance reporting has been used in the justification of resource requests and in the assessment of cost and work progress where activities are fairly routine and repetitive. Under this approach, units of work are identified, and changes in quantity (and, on occasion, quality) of such units are measured as a basis for analyzing financial requirements. The impact of various levels of service can be tested, and an assessment can be made of changes in the size of the client groups to be served. This approach is built on the assumption that certain fixed costs remain fairly constant regardless of the level of service provided and that certain variable costs change with the level of service or the size of the clientele group served. *Marginal costs* for each additional increment of service provided can be determined through such an approach. With the application of appropriate budgetary guidelines, these costs can then be converted into total cost estimates.

For example, if the annual operating costs of a welfare program is $350,000 and the fixed costs are determined to be $50,000, then the variable costs would be $300,000. If the program in a given year involves 1,000 cases, the variable cost would be $300 per case. If the caseload is expected to increase by 20% in the coming year, then the program's budget should be set at $1,200 \times \$300 = \$360,000 + \$50,000 = \$410,000$.

Variances, budgeted results, and other techniques of managerial accounting are relatively neutral devices. When viewed positively, they can provide managers with significant means of improving future decisions. They can also assist in the delegation of decision responsibility to lower levels within an organization. These techniques, however, are frequently misused as negative management tools, as means of finding fault or placing blame. This negative use stems, in large part, from a misunderstanding of the rationale of managerial accounting.

Passing the buck is an all-too-pervasive tendency in many large organizations. This tendency is supposedly minimized, however, when responsibility is firmly fixed. Nevertheless, a delicate balance must be maintained between the careful delineation of responsibility, on the one hand, and an overly rigid separation of responsibility, on the other. Many activities may fall between the cracks when responsibility is too strictly prescribed. This problem is particularly evident when two or more activities are interdependent. Under such circumstances, responsibility cannot be delegated too far down in the organization, but must be maintained at a level that will ensure co-operation among the units that must interact if the activities are to be carried out successfully.

5 OPERATIONS SCHEDULING AND CONTROL

The timing of costs—that is, when various expenditures will be incurred—often is a critical factor in strategic management decisions. The coordination of the various cost components involved in the conduct of a program or project often requires the orchestration of multiple tasks or activities, carried out by different staff members or work crews, which may have significant interdependencies. Many programs of public and nonprofit organization operate at far less than full efficiency, however, as evidenced by (1) missed deadlines—often because they were unrealistic in light of the scope of work, (2) programs that require substantial time extensions because the anticipated results have not been achieved, and (3) the all-too-familiar practice of dropping items from a project schedule in order to meet overall budget constraints. Much of this continued inefficiency can be attributed to a lack of understanding of and/or confidence in the techniques of operations scheduling and control.

5.1 Three Fundamental Elements

Many activities of public and nonprofit organizations are "process-oriented" and therefore do not result in an "end product" as such. However, most processes of such organizations have some objective that can be held analogous to a project completion; for example, number of cases processed within a given time period;

miles of streets resurfaced annually; or the number of inspections conducted per month. Further, a range of cost and time constraints can be associated with most of these activities. Through effective programming and scheduling, it should be possible for managers to organize these activities in a more optimal manner. Costs can be more clearly defined and controlled, and time constraints can be utilized more effectively. Firmer assurances can be provided that the work will be completed within anticipated schedule deadlines. Assuming that the operations schedule is followed, the time saved by minimizing inefficiencies should enable new and varied activities to be undertaken without appreciably increasing staff size.

If a program or project is to be implemented successfully, three diverse and often contradictory elements must be coordinated in an *operations plan* in order to permit the work to be completed in the "best" time, at the least cost, and with the smallest degree of risk and uncertainty.

1. *Operations:* Things that must be done (tasks, activities, or jobs), each with a sequential relation to other operations and each requiring resources for some time period.
2. *Resources:* Things utilized in a program or project, often reduced to a common standard of cost, but including personnel, equipment, materials, and time.
3. *Constraints:* Conditions imposed by outside factors (i.e., budgetary limits, completion deadlines, availability of staff resources, and inputs from other units).

The primary purpose of an operations plan is to provide a mechanism for the continuous control over the operations of a program or project. An operations plan defines the sequence in which all activities must be performed to complete a given program or project.

Operations scheduling involves determining the calendar dates or times that resources will be utilized in accordance with the total resource capacity assigned to the project or program. Two basic requirements for the development of an effective operations schedule are:

1. The ability to clearly state an operations plan or work program (including the delineation of tasks into specific activities, jobs, or work elements) directed toward one or more defined objectives.
2. The skill to attach cost and other resource requirements or constraints to each activity in the operations plan or work program.

An operations schedule must reflect the availability of resources, the sequence of activities or jobs, the resource requirements, and possible starting times for each activity. An efficient schedule must establish a time period (duration) for each activity with varying levels of resources to be utilized so that the program or project will remain within the limits of peak efficiency. This approach should yield a minimum cost for each activity and, presumably, for the total program or project.

5.2 Work Breakdown Schedule

The first step in formulating a project plan is to identify the major tasks and the supporting activities for the entire project or program. Tasks and activities must be linked together so that the project can be seen in its true perspective—so that relationships among all of the procedural steps are clear. A work breakdown schedule (WBS) is one important technique for developing a preliminary outline or "schematic" of the way in which supporting activities mesh together to ensure the attainment of the major tasks.

The basic idea of a work breakdown schedule is to divide the total project into major tasks, then to subdivide these tasks into subtasks and into activities. Tasks should be subdivided into smaller units according to their interrelatedness. The project may be subdivided through as many stages or levels as necessary to provide final work units of the desired size. At the lowest level, the work units should be small enough to permit adequate visibility and control without creating an unwieldy administrative burden. Excessive zeal in pushing the WBS into too many subdivisions may result in an unproductive management structure. It is not necessary to extend the WBS to the same number of levels for all tasks.

The initial division of work should not be made along organizational lines—this nullifies much of the usefulness of the WBS. Any schedule below the first level will only reflect what the separate organizational units require and will not reflect the dependencies or obligations among these units.

The structure of the WBS should be flexible enough that it can be expanded over time in both depth and scope. An early version of a WBS—containing only two or three levels of task subdivision—may provide a sufficiently sound basis for project planning. When certain parts of the project are initiated, tasks can be further subdivided into additional levels as may be appropriate for cost and schedule control. Thus, managers with different responsibilities can look at segments of the project in varying degrees of detail.

A WBS should be structured in a consistent manner, according to some orderly identification scheme that will also provide the flexibility for expansion, if necessary, during the time required to complete the project. The so-called *indented decimal system* provides such a structured approach. This straightforward system is relatively simple and readily understood. The decimal format makes it easy to build the WBS into an information management system and to develop managerial accounting procedures useful to the project manager. For example, accounting codes can easily be expanded to include the numerics of a project's work breakdown schedule so that the project manager can monitor costs at various levels of activity.

The first subdivision (1.0, 2.0, 3.0, etc.) represents the major tasks of the project associated with the major operational objectives. The second level (1.1, 1.2, 2.1, 2.2, etc.) represents the further breakdown of major tasks into subtasks. The third level (1.1.1, 1.1.2, 1.1.3, etc.) begins to identify specific activity clusters or job assignments that are required to successfully carry out the subtasks (see Table 10.9).

The work specified in each division is logically the sum of all the work described in the elements contained in that division or its subdivisions. Subtasks and activities are the logical divisions of larger tasks and should be distinct from each other. For this reason, each entry in the WBS should have its own, unique descriptive title that provides a brief identification of that work unit so that it is distinguishable from other work units. These descriptive labels need not be long and complicated. In no case, however, should the title of one level repeat words used in the subdivision. The numerical designation provides the traceability to larger groupings of work units at higher levels.

TABLE 10.9 Work Breakdown Schedule for Prenatal Health Care Clinic

1.0 Secure and equip space for the clinic.
    1.1 Locate appropriate space for the clinic.
    1.2 Negotiate rental contract on clinic space.
    1.3 Equip office and clinic space.
        1.3.1 Make physical modifications to rental space, as necessary, to accommodate clinic layout.
        1.3.2 Order office equipment for the clinic.
        1.3.3 Order medical supplies, drugs, and other materials.
        1.3.4 Order office supplies and materials.
    1.4 Open clinic to eligible applicants.

2.0 Train and certify clinic staff.
    2.1 Hire/assign clinic staff.
    2.2 Orient staff to agency procedures.
    2.3 Train staff in clinic operations.
    2.4 Certify professional and volunteer staff members.

3.0 Publicize programs and screen applicants.
    3.1 Develop informational materials on clinic programs.
    3.2 Publicize the availability of the clinic and its programs.
    3.3 Screen initial applicants for eligibility and complete their enrollment in the program.

It should be evident that no task should be "divided" into a single subtask, and no subtask should be "subdivided" into a single activity. Failure to adhere to this basic rule accounts for many shortcomings in the application of the WBS approach. It is also important to maintain the integrity of the task hierarchy to guard against the misplacement of activities under an inappropriate subtask or to repeat the same activity under more than one subtask.

With the addition of narrative descriptions of each of the major tasks and subtasks, a WBS can serve as a more detailed project plan. Individuals with various functional responsibilities in the organization should be able to refer the WBS as a common source of information for the fulfillment of their planning and control responsibilities. Since there is no need to provide the same level of subtask division for each task, flexibility of the schedule can be maintained. This is especially important in the early developmental stages of a project. In fact, the WBS can be sent out to various personnel with the work only divided into major tasks. As the planning of the project is further refined, the major tasks can be subdivided. By issuing a "first draft" of a WBS, the project manager also allows for the fuller participation of affected personnel. Such a process may result in a better WBS and a more successful project. At a minimum, however, such a process allows relevant personnel to participate in the development of the operations schedule and the monitoring and control devices that will be applied to the project. By providing for such participation, greater cooperation and understanding of the project may be anticipated, as well as a greater potential for realizing a successful project.

5.3 Network Analysis Techniques

Network analysis offers a useful and straightforward approach by which to "map" the various steps required to implement a project or program. Network analysis provides a basis for determining the order in which activities should be undertaken—either their sequence or priority—and the critical linkages among activities. Even the most detailed and apparently complex networks are merely composites of a number of relatively simple networks. By understanding the basic techniques of network analysis, a program manager should be able to convey specific assignments to those responsible for carrying out activities.

Contemporary techniques for operations scheduling and control can be traced back to the work of pioneers in the field of scientific management, such as Frederick Taylor and Henry Laurence Gantt. Taylor's time and motion studies are familiar to students of industrial engineering and business administration. Gantt charts form the basis for many current production scheduling systems. The relative simplicity of the Gantt chart is one reason why this technique continues to receive widespread application. The so-called *time-line diagram* is one of the more common forms of Gantt charts used today.

5.4   Arrow Diagrams: First Step to the Critical Path

An arrow diagram provides the initial portrayal of a critical path network. Elements of a project—*activities*—are represented by arrows on a network diagram (see Figure 10.4). An activity may represent a process, task, procurement cycle, or waiting time and may simply represent a connection or *interdependency* between two events on the network. An *event* is a specific, definable accomplishment in an operations plan, recognizable at a particular point in time. An activity cannot be started until the event preceding it has occurred. Events do not consume time or resources and are normally represented in the network by circles, squares, or rectangles (called *nodes*).

If an activity is denoted as a direct link between two nodes (events) in a network, an arrow (symbolizing the activity) indicates the direction of dependency and time flow from one node to another. A dependency relationship is assumed to mean that, before the dependent activity can be initiated, the other related activity must be completed.

Since the nodes in the arrow diagrams represent the completion of activities (i.e., events), the term "start" often is used to anchor the initiation of the network. Since each arrow represents a linkage between events, more than one arrow can designate the same activity. For example, two arrows that terminate at the same node represent the same activity. This approach has certain advantages in determining time durations and in delimiting the critical path, as will be subsequently illustrated.

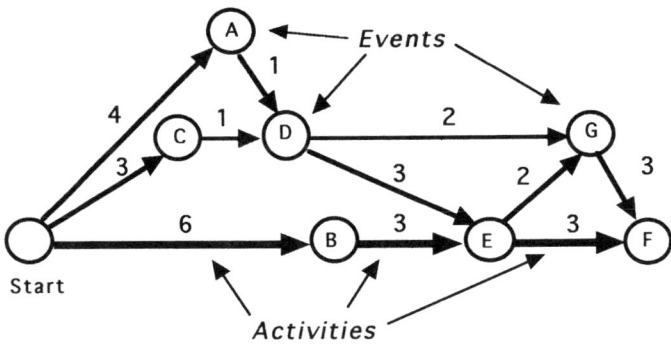

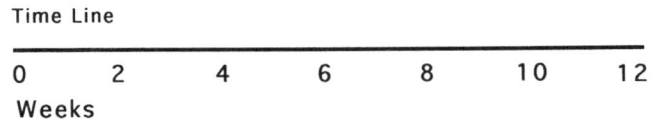

FIGURE 10.4   Arrow diagram illustration.

An arrow diagram is composed of a series of sequential relationships or *paths*. Each path should be completed in the indicated sequence in order for the various activities to be carried out in proper relation, one to another, and for the overall project to be successfully implemented. Once the various connections have been drawn, a critical path can be determined and progress can be more easily measured against key checkpoints or milestones.

Associated with each arrow (activity) in the network is a time estimate called its *duration*—the amount of time required to complete the activity represented by the arrow. The next step, therefore, is to assign time estimates to each of the paths or arrows. Each arrow (activity) leading to a given node (event or activity completion) is assigned the time duration for the designated activity. In this way, all of the possible paths to that node can be easily traced.

The time duration for each path should be summed to determine:

1. The earliest possible time that an activity that terminates at a give node can be completed—known as the *earliest possible occurrence* or EPO.
2. How long it will take to complete the entire project (*project duration*).
3. Which activities establish and control the project duration (the *critical path*).
4. How much leeway (*float*) exists for those activities that do not control the project duration.

5.5   Operational Leeway: Float

The *float* of a given activity is the amount of time that the activity can be delayed or its duration extended without affecting the EPO of any other activity. To determine this operational leeway, calculations must be made by taking the EPO of the final activity node and subtracting the time durations back to the nodes that lead to this final activity. This process is repeated for each node, in turn, back to "start." These calculations determine the *latest possible occurrence* or LPO, that is, the latest time that all of the activities terminating at a given node can finish without causing the project to exceed the originally determine duration.

Whereas the EPO is the longest path from "start" to a given node, the LPO is the shortest path from the termination of the project back to a given node. The difference between the EPO and LPO represents the float for that activity.

5.6   The Critical Path

It should be clear that the duration of the entire project cannot be controlled by any activity with a positive float. The durations of these activities can be extended by an amount equal to the float that they possess without affecting the

EPO of any other activity. This means that the EPO of the last activity node will not be affected and, hence, that the project duration will not be altered. This characteristic of float limits the search for "critical" activities to those that have a float of *zero*.

Not all activities with zero float control the project duration, however. The activities that do control the project duration are those that have zero float *and* form a continuous path, starting at the first activity and ending at the last one.

5.7   Case Study

To illustrate these procedures, assume that the Board of the Public Library has authorized the development and installation of a computerized database of library holdings. The change over in the current cataloging and retrieval procedures will require the formulation of appropriate computer software (or the adaptation of "off-the-shelf" programs). It will also require hiring and training of personnel to operate the system, acquiring and installing computer equipment, and debugging and installing the database and database management system. The library staff further delineates these basic tasks as a series of activities required to complete this project. The relationships among these activities and preliminary estimates of the time duration required for each activity are shown in Table 10.10. The

TABLE 10.10   Linkages and Predecessor Relationships for the Installation of a Library Database

Activity	Description	Preceded by	Duration (in weeks)	EPO	LPO	Float
A	Position recruiting	None	4	4	5	1
B	Systems development	None	6	6	6	0
C	Equipment acquisition	None	3	3	5	2
D	Equipment training	A, C	1	5	6	1
E	Systems training	B, D	3	9	9	0
F	Computer–personnel interface	E	3	12	12	0
G	Manual system test	D, E	2	11	15	4
H	Preliminary systems changeover	F	3	15	15	0
I	Equipment modification	F	2	14	15	1
J	Equipment testing	J	1	15	16	1
K	System debugging and installation	G, H	1	16	16	0
L	Equipment changeover	K, J	3	19	19	0

EPO, earliest possible occurence; LPO, latest possible occurence.

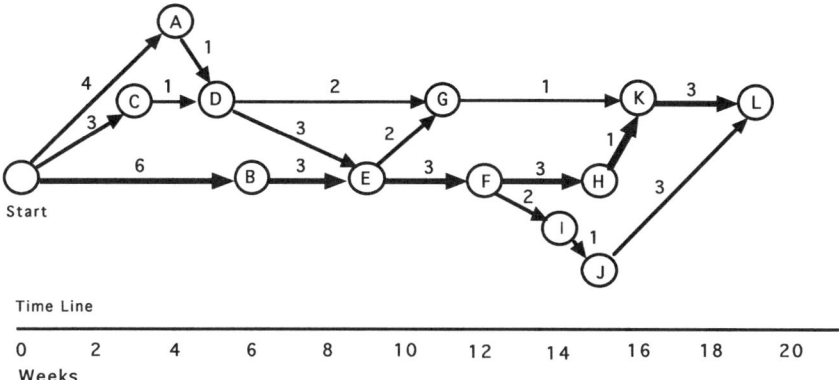

FIGURE 10.5 Arrow diagram for library project.

arrow diagram that delineates the sequential relationships among these activities is shown in Figure 10.5.

Three activities—recruitment, systems development, and equipment acquisition—can be initiated concurrently at the outset of the project. The development of software has the longest estimated duration of these three activities (6 weeks). However, initial training in the use of the computer equipment can begin in the fourth week after the equipment is purchased and delivered (3 weeks), and the new personnel are recruited and hired (4 weeks). Then, the training in the use of the software can begin in the sixth week. While the manual systems test cannot be initiated until the staff has been trained in the use of the software (at the end of week 9), this activity is not on the critical path (i.e., it has float). Equipment modification and testing are dependent upon the completion of the computer–personnel interface. However, these two equipment-related tasks also have float. Thus, the critical path is comprised of the sequence of activities: B, E, F, H, K, and L. This path can be confirmed by determining the LPO's for each of the activities in this sequence. The project duration, given the assigned times, is 19 weeks.

5.8 Dynamic Control Mechanism

Once the actual program or project is implemented, the critical path can be continuously monitored so that potential delays can be identified before they occur. Such delays can be avoided by shifting personnel, materials, or other resource inputs to the critical path from those paths that have "float." Therefore, the identification of the critical path also provides the program manager with a dynamic control mechanism.

In addition, a critical path network offers a convenient form of shorthand to express a complex set of relations. It offers a medium of communication and prediction. And it facilitates the subdivision of work so that each person involved can proceed with the more detailed planning of their part of the program or project.

The critical path approach provides a basis for an analysis of the costs involved when efforts are launched to utilize float time in order to reduce overall project costs. Or in those instances when a project deadline is imposed, the critical path approach can assist in the determination of the cost of "*crash scheduling.*" In general, the critical path approach determines: (1) the sequential ordering of activities, (2) the maximum time required to complete the project or program, (3) the costs involved, and (4) the ramifications in time and costs for altering the critical path.

6 SUMMARY: STRATEGIC MANAGEMENT AND ORGANIZATIONAL CONTROL

Control systems are an integral component of strategic management, providing tools to determine whether an organization is proceeding toward established objectives and to alert decision makers when actual performance deviates from the planned performance. *Strategic controls* are used to evaluate the overall performance of an organization. *Management control* involves the measurement and evaluation of program activities to determine if policies and objectives are being accomplished as efficiently and effectively as possible. *Operational controls* seek to ensure that specific tasks or programs are carried out efficiently and in compliance with established policies.

Accounting has always been an important component of the control functions of organizations. The primary concern of *financial accounting* is the accurate and objective recording of past events (financial transactions). *Fund accounting* provides the primary mechanism for the control and reporting of financial activities through the use of standard fund designations. An emphasis on budgetary control through the application of *budgetary accounting* procedures is a major distinction between governmental accounting and for-profit accounting. The basic objective of *cost* and *managerial accounting* is the provision of information for improved financial management decisions.

Whenever the full cost of a service or product must be determined, costs must be allocated according to their fixed, variable, direct, and indirect components. Fixed costs of any project remain constant as the volume of activity increases; on a per unit basis, these costs become progressively smaller. Variable costs are more or less uniform per unit, but the total of these costs increases as the volume of activity increases. A direct cost is incurred in support of a specific, identifiable purpose. An indirect cost is associated with more than one activity or program and cannot be traced directly to any individual activity.

An important step in controlling costs is to determine how they function under various conditions. This process, called cost approximation or cost estimation, involves efforts to find predictable relationships (cost functions) between a dependent variable (cost) and one or more independent variables (organizational activities). Several methods for approximating cost functions were discussed in this chapter, with the most reliable being the regression method.

A primary objective of operations scheduling and control is to organize work activities in a more optimal manner and to more clearly define and control costs. An operating schedule promotes the more effective use of time, thereby facilitating the completion of work assignments within anticipated deadlines. The time and effort saved by minimizing inefficiencies should enable a public and nonprofit organizations to undertake new and varied activities within the constraints of limited resources.

ENDNOTES

1. Peter F. Drucker. Management: Tasks, Responsibilities, Practices. New York: Harper & Row, 1974, p. 494.
2. Peter F. Drucker. Management: Tasks, Responsibilities, Practices. New York: Harper & Row, 1974, p. 496.
3. Charles W. L. Hill and Gareth R. Jones. Strategic Management—An Integrated Approach, 4th edition. Boston: Houghton Mifflin Co., 1998, chapter 12.
4. For a more complete discussion of the new GASB financial reporting requirements see: Alan Walter Steiss and Emeka O. C. Nwagwu. Financial Planning and Management in Public Organizations. New York: Marcel Dekker, Inc., 2001, chapter 10.
5. For a discussion of accrual accounting procedures see Leo Herbert, Larry N. Killough, and Alan Walter Steiss. Accounting and Control for Governmental and Other Nonbusiness Organizations. New York: McGraw-Hill Book Company, 1987, chapter 1.
6. Robert N. Anthony and James S. Reese. Management Accounting: Text and Cases. Homewood, IL.: Richard D. Irwin, 1975, p. 422.
7. James H. Rossell and William W. Frasure. Managerial Accounting. Columbus, OH: Charles E. Merrill, 1972, p. 4.

11

Performance Evaluation

A critical component of strategic management involves the application of strategic controls to evaluate the overall performance of an organization. Strategic controls should assist in determining the extent to which strategic objectives have been achieved and in identifying appropriate corrective actions to deal with unanticipated changes in the broader environment. When an organization fails to achieve its strategic objectives, the remedies may include recasting these objectives, reformulating plans and programs, modifying organizational structure, and improving internal and external communications.

1 DETERMINANTS OF PERFORMANCE EFFECTIVENESS

The effectiveness of an organization's performance is dependent upon the ability of management to develop, implement, and sustain critical programs and projects. To be effective, the performance of management must have utility and relevance to the overall mission of the organization. Even though the efforts of management may have internal consistency—a frequently cited test of effectiveness—if such efforts contribute little or nothing to the achievement of organizational purpose, they are obviously of limited value. In short, an examination of an organization's performance in terms of the achievement of its strategic objectives must begin with a critique of the management style or approach that has been adopted. The nature and quality of management is largely a function of three basic sets of concerns.

1. *Systemic concerns:* organization purpose, stability, comprehensiveness, and responsiveness to the larger environment in which the organization operates.
2. *Concerns for risk:* including responses to opportunity and application of innovation.
3. *Time concerns:* time perspectives adopted in dealing with problems and preparing for resource commitments.

A detailed examination of these three basic areas can provide a fuller understanding of the possible attitudes that managers may adopt in the performance of their responsibilities—how they seek out facts, share information, and communicate with one another. This examination, in turn, can assist in determining the basis for a successful and effective performance in terms of specific programs and projects.

1.1 Systemic Concerns

In every human situation, there is an inherent desire to put things in order, establish priorities, relate specific activities to broader purposes, and provide mechanisms for measuring success. Three key ingredients are at the core of these concerns.

1. *Purpose:* Concern for the relevance of specific occurrences to overall goals, objectives, and orientation. An attempt must be made to place objectives into a future-oriented priority system.
2. *Stability:* Desire to reduce the effects of chance or randomness in the operations of the organization. Every organization seeks to develop a set of expectations—norms, standards, rules, policies, and procedures—for determining appropriate courses of action or for dealing with specific problems. The desire for stability is reflected in the need to establish order, sequence, and predictability, to anticipate events, and to establish procedures to deal with problems as they arise.
3. *Comprehensiveness:* Concern for an organization as a total entity. An organization, institution, or community is a complex system composed of related and interdependent subsystems (smaller units within the total entity). In order to maintain direction and stability, information from one part of the organization must be linked to information from all other parts to create a comprehensive whole.

These three components of systemic concern—purpose, stability, and comprehensiveness—are closely linked. The greater the awareness of the entire system, the more management can plan and work in terms of the system's purpose and stability. Conversely, if management personnel do not appreciate the overall purpose and goals of the organization, it is very difficult for them to carry out their responsibilities in a way that will maximize their contributions to the total system.

Every individual in an organization should have systemic concerns on some level—concerns for maintaining direction, achieving stability, and dealing with the total system. These concerns may be with specific *elements* without parallel concerns for their interrelationships. Or they may be with the *total system*, with explicit recognition of the linkages among elements and subsystems. An individual may take a position somewhere between these two endpoints, manifesting a concern for *events* or combinations of elements, or a concern with *subsystems* or combinations of events, without recognizing that they comprise a system or combination of subsystems. In short, degrees of concern for the system adopted by individuals or groups within an organization can be arrayed on a continuum, ranging from high concern (positive) to low or negative concern (resistance to systemic considerations), as shown in Figure 11.1.

As an illustration, consider the City Manager who has been asked by the merchants association to solve the parking problem downtown, which the merchants maintain has caused them to lose business. The City Manager might respond in several ways.

1. Instruct the public works department to install parking meters along Main Street to promote greater turnover of on-street parking (concern for elements).
2. Initiate an off-street parking study to determine the feasibility of municipal parking facilities adjacent to the downtown area (concern for events or combinations of elements).
3. Launch a major thoroughfare and parking study to determine whether re-routing through traffic, in combination with one-way streets and off-street parking, would make the downtown business district more accessible (concern for subsystems).
4. Request the planning department to undertake a comprehensive analysis of the downtown area, including a study of competition from outlying shopping centers to determine the feasibility of renewal and redevelopment programs. These programs would involve both public and private investments to make the downtown area more attractive to shoppers and to stimulate new business ventures (concern for the total system).

It is likely that the most feasible solution to the problem will be found somewhere in the subsystems. However, if studies show that the current merchandising practices of downtown businessmen are outdated, then a solution to the real,

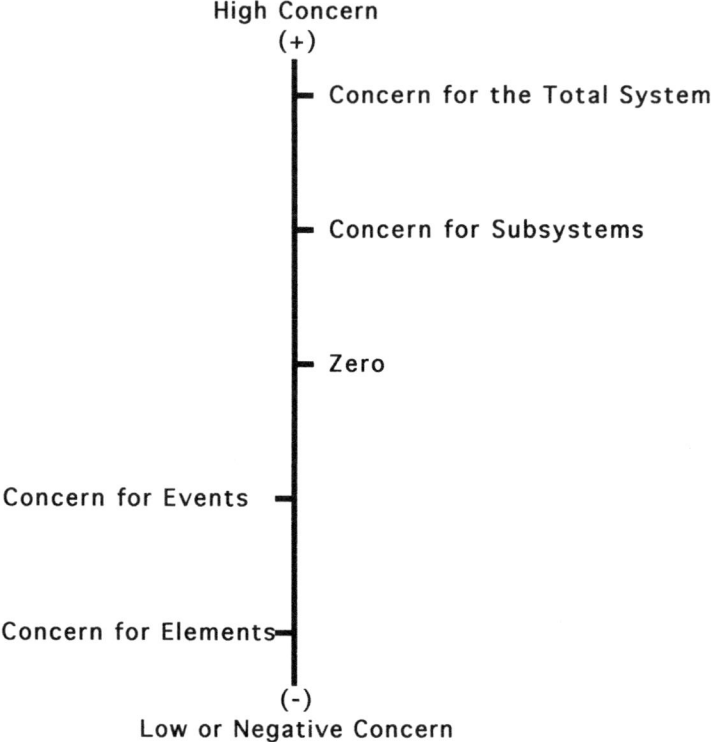

Figure 11.1 Continuum of systemic concerns.

long-term problem is not likely to be found in providing more parking, but rather in making changes in these practices.

Concern for the total system, of course, can lead to a major digression into larger and larger systems. In most cases, managers will draw boundaries that are contiguous with their scope of authority. However, it may be well to consider the full range of spillover effects, particularly in the early planning stages.

1.2 Concern for Risk

Managers must continually consider opportunities for innovation, change, and their associated risks. Sometimes the risks are personal; at other times, they affect the entire organization. From an organizational standpoint, the risks associated with a new policy or program generally include the possibility of higher costs, reduced effectiveness, program failure, and negative public reaction. Innovation and risk-taking are inevitable bedfellows. An effective manager understands the

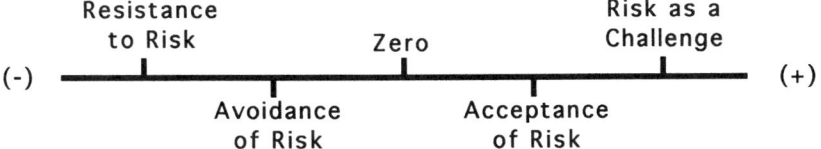

FIGURE **11.2** Continuum of concern for risk.

interrelated nature of opportunity, innovation, and risk, and is willing to take risks appropriate to their level of responsibility. The ultimate decision to take risks should be based on the weighing of available *information*, the exercise of *logic*, the assessment of *uncertainty*, and an estimate of alternative *payoffs* or *gains*.

In the same manner that the degrees of systemic concern can be represented schematically, attitudes and assumptions regarding risk can be arrayed on a continuum, as illustrated in Figure 11.2. At the right-hand (positive) end of the scale, risk is synonymous with challenge or the opportunity to develop or exploit situations in the best interests of the organization. At the opposite (negative) end of the continuum, there is strong resistance to risk. Between the positive extreme and the mid-point of the continuum are various degrees of acceptance of risk; from the mid-point to the negative end of the continuum there are various degrees of avoidance of risk.

Risk becomes highly significant when the probable *utility function* of a given decision is considered. Von Neumann and Morgenstern derived the concept of "standard gambles" from the theories of probability and risk [1]. This concept suggests that when potential returns are great, the marginal utility is positive for the risk acceptor and negative for the risk avoider. The opposite is true when the potential returns are low, a result of the risk acceptor placing a higher-than-expected value on potential returns.

Since the possibility of windfall returns is relatively low in the public sector, the acceptance of risk has been relatively limited. As accelerated change makes the future increasingly uncertain, however, public officials may find significant risk involved in even relatively simple, straightforward management functions.

1.3 Time Continuum

It is important to be aware of various time dimensions associated with decisions and the commitment of organizational resources resulting from these decisions. Some problems demand immediate solutions and have a relatively short-range effect. They involve elements that can be altered with relative ease if the initial decision proves to be incorrect. Although long-range approaches may be necessary to identify the causes and implications of such problems (and to develop appropriate strategies to prevent their reoccurrence), the urgency of these problems may demand immediate responses. Other problems—particularly those involving fixed capital investments—have relatively long-term time dimensions. Decisions associated with such projects can subsequently be modified only at considerable expense. Thus, the time dimensions of different problems and issues may invoke different approaches along a continuum, with short-range, day-to-day dimensions at one end, and long-range time dimensions associated with forecasting and planning at the other.

Over the past several decades, the differences between long-range and short-range decisions have become less significant. Reasons for this include:

Increasing acceleration of social change.

Increasing awareness of the longer-term consequences of even fairly rudimentary decisions.

Increasing appreciation of interlocking and therefore cumulative impacts of small or incremental changes.

Given the effects of time on basic management decisions, there is an increased need for careful planning in order to expand the time horizons of parochial decision making. Although evidence suggests that such planning is on the rise in the private sector, many public officials have yet to fully develop their inherent planning capabilities.

2   A PARADIGM OF MANAGEMENT ATTITUDES

A descriptive paradigm can be organized around these three basic sets of concerns to facilitate an understanding of the alternative approaches to management responsibilities. Such a paradigm reflects the following key issues:

The extent to which managers should be concerned with the total system, that is, the organization, institution, or community.

The degree of risk, innovation, and opportunity managers should be willing to accept.

The extent to which managers should take a long-range view in formulating policies and programs.

How managers should relate these basic areas of concern in their use of information.

2.1   The System-Time Continua

The first step in formulating a paradigm of management attitudes is to combine the continua representing the concern for system and time concerns, as illustrated in Figure 11.3. For reasons that will become evident, the two axes have been

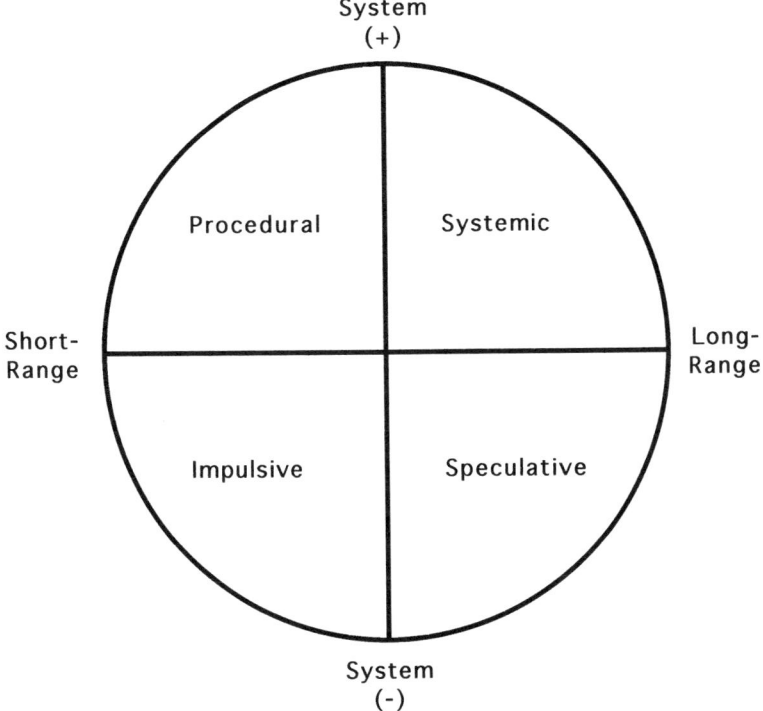

System
(+)

Procedural   Systemic

Short-   Long-
Range   Range

Impulsive   Speculative

System
(-)

FIGURE **11.3** Combined system-time continua.

enclosed in a circle, with the mid-point between (−) and (+) on each axis (the zero point) now forming the center of the circle.

The *impulsive approach* (lower left-hand quadrant of the system–time continua) reflects a very short-range concern for time. In addition, individuals who have lost touch with the overall purposes of the system often make this response. No attempt is made to limit risk or to weigh it against potential gains. The impulsive manager responds to whatever comes along. Their behavior is unpredictable, since few internal ground rules exist and established precedent and policy tend to be ignored. The impulsive manager operates almost entirely in the present; in extreme cases, they may do almost anything that comes to mind. Financial administration may be very erratic—a spending spree at one moment and tight fiscal controls at another time.

The *procedural approach* reflects a desire to apply established policies and practices to current problems. The question asked is, "How can this present situation be handled by applying past experiences and procedures?" The procedural manager is concerned with maintaining the system but focuses on short-range, immediate problems (characteristic of the incrementalist). Long-term commitments to capital investment are to be avoided, and as long as the next move is closely related to the past, the organization cannot get into too much trouble. Decisions are processed incrementally within the safe boundaries of established values, policies, rules, and regulations.

The *systemic approach* reflects a concern for the total organization, for the relationship between the parts and the whole, and for long-range direction as well as short-term purposes within this longer time dimension. The systemic manager asks, "Where are we going and how can we best get there?" Planning for particular events, operations, or activities is thought through carefully with concern for the total system. Investment decisions are considered in terms of long-range plans of the system. Information is gathered and analyzed in an effort to reduce future uncertainty. All available methods of analysis may be applied to define problems and seek their solutions. However, the systemic manager may move too cautiously to meet more immediate demands.

The *speculative approach* is characteristic of individuals whose eagerness to take chances move them beyond merely opportunistic behavior to actual speculation or gambling. Although little concern is shown for the impact of risk or experimentation on the overall system, the speculative manager exhibits a long-range perspective in the attitude that chances must be taken now in order to reap significant gains in the future. The general attitude is "You've got to take chances if you want to get ahead, so let's give it a whirl." Indeed, the speculative manager may attempt to create opportunities where none exist (for example, by committing organizational resources to projects in hopes that such commitment will stimulate further investment from the private sector). As one moves further and further from any systemic considerations of goals and objectives, one moves from calculated risk, to somewhat risky exploitation, to pure speculation.

2.2 The Risk-Time Continua

The four quadrants of the risk–time continua are identified in Figure 11.4. The *fire-fighting approach* characterizes individuals who see each event as a distinct, short-range problem to be contained or controlled. Such individuals are unwilling to take risks; they consider each incident as lacking precedent or antecedent. Therefore, they deal with each problem without reference to long-term purpose. The concern is with solving the problem as quickly as possible, with minimal cost and risk. In the short run, this approach may be an effective way of dealing with certain problems or managing certain programs. In the long run, however, resources often are used inappropriately, unfortunate obligations may be established, important opportunities may be lost, and the organization is barely sustained.

The *entrepreneurial approach* exhibits an affinity for risk—for new opportunities—often, although not always, at the expense of long-term direction and

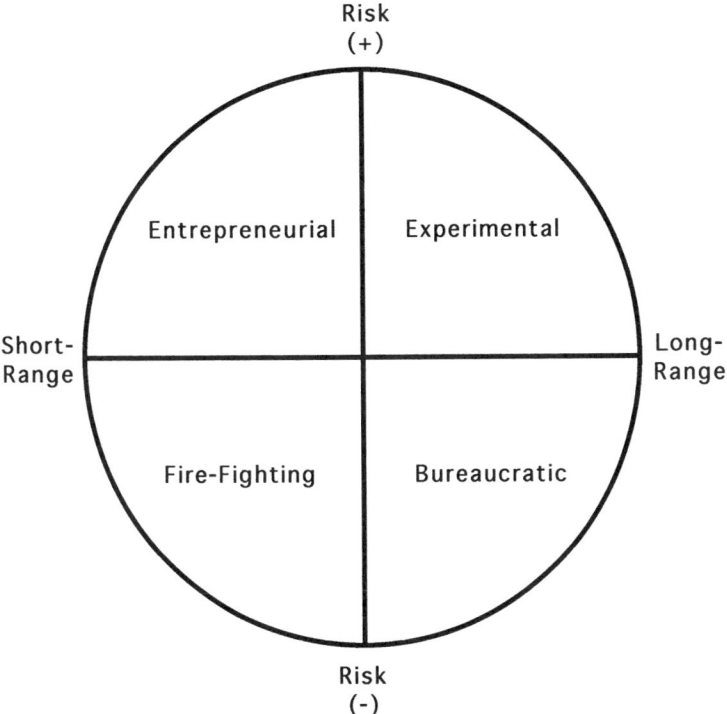

Risk
(+)

Entrepreneurial | Experimental

Short-
Range | Long-
Range

Fire-Fighting | Bureaucratic

Risk
(-)

FIGURE 11.4 Combined risk-time continua.

purpose. Commitments may be quickly abandoned (or not adopted at all) when new opportunities are detected. The primary orientation is "How can we make a quick deal and exploit an opportunity?" rather than "How can we determine if this is an appropriate opportunity for building toward our long-range objective?" Consequently, investments involving long-term obligations may be made without sufficient attention given to their impacts on limited resources or the long-range demands for such facilities.

The *experimental approach* characterizes those individuals who maintain an analytical attitude in their attempt to deal with risk and to exploit opportunities that may contribute to the achievement of some long-term objectives. Managers pursuing this approach seek facts and information on which to base their decisions about what to do and how best to do it. They avoid the pitfalls of both compulsive and overly rigid behavior by maintaining a long-range, purposeful outlook. However, the cost of information gathering may result in a substantial increase in the total commitment required to resolve any problem.

The *bureaucratic approach* involves avoidance of any kind of risk, while maintaining the long-term consistency and continuity of the organization. The objective is not to determine how to best apply established practices to changing situations; rather, past precedents are blindly applied. The bureaucratic response results in tighter control and rigidity based on an adherence to tradition (a long-range time perspective in reverse). Bureaucratic managers may state flatly, "There doesn't have to be a reason for it, it's just the way we have always done things." Consequently, new approaches to policy and programs seldom are considered, and established patterns are maintained unquestioned.

2.3 Combining the Continua

It should be evident that the quadrants in Figure 11.3 and 11.4 represent paired subsets of broader descriptive categories. By combining the three basic areas of concern—systemic, risk, and time—the paradigm can be further expanded, as shown in Figure 11.5. The basic characteristics of the four quadrants can be summarized as follows.

1. *Traditional approach:* High concern for the system and its stability coupled with a desire to avoid risk and innovation. In this quadrant, the concern is primarily with maintenance of the system, the status

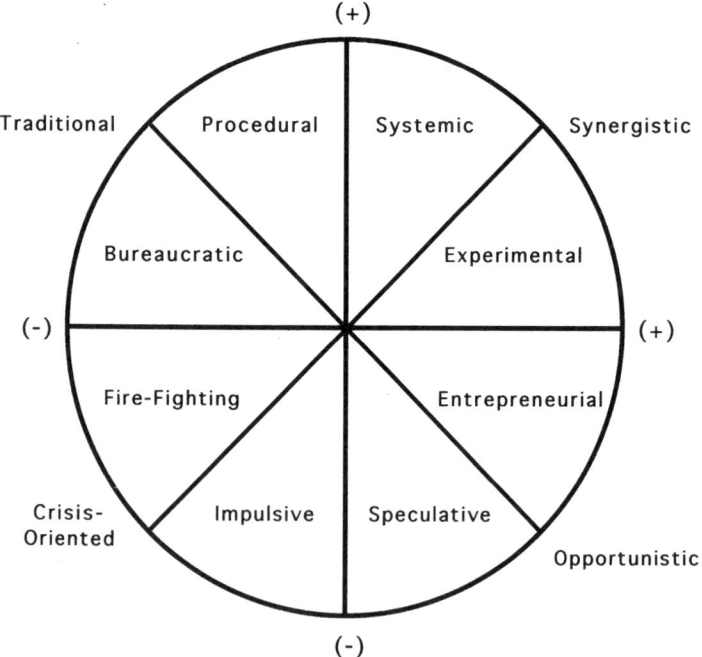

FIGURE 11.5 Attitudinal paradigm of public management.

quo, support for traditions and precedents, and minimization of risk and uncertainly.

2. *Crisis-oriented approach:* Low or negative concern for the system, coupled with either a desire to avoid risk or a lack of concern about risk. In this quadrant, every problem is treated as the most important job facing the manager, regardless of its magnitude or its relevance to the organizational purposes or growth opportunities.

3. *Opportunistic approach:* Low or negative concern with the system and its stability coupled with a desire to take advantage of opportunities and a willingness to accept risk. In this quadrant, management is preoccupied with growth, exploration, and speculation.

4. *Synergistic approach:* High concern for the system (purpose, stability, and comprehensiveness) coupled with a willingness to accept risk and a desire to take advantage of opportunities. In this quadrant, a sense of total system purpose and direction is integrated with a desire for experimentation, innovation, and increased interaction with the broader environment. Emphasis is on the long-term growth of the system.

Traditional approaches emphasize stability, precedent, and control at the expense of opportunities for innovation and growth. Such an approach becomes rigid, formal, and tradition-bound. Procedures, policies, and practices that were developed to deal with past problems are still applied even though they may be irrelevant to current situations. These traditional practices are seen as safer and more likely to succeed because, after all, they worked before. Review is resisted because it may distract from what is believed to be the basic need of the organization to stay on its current path. Any significant innovation usually is repressed. The question is not: "Where are we going and how do we get there?" but rather: "How can we stay on the previously determined course, avoid rocking the boat, control deviations from established patterns, and eliminate risk?"

Crisis-oriented responses reflect a distorted concern for stability and a strong reluctance to accept risk. Every problem is defined as ultimate and of the highest priority. Every incident is seen as an unrelated event requiring quick, firm handling. To minimize risk, managers adopting this approach must maintain constant surveillance over situations and personnel for whom they are responsible, and must apply tight resource controls even at the expense of the overall needs and objectives of the organization.

Opportunistic responses reflect a concern for innovation with little or no regard for its impact on the long-term purposes of the organization or the community. The term opportunistic here refers to individuals who react too quickly or compulsively to what they perceive to be growth opportunities, without adequate consideration of the total system or of the distribution of impacts. Such individuals constantly seek new breakthroughs, especially short-term, quick-return opportunities. A typical concern is "How can we move quickly on this opportunity?" Long-term, systemic considerations are overlooked in an eagerness to keep assets liquid and to be ready to seize any opportunity. As a consequence, inappropriate risks may be taken or the organization may be overextended on projects unrelated to overall purposes or to long-term direction.

Synergistic responses seek to strike a balance between stability–direction and risk–opportunity and also attempt to integrate these dimensions. Such responses address the overall objectives of the organization or community, but system and stability are not seen as ends in themselves nor merely as means for minimizing risk. Rather, they are seen as important for maintaining a sense of direction and purpose. When growth opportunities entailing some risk arise, the synergistic manager seeks information by which to evaluate their potential contribution to the broader system.

Differences among these basic approaches can be further clarified by examining the actions and attitudes generated in response to various areas of managerial responsibility, as summarized in Table 11.1 and the discussion that follows.

2.4   Organization Structure and Control

The traditional manager seeks an organization structure that permits the explicit definition of essential staff functions and responsibilities, thereby providing stability and preventing undisciplined action. The procedural manager achieves this objective through formal rules and regulations. The bureaucratic manager seeks organizational stability through a formal hierarchy of authority (the organization chart) in which the precise role of each person is clearly defined. The rewards and sanctions of the organization reinforce these mechanisms. Communication channels are clearly defined by the organization's chain of command and by established protocol—rules and regulations created to support the hierarchy of authority.

The crisis-oriented manager seeks to structure the organization with accountability as the foremost issue. Fire-fighting managers may assign staff specific responsibilities to identify problems, alter procedures when errors occur, and take necessary steps to "solve" problems within defined areas of jurisdiction. Since staff members are judged by impulsive managers on the basis of their ability to circumvent problems, rivalries may develop as individuals and groups vie for feasible "quick fix" solutions. Information is collected and communicated as current problems indicate a need to determine causes, establish responsibility, and identify the required action.

The opportunistic manager avoids formal organizational structure, such as job descriptions and organization charts, in favor of freedom and flexibility

TABLE 11.1 Profile of Attitudes Toward Management Responsibilities

	Traditional	Crisis-oriented	Opportunistic	Synergistic
Organizational structure	Clear-cut chain of command; hierarchy of authority.	Organization structured for trouble-shooting.	Formal structure avoided so as to promote flexibility.	Organization structured to promote flow of communication.
Controls	Close control maintained through established procedures to ensure minimum deviations.	Close control to ensure that mistakes do not hurt the organization.	Loose control since the staff needs to use imagination and initiative.	Control must be consistent with organization purpose with flexibility for initiative.
Problem identification	Bias toward low risk, broadly defined problems; problems often stated in "how-to" terms.	Problem statements with built-in action-oriented solutions.	Future-oriented, but on an elemental level; tends to "take a flyer."	Reflects concern for total purpose and building in opportunities for innovation.
Planning	Systematic efforts, building on established practices; planning provides control mechanisms.	Impossible because of unpredictable nature of the future.	Impractical since events are random; planning restricts freedom.	Provides stability and sound direction; should be systematic yet flexible.
Data collection	Seeks data that will cast light on deviations from predetermined patterns; detailed information to reduce risk.	Focus is on current problems, causes, risks, and responsibilities.	Seeks data to confirm quick and easy set of solutions; reliance placed on intuition and judgment.	Strong reliance on data collection and information analysis.
Alternative solutions	Limited by the parameters of precedent and existing standards; low risk, "safe" solutions.	Limited in number, rarely contain innovation; tend to be defensive and responsive to momentary considerations.	Seeks opportunities for quick gain; focus on elements; quick solutions may work against greatest gains.	Concern for long-term solutions and appropriate avenues of growth.

to respond to opportunities. Entrepreneurial managers may collect a relatively limited amount of information, relying instead on experience, intuition, and personnel judgment for detecting opportunities and solving problems. Relatively few organizational controls are imposed; staff members are free to use imagination and initiative in dealing with problems. They are not encumbered with restrictive rules and regulations.

The synergistic manager gives particular attention to the flow of information in the structuring of the organization. The communication system is a vital link and is structured so that the organization's resources can be quickly mobilized to handle both short- and long-range problems and opportunities. Information is collected to assist in maintaining a sense of direction and control and to provide a basis for planning ahead. A control mechanism, however, must leave room for the exercise of initiative to guide actions relevant to perceived needs.

2.5   Problem Identification

A key issue in the identification of problems is the tendency of problem solvers to include their prejudices regarding the solution in the statement of the problem. When seeking to improve efficiency, for example, a manager may state the problem in terms of reducing costs. Problem statements may have much more subtle indications of direction, which nonetheless limit the number of potential alternative solutions that may be examined.

A related pitfall is the tendency to couch problem statements in terms of how to solve the problem. Ideally, a problem statement should not include any bias toward a particular solution, nor should it offer specific "how-to" elements. Such elements should be part of the programming effort once the specific solutions are proposed.

Maintenance of the status quo is a primary pressure on the traditional manager. Therefore, their problem statements often are biased toward keeping things in line with predetermined standards or precedents. This characteristic may be seen in the expression of some "how-to" steps along with the problem statement. For example, a traditional manager's response to a cost overrun may be, "How can we get costs back in line with established standards by reducing nonessential expenditures."

A lack of concern for existing standards and traditions, coupled with a desire to avoid risk, leads the crisis-oriented manager to formulate problem statements with built-in action-oriented solutions on an elemental level. For example, the cost-overrun problem may be stated, "How can we reduce costs of Operation Y in Program X?" Such a problem statement includes a clear bias toward a solution, although the true problem may be the quality of outputs rather than costs.

With limited concern for the system, the opportunistic manager tends to direct attention toward those aspects of a given operation where growth seems possible. Problem statements show a bias toward solutions that are gain-oriented, but may not be well connected to the overall purpose of the organization.

The synergistic approach is least likely to include any predetermined indications of how the problem should be solved. In the cost-overrun example, a synergistic first statement may be, "What steps need to be taken in this situation to determine the effectiveness of our present operations?" Thus, the synergistic manager begins with a means–ends analysis to clarify objectives and identify measures of effectiveness which, in turn, may lead to cost-oriented solutions. Possible solutions may also include an improvement in methods, a change in program emphasis, or a redefinition of program goals.

2.6 Orientations Toward Planning

For the traditional manager, planning provides the organization with stable and sound direction and should involve the establishment of specific checks and balances to ensure that actions conform to existing procedures and practices. The procedural manager is likely to give priority to the maintenance of a stable organization, whereas the bureaucratic manager may see planning as a means of developing structures and programs to minimize risk. Thus, while their motives may differ slightly, the results often are the same: a fairly conservative plan (perhaps more appropriately labeled a "trend projection") that builds in linear fashion on the accumulated conditions of the past and attempts to alter these conditions only when they threaten the status quo.

In the eyes of the crisis-oriented manager, long-range planning is impossible—a waste of time and resources—because the future is unpredictable. The organization will do all right, asserts the crisis-oriented manager, if current situations are dealt with promptly. Uncertainty and risk associated with future conditions will be problems soon enough; there is no need to look for trouble.

The opportunistic manager sees planning as impractical, since events are random and disconnected. Furthermore, planning tends to restrict freedom; action is the key to organizational success. Since both the entrepreneurial and the speculative manager place high priority on opportunities for growth and improvement, they frequently hold that the long-run future can best be addressed by sensitive and creative individuals who are able to spot trends and take appropriate actions to capitalize on opportunities.

For the synergistic manager, planning provides stability and sound direction. Although opportunities are welcomed and risk accepted as a necessary consequence of innovation, the synergistic manager considers sound planning to be the basis by which to evaluate opportunity and to judge the acceptability of risks. This type of manager undertakes long-range planning in a systematic and comprehensive fashion, while allowing sufficient flexibility for innovation. In short, the planning emphasis of the synergistic manager is on the maintenance of sound direction, while building a basis for organizational growth.

2.7 Collection and Analysis of Data

The traditional manager, in large measure because of the way in which problems are stated, tends to collect data that will cast light on deviations from standards or predetermined pathways. When there is a cost problem, for example, data may be collected to indicate why expenditures vary from the established budget. If there is a gap in expected performance, the tendency is to see how that performance compares with written job descriptions. As a consequence of a pre-occupation with minimizing risk, the traditional manager often collects a great deal of data systematically. Often bureaucratic organizations have floundered in the "syndrome of data collection" in which the assemblage of detailed information becomes an end in itself.

Most of the energy of the crisis-oriented manager is devoted to action rather than to data gathering and analysis. The paradox is that when action is impossible, such a manager may become preoccupied with surveillance and careful scrutiny of all kinds of detailed data on an elemental level in an effort to avoid or reduce risk.

The opportunistic manager tends to collect relatively little data, and the data gathered are oriented toward gains rather than toward a comprehensive analysis of possibilities. The sequence and ordering of data is unimportant, since the opportunistic manager is primarily seeking a basis for action.

The critical data issue for the synergistic manager is relevance. This focus largely dictates the nature, amount, and sequence of data collected. The synergistic manager seeks information that will shed light on general direction and provide guidance for long-term course corrections. Clearly, traditional and synergistic managers are disposed to collect more data and to be more concerned with comprehensiveness and overall objectives. However, the traditional manager's orientation away from risk means that the data collected are similar to that of the crisis-oriented manager.

2.8 Selecting Alternatives

To a large extent, the pressures on the manager, the way in which problems are stated, and the types of data collected determine the range of alternatives that emerge. Traditional and crisis-oriented managers seldom include opportunities for significant breakthroughs or innovations as potential decisions. The opportunistic manager tends to focus on breakthrough strategies, but often deals only with pieces of the total problem, frequently ignoring preventive measures that might yield better solutions than gain-oriented initiatives.

In an effort to keep the organization on track, the traditional manager rarely pursues the possibilities that offer the highest payoff; rather, the emphasis is on safe solutions—compromises between maximum and minimum possibilities. Choices may be greatly influenced by what has worked in the past, although the very fact that something has worked in the past may be a good indication that it will not work as well in the future. The perpetuation of past solutions may be a major part of the problem.

The crisis-oriented manager often finds appeal in elemental solutions, oriented toward dealing with immediate problems and reducing risk. Such solutions, however, often are inappropriate in terms of the one thing they are most worried about: survival.

The opportunistic manager tends to select the alternative that promises the quickest gain at an elemental level. Paradoxically, the temptation to choose the quickest solution may work against the desire for the greatest gain, if gain is measured in terms of total organizational purpose.

The synergistic manager seeks to optimize the process—to choose the higher payoff when calculated risk is appropriate to that payoff. Low risk per se is not a goal; rather, calculated risk, based on careful analysis of alternative payoffs, is optimal. The synergistic manager identified the decision-making process as a key component in establishing and maintaining sound direction toward overall objectives. While every decision involves a certain amount of intuition, this factor is limited by the array of alternatives under consideration. A given solution might "feel good" to an experienced manager, providing that solution is included in the decision array. In the early stages of problem solving, therefore, synergistic managers are concerned with uncovering data, assessing the probabilities of risk, and identifying potential opportunities so that personal knowledge, sensitivity, and intuition can more appropriately be brought to bear on the ultimate decision.

3 SELECTION OF A MANAGEMENT APPROACH

Ultimately, any decision must be analyzed in terms of its effects. Although the paradigm outlined here clearly favors the synergistic approach, there are many management situations in which judgment, sensitivity, imagination, and intuition may be more effective tools than the rational emphasis of the synergistic approach. An opportunistic manager, in the right place at the right time, may produce a higher payoff for the organization. Similarly, a crisis-oriented or traditional manager, in the right place at the right time, may take the most appropriate steps to avoid serious problems.

3.1 Guidelines for Selection

A number of guidelines may be applied in selecting an appropriate management approach to a particular situation. Among these are consideration of the estimated gain or loss, severity of the problem, frequency with which the problems are encountered, and the spillover effects of decisions.

A key question in any decision situation is "What is the worth of any additional information derived from further study?" Frequently, the amount of time and energy required will be greater than the potential gains. Accordingly, there may be no point in working through to a "best" solution in a synergistic fashion. Traditional or crisis-oriented responses may yield a quick solution that will suffice, especially if the consequences are not great. A manager operating initially in the synergistic quadrant may decide to adopt a less than optimal alternative if the potential gain from experimentation and fact-finding is limited, or if the costs (and hence the potential loss) of such additional data collection are high.

Gain or loss often is affected by the severity of the problems encountered. Severe problems may require a relatively quick solution to avoid further adverse effects on the system—it may be necessary to "stop the bleeding" before a more systemic solution can be found. Or such problems may involve complications that prevent the identification of a "best" solution. The phrase "real and immediate threat" is a good test of the severity of the problem. When this test is met, a crisis-oriented response may be required. Applying such an approach, however, should not preclude a search for long-term causes, experimentation with new methods, and development of new policies and procedures appropriate to avoiding the re-occurrence of the problem.

If a problem is encountered frequently, considerable potential gain may result from a search for the "best" solution—one that could be applied whenever the problem arose. If the problem is encountered infrequently, it may or may not warrant the detailed fact-finding and analysis of synergistic behavior. An infrequently encountered problem, however, may be the first manifestation of a more generic problem that will occur with greater regularity in the future.

Many aspects of a decision affect gain or loss, although often obscurely— these are the spillover effects. A decision with a spillover effect is one that has significant impact beyond the immediate situation in which it is made. Such decisions and their effects are inevitable when managers fail to consider appropriate aspects of the total system. Thus, a single act, intended to have limited impact, may spill over into other areas and become an even more costly headache.

3.2   Organizational Implications

The discussion of this paradigm has focused on its application in understanding the attitudes and motivations of individual managers. Any organization is the sum of the individuals who work in it and, therefore, many organizations can be characterized by the prevailing attitudes manifested in one of the four quadrants of this paradigm. The classes of problems that confront an organization (or units within a larger organization) may contribute to the particular manifestations of attitudes and responses. Regulatory agencies, for example, tend to be more traditional (bureaucratic or procedural) in their orientation, whereas development agencies may adopt an opportunistic approach.

In addition, this paradigm may be used to trace the evolution of an organization. Many new organizations are created in response to a particular problem or opportunity. Once the crisis is past or the opportunity has been seized, the organization may be dissolved. More often, the organization continues, moving to the next stage in its development. Crisis-oriented organizations may seek new opportunities, whereas opportunistic organizations may seek to solidify their gains by adopting more systemic concerns, that is, by exhibiting more synergistic attitudes. Long-range goals and objectives may be defined and specific steps taken to formalize the organizational structure. Eventually, synergistic organizations tend to become more traditional in their perspective unless specific efforts are made to counter this tendency. Rules, regulations, and practices designed to support systemic concerns may become more rigidly codified, limiting the flexibility to respond to new opportunities. Risk may become less of a challenge and more of a threat. Depending on the demands that affect the organization, the emphasis of the traditional approach on the status quo may be inappropriate as an organizational response. As problems arise, managers may lose their overall sense of purpose and respond to new situations in a crisis-oriented fashion, seeing traditional responses as inappropriate but still attempting to avoid risk. As new situations become more frequent and intense, the crisis-oriented organization may be unable to survive and may be replaced by a new or significantly modified organization.

In short, the evolution of many organizations can be described as a counterclockwise cycle through the four quadrants of the paradigm. This is not to say that all organizations complete this cycle. There may be conscious efforts to stabilize the organizations in one of the quadrants or attempts to reverse the direction as the organization slips from one quadrant to another. Since the traditional or bureaucratic mode is most stable (least subject to volatile shifts in direction), many public organizations settle in this quadrant, emphasizing systemic concerns and avoiding risk.

3.3 The Futurity of Decisions

In the literature of public administration, the management process often is depicted as a well-defined set of procedures applicable to all situations. The message seems to be that there is always one best way to manage. In this discussion, the focus has been on a variety of approaches that may vary, depending on attitudes, assumptions, and concerns. The paradigm built around three basic sets of concerns is an attempt to show how particular management responses may come about. Obviously, the synergistic approach is considered most effective in terms of the dimensions outline in the paradigm. However, the best approach for a manager to take in any particular situation is the one most appropriate in terms of the relative importance of and interrelationship among a number of factors.

The problem-solving and decision-making process can be considered as a series of open loops (involving subsystems) which contribute to the totality of the organization. In effect, every decision predetermines the degrees of freedom presented for the next decision. Viewed as a social system, any organization is continually influenced by a series of small decisions that accumulate to produce an overall decision-climate. This climate involves a set of parameters that to some extent determine the range of alternatives available for future decisions.

In terms of the criteria by which an organization is evaluated, things that happened sometime in the past may determine its success or failure. Strategic decisions that are made today will probably not have their true impact for five years. In industry, for example, today's profits are often the result of decisions made three to five years ago regarding new product development, marketing strategies, selection of personnel, and a wide-range of other operating and financial choices. When things are going well within an organization, it may be assumed that good decisions currently are being made. In fact, the organization may be benefiting from good decisions made several years ago. The assumption that the good things happening now reflect current wise decisions may be both false and dangerous. To paraphrase Peter Drucker, strategic management does not deal with future decisions. It deals with the futurity of present decisions. It involves more than doing things right. It is concerned primarily with doing the right things.

The statement frequently is made that continued corporate profits are impossible without change and innovation. The same may be said about public and nonprofit organizations, substituting the term effectiveness for profits. In this context, effectiveness is defined in terms of the organization's capacity to handle problems in an ever-changing decision environment and to deal with its mission in an efficient and effective manner. To determine an organization's capacity to recognize and accommodate change, it is essential to evaluate the relative success (or lack of success) of its current processes and programs.

4   PERFORMANCE EVALUATION DEFINED

For the purposes of this discussion, a performance evaluation can be defined as an assessment of the effectiveness of ongoing and proposed programs and processes in achieving agreed-upon goals and objectives. Performance evaluation brings the strategic management process full circle by determining the need for improvements in current programs and processes and by identifying opportunities for further organizational development. An evaluation must take into account the possible influence of external as well as internal factors that affect the overall performance of an organization.

4.1 Types of Evaluations

The first major task is to decide what to evaluate and how to evaluate it. Not all programs or projects can be or should be evaluated in depth. Short-term programs or programs that may be politically vulnerable, for example, may not warrant a detailed evaluation. As Wholey noted, "From the point of view of decision-makers, evaluation is a dangerous weapon. They don't want evaluation if it will yield the 'wrong' answers about programs in which they are interested [2]." In such situations, political pressures frequently override empirical evidence available from formal performance evaluations. Nevertheless, decision makers may welcome evaluations that provide basic descriptive information on a consistent basis.

Evaluations range from simple data collections to complex analyses. Perkins identified six basic types of evaluation [3].

1. *Impact evaluations* deal with program delivery systems and the relation between program results and program objectives.
2. *Management evaluations* focus on the efficiency and effectiveness with which available resources are deployed to achieve program objectives.
3. *Design evaluations* test the measurability of program assumptions, the overall logic of the program approach, and the assignment of responsibility and accountability for program results.
4. *Intervention effect assessments* attempt to establish the relation between program intervention and outcomes, or, in some cases, the processes involved in producing those outcomes.
5. *Compliance evaluations* examine the consistency of program objectives with broader legislative aims and attempt to ensure that funds are allocated in accordance with policy guidelines.
6. *Strategic evaluations* are concerned with underlying causes of social problems and focus on "implicit theories" as a basis for broad ameliorative programs.

While each of these basic evaluative approaches has potential application in the context of strategic management, the first four types are perhaps most relevant. Compliance evaluations often are required by law, are undertaken by oversight authorities (e.g., independent certified public accountants serving as external auditors), and may be submitted to a regulating agency (such as the Auditor of Public Accounts), as well as to the organization's governing body. Strategic evaluations focus on relatively high-order assessments of the effectiveness of major policy decision and may involve extensive scholarly research evolving over a number of years [4].

A performance evaluation can focus on *process*—the extent to which a program is implemented according to predetermined guidelines—or on *impact*—the extent to which a program produces change in the intended direction. The key product of an evaluation may be knowledge about the implementation of the program (rather than the program itself) or the quality of the larger system in which the program is located. Evaluation also may produce a more complete understanding about a program among constituents who may be at odds with one another. This information, in turn, can make consensus-building another important outcome of a performance evaluation.

It is necessary to decide whether the program or the organization responsible for the program is to be evaluated. A program may be evaluated in terms of its effectiveness and costs. However, an organization should not be evaluated solely on the basis of its success (or failure) in carrying out a particular program. As Quade observed, an organization should be judged not by an initial program failure, but by its capacity to learn from failure and to improve the operation of the program [5].

Evaluations may look at specific aspects of a program or at a whole program. Components may be compared across programs, or a number of programs may be compared across application sites. Such comparisons provide the basis for determining if a program worked, or if one program worked better than something else did. Complex comparative evaluations can be expensive to conduct, involving consultants, programmers, and statisticians who may not be readily available on agency staffs. Good, useful, credible evaluations, carried out on a more limited scale, often can yield critical process or program data.

The scale and time frame of evaluations must be such that the organization is assisted in formulating viable improvements to its programs or processes. Moreover, problems and issues must be specified in evaluations in a way that provides clear indications of alternative courses of action to resolve them. As Clark observed, unless an evaluation is keyed to meeting specific information requirements and decision-making needs in a timely fashion "... it risks being irrelevant—a monument to what might have been [6]."

The purpose of many evaluations has been to improve efficiency. Questions of efficiency often are defined and answered strictly in *least-cost* terms. Minimal consideration may be given to the relative worth of the programs pursued in terms of its effectiveness. It is possible to do things very efficiently, but if they are the wrong things to do, they will have little positive impact on the problems to which the program is directed. Improving efficiency may not require any drastic changes in program strategies. However, increasing effectiveness often entails significant program adjustments—one reason why recommendations of evaluations that focus on effectiveness may not be fully utilized.

The notion of a criterion of efficiency, first formulated by Herbert Simon, asserts that a choice among alternatives should be made in favor of the course of action that produces the largest result for a given application of resources [7]. To guide this choice, however, Simon noted that it is necessary to determine appropriate levels of goal attainment or program adequacy (e.g., a minimum acceptable level of performance). In the absence of such definitive statements of goals and objectives, measures of efficiency cannot provide the insights necessary to make appropriate judgments about program achievements or benefits.

4.2 Formative and Summative Evaluations

A comprehensive evaluation should be based on both formative and summative techniques. *Formative evaluations* provide information necessary to design and/or modify processes, programs, and service delivery systems. Such evaluations include (1) an analysis of the needs to be met or the problems to be solved, (2) a determination of whether or not a process or program should be initiated to meet such needs, and if so, (3) how the process or program should be designed. *Summative evaluations* measure performance and program impacts. These two types of evaluations are closely interrelated. Information derived from summative evaluations of program impacts provides input for continuing formative evaluative efforts.

At first glance, designing a measurement system capable of providing such evaluative information may appear to be an awesome undertaking. When seen in a historical context, however, the provision of practically all public services are the result of decisions made over time, based directly on such formative and summative information. The mix of services provided by local government reflects a variety of commitments made by the governing body, regulations imposed by other levels of government, and administrative decisions made by appointed officials. The current programs of nonprofit organizations are similarly the cumulation of previous decisions and commitments.

Formative decisions are expressed through local ordinances, budget documents, state statutes and regulations, intergovernmental contracts and agreement, federal laws, and so on. While managers can make important contributions to these decisions, it is more likely that formative evaluations will be useful in developing better decisions concerning the improvement of service delivery systems once these broader commitments are made. As Weiss noted, "The analysis of program variables begins to explain why the program has the effect it does. When we know which aspects of the program are associated with more or less success, we have a basis for recommendations for future modifications [8]." In short, effective evaluation not only describes what is happening, it also helps to determine which features of a program are successful and which are not.

Both input and intervening variables must be measured in order to make such determinations. *Input variables* include information that might be considered extraneous to the program itself. Analysis of input variables, however, can provide information necessary to identify more clearly why a program may or may not be successfully implemented in a particular setting or context. Data collection on input variables should be undertaken with the limitations of time and cost constraints in mind. As Weiss suggested, "... most evaluations have limited resources, and it is far more productive to focus on a few relevant variables than to go on a wide-ranging fishing expedition [9]."

Two kinds of *intervening variables* must be measured: (1) program operation variables, and (2) bridging variables (i.e., the intermediate steps selected as a means to achieve program objectives). A clear understanding of the causal relationships between intermediate activities and their consequences has a direct impact upon the ability of an organization to meet its objectives [10]. A poorly conceived program or process, no matter how effectively implemented, contributes relatively little to the overall effectiveness of an organization.

Organizational constraints again will limit the time and resources that can be devoted to the analysis of intervening variables. One approach is to involve program managers, either through formal or informal procedures, in seeking answers to such questions. Whether or not the connections between program design and objectives are formally determined, "there are almost always some prevailing notions, however unexplicit, that certain intermediary actions or conditions will bring about the desired outcomes [11]."

Complete clarity as to the anticipated program impacts seldom comes from an examination of the final statements of the planning process. Therefore, before an evaluation can be initiated, it often is necessary to determine the exact character and intent of specific program objectives. Ten criteria for clarifying program objectives were identified by Shortell and Richardson (see Table 11.2).

Final product of the formative evaluation process should be a *service delivery plan*, based on an understanding of the causal relations between the activities to be performed and the desired results. A formative evaluation should also yield a set of *strategic objectives*, outlining a course of action in broad terms and supporting *management objectives*, which provide for the quantification of progress toward goal achievement. Objectives developed through formative evaluation techniques should represent the best available solution for a particular problem (within the constraints of available resources). They should also provide a foundation for the subsequent development of mechanisms with which to measure the actual performance of programs and their broader impacts. However, as previously discussed, the complexities inherent in an analysis of the relationships that exist between programs and desired results and the difficulties surrounding the development of appropriate objectives represent a significant challenge to the strategic manager.

TABLE 11.2   Criteria for Clarifying Program Objectives

Nature or content of the objective. It is important to determine the intended changes to be brought about by the program.

Ordering of objectives. Objectives should be clearly presented at each level of abstraction, with corresponding operational indicators to determine if the objectives have been met.

Target groups. The specific group(s) to which the program is directed should be identifiable in terms of age, sex, ethnic categories, geographic boundaries, etc.

Short-term versus long-term effects. The short-term impacts and the long-term effects of any program should be documented.

Magnitude of results. It is necessary to determine how large (or small) an effect will be acceptable as a positive indicator of success.

Stability of outcomes. For many programs, the effects are meant to be lasting; for others, particularly programs involving behavioral changes, additional exposure (reinforcement) to the program may be necessary.

Multiplicity of objectives. It is important to clarify objectives to the extent that possible conflicts among them can be identified and addressed.

Importance. While objectives often differ in importance, and individuals may disagree on their relative value, some attempt should be made to place objectives in some general priority order.

Interrelatedness. Linkages should be identified especially when a set of lower-order objectives may serve as an important component in the achievement of higher order objectives.

Second-order consequences. It is important to identify possible side effects of the program—effects not intended but anticipated, or even unanticipated, by the initiators of the program.

Source: S. M. Shortell and W. C. Richardson. Health Program Evaluation. St. Louis, MO: Mosby, 1978, pp. 18–20.

5   BASIC APPROACHES TO EVALUATION

Ideally, a performance evaluation seeks to compare *what actually happened* to *what would have happened if* the program or process had not been initiated. Since it often is difficult, if not impossible, to determine exactly "what would have happened if ..." the problem is to apply evaluative procedures that can approximate this state. Standard approaches for conducting an evaluation include (1) before-and-after comparisons, (2) time-trend-data projections, (3) with-and-without comparisons, (4) comparisons of planned versus actual performance, and (5) controlled experimentation.

5.1   The First and Final Steps

Each performance evaluative approach begins and ends with the same procedural steps. The first step is to identify the *relevant objectives* of the process, program, or activities under evaluation and the corresponding evaluative criteria or effectiveness measures. The final step should include an explicit and thorough search for *other plausible explanations* for the observed changes and, if any exist, an estimate of their effects on the data.

The major purpose of evaluation is to identify changes in those criteria that can be reasonably attributed to the process, program, or activities under study. A major problem, however, is that other factors—such as external events or the simultaneous introduction of other related programs—may have occurred during the time period covered by the evaluation. One of these factors may have been the significant cause of the observed changes and not the program or process under evaluation. Explicit provisions for controlling at least some of these exogenous factors are included in the second, third, and fifth approaches described below.

Rossi and his colleagues identified a number of "competing processes" that may influence program effects (see Table 11.3). The outcome of any program is a function of net program effects and these confounding elements. Competing processes must be isolated and addressed in each of the evaluation approaches described in the following sections.

Evaluators need to be aware of the history, trends, politics, policies, values, and philosophies behind public programs. For example, programs that deal with juvenile justice may reflect bias toward treatment or punishment or may focus on the youth or on the family. It is necessary to know how all of the forces impact on whatever services are being evaluated. Evaluators may have to deal with client groups that receive services from many different programs. Such multiple service systems may have competing and contradictory orientations.

5.2   Before-and-After Comparisons

Before-and-after comparisons are the simplest, least costly, and most common evaluative approaches. Such comparisons involve the examination of conditions in a given target population at two points in time—immediately before a program or process is introduced and at some appropriate time after its implementation. The assumption is that any changes in the "after" data, as measured by appropriate evaluation criteria, have occurred as a consequence of the new program or process. This approach is valid only in situations where changes related to the program or process are clearly measurable and where comparisons are not likely to reflect short-term fluctuations.

The effectiveness of this approach can be increased if the evaluation is carefully planned prior to the implementation of the program. In this way,

TABLE **11.3** Competing Processes That Influence Program Effects

Endogenous change: Conditions for which the program is seen as a remedy or enhancement may change of their own accord. In medical research, the phenomenon is known as "spontaneous remission."

Secular drift: Relatively long-term trends in the target population or in the broader community may produce changes that enhance or mask the effects of the program.

Interfering events: Short-term events also may produce enhancing or masking changes.

Program-related effects: Actual evaluation effort may contribute to a bias in program results—the problem for an evaluator is to maintain the role of an 'uninvolved observer."

Stochastic effects: Chance or random fluctuation in any measurement effort may make it difficult to judge whether a given outcome, in fact, is large enough to warrant attention. Sampling theory can identify how much variation can be expected by chance.

Unreliability: Data collection procedures are subject to a certain degree of unreliability. A major source of the problem may be the measurement instrument itself.

Self-selection: Segments of the target population easiest to reach are those most likely to change in the desired direction for other reasons. Similar processes in the opposite direction may lead to differential attrition. Dropout rates vary from project to project, but are always troublesome in evaluations.

Maturation trends: Programs directed toward changing persons at various stages in their life cycle must cope with the fact that considerable changes also are associated with the process of maturation.

Source: Peter H. Rossi, Howard E. Freeman, and Sonia Wright. Evaluation: A Systematic Approach. Beverly Hills, CA: Sage Publications, 1979, pp. 172–175.

appropriate data can be collected as a basis for the evaluation criteria. Reliance on data available in established collection procedures seldom provides an adequate basis for such evaluations. Special data collection procedures will increase the cost of the evaluation, but this approach is still the least expensive of the methods outlined.

5.3 Time-Trend Data Projections

Time-trend data projections draw comparisons between actual data and extrapolated data that suggest conditions that would have prevailed without the program or process. Data on each evaluative criterion should be obtained at several intervals before and after the initiation of the new activities. Data obtained prior to implementation are projected to the end of the evaluation period by means of standard statistical methods. Actual and projected estimates are then compared to determine the amount of change resulting from the introduction of the program or process.

This approach is most appropriate when an underlying trend can be identified over a period of time that would likely continue if the new program or process had not been introduced. The objective is to change the direction of the trend—to dampen some undesirable condition or to amplify some desirable change. Statistical projections may be relatively meaningless, however, if data for prior years are unstable. Likewise, if there is strong evidence that underlying conditions have changed in very recent times, data for prior years probably should not be used.

The time-trend approach adds two cost elements to the first method: (1) the cost of technical expertise to undertake the statistical projections, and (2) the added data collection for prior years. This latter requirement may become problematic in assuring that preprogram data are compatible with current or postprogram data.

5.4   With-and-Without Comparisons

With-and-without comparisons examine a population to which a particular program has been applied and one or more "control groups" to which comparable programs have not been applied. This approach can be used, for example, if some segment of the population within a community is to be served by a given program while others are not, as is the case when a pilot program is tested. Changes in the values of the evaluative criteria (rates of change as well as amounts) for the "with" and the "without" groups form the basis for this comparison. The characteristics determining the choice of comparative groups will vary with the types of programs under evaluation. The choice ultimately is based on the judgment of the evaluator as to what factors that are not related to the program may influence the effectiveness of the program under study. Although this approach controls some important external factors, it generally is not a fully reliable measure of program effects. It is best applied in conjunction with other evaluative methods.

Identification of comparable populations may require considerable effort. The cost may be reasonable if standard data categories are adequate (such as similar population size, proximity, and so on). The costs may rise significantly, however, if populations are selected for particular combinations of characteristics or to ensure that a similar program effort does not exist in the "without" populations. The availability of comparable data may be severely limited since the type of data collection and the precision of these data is likely to vary from group to group. Thus, the cost of this approach will be considerably higher if special data-collection efforts are required.

5.5   Comparisons of Planned Versus Actual Performance

After-the-fact comparisons involve rather straightforward procedures and yet are surprisingly rare in their use. This approach requires that specific, measurable objectives or targets be established prior to the initiation of the program or process. Targets should be identified for a specific achievement within specific time periods (for example, "A reduction in the incidence of juvenile delinquency by 15% in two years," rather than, "The elimination of juvenile delinquency"). The actual performance (program outcomes) is then compared to these targets. Such evaluations can be readily undertaken if targets are expressed in terms of effectiveness measures. This evaluative approach is commonly used in conjunction with Hoshin planning.

Like the before-and-after approach, this method provides no explicit means of indicating the extent to which changes in the values of effectiveness criteria can be attributed solely to the new program or process. As with other techniques, an explicit search should be made for other plausible explanations as to why the targets have been met, exceeded, or not met.

Appropriate, realistic objectives must be established as the basis for evaluation criteria. The task of setting objectives may not be taken seriously if the evaluations are not used seriously—a problem with all evaluation techniques. Targets may be overstated and, therefore, unattainable, or they be understated to make the program achievements look better. If the findings of the evaluation are seriously used by decision makers, however, a valuable spin-off of this approach is that the establishment of targets is likely to become an important issue. Higher-level officials, as well as program managers, should participate in this process, and the targets should explicitly encompass all key program effects.

The after-the-fact approach can be applied more widely once provision is made for the regular collection of the data necessary for measuring effectiveness. This approach is particularly useful for annual performance evaluations. Targets can be set each year for one or more future years. Much can be learned from a careful, systematic examination of the immediate, short-term consequences of a program, even if a more elaborate evaluation method is not applied.

This evaluative technique is relatively inexpensive compared to other methods. Costs depend primarily on the expenditures necessary to gather additional data for the evaluation criteria selected. Setting appropriate (measurable) objectives is likely to entail relatively small cost—at least in dollar terms.

5.6   Controlled Experimentation

Controlled experimentation is by far the most potent approach to evaluation. Unfortunately, it also is the most difficult and costly to undertake. The procedures may involve many steps of experimental design techniques and can become very complex with respect to a particular performance evaluation. The basic steps are outlined in Table 11.4.

The controlled experiment is most appropriate for the evaluation of programs directed toward specific individuals, such as health programs, manpower training, etc., and for a variety of treatment programs such as those of drug and alcohol abuse, correction and rehabilitation, or work-release. It is not likely to be appropriate, however, for programs requiring large capital investments in equipment or facilities.

An important variation on this approach involves the comparison of different geographical areas. Many programs can be introduced initially in some localities and not in others. For example, new crime prevention programs, solid waste collection procedures, programs of traffic control, and so forth often are tried out and evaluated in a few areas before receiving widespread application. If it is possible to identify areas with similar characteristics with respect to the program being tested, some of these areas may be designed as program recipients. If trends in the evaluation data before and after the new program was implemented show significant improvements in those areas with the program, then a basis would be provided for attributing the change to the introduction of the program.

TABLE 11.4 Basic Steps of the Controlled Experiment Approach

1. Identify relevant objectives and corresponding evaluation criteria.
2. Select target populations that have similar characteristics with respect to their likelihood of being effectively treated by the program.
3. Assign target population (or a probability sample of that population) to control and experimental groups in a scientifically random manner.
4. Measure the preprogram performance of each group using the selected evaluation criteria.
5. Apply the program to the experimental group, but not to the control group.
6. Continuously monitor the operations of the experiment to determine if any actions occur that might distort the findings.
7. Adjust any such deviant behavior, if appropriate and possible; if not, at least identify and estimate its impact on eventual findings.
8. Measure postprogram performance of each group using the selected evaluation criteria.
9. Compare pre- and postprogram changes in the evaluation criteria of the groups.
10. Search for plausible alternative explanations for observed changes and, if any exist, estimate their effects on the data.

Adapted from: Harry P. Hatry, et al., How Effective Are Your Community Services? Washington, D.C.: The Urban Institute, 1977, pp. 207–213.

This approach can produce some special problems that may bring the observed results into question.

1. Members of an experimental group may respond differently to a program if they realize they are part of an experiment. This problem is known as the Hawthorne effect, after studies by Dickson and Roethlisberger in the late 1920s at the Western Electric Company's Hawthorne Works in Chicago. In these studies, the productivity of the test group increased even under adverse conditions as a consequence of their selection for evaluation. To help reduce this problem, it may be necessary to inform members of the control group that they too are part of an experiment.
2. Results may differ significantly when the program is shifted from a pilot basis to full-scale application. For example, a new crime prevention program introduced on a pilot basis may merely cause a shift in the incidence of crime to other parts of the community. As a result, there may be no reduction in the overall crime rate.
3. In some situations, political pressures may make it impractical to provide services to one group, while withholding these services from others. Testing variations of a program in several locations rather than allocating program resources on an all-or-nothing basis may lessen such problems.
4. It may be considered morally wrong to provide a service temporarily if the service may cause dependency and leave individuals worse off after the program is withdrawn.
5. If persons are permitted to volunteer to participate in the experimental group, the two groups are not likely to be comparable. A self-selected group will probably be more receptive to the program and thus may not be typical of the whole target population.
6. Administrative problems may introduce a bias into the program results. For example, a specially trained staff may be able to deliver the pilot program at a level that cannot be sustained by regular agency personnel who will be called on to administer the full-scale program.

The use of the controlled experiment approach generally costs considerably more than the other evaluation techniques. These higher costs are because of the greater time required to plan and conduct the experiment and to analyze the data and the higher level of analytical and managerial skills required. This approach also implies certain indirect costs arising from the temporary changes made in the way the program operates in order to achieve differential benefits. Innovative projects can be evaluated more readily because pools of "unexposed" potential targets usually are available. Established projects, on the other hand, may require statistical methods that measure the effects in degrees of exposure, as well as by reflective controls that utilize time-series analysis [12].

5.7 Combined Approaches

The selection of an appropriate approach will depend on the timing of the evaluation, the costs involved and resources available, and the desired accuracy. It should be evident that these approaches are not either/or choices. Some or all of the methods can be used in combination. The before-and-after method is relatively weak when applied alone, but becomes much more useful in combination with other approaches. The after-the-fact approach, involving comparisons of planned versus actual performance, is likely to be used more extensively once information management systems become more widely accepted and implemented in public and nonprofit organizations. Although the experimental approach provides the most precise evaluation, its costs and special characteristics result in its being applied on a very selective basis.

Decisions about public programs inevitably are made under conditions of considerable uncertainty. Evaluations can reduce this uncertainty, but cannot eliminate it totally. Even though it may not be possible to isolate the effects of a program from other concurrent events, it may be unnecessary to be overly concerned if the evaluation indicates significant benefits to the community or target population.

6 APPLICATIONS OF EVALUATION FINDINGS

Performance evaluations are little more than academic exercises if their findings have no impact on the processes by which policies are made and programs are developed. As Rossi observed: "Evaluations cannot influence decision-making processes unless those undertaking them recognize the need to orient their efforts toward maximizing the policy utility of their evaluation activities [13]." At the same time, the need for evaluation must be recognized and accepted by those individuals with responsibility for the development and implementation of programs and policies. Management and performance audits are examples of mechanisms for the further application of findings of evaluations.

6.1 Management and Performance Audits

The American Accounting Association defines auditing as

> ... a systematic process of objectively obtaining and evaluating evidence regarding assertions about economic actions and events to ascertain the degree of correspondence between those assertions and established criteria, and communicating the results to interested users [14].

The traditional focus of auditing has been an assessment of fiscal transactions for accuracy, legality, and fidelity—on issues of financial compliance. There are two basic types of financial audits. *Internal audits* are conducted periodically by in-house staff and result in reports for internal control purposes. *External audits*, normally required by state law, are conducted by independent certified public accountants after the fiscal year has been completed. An external audit may be submitted to the regulating state agency (such as the Auditor of Public Accounts), as well as to the local governing body. The governing body, in turn, should review the audit findings to ensure that revenue and expenditure activities have been conducted in accordance with the intentions of the budget and appropriation ordinance.

The scope of auditing is expanding because the notion of accountability has been expanding. More emphasis is being placed on audits that ask, "Were the program milestones achieved in the most efficient and economical way possible?" *Management audits* involve an assessment of resource utilization practices, including an examination of the adequacy of information management systems, administrative procedures, and organizational structure. A *performance audit* extends the focus of a management audit to include an examination of program results to determine whether (1) the desired benefits were achieved, (2) program objectives were met, and (3) alternatives were considered that may yield the desired results at a lower cost. A performance audit generally is undertaken when a program or project has been completed or has reached a major milestone in its funding. In some instances, the performance of agencies or programs is audited because standards of performance accountability are spelled out in legislation, regulations, or other governmental guidelines.

The distinctions among three basic types of audits, as described by the U.S. Comptroller General, are shown in Table 11.5. Regardless of the scope or emphasis, an audit must include the following elements.

1. *Audit objective:* A question or a statement at the start of the detailed examination concerning the results expected.
2. *Audit criteria:* Appropriate standards that can be used to measure the actions of management, employees, or their delegated agents in any audit situation.
3. *Causes:* Actions that took place or that should have taken place to carry out assigned program responsibilities.
4. *Effects:* Results achieved as determined by comparing actions taken (causes) with the appropriate standards (criteria).
5. *Audit evidence:* Facts and information used by an auditor as a basis to come to a conclusion on the audit objective.

The information that constitutes the audit evidence must be relevant, material, and competent. The auditor cannot reach a conclusion from evidence unless

TABLE 11.5 Types and Characteristics of Audits

Financial and compliance. Determines whether financial operations are properly conducted, the financial reports of an audited entity are presented fairly, and the entity has complied with applicable laws and regulations. Sufficient audit work must be carried out to determine whether the audit entity is:

1. Maintaining effective control over revenue, expenditures, assets, and liabilities.
2. Properly accounting for resource liabilities and operations.
3. Providing financial reports that contain accurate, reliable, and useful financial data that are fairly presented.
4. Complying with the requirements of applicable laws and regulations.

Economy and efficiency. Determines whether the entity is managing or utilizing its resources (personnel, property, space, and so forth) in an economical and efficient manner with due consideration to conservation of its resources and minimum expenditure of effort. Causes for any inefficiencies or uneconomical practices should be identified, including inadequacies in information management systems, administrative procedures, or organizational structure. Examples of uneconomical practices or inefficiencies include:

Procedures, whether officially prescribed or merely followed, which are ineffective or more costly than justified.

Duplication of effort by employees or between organizational units.

Performance of work which serves little or no useful purpose.

Inefficient or uneconomical use of equipment.

Over-staffing in relation to the work to be done.

Faulty buying practices and accumulation of unneeded or excessive quantities of property, materials, or supplies.

Wasteful use of resources.

Program results. Determines whether the desired results or benefits are being achieved, the objectives established by the legislature or other authorizing body are being met, and the agency has considered alternatives that may yield desired results at a lower cost. The auditor should consider:

1. Relevance and validity of the criteria used by the audited entity to judge effectiveness in achieving program results.
2. Appropriateness of the methods followed by the entity to evaluate effectiveness in achieving program results.
3. Accuracy of the data accumulated.
4. Reliability of the results obtained.

Adapted from: The Comptroller General of the United States. Standards for Audit of Governmental Organizations, Programs, Activities, and Functions. Washington, DC: General Accounting Office, 1974, pp. 2, 11, 12.

fairly specific guidelines are available as to the nature of what is to be audited. Evidence should only be gathered relating to the specific objectives of the audit. The evidence gathered should permit the auditor to reach a conclusion on the audit objective.

An example of an audit objective might read as follows: By contracting with a consulting firm for the development, implementation, and conversion of its accounting and administrative records system to a computerized system (causes) upon completing the design and systems specifications (criteria), will the City be provided with a workable system after spending the total cost of the contract of $200,000 (effects)?

Assume that the audit evidence indicates that the information system, as delivered by the consultants, has encountered a number of problems and, in fact, has resulted in additional billings by the consultants in an effort to address these problems. Further investigation reveals that the design and systems specifications that were to be undertaken by the city were only about 75% complete at the time the contract was entered into with the consultants. City personnel also took excessive amounts of time in reaching decisions necessary to resolve various problems that arose during the development of the information system. As a result, significant delays were encountered in implementation of the new information management system.

The audit conclusion drawn from the audit objective and the evidence may be as follows: By not providing complete design and systems specifications and proper and timely review of the consultant's work at each stage of the system's development (causes), the City was forced to spend an additional $75,000 beyond the original cost of $200,000 to address problems encountered with the operation of the system (effects), and now finds that an additional cost of over $50,000 will be required to bring the system to an acceptable level of performance (effects).

The *audit report* would contain the audit conclusion, along with sufficient evidence to demonstrate that the conclusion is correct. In addition, the report would likely include recommendations regarding procedures for preparing, managing, and monitoring software development contracts in the future. The report may also recommend the establishment of proper review and approval procedures to monitor each phase of the software development. And appropriate clauses to be included in contracts may be suggested to ensure the ability of the City to deny payment when a contractor does not perform properly.

6.2 Program Reconstruction

Program terminations are rare. Complex organizations have an uncanny instinct for survival, and as a consequence, programs may be constantly adapted to emerging situations in order to avoid termination. Given the hard-fought battles necessary to obtain a policy or program in the first instance, officials have a natural reluctance to consider the issue of termination. Significant political and/or client groups often support programs beyond their span of effectiveness. And programs have certain rights of "due process." Thus, mounting campaigns for termination often can be costly, both monetarily and politically.

The real art of program improvement is not the bold guillotining of unpromising programs, but rather reconstructing or renegotiating the program development process. The concept of *program reconstruction* is based on the feedback stage of the strategic management process, wherein initial program outputs are modified in response to the reactions of affected groups and sources of support. Reconstruction suggests a refining and retargeting of programs (and policies) rather than setting totally new directions.

Strategic reconstruction often is possible, particularly if such adjustments are amenable to entrenched interests. Peter de Leon offered several guidelines for program modification:

1. Modification and/or termination should be viewed as an opportunity for program or process improvement and not as the end of the world.
2. Modification and/or termination should coincide with systematic evaluation.
3. Policies and programs have certain "natural points"—times and places in their life spans—where reconsideration is more likely and more appropriate.
4. The time horizon for gradual change is a significant factor.
5. The structure of incentives may be changed to promote modifications (for example, agencies may be permitted to retain a portion of the program funding that they voluntarily cut).
6. Agencies may employ a staff of "salvage specialists," trained in reallocating resources [15].

Increasingly, government activities are constrained by fiscal circumstances. Therefore, termination, or at least reconstruction, is becoming more viable.

6.3 Balanced Scorecard

According to Kaplan and Norton, the primary objective of an evaluation should be to provide a balance "between short- and long-term objectives, between financial and non-financial measures, between lagging and leading indicators, and between external and internal performance perspectives [16]." They suggested that traditional performance measures, derived from accounting data, quickly become obsolete. Therefore, a more comprehensive approach is required to provide organizations with more efficient evaluative tools. Kaplan and Norton proposed four different perspectives from which an organization's activities should be evaluated.

1. Financial perspective. (How does the organization perceive its stakeholders?)
2. Customer perspective. (How does the organization perceive its customers?)
3. Process perspective. (In what processes should the organization excel in order to succeed?)
4. Learning and innovation perspective. (How will the organization sustain its ability to change and improve?)

These four perspectives are incorporated in the balanced scorecard approach to performance measurement. The balance scorecard supports strategic planning and implementation by consolidating the actions of all parts of an organization around a common understanding of its goals and objectives. It facilitates the assessment and upgrading of the organization's strategies. It enables management to monitor the determinants of stakeholder values, such as customer satisfaction, quality of service, response time, and long-term strategic vision. Scorecard applications are used to drive more effective performance from the top throughout the organization, linking employee action to the organization's mission.

A balanced scorecard starts from the organization's vision statement and related strategic objectives. Critical success factors are defined, and measures (metrics) are constructed that can assist in setting targets and measuring performance in areas critical to the strategic objectives. A limited, yet comprehensive set of performance measures is identified to assist senior executives in directing the operations of the organization. Operational excellence is achieved by:

Focusing on the deployment of an organization's long-term strategies in addition to meeting its short-term targets.

Recognizing that success is measured by a total spectrum of performance measures—financial, customer, internal process, and innovation and learning. Financial results are only one measure of success.

Becoming more forward-looking by concentrating on leading indicators rather than focusing on the past (lagging indicators).

Expanding the outlook of management beyond an organization's internal structure.

The balanced scorecard approach is intended to communicate strategies to the rank and file of the organization so that everyone can understand how they can contribute to achieving the organization's objectives. In the private sector, compensation often is tied to achieving strategic targets.

The metrics of the balanced scorecard require modification when applied to public and nonprofit organizations. Government agencies do not strive to achieve a competitive position and thereby, maximize profits, but rather they seek to fulfill their charter or mission, which is an "inherently governmental function [17]."

> The key metric for government (or nonprofit) performance, therefore, is not financial in nature, but rather *mission effectiveness*. But mission effectiveness is not a definite and static thing. Usually, an agency has a rather broad general mission, which incorporates many specific sub-missions or departmental missions within it [17].

Thus, to evaluate the performance of public or nonprofit organizations, the criteria or metrics of the balance scorecard should focus on the following categories.

1. Strategic control measures.
2. Process-specific effectiveness measures.
3. Measures of operational efficiency.

Strategic control measures provide a basis on which to assess the current and future needs of the organization in terms of its overall mission effectiveness. This assessment includes an analysis of the broader environment within which the organization must operate. SWOT analysis and gap analysis techniques often are applied in this broad area of performance evaluation. Process-specific effectiveness measures should focus on the health and viability of those processes or programs that will be required to sustain the organization's growth and vitality now and in the future. Measures of operational efficiency should be selected to assess the quality of operational functions in support of the strategic objectives of the organization. Efficiency measures are concerned with minimizing cost and often are derived from benchmarking and best practice initiatives.

The four basic evaluative perspectives of the balanced scorecard approach, as identified by Kaplan and Norton, require some modification when applied to public and nonprofit organizations (see Figure 11.6). The financial perspective is focused primarily on the budget process—on the management of public resources and on the control of costs. The achievement of customer satisfaction is still an important objective to evaluate. However, as has been discussed previously, the customer (or constituents) of public and nonprofit organizations differ considerably from those of for-profit entities. Internal processes in public and nonprofit organizations often focus on economies of scale, cost reduction, efficiencies, and standardization of services. The learning and innovation perspective is the least developed component of the balanced scorecard approach as applied in the public sector. Private entities actively pursue creativity and innovation, uniqueness and product recognition, and the application of advanced technology

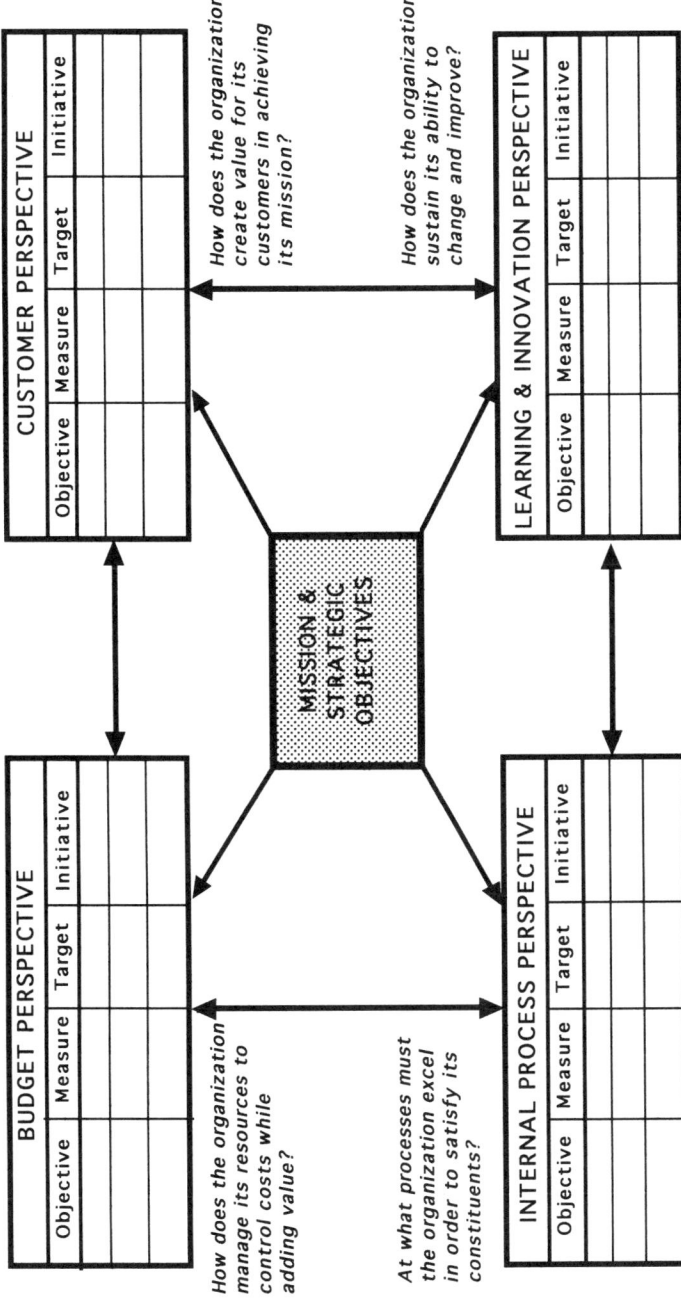

FIGURE 11.6   Balanced scorecard perspectives for public and nonprofit organizations.

to remain competitive. Issues of accountability, equity and fairness, and integrity are more likely reflected in the values of public and nonprofit organizations.

The balanced scorecard method provides public and nonprofit organizations with the ability to:

Define strategic performance and analyze current programs and processes in terms of this performance scorecard.

View critical interdependencies among the organizational units that deliver value to customers or constituents.

Communicate and implement the organization's strategies.

Track key milestones relating to strategic initiatives and projects.

Capture and communicate both obvious and tacit knowledge for exception-driven problem solving.

Integrate enterprise data sources and systems and deploy the same information technology applications across multiple platforms.

A balanced scorecard helps align key performance measures with strategies at various levels within an organization. Management is provided with a more comprehensive picture of organizational operations. Greater visibility is created in terms of how stakeholder values are influenced by nonfinancial drivers within the organization. The balanced scorecard approach helps reduce to the essentials the vast amount of information that an organization's information management systems must process. And it provides strategic feedback and learning.

The balanced scorecard is not without its limitations, however. By focusing on a limited set of measures, an organization may be blindsided by other factors. Experience has shown that a limited set of performance measures cannot provide a complete and definitive understanding of an organization's performance. It also is human nature to choose measures that will confirm our belief set. However, these selected measures may not provide the objective data necessary to identify the need for and assist in making major changes in performance.

Many organizations often seem to measure for measurement sake. Collecting data is generally wasteful to an organization that does not act on the data. Reacting to random variation (noise) as if it were a signal to implement change will lead to wasted efforts and actions that are, at best, inappropriate, and at worst, completely contrary to the proper course of action.

Performance measures often remained unbalanced with a prejudice toward financial measures. To report that an organization had such and such a profit or loss is relatively easy to comprehend. However, to evaluate the combined impact of unhappy employees and dissatisfied customers is much more difficult to conceptualize. Often the secret to improved performance is to focus on measuring the process rather than performance results. Multiple dimensions of results could and should be measured for any process, necessitating the need for a more exhaustive list of performance measures.

The concept of leading and lagging indicators was introduced into the performance measurement lexicon to minimize the impact of historical analysis. A lagging indicator focuses on what happened in the past. A leading indicator, on the other hand, measures factors that cause the subsequent results. All too often, a leading indicator is still a historical measure that is assumed to have forward-looking powers. What is needed are real-time indicators that statistically infer upcoming events—to know what certain events will follow. These future-oriented indicators should allow management to be proactive rather than drawing inferences after the fact.

7 SUMMARY AND CONCLUSIONS

Performance evaluation involves the application of strategic controls to significant components of an organization. The strategic management process must be continually evaluated as a series of activities that can operate with varying degrees of effectiveness. An evaluation of an organization's performance must begin with a critique of the management style or approach that has been adopted. The nature and quality of management is largely a function of systemic concerns, concerns for risk, and time concerns. An examination of these basic areas can provide a fuller understanding of the possible attitudes that managers may adopt in the performance of their responsibilities. This assessment, in turn, can assist in determining the basis for a successful and effective performance in terms of specific programs and projects.

In applying the techniques of performance evaluation, the effectiveness of ongoing and proposed programs is examined in terms of agreed-upon goals and objectives. Areas needing improvement through program modification are identified, including the possible termination of ineffective programs. A performance evaluation must take into account the possible influence of external as well as internal organizational factors.

Formative evaluations provide information necessary to design or modify service delivery systems and to set goals and objectives for these systems. Summative evaluations measure performance and program impacts. Information derived from summative evaluations of program impacts provides input for continuing formative evaluative efforts.

The repertoire of evaluative techniques include (1) before-and-after comparisons, (2) time-trend data projections, (3) with-and-without comparisons, (4) comparisons of planned versus actual performance, and (5) controlled experimentation. An evaluation should begin with an identification of the relevant program objectives and the corresponding evaluative criteria. The major purpose of evaluation is to identify changes in those criteria that can be reasonably attributed to the program or activities under study. Other factors—such as external events or the simultaneous introduction of other related programs—may have precipitated the observed changes and not the program under evaluation. Thus, the final step in any evaluation should include an explicit search for other plausible explanations for the observed changes and, if any exist, an estimate of their effects on the data.

Management and performance audits can provide significant insights regarding the effectiveness of an organization's strategic management system. Issues regarding the overall "fit" of strategic management with the organization's management paradigm should be carefully examined as part of such evaluations.

Program terminations are rare. The real art of program improvement involves the reconstructing or renegotiating of programs (and policies) rather than setting totally new directions.

The balanced scorecard approach is a performance measurement system for translating strategy into action at all levels of the organization. It supports strategic management by focusing all components of an organization on a common understanding of goals and objectives and by facilitating the assessment and upgrade of an organization's strategies. Scorecard applications drive more effective performance from the top throughout the organization, linking employee action to an organization's strategic vision.

ENDNOTES

1. John von Neuman and Oskar Morgenstern. Theory of Games and Economic Behavior. Princeton, NJ: Princeton University Press, 1947.
2. Joseph S. Wholey. What can we actually get from program evaluations? Policy Science. Vol. 3, No. 3, 1972, pp. 361–369.
3. D. N. T. Perkins. Evaluating social intervention: A conceptual schema. Evaluation Quarterly. Vol. 1, November 1977, pp. 642–645.
4. The findings of these evaluations may not be fully utilized because (1) the evaluators are "outsiders" (academic types) often with different perceptions and opinions about the objectives of the policy or program, (2) the evaluations tend to be postmortems, useful in developing a conceptual basis for evaluations but providing little basis on which to improve ongoing policy formulation, and (3) evaluators tend to focus on the negative aspects and rarely offer constructive advice. For a further discussion of these points see: Rehka Agawala-Rogers. Why is evaluation research not utilized? Evaluation Studies. Vol. 2, Beverly Hills, CA.: Sage Publications, 1979; Carol Weiss and Michael J. Bucuvalas. The challenge of social research to decision-making. In Using Social Research in Public Policy Making. Carol Weiss (ed.). Lexington MA: Lexington Books–D.C. Heath and Co., 1977, pp. 213–234.
5. E. S. Quade. Analysis for Public Decisions. New York: American Elsevier Publishing Company, 1975, p. 235.
6. Robert Clark. Policy implementation: Problems and potentials. The Southern Political Science Association Meeting, October 1976.
7. Herbert A. Simon and C. E. Ridley. Measuring Municipal Activities. Chicago: International City Managers' Association, 1938.

8. Carol H. Weiss. Evaluation Research. Englewood Cliffs, NJ: Prentice-Hall, Inc., 1972, p. 46.

9. Carol H. Weiss. Evaluation Research. Englewood Cliffs, NJ: Prentice-Hall, Inc., 1972, p. 47.

10. John Dickey developed a computer-based model called Quantitative CyberQuest (QCQ), the objective of which is to identify the complex interactions among strategic objectives, program strategies, external factors, intermediate variables, and reaction times. For further discussion of this model and its applications, see: John W. Dickey. Quantitative CyberQuest: A new tool for analytical discovery. Proceedings of the International Conference on Computers in Urban Planning and Urban Management. R. Wyatt, ed. Melbourne: University of Melbourne, 1995.

11. Carol H. Weiss. Evaluation Research. Englewood Cliffs, NJ: Prentice-Hall, Inc., 1972, p. 50.

12. Peter H. Rossi, Howard E. Freeman, and Sonia Wright. Evaluation: A Systematic Approach. Beverly Hills, CA: Sage Publications, 1979, p. 224.

13. Peter H. Rossi, Howard E. Freeman, and Sonia Wright. Evaluation: A Systematic Approach. Beverly Hills, CA: Sage Publications, 1979, p. 283.

14. American Accounting Association. Report of Committee on Basic Auditing Concepts. Sarasota, FL, 1971, p. 15.

15. Peter de Leon. A theory of termination. The American Political Science Conference, September 1977.

16. Robert S. Kaplan and David P. Norton. The Balance Scorecard: Translating Strategy into Action. Cambridge, MA: Harvard Business School Publishing, 1996; The Strategy-Focused Organization: How Balanced Scorecard Companies Thrive in the New Business Environment. Cambridge, MA: Harvard Business School Publishing, 2000.

17. Paul Arveson. Translating performance metrics from the private to the public sector. Rockville, MD: Balanced Scorecard Institute, 1999, p. 1.

12

Information Management and Decision-Support Systems

Relevant management information is essential to the effective planning and control of any strategy, process, project, or program. Timely information is required to understand the circumstances surrounding any issue and to evaluate alternative courses of action to resolve any problem. Information is the raw material of intelligence that triggers the recognition that decisions need to be made. Such incremental knowledge can help to reduce uncertainty in particular problem situations.

1 INFORMATION MANAGEMENT SYSTEMS

Vast amounts of facts, numbers, and other data usually are processed in any organization. What constitutes *management information*, however, depends on the problem at hand and the particular frame of reference of the manager. Accounting data, for example, can provide important management information when arrayed appropriately in balance sheets and financial statements. Traditional accounting data may be relatively meaningless, however, if the objective is to evaluate the overall performance of a new strategy or process. Quantitative data, in general, may be insufficient to assess the effectiveness of program activities designed to bring about qualitative change. All-too-often, a significant time lag exists between the emergence of major problems and the recognition of those problems in an organization's information system [1]. Therefore, information required to make more effective strategic decisions must be both *relevant* and *timely*.

1.1 Objectives of an Information Management System

An information management system (IMS) often is vaguely described and broadly misunderstood. Some people tend confuse an IMS with an electronic data-processing system, thinking that the all-knowing computer will provide the answers to complex problems *if* and *when* managers simply learn to press the right buttons. Most information management systems make effective use of modern data-processing software and hardware. However, an IMS is much more than an electronic "black box" that assists in directing and controlling the operations of complex organizations.

Traditionally, information management systems have been developed as tools for operational management. Data are recorded and tracked in some detail to measure various aspects of an organization's day-to-day operations. Strategic decisions differ from operational decisions along several dimensions and, therefore, the information necessary for strategic management varies from the more traditional IMS used for operational control.

The concept of IMS can best be understood by examining separately the three terms: information, management, and system. Taking these words in reverse order may enhance this understanding.

A *system* is a set of component parts joined together to attain a common objective. A system often is made up of a number of *subsystems*, which, in turn, are composed of basic *elements* that define the purpose and capacity of the total system. A properly functioning system is characterized by *synergy*. That is, all elements and subsystems work more effectively together in a system than if they were operating independently. An integrated system's output may be expected to be far greater than the sum of the outputs of its constituent elements. To understand these output relationships, however, it is first necessary to identify and understand the elements and subsystems that serve as the components of the larger system. One reason why "systems" often are so misunderstood stems from a failure to penetrate beyond the surface.

For purpose of an IMS, *management* consists of the activities carried out by managers. Managers must plan, organize, implement, and control those operations within their realm of responsibility. Managers must continually develop, adapt, and implement strategic, tactical, and technical decisions to enhance the capacity of the organization to meet the demands that impinge upon it. The specific objective of an IMS is to communicate information for decision making in a synergistic fashion, where the whole becomes greater than the sum of the individual parts.

Information is different from data and this distinction is very important. Data are facts and figures that are not currently being used in a decision process. Files, records, reports not under immediate consideration are examples of data. By contrast, information consists of classified and interpreted data that are being used for decision making. Thus, the "memory" of an information management system is a repository for information concerning past experiences, for programmed decisions, for information by which "right" decisions can be tested for acceptability, as well as for raw data.

1.2 Storage of Information: Function of the Memory Bank

Information is not subject to the laws of conservation of matter and energy. Information can be created and destroyed—although it cannot be created from nothing nor completely wiped out. Since information has physical reality, its storage—memory—is a physical process that can be represented in seven distinct stages (Table 12.1).

Only part of past experience is selected for storage. In human memory, a selection of what we would like to remember is combined with a selection of what our subconscious mind chooses to emphasize. Information and experience can be broken down into their component parts for storage, and then reassembled into new patterns that are quite different from the intake from the outside world. If improbable combinations and associations turn out to be highly relevant to a particular situation and lead to significant actions, they may be called strokes of genius, flashes of insight, or innovations.

Like human memory, a selective process characterizes organizational "memory"—items are retained that may have some future application. And since

TABLE 12.1 Seven Stages of Information Storage

1. Incoming information is abstracted or coded through the use of appropriate symbols.
2. These symbols are stored using some recording device—distribution of written symbols on paper, activity patterns of cells in nerve tissues, or patterns of electrical charges in electronic devices.
3. Some of the information is dissociated from the rest.
4. Some of the dissociated items, as well as items that have been combined into large assemblies, are recalled.
5. Some of the recalled items may be recombined into new patterns that were not among the inputs into the system.
6. Recombined items are further abstracted or coded, preserving their new pattern, but obliterating their combinatorial origins.
7. New items are transmitted to storage or applied to achieve some desired action.

the future is uncertain, organizations tend to retain more data than can possibly be used as information, thus complicating the retrieval process. Organizational memory also is *dissociative* and *combinatorial*. Stored information can be reassembled into new patterns to more effectively meet particular decision situations and the overall needs of the organization. Collecting and analyzing data and estimating that particular combinations are worth pursuing is one of the fundamental responsibilities of strategic management, resulting in information that better meets an organization's decision needs.

Memory serves a number of important functions in the process of strategic management. It is involved in the screening and selection of *inputs* (the myriad of data that impinge on the organization) to determine *intakes* (information that is taken into the system). Selected information is transmitted to memory and stored for possible recall at later stages in the decision process. In defining a problem, selective recall serves to classify the general nature of the problem and to identify the constraints and boundary conditions of possible solutions. Combined information may be recalled from the memory bank of the IMS, and further input is generated and stored for future recall.

Once preliminary decisions are reached as to the appropriate actions to be initiated, selective information combinations are recalled and applied to modify these decisions in light of what is judged acceptable and feasible. In this process, normative decisions—what should be done—are measured against past experiences (drawn from memory) as to what may be the limit of appropriate action. This process of combining selected data and memories with the "right decision" to achieve an acceptable decision constitutes a second screening process. The screen is continuously modified by the outputs of the system, that is, by the results of decisions that are translated into action.

1.3 IMS, DBMS, and Computers

Computers have made possible the collection and dissemination of greater quantities of information through their ability to store, quickly retrieve, and carry out rapid data computations. Computerized databases provide the basic source of information for organizations in today's fast-paced decision environment. An IMS is composed of *databases* and the *software packages* (computer programs) required to manage them. A database is a collection of structured and related information stored in the computer system. Different software packages facilitate the access and management of these data, along with the tools necessary to conduct analyses and generate reports.

However, data may suffer from significant incompatibilities across different computing platforms—hardware and supporting software—and even within the personal computer environment. Multiple users must be able to share much of the same data in a consistent, accurate, up-to-date, and secure format, regardless of the origin and purpose such data. The primary objective of a *database management system* (DBMS) is to facilitate this sharing function. Bassler defined a DBMS as,

> A software system that provides for a means of representing data, procedures for making changes in these data (adding to, subtracting from, and modifying), a method for making inquires of the data base and to process these raw data to produce information, and to provide all the necessary internal management functions to minimize the user effort to make the system responsive [2].

A database management system should include a high-level, interactive query language facility; word-processing software; and statistical analysis capabilities. A DBMS may also include an interactive analytical package that permits the exploration of "what if" scenarios; a package that supports modeling and simulation; and, possibly, customized software related to specialized management needs. In the past, such systems have been limited to large mainframe computers with collections of extensive and often expensive software packages. This limitation is one major reason why information management systems have been used primarily for operational decisions and not for strategic management decisions.

Data sharing is achieved through file servers housed in local area networks (LAN). Files are shipped from a DBMS residing centrally on the network to be processed locally. Whole files may be downloaded and selectively accessed. This approach can be inefficient, however, especially when only a few records are required by the requesting applications. Moreover, the integrity, security, concurrency, and recovery of such files can be difficult to manage under this approach.

Similarly, the connection of microcomputers to other platforms is limited to host links. Conversion problems and the resulting data redundancy may accompany the transfer of data files of different formats for processing and storage.

Unfortunately, many popular so-called DBMS are essentially programmable filers, leaving most of the job of managing data to the users and providing relatively unproductive tools to assist in this undertaking. Except for elementary data manipulations, the results often cannot be accessed directly. To obtain the desired results, internal procedures must be created for the system to follow. Much of the procedural detail consists of explicit references to internal storage structures, addressing mechanisms, and so on—tasks that are irrelevant to logical database operations. Thus, the user must become involved in machine complexities and performance considerations. Most people are ill-equipped to handle these programming requirements and should not have to bother with them anyway.

Technical personnel often must mediate between end-users and their data. The natural language of the end-user differs considerably from the procedural machine-oriented tools that traditional DBMS products provide. Communication between the user and the DBMS often is time-consuming, inefficient, and ineffective. The development of procedural applications frequently is difficult and error-prone. A database that tracks the property tax records of a medium-sized city or county, for example, may require the attention of a programmer or systems analyst for 20 to 30 hours a week. This programming intervention is necessary not only to access the data for various management reports, but also to ensure that data consistency is maintained so that the information generated is consistent over time.

Without systematic guidelines drawn from a theoretical foundation, database products have been developed largely on an ad hoc basis. The result has been a proliferation of different solutions to a generic set of problems. Most of the available products were originally designed to operate in a stand-alone mode. Furthermore, these products are proprietary, and despite some similarities, each approaches the same data tasks in its own unique way. As a result, the user ends up having to fill the gaps with their own programs and often must accept disruptive revisions that often result in additional programming requirements to deal with further incompatibilities. Implementation of revisions to the DBMS results in the imposition of further maintenance burdens on their applications. The ability to transfer or distribute data and applications may be limited because such details tend to vary across computing platforms.

Various attempts have been made to overcome these limitations within the constraints of the personnel computer environment. However, in these approaches, the overall purpose of the data operations may not be obvious to the database system, and thus, these operations cannot be optimized. In addition, personnel computers often lack vital information about the current state of the decision environment and the intelligence on which to base optimal decisions.

Issues of integrity, security, concurrency, and recovery must be properly addressed in the development of a more effective DBMS. The power to ease-of-use ratio must be improved. As the capacity of mainframe computers for even more rapid data processing developed, the ability of end-users to access data without extensive programming skills often diminished. Maintenance burdens must be minimized, while performance is maximized, especially over various information networks. Moreover, a variety of nondatabase software packages, which store and manage their own disparate data in different formats, must be more fully integrated into an effective DBMS.

1.4 The Relational Model

The interrelated nature of data had been recognized from the beginning of computing. Prior to the 1970s, however, the most advanced approaches for organizing data were hierarchies—relatively complex programming structures that limited the ability to transfer data from one hierarchy to another. In 1969, Edgar F. Codd, an IBM mathematician, developed a relational theory of data, which he proposed as a universal foundation for database systems [3].

Codd's model covered the three primary aspects that any DBMS must address: *structure*, *integrity*, and *manipulation*. It is based on the mathematics of relations and first-order predicate logic—a rigorous definition of the "set operations" that a relational database should support for manipulation of tables. Codd's theories were so radical for the time that they were met with skepticism. However, the simplicity of the relational model won over many software designers and relational database management systems (RDBMSs) were developed.

As originally presented, the meaning and implications of Codd's relational model were largely misunderstood. Therefore, Codd supplemented his model in 1985 with the now-famous "fidelity rules" to guide the implementation and evaluation of relational DBMS software [4]. The rules cover matters ranging from the database access that must be provided for users to issues of data security. These rules are shown in simplified terms in Table 12.2. Since Codd proposed these rules, the relational model has been refined, clarified, and extended in many ways, but the initial features and rules are still valid.

All relational databases share the following basic technology.

1. A clear distinction is maintained in the database system between the logical views of the data presented to the user and the physical structure of the data stored in the system. The user does not need to

TABLE 12.2 Codd's 12 Fidelity Rules

---

1. Data should be presented to the user in table form.
2. Every data element should be accessible without ambiguity.
3. A field should be allowed to remain empty for future use.
4. The description of a database should be accessible to the user.
5. A database must support a clearly defined language to define the database, view the definition, manipulate the data, and restrict some data values to maintain integrity.
6. Data should be able to be changed through any view available to the user.
7. All records in a file must be able to be added, deleted, or changed with a single command.
8. Changes in how data are stored or retrieved should not affect how the user accesses the data.
9. The user's view of the data should be unaffected by its actual form in files.
10. Constraints on user input should exist to maintain data integrity.
11. A database design should allow for distribution of data over several computer sites.
12. Data fields that affect the organization of the database cannot be changed.

Source: Adapted from Ref. 4.

understand the physical structure of the data in order to access and manage data in the database.

2. The data structure is based on a simple logic that is easily understood by users who are not database technologists. Data are stored in tables, the rows of which must have unique storage addresses or ordering. Each cell of a table contains a single *attribute value*. Attributes in the same column are members of a set. Attributes in the same row are members of an *ordered n-tuple*.

3. The *n*-tuples in the table form a relation. Each table has one or more columns that contain the key to the table. The attributes in the key uniquely identify each relation. The DBMS—and not the user—must ensure that all database tables comply with these requirements. When these requirements are met, mathematical operations and strict logic can be applied to manipulate the tables.

4. A high-level language is provided for accessing the sets (rows and columns) of the table and for joining (combining) tables that have a common set of attributes (one or more columns containing the same attributes). The American National Standards Institute (ANSI) has standardized the structured query language (SQL) to fulfill this role. However, most vendors of relational database also provide other methods for accessing data.

The characteristics of a relational database eliminate deficiencies of traditional databases and offer significant practical benefits. The tabular structure is simple and relatively "user friendly." It is sufficiently general that most types of data can be represented. It is independent of any internal computer mechanisms. And it is flexible, because the user can readily restructure tables vertically, horizontally, or both ways, through either splitting or joining data. In fact, table manipulation always yields results that are tables themselves. By supporting a well-defined set of mathematical operations and some useful combinations— restrict, project, natural join, division, product, union, difference, and intersect— data access no longer needs to be limited by predetermined reporting procedures.

To derive the desired information (as a table), a data request can be specified in terms of the operations that must be performed on the tables within the database. The DBMS then transparently translates these logical requests into an efficient internal-access strategy. A relational DBMS is built upon a catalog, which is a set of tables dynamically maintained by the system. It can use information about the database (e.g., statistics) in its catalog to optimize the logical operations.

Relational databases have been widely applied in the areas of operations and control, with a particular emphasis on processing transactions (e.g., accounting data that track financial transactions). To be successful in this application, a premium is placed on the efficient and rapid execution of a large number of relatively small transactions with a minimum level of errors.

A prominent aspect of relational database theory is the concept of *normalization*—how data should be organized in order to make the database as compact and as easy to manage as possible and to ensure that consistent results are produced. Normalization rules provide design guidelines (or schema) by specifying how a relational database should be divided into tables and how these tables should be linked together. The two major objectives of normalization are:

1. Minimize the duplication of data.
2. Minimize the number of attributes that must be updated when changes are made to the database, thereby making the maintenance of the data easier and reducing the possibility for errors.

Codd initially defined three ways in which data in a database can be normalized [5]. Subsequently, two other approaches have been identified as *normal forms*. In order for a database to conform to the *first normal form*, an attribute cannot be a set, list, or, most importantly, a complex object or table. This restriction means that a table cannot be "nested" in a first normal form database—separate tables must be created for each data set and a relation in each table must be established for the attributes that form the keys in the other tables.

Conformance with the first normal form often increases the amount of storage required and makes maintenance more difficult. It also greatly increases the processing time required, since separate tables must be maintained and often must be joined to produce the desired information. Joins are highly compute-intensive operations. The second through fifth normal forms each define increasingly stringent conditions that must be met in order for the database to conform to that normal form. However, these more stringent requirements reduce the storage space needed in the database and the number of updates required [6].

1.5 Relational Fidelity and Standard Compatibility

A relational database management system (RDBMS) requires that strict and comprehensive integrity constraints be enforced in the database to ensure data accuracy and consistency. However, the user is relieved from having to develop or maintain integrity code in their specific applications. As a consequence, the RDBMS offers a level of reliability and productivity that is superior to that achieved in traditional database management systems. The relational model also requires the support of logical units of work, as well as self-recovery from operational failures that could corrupt the database.

The structure, integrity, and manipulative features must be incorporated in the DBMS engine for the practical benefits of the relational model to materialize.

These features are highly interdependent, and the lack of any one feature affects the support of the others. It is not possible to provide all of the intended benefits by arbitrarily implementing only some of the features or by simply adding an interface to nonrelational engines. The fidelity rules were devised to clarify this important point.

A standard based on the relational model would yield the best of both worlds: products that complied would offer both relational fidelity and standard compatibility. The underlying database functions would be the same for all products, regardless of whether they were stand-alone or multi-user. The kind of front-end tools and applications they offer would not affect these database functions. In addition, front-end tools, such as spreadsheets and word processors, could all operate on databases, not only on disparate files.

The structured query language (SQL) is the concrete expression of the relational model that has gained industry acceptance [7]. SQL interacts with relational databases, but is not a full application development language. As a result, the well-defined, set-oriented database foundation is kept distinct from the less precise, procedural character of existing programming languages. The need to create yet another general-purpose language is eliminated. By trying to be everything to everybody, such a general-purpose language often becomes too complex to master and invites compromises. This approach avoids the lengthy process that would be required to extend standard procedural languages, such a COBOL and FORTRAN, with relational database functions [8].

1.6 On-Line Analytical Processing

On-line analytical processing (OLAP) is a category of software technology that is built on the conceptual foundations of the relational theory of data. OLAP enables analysts, managers, and executives to gain insight into data through fast, consistent, interactive access to a wide variety of possible views of information. Raw data are transformed into information that reflects the functional dimensions of the organization, as understood by the end-users. OLAP provides an ability to conduct dynamic analyses of consolidated data, while supporting the analytical and navigational activities of end-users (see Table 12.3).

The functionality of an OLAP system should include:

Capacity to perform calculations and apply models across multidimensions, through hierarchies, and/or across component units.

Ability to perform trend analysis over sequential time periods.

Capability of slicing subsets of data for on-screen viewing.

Ability to drill-down to deeper levels of data consolidation and to reach through to underlying detail data.

Capacity to rotate to new dimensional comparisons in the viewing area (OLAP cubes).

TABLE 12.3 Basic Characteristics of On-Line Analytical Processing

Fast: An on-line analytical processing (OLAP) system should deliver most responses to users within about five seconds, with the simplest analyses taking no more than one second and very few complex analyses taking more than 20 seconds. This speed is not easy to achieve with large amounts of data, particularly if on-the-fly and ad hoc calculations are required.

Analysis: An OLAP system should be capable of coping with any operational logic and statistical analysis that is relevant for the application and the user. Although some preprogramming may be needed, the user should be allowed to define new ad hoc calculations as part of the analysis and to report on the data in any desired way, without having to undertake extensive programming.

Shared: An OLAP system should be able to implement all security requirements for confidentiality. If multiple data entry access is required, the system should have the capability of locking the concurrent update at an appropriate level.

Multidimensional: An OLAP system must provide a conceptual view of the data that includes full support for hierarchies and multiple hierarchies.

Information: An OLAP systems should be capable of providing all of the data and derived information needed, wherever it is, and however much is relevant for the application.

OLAP facilitates decision making about future actions. A typical OLAP calculation is more complex than simply summing data, for example, "What would be the effect on local property tax revenues if the millage rate was increased by 5%, assessed values of property increase by 7%, and the rate of new residential construction increases by 2.3%?"

OLAP is implemented in a multiple user client/server mode. It offers rapid response to queries, regardless of the size and complexity of the database. OLAP helps users to synthesize organization-wide information through comparative viewing that is personalized to the perspective of the end-user. It also provides a basis for the analysis of historical data and data that are projected in various "what-if" scenarios. This analysis/synthesis is achieved through use of an OLAP server.

An OLAP server is a data manipulation engine that is specifically designed to support and operate on multidimensional data structures. It is structured to accommodate multiple users in a high-capacity processing environment. The design of the server and the structure of the data are optimized for the rapid ad-hoc retrieval of information in any orientation. Every data item is located and accessed on the basis of the intersection of the dimensions that define that item. An OLAP server is also designed to facilitate the flexible calculation and transformation of raw data through formula-based relationships.

OLAP applications require the following key features.

1. *Multidimensional views of data.* Rarely are analyses limited to only one or two dimensions. Managers typically look at financial data by line items, by organizational units, by scenario (for example, actual vs. budget), and by time. A multidimensional view of data must provide the foundation for analytical processing through flexible access to information. Managers must be able to analyze data across any dimension, at any level of aggregation, and with equal functionality and ease.

2. *Calculation-intensive capabilities.* OLAP databases must be able to do more than simple aggregation of data. Examples of more complex calculations include share calculations (percentage of total) and allocations (which use hierarchies from a top-down perspective). The ability to model complex relationships is key in analytical processing applications.

3. *Time intelligence.* OLAP systems must understand the sequential nature of time. Performance is almost always judged over a time period (for example, this month vs. last month, this month vs. the same month last year). Concepts such as year-to-date and period over period comparisons must be easily defined in an OLAP system.

A key indicator of a successful OLAP system is its ability to provide information as needed, that is, its ability to provide "just-in-time" information for effective decision making. Just-in-time information is computed data that usually reflects complex relationships and is often calculated "on the fly". Analyzing and modeling complex relationships are practical only if response times are consistently short. In addition, because the nature of data relationships may not be known in advance, the data model must be flexible. A truly flexible data model ensures that OLAP systems can respond to changing information requirements as needed for effective decision making.

1.7 Data Warehouses

A data warehouse involves copies of transaction data (e.g., financial transactions recorded in an accounting system, payroll data from a personnel system) that is specifically structured for querying and reporting. A data warehouse stores tactical information that answers "who?" and "what?" questions about past events. A typical query submitted to a data warehouse is, "What was the total revenue derived from licenses and fees in the first six months of the fiscal year?" While nontransaction data may also be stored in a data warehouse, typically 95 to 99% is transaction data. The chief output from data warehouse systems are either tabular listings (specific queries) with minimal formatting or "formal" reports that adhere to predetermined formats.

The form of the stored data has nothing to do with whether a data storage system is a data warehouse. A data warehouse can be normalized or denormalized. It can be a relational database, multidimensional database, flat file, hierarchical database, or object database. Data in a data warehouse are often updated and changed. And a data warehouse may focus on a specific activity or entity.

The overwhelming uses of data warehouses are for relatively mundane, nondecision-making purposes, rather than for making strategic decisions with wide-ranging effects. Most data warehouses, in fact, are used for post-decision monitoring of the effects of decisions (i.e., for tracking "operational" issues). While the role of data warehousing may be promoted by vendors and many industry experts as a vital tool for strategic decision making, in reality, a clear understanding of the full potential in this area of application has yet to emerge. For more on this perspective, see the writings of Peter Keen and Marc Demarest [9]. Damarest suggested that,

> The 'data warehousing' marketplace is concerned largely with plumbing— with technology associated with data movement and storage—rather than business value: with the building of decision support systems that materially effect the quality and quantity of commercial decisions. In other words, from a bright beginning in the early 1990s, when 'DSS' meant the promise of real returned business value from open systems technology, we have retreated to a largely technical, largely insular state in which the objective of DSS is not decision support, but dumping data on the Windows® desktop in hopes that the person using that desktop knows what to do with that data [9].

1.8 Centralized Data Processing Centers

Computers can help to achieve better management information if used to process properly designed information flows. However, they are not the automatic answer to the need for better information. In fact, undue preoccupation with how data will be processed and with the characteristics of the processing hardware and software often can inhibit the design of an effective information management system.

When thinking about an IMS, hardware should be one of the last things to contemplate. The first consideration is what kind of information is needed— how much, how soon, and how often. Management information must include explicit attention to nonquantifiable inputs, as well as those inputs that result from computerized data processing applications. The kind of equipment that will best serve these needs is a secondary, although important, consideration. Concentrating first on the information and communication requirements can dispel many early wrong notions about data processing. In so doing, plans for computer hardware often shrink to more a realistic size.

The desirability of large centralized data processing centers depends more on the size and nature of the organization than on the purposes of an IMS. Many excellent information management systems are serviced by relatively simple, local data processing operations, tailored to the particular needs of the users. With the further miniaturization and mass production of computer systems, the cost of mainframe capabilities has decreased dramatically. Through the introduction of more and more powerful desktop equipment, the power of the computer is now more readily available to resource managers in most organizations.

An IMS goes beyond the objectives of centralized data collection and retrieval, however. As Kennevan suggested, an IMS is,

> an organized method of providing past, present, and projection information relating to internal operations and external intelligence. It supports the planning, control and operational functions of an organization by furnishing information in the proper time frame to assist in the decision-making process [10].

According to Michael Hammer, modern databases, expert systems, and telecommunications networks provide many, if not all, of the benefits that once made internal specialization of administrative functions like personnel, finance, accounting, and so forth attractive [11]. Hammer claimed that work assignments in today's organization should be designed around an objective or outcome instead of a single function. Functional specialization and sequential execution are inherently harmful to the expeditious processing of information. Parallel activities should be coordinated during their performance and not after they are completed. The people who produce information should process it, since they have the most basic need for the information and the greatest interest in its accuracy. Information should be captured once and at the source. And according to Hammer, the people who do the work should be primarily responsible for decision-making [12].

2   DECISION-SUPPORT SYSTEMS

Advances in information technology—represented by more powerful and more user-friendly capabilities for data retrieval, database management, modeling, and graphics—have afford nontechnical users an opportunity for relatively effective, *ad hoc* use of computers to support a variety of management-related functions. In this context, the "conference room of the future" has been the subject of considerable discussion concerning the role that computer software and hardware will play in assisting decision makers on a "real-time" basis.

Decision-support systems (DSS), like information management systems before them (and electronic data processing systems that preceded IMS), represent a new stage in the "computer revolution." These emerging systems are supported partly by technological advances and partly by a long-standing conviction that such capabilities are possible.

2.1 DSS Defined

According to the proponents of decision-support systems, the ultimate mission of the computer should be to *interact* effectively with management so as to *influence* decisions on a day-to-day basis. Decision-support systems deal with the use of information technology to support human decision-making processes. Michael Scott-Morton, who is credited with originating the concept of DSS in the early 1970s, offered this definition,

> Decision-support systems couple the intellectual resources of individuals with the capabilities of the computer to improve the quality of decisions. It is a computer-based support system for management decision-makers who deal with semi-structured problems [13].

Software packages currently available do incorporate powerful technical tools that may make it possible to realize the potential suggested by the notion of "computerized decision support." However, as one manager of a DSS service observed,

> DSS is a philosophy. It provides users with an effective way to get information without intermediaries. It's software, it's support, and it's an organization that coaches the user as he continually changes and improves his decision-making models [14].

In short, there are no magic solutions that will create the kind of interface between humans and computers that would be necessary for true decision support.

A primary objective of DSS is to provide decision support for problems within an organization that are continually changing—problems that often have more than one "right" answer. Some computer professionals do not feel comfortable with such relatively unstructured problems. More conventional methods of programming seek to "freeze" the specifications of a problem as soon as possible, so that the programmer can "build the solution" (the information system) in relative isolation from the problem.

Decision-support systems, however, must be constructed through an interactive approach in which the problem specifications may never be "frozen." As Ralph Sprague noted,

> If I were to try to build the system the old way, I would go to the decision-maker and ask him what his requirements are. The problem is, he won't

> know. You ask him what information he needs—again, he won't know. Now,
> by contrast, the iterative approach says, 'OK, give me a small problem, and
> I'll help you in the process of using and changing the system as your
> requirements grow and evolve over time' [15].

Management problems often are relatively short-lived. Therefore, more traditional methods of building relatively large information management systems to deal with such problems may result in the delivery of "too much, too late." The development and maintenance of elaborate databases to provide inputs into sophisticated simulation models requires substantial resource commitments. If the problems that management must address are "moving targets," the response time may be too long to provide useful answers.

DSS represents a major break with the tradition whereby individuals and groups participate in the decision-making process based on "ownership" of (access to) certain data and information.

> The distribution of ... information ... may have a significant bearing on
> authority relations in any given situation. The participation (and relative
> influence) of an individual is conditioned, in part, by how much he knows.
> As a consequence, the withholding of information and the jealous guarding
> of informational resources are strategies frequently employed to gain greater
> influence in decision-making situations [16].

Armed with user-friendly technology, managers are making stronger claim to available data and information—with or without the blessings of those in the organization responsible for gathering and recording this information.

The relation between decision-support and decision-making cannot be considered clear-cut, however. As Steven Alter stated,

> The development of modeling and data-retrieval technologies is not inex-
> pensive, and the immediate benefits are not always clear. The justification
> for much of the initial work is necessarily based on pure faith. It is diffi-
> cult to quantify the benefits from such efforts, even after they have attained
> momentum: What is a good decision worth [17]?

It is not surprising in light of such uncertain payoffs that much of the pioneering work in decision-support research has been dedicated to understanding the intricacies of just how managers go about making decisions.

Over the past decade, decision theorists have developed a fairly useful generic model of decision-making that makes sense, as a normative model. Any decision can be understood as a seven-phase process [18]:

1. *Screening decision demands to determine intakes:* Information required to structure, evaluate, and make a decision is gathered in response to some change that has occurred (or is anticipated) within the
   organization or its operating environment.

2. *Identification of constraints and boundary conditions:* The parameters to which the decision must conform are identified and examined for implications, dependencies, and links to other decisions.
3. *Formulation of alternatives:* Alternative scenarios are developed and analyzed—each of which might serve as an appropriate response to a particular decision-demanding situation.
4. *Search for a best solution:* One or a few alternatives are selected as possible "best solutions" to the problem at hand. This phase typically involves multiple cycles, during which the selected alternatives are discussed among groups, are modified, tested, and enhanced or even discarded.
5. *Modification to gain an acceptable solution:* A reconnaissance is made of the expectations of those most likely to be impacted by the proposed decision and necessary accommodations are made to arrive at an acceptable solution.
6. *Converting the decision into action:* Converting a decision into action requires that several distinct questions be answered: (1) Who must know the decision? (2) What action must be taken? (3) Who must take this action? (4) What does the action need to be, so that the people who must do it can do it? All too often, the first and last of these questions are overlooked, with dire consequences.
7. *Feedback phase:* Implementation of a particular decision is tracked and its effects on the state of the organization relative to its objectives are measured and evaluated.

Possible contributions of DSS to improved organizational decision making are just beginning to be identified. It has been suggested that DSS can provide important data inputs required by the decision-making process (what most data warehouses supply today). DSS can provide tools and models for arranging the data inputs in ways that make sense to frame the decision parameters. These tools include fault tree analysis, Bayesian logic, and model-based decision making predicated on things like neural networks. DSS can also provide tools and mechanisms for capturing information about constituencies (who will be affected by the decision), outcomes and their probabilities, and other elements of the larger decision-making context.

As Holsapple and Whinston pointed out, decision-support systems differ with respect to the kinds of knowledge they help manage [19]. Conventional decision-support systems, for the most part, were developed primarily to assist in the management of knowledge that was either descriptive (data and information) or procedural (specifying how to accomplish various tasks). Expert systems and artificial intelligence (AI) environments, on the other hand, are concerned mainly with representing and processing reasoning knowledge. This type of knowledge provides significant insights into the validity of certain conclusions under particular circumstances. Part of the decision-making process may be automated using these AI techniques, and evaluations may be made regarding the optimal decision. To date, however, these approaches have functioned successfully in only very limited cases. Some fundamental problems in AI technology remain—for example, an inability to deal with nonbinary, or fuzzy choices, which traditional AI-based systems cannot code.

Finally, DSS can be used to monitor decision outcomes to determine if (1) the decision was successfully implemented, and (2) if the effects of the decision are as anticipated. Studies also have shown that decision-support systems can lead to better communications among managers. These improvements, in turn, can contribute to a more unified approach to problem solving by providing a broader consensus as to goals and objectives and underlying assumptions concerning problems confronting the organization.

2.2   The Right Problems/People/Tools/Process

Certain basic conditions must be met if a DSS is to have the desired impact on the decision-making process of an organization [20]. The right problems must be addressed and the right people must participate in the development of the decision-support system. The right tools must be used and the process must be able to evolve as decision situations and technology change. To meet these conditions, conflicting interests often must be balanced in terms of the available technology, the cost of systems development and maintenance, and the ever-present issues of data ownership and inherent prerogatives to participate in the decision-making process.

> ... the line between advisory and prerogative-based participation often becomes blurred and, over time, advisory participants often become "prerogative" participants. Further, they come to expect this relationship to exist in any decision-making situation in which their technical expertise may be required [21].

The right problems. Should a DSS focus on well-defined, specific problems, or should it be designed as a flexible system with wide-ranging applications? Sprague and Carlson asserted that,

> Because of the variety of decision-making process, a DSS is more likely to be useful and cost-effective if it supports multiple processes. If a specific DSS is designed for only one type of decision, any change in the decision requires a change in the DSS to accommodate changes in the information-processing requirements [22].

However, decision support often is difficult to justify in terms of cost. Therefore, a DSS should address, at the very least, the specific problem situations that top officials deem to be most important. A DSS should be *demand-driven* rather than *supply-generated*. That is to say, the demand for decision support must come from top-level management rather than being "force-fed" on the basis of available data.

The right people. Participants in the development of the DSS must have a general understanding of management principles, as well as the technical skills to solve problems as they arise. Lacking an appreciation for technical considerations, management can be "sold" on the purchase of extensive software and hardware systems that may have very little immediate use in the decision-making processes of the organization. On the other hand, cost consideration can unduly influence the purchase of computer equipment and software that may not serve the real decision needs of the organization.

The right tools. An effective way to reduce the "burden" on the technical experts is to bring in technical tools that are as easy to use as possible. Recent developments in computer software have introduced more "user friendly" products that have the ability to "understand" natural English, so that users do not need to learn special languages or elaborate sets of commands in order to use the system.

A price must be paid for such "user-friendly" systems, however, beyond the purchase cost of the software. The easier a system is to use, the heavier the load it tends to place on computing hardware in terms of machine cycles. A separate computer often may be required to support the DSS. As an alternative, some organizations are switching from large mainframe systems to distributed microsystems, supported by PC hardware. While such microsystems are slower in terms of processing time, the hardware costs can represent a significant trade-off when compared to the "care and feeding" of a typical mainframe.

This approach is not without its own risks, however. While desktop, personal computers can provide significant analytical tools, the decentralization of computational capacity exacerbates the need to manage information more carefully. With the proliferation of microsystems, it is possible that the organization will miss out totally on one of the primary advantages afforded by decision-support systems—more effective communications and the sharing of assumptions regarding problems confronting the organization. A shared resource on a mainframe system encourages and supports such communications. Distributing the resource among microsystems may not yield the same results.

The right process. A DSS must be a dynamic mechanism, capable of continual evolution in new and often unanticipated ways as problems evolve. Such an "evolution" can result in considerable stress within an organization, however, which, in turn, can adversely affect the momentum in support of DSS. This problem often arises when controls must be installed to bring the demands placed in the DSS into more manageable bounds. During the early stages of development in particular, it is important that *user support* stays ahead of *user demands.* Often the tendency is to spread access to the system as broadly as possible—to promote the adoption of the software by providing hardware to as many people in the organization as possible. Communication links often become overloaded, however, and users incur significant delays in response time (or difficulties in "logging on" to the system). Confronted with such delays, users frequently abandon the system and return to their prior approaches to making decisions.

Many proponents argue that it is inappropriate to think of DSS as a deliverable product—it is an evolving process. Nevertheless, users do not want to have to learn new commands every few weeks in order to access the system. For these users, who may well be in the majority in any organization, it may be appropriate to provide a DSS as a relatively stable product. Major changes in "language" or in presentation formats may be very disconcerting to those users who view the system as a "tool" and not as a "vocation." At the same time, a select group of users may be treated as "iconoclasts," by being exposed to the latest versions of software as they become available. As more is known about the system, it may be perfectly natural for a DSS to stabilize.

The development process often is viewed as unwieldy from the stand-point of getting useful decision-support systems designed and built quickly. The conventional wisdom concerning DSS is to eschew the more formal systems analysis and design procedures, so as to avoid inhibiting the process of managerial learning and systems evolution. As Moore and Chang pointed out, however,

> The unfortunate side effect of this is that informal and ad-hoc design approaches, so desirable from a design and implementation standpoint, highly personalize the DSS design process and the DSS itself, thereby subjecting the DSS designers and users to greater buffering, whipsawing, and other organizational turmoil [23].

2.3 Quantity of Data Versus Quality of Information

For all the risks and uncertainties, the prospect of computerized decision support is nevertheless an exciting one. No matter how good the system, however, a DSS will not miraculously transform bad decision makers into good ones. Good decision makers are meticulous about facts, but also have the ability to develop and apply intuitive insights. They have a feel for the "big picture" and are able to delegate responsibilities so they do not "micro manage." They have the capacity to distinguish between genuine merit and unreasonable bias. The fundamental objective of a DSS is to enhance these attributes of good decision making and not to devalue them by substituting *quantity of data* for *quality of information.*

The emerging technology of expert systems shows promise as a step beyond DSS to assist in enhancing productivity and in safekeeping of one an organization's most valuable resources—its human expertise [24]. At a more fundamental level, the establishment of organization-wide, integrated databases have made information more accessible, more timely, of better quality, and wider in scope than was formerly available.

Of course, the foregoing portrays an ideal state of affairs. In actual practice, many organizations and their managers do not maximize the potential of computer-based information systems. In such organizations, both top management and the managers of information systems must share in the blame. The IMS department of these organizations often is under the misconception that the information needs of management can be fulfilled by the reports that are produced as by-products of the processing the daily transactions. Allowing the misconception to persist accounts for a major portion of top management's share of the blame.

A different approach is needed to escape from this quagmire. Managers often wrestle with the question "Why do we have dozens of reports and yet very little of the 'real' information we need to manage?" Instead of using the requirements for processing transactions to establish an organization's information system architecture, a top-down approach is needed, where the information needs for strategic management, planning, and control define the required architecture.

This approach to information development and reporting calls for a new breed of managers, however. Managers must be neither in awe of the technology of information systems nor estranged by the jargon of information systems professionals. And they must hold the IMS department accountable for providing them with the "real" information they need to manage.

As Stephen Maclin observed,

> For public managers, the phenomenal growth of the new cyber-technologies has been accompanied by a growing frustration as to how these technologies might be effectively integrated within existing technological structures. Part of the difficulty has been managerial—ensuring that the new technologies neither duplicate nor undermine those that already work successfully. However, some interesting questions have been raised for public managers and how they carry out some of their normal functions now that cyber-technologies have, seemingly forever, changed their working environments [25].

Marc Demarest suggested that DSS vendors have solved the "data access" problem, at least conceptually. Therefore, rather than focusing on issues of data movement and storage, infrastructure, or functionality, they now should target their technology to specific classes of decision-making problems. He further observed that the challenge is to focus explicit attention on a class of decisions that management understands and knows how to support in order to achieve improvements in the quality of decisions made. Finally, Demarest asserted that,

> The organization as a whole must enforce a set of decision-making poli-
> cies that ensure that decisions are made according to standardized models,
> methods and practices, and then implemented with measurement and man-
> agement regimes in place so that the decision, once taken, is implemented
> and its effects on the organization monitored and assessed [26].

3   ENTERPRISE RESOURCE PLANNING

Enterprise resource planning (ERP) is being touted as the foundation for an integrated enterprise-wide information systems, designed to link together an organization's total operations including financial management, human resources, production, and distribution. It is also intended to connect the organization to its constituents or customers and suppliers [27]. ERP is envisioned as the next stage in the evolution of information management systems. While the major impetus for ERP has come in the manufacturing sector, other public and private organizations with multiple databases and data sources have begun to experiment with enterprise-wide approaches to information management (see Table 12.4 for a glossary terms associated with enterprise resource planning).

3.1   The Need for Systems Integration

Many large organizations have followed a "best of breed" approach in selecting software applications to meet their diverse data processing and analytical needs. Under this approach, various functional areas within the organization have identified the software packages (and, at times, the hardware platforms) best suited to their particular data processing requirements. Specialized information management systems have been established and enhanced to serve the data storage and analytical needs of individual functional areas—accounting, budgeting, personnel, engineering, purchasing, and so on. The inevitable result has been multiple databases that are unable to communicate with one another or share critical information across platforms.

Systems integration has moved to the forefront as a primary requirement of successful operations in the rapidly changing world of electronic commerce (e-commerce). Many private organizations traditionally have relied on business plans that forecast production requirements on a time frame of six months to one year. In such a decision environment, there is little impetus to tie together business systems because inventory levels can be used to smooth out problems. For years, business systems have been implemented to control factories, production, and, more recently, entire enterprises. During all that time, companies have managed to grow without having tight system integration.

TABLE **12.4** Enterprise Resource Planning Glossary

Automated data collection (ADC): Technologies that automate data collection at the source such as bar codes, biometrics, machine vision, magnetic stripes, optical card readers, voice recognition, smart cards, and radio frequency identification.

Application programming interface (API): An interface used by one application program to communicate with programs of other systems.

Bolt-on: A software application that performs specific tasks and interfaces with an ERP system.

Function library: A collection of ready-made, reusable units of code for specific programming tasks.

Legacy system: Existing systems and technology in which an organization has considerable investment and which may be entrenched in the organization. Some legacy systems have been in place for many years and are based on outdated or inadequate technology.

Middleware: Software interfaces or links that enable data to pass from the source to a client.

Open applications group (OAG): A non-profit, vendor-focused consortium formed by leading enterprise software vendors to create more open application integration by establishing and publishing standards for integration of business objects across an enterprise.

Open applications integration (OAI): The OAG's term for business object integration, defined as integrating the software that automates the direct business functions occurring in an enterprise.

Open database connectivity (ODBC): Microsoft's strategy for open database interface. ODBC makes it possible to access both relational and non-relational database management systems in a heterogeneous PC environment with minicomputers linked to a mainframe.

Object linking and embedding (OLE): A "de facto" standard that describes communication between various applications.

Portability: The ability of an ERP system to run various operating systems, databases, and networks without requiring any major adjustments or sacrificing any functionality.

Real-time: The immediate availability of data to an information system as a transaction or event occurs.

However, those days are over. As a consequence of the Internet, the world wide web, and widespread interest in e-commerce, consumers and businesses now expect instant gratification—they want what they want, when they want it, and at the price they want to pay for it. As Mitchell Vaughn, Marketing Manager for USDATA Corporation, observed,

> Everybody's talked about [integration] for years, from the computer-integrated manufacturing days. The difference now is that businesses are facing performance level demands that are impossible without greater integration [28].

Web-based orders have forced many companies to adopt a "make to order" or "engineer to order" approach to doing business. Existing business systems cannot adequately compress processing time in this environment.

> As we head down to weeks and days, [we are] beyond what business systems can do alone. We've basically soaked out what we can from the business systems. To go any further, we have to tightly integrate [29].

Not only are companies feeling pressure to integrate factory floors with enterprise applications such as ERP systems, but also there now is the additional need to connect supply chain software and customer relationship management software to transaction systems.

The e-commerce mandates coming from many boardrooms will force managers to focus on processes rather than systems. The demand for greater integration is being driven by the need to take the slack out of the order flow process. Business on the web creates expectations of immediate attention, and therefore, corporations must find ways of knowing in real-time whether they can fulfill a customer order.

While the need for systems integration is most apparent in manufacturing and other business enterprises, it is no less essential in public and nonprofit organizations. As local governments purchase and install new software to meet the new financial management requirements of the Government Accounting Standards Board, for example, care must be taken to ensure that this software can be integrated with inventory controls, treasury and asset management requirements, payroll systems, and other human resource needs. Many localities have suffered considerable embarrassment when they have been unable to mail out property tax bills on a timely basis or have double billed property owners because of "glitches" in their new computer software. In many cases, these problems stem from a lack of integration between the database that tracks property ownership for assessment purposes and the database that maintains property tax billing records.

In 1999, the National Association of Counties (NACo), the International City/County Management Association (ICMA), the National League of Cities, and Public Technologies, Inc., co-sponsored a meeting to explore the impact of information technology in the public sector. Participants discussed key trends that may well define government in the future including integrated service delivery, self-service government, effective outsourcing, and the use of e-commerce technology. Tom Goodman, the NACo Director of Public Affairs, observed that, "Technology changes on a daily basis. We need to understand and deal with that in a positive way to make government more effective."

In 2000, ICMA and Public Technologies, Inc., conducted a survey of city and county governments concerning the use of electronic government. This survey defined electronic government as "the delivery of services and information, electronically, to business and residents, 24 hours a day, seven days a week." The survey was sent to 3,749 local governments, of which 1,881 (50.2%) responded. While only 8.8% of the responding governments indicated that they currently had an overall e-government strategy and/or plan to guide future e-government initiatives, 60% indicated that they were considering the development of a formal e-government strategy or plan within the coming year. The executive summary of the survey results concluded that,

> "We anticipate that as e-government applications become more extensive and sophisticated, local governments will experience (at least initially) increases in information technology expenditures and technical staffing requirements. On a more positive note, more extensive and sophisticated e-government also should promote greater efficiency, effectiveness, and responsiveness in mission-critical programs [30]."

Achievement of these important objectives, in large measure, will depend upon a more complete integration of the information management systems currently in use in local governments.

3.2 ERP Implementation

The term "enterprise resource planning" (ERP) is something of a misnomer. ERP software does not provide a mechanism for planning per se, nor does it focus on resources, except in the most generic sense. The primary mission of ERP is to integrate all functions and departments across an organization into a single information system that can serve the particular needs of all those different departments. It involves a single software system that can serve the needs of finance as well as it does human resources, the requirements of procurement and asset management, and the needs of engineering and public works. Each functional unit within an organization typically has its own information system. And each system seeks to optimize its applications for the particular ways in which the unit operates. ERP seeks to serve the requirements of these separate systems by using an integrated software package that runs off a common database so that various units can more easily share information and communicate with each other.

The software packages provided by ERP vendors are generic representations of the ways a typical organization operates. While most packages strive to be comprehensive, each organization has its quirks and idiosyncrasies that make it unique. Most ERP systems currently available are designed for use by manufacturing industries (companies that make physical things that can be counted). Organizations that measure their products by flow rather than individual units (e.g., oil, chemical and utility companies) have only recently become involved in the implementation of ERP systems. Each of these processing industries has struggled with different vendors to modify core ERP programs to meet their specific needs.

ERP vendors, in turn, have begun to look to public and nonprofit organizations as a major new market for their products. Three of the four major vendors—SAP, Oracle, and PeopleSoft—have developed software products designed to address the specific requirements of organizations in the public sector [31]. SAP is the world's largest inter-enterprise software company and is headquartered in Walldorf, Germany. Its software package, mySAP Public Sector, "turns e-government hopes into public service reality" and "helps public sector organizations meet the challenge of serving the public today." Oracle offers a wide range of software to local, state, and regional governments with "the vision, the solutions, and the expertise to help (governments) realize the advantages of becoming an e-government organization." PeopleSoft announced the formation of its Education and Government Division in November 1998 and works with a number of consulting firms to install and maintain its public sector software applications.

There are four major reasons why organizations install an ERP approach.

1. *Integrated financial data.* Many different versions of "the truth" may be encountered in attempting to understand an organization's overall fiscal performance. Finance has its own set of revenue numbers, sales has another version, and different organizational units may each have their own versions of how much they contributed to the revenue stream. ERP creates a single version of the truth that cannot be questioned because everyone is using the same system.
2. *Standardized processes.* Multiple units across a given organization may offer the same service or make the same product using different methods and may track data about these processes through different systems. Standardizing those processes and using a single, integrated information system can save time, increase productivity, and reduce divergent outputs.
3. *Standardized human resources information.* Especially in organizations with multiple units, the human resources office may not have a

unified method for tracking employees and communicating with them about benefits and services. ERP can address these problems.

4. *Standardize customer/constituent information.* Information about individuals who are customers or constituents of an organization may exist in a number of formats and, in some cases, may be incomplete or contradictory. Capturing consistent information "at the source" reduces the chance of errors and improves customer service. By maintaining this information in one location in the database, much of the data will not have to be re-entered as individuals change their status.

A major public university recently installed an enterprise-wide information management system. In developing a strategic data plan, it was determined that the university had 17 different databases for tracking students and three databases for tracking faculty and other employees. It had five databases for tracking externally funded activities (e.g., sponsored research, development foundation support, and alumni support). Separate databases existed for tracking budget allocations to schools and colleges, for managing assets, for maintaining inventory data, and for issuing and controlling parking permits. And none of these databases were capable of communicating effectively with one another.

Once an organization has chosen to improve its performance by selecting an ERP software application, a number of crucial elements still must be addressed. A decision concerning project management must be made that will produce one of three predictable approaches for the implementation of the ERP system:

Use internal resources to do it "in house."
Rely on the software vendor for project management guidance.
Contract with third-party consultants to facilitate project management.

Relying upon internal resources to handle project management activities usually slows the project implementation to a crawl and causes project-related expenses to increase significantly. This approach often results in a never-ending project in which many participants quickly lose interest. The reasons that this approach almost never works are:

Lack of project management experience.
Lack of time—daily operations come first; project management activities are handled only if time is available.
Significant delays encountered by the software vendor as a result of the slow manner in which the organization reaches decisions and the lack of interest that occurs when the project starts to crawl.

The strength of the software vendor lies in understanding the application software that is to be install. Electing to rely on the ERP software vendor to supply project management skills, however, often leads to significant problems for many reasons, some of which are listed below:

ERP software vendor employees are trained to be product specialists, not process analysts. Usually relatively little effort is devoted to a process review. As a result, the undertaking quickly becomes a software project.

Software vendors have generic approaches to handle the installation of software based on past experiences; they often lack the experience needed to see the bigger picture that project management requires.

A lack of common expectations and resulting miscommunications often result in deadlocks or, even worse, in costly modifications to the software.

Development of task lists, schedules, budgets, and third party software agreements must be carried out by the client organization.

A number of software vendors have come to recognize the shortcomings of this approach and have developed contractual relations with third-party consultants to serve as project managers in the implementation process. A problem is for whom does the facilitator work—the software vendor or the organization installing the ERP system?

The primary benefits of contracting directly with a third party facilitator for project management are:

The facilitator is dedicated to planning, managing, and overseeing the project; attention is not divided between the project and dealing with the daily operations of the organization.

The facilitator has the experience to define the scope of the implementation.

The facilitator has the expertise needed to develop task lists, schedules, and monitors the project budget and other resources.

Project facilitators understand the resources that the organization will be called upon to supply to the implementation of the project. They also understand that software vendors supply expertise regarding their product. Additionally, the facilitator often is called upon to serve as a translator and referee between the client and the software firm. For example, misunderstandings often develop as a result of expectations that are never clearly defined by the client organization. The facilitator should work with the client's project team to produce a flow chart to determine the staging of the implementation. In so doing, the facilitator should seek to determine what expectations exist with regards to improved customer services. The facilitator, in turn, should document these expectations and share them with the software vendor. The software vendor may have a standard sequence for implementing the various components of the ERP, for example, that may be at odds with the organization's expectations. The facilitator must then play the role of referee by bringing together the client and the software vendor to establish realistic expectations that both parties can agree upon and that can be measured. Clear targets with clear performance expectations must be developed for every step of the project as well as every member of the project team.

The implementation of an ERP approach is much more than installing a software application. It takes implementation experience to be able to combine the talents of employees, software vendors, and hardware vendors in a cohesive task force. Task lists, project plans, and issue logs are the working tools of a consultant, whose reputation relies upon the ability to manage the implementation project. The role of the facilitator is to identify expectations, manage those expectations, and deliver the agreed-upon results. The appropriate use of third-party facilitators should maximize return on investment, while ensuring that the daily operations of the organization continue with a minimum of interruptions. The organization is then in position to achieve the higher levels of productivity that are expected out of an ERP system.

3.3 Installing an ERP

Three commonly used ways of installing an ERP system are (1) an "across-the-board" approach, (2) a franchising strategy, and (3) a fast start approach. The first approach is the most ambitious and difficult to undertake; the second approach may be appropriate for large or diverse organizations that do not share many common processes across units; and the third approach focuses on a few key processes, permitting the organization to grow into ERP.

Under the "across-the-board" approach, all legacy systems are eliminated at one time and a single ERP system is implemented across the entire organization. This method dominated early ERP implementations. Today, few would dare to attempt this approach because it requires that the entire organization change at the same time. Most of the horror stories from ERP implementations in late 1990s provide ample warning about using this strategy. Getting everyone to cooperate and accept a new software system at the same time is a tremendous effort. No one within the organization has had any experience using it, and no one is sure whether it will work. The implementation of ERP inevitably involves compromises. Many departments have information systems that have been finely honed to match the ways they work. In most cases, ERP offers neither the range of functionality, nor the comfort of familiarity that a custom legacy system can offer. Frequently, the speed of the new system may suffer because it is serving the entire organization rather than a single department.

Under a franchising strategy, independent ERP systems are installed in each unit, while common processes, such as financial record keeping, are linked across the organization. This approach has emerged as the most common way of implementing an ERP system. In most cases, each unit has its own ERP— that is, its own separate IMS and database. The systems are linked together only to share the information necessary for the organization to get the "big picture" across all units or for processes that do not vary extensively from unit to unit (for example, employee benefits). Implementation usually begins with a demonstration or "pilot" installation in a unit that is particularly open-minded and patient. This unit is often selected on the basis that the core business of the organization will not be significantly disrupted if something goes wrong. Once the system is up and running and all the bugs are worked out, the project team begins selling other units on ERP, using the first implementation as an in-house customer reference. This strategy usually takes a relatively long time—several years—to complete the full implementation.

The objective of the third approach is to get ERP up and running quickly and to avoid extensive process reengineering in favor of the "canned" processes included in the ERP system. Often the new information system is installed in a central unit, with few if any procedural changes disseminated to end-users. A number of organizations confronted by the so-called "millennium problem" adopted this approach in upgrading their financial systems—accounting, payroll, purchasing, and so forth. Operating units in the organization continued to process transactions in the "traditional" manner (e.g., hardcopy, paper forms), with the ERP interface occurring in the central unit.

Only a few organizations that have approached ERP in this way have claimed much payback from the initial installation of the new system. Most use it to support more extensive installation efforts down the road. An ERP system installed on a "fast start" basis may be better than the legacy system that it replaces, because employees are not required to change many of their old habits. However, undertaking the hard work of process reengineering after the ERP system is in place can be more challenging than if there had been no new system at all, because at that point, few people in the organization will have felt much benefit.

The most common reason that organizations abandon ERP projects is that they discover the software does not support one of their important processes. At that point, two things can be done:

1. The process can be changed to accommodate the software, which will likely mean significant changes in long-established methods of doing business (methods that often provide competitive advantage) and significant changes in roles and responsibilities (something that few organizations are interested in undertaking).
2. The software can be modified to fit the process, which will slow down the project, introduce bugs into the system, and make upgrading the software to the ERP vendor's next release more difficult, because the customizations will need to be rewritten to fit with the new version.

For most ERP systems, client organizations cannot determine in detail how all of the functional procedures should be set, making thousands of decisions that affect how the system will behave in conjunction with their own activities. Most ERP systems are preconfigured—the client is able to make just hundreds (rather than thousands) of procedural settings. As a consequence, when it is discovered that the software does not support an important process, for the most part, the process is reengineered to fit the ERP system and not the other way around.

4 IMPLEMENTATION OF AN INFORMATION MANAGEMENT SYSTEM

Implementation of an information management system can be a traumatic experience. At a minimum, procedural changes will impact the ways in which plans are made, programs are developed, and performance is evaluated within the organization. New patterns of communications will emerge, and new—presumably better—information will be available to assist in carrying out decision-making and management responsibilities. Efforts to improve the IMS may also uncover the need for organizational changes, which may be even more unsettling than the changes in procedures necessary to implement the system. The introduction of an IMS may represent substantial change in the established way of doing business, which can be viewed with considerable alarm (and generate significant resistance) by those within the organization.

4.1 An IMS for Strategic Management

The basic components of an IMS applicable to the information needs of strategic management are illustrated in Figure 12.1. Basic research and analysis of data is essential to effective strategic management. Data must be systematically collected and stored for future use and reference. Data can be generated externally (e.g., macro-trend analyses, benchmarking and "best practices," etc.) or internally (e.g., accounting and other financial management data). Basic analyses can be carried out using various modeling programs available in a well-constructed IMS.

Three specific data sources provide significant inputs for strategic management:

1. *Environmental intelligence:* data about the broader environment of which the organization is a part, including assessments of client needs.
2. *Autointelligence:* data about the component elements of the particular organization, including an evaluation of organizational resources and its capacity to respond to client needs.
3. *Historic data:* compilation and analysis of lessons learned from past experience.

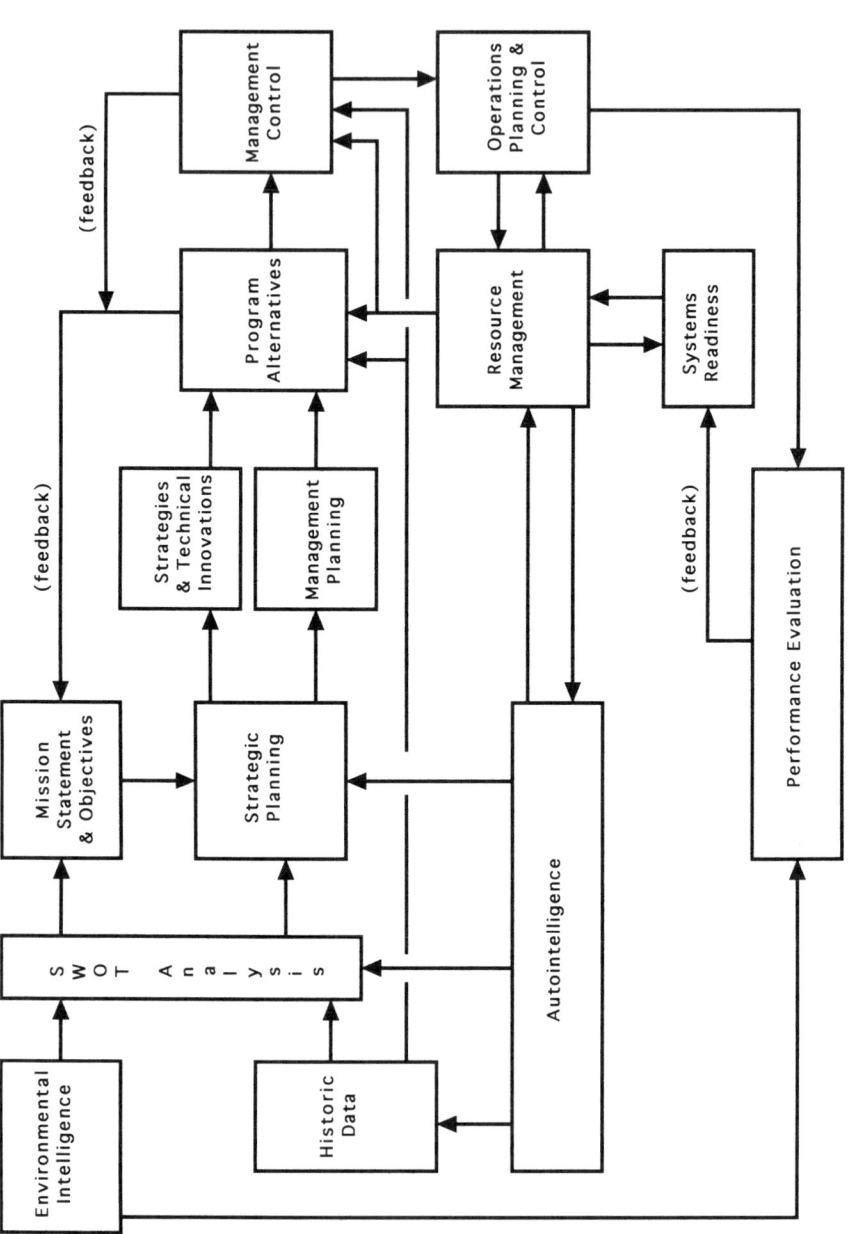

FIGURE 12.1 Components of an IMS for strategic management.

These data are stored in the organization's memory banks (i.e., in a data warehouse and OLAP server) to be retrieved when particular decision situations arise or when a broader assessment of the overall goals and objectives of the organization is appropriate.

The compilation of data about an organization's strengths and weaknesses, and data that highlight critical external issues—opportunities and threats—form the basis for a SWOT analysis. A key component of a SWOT analysis is an evaluation of the efficiency and effectiveness of the organization's current programs and processes. This assessment should include process evaluations based on quantitative data (review of records, descriptive statistics related to various indices, formal performance evaluations) and qualitative data (constituents or clients opinions about the organization's programs). The diagnosis of trends can be aided, in part, by the modeling and simulation programs and statistical analysis packages. The results can be stored in the OLAP database for reference and updating. Forecasts of probable outcomes—assuming the continuance of existing trends into the hypothetical future—can be developed on these analytic foundations. The SWOT analysis and related forecasts provide an important input in determining an organization's mission statement and its strategic objectives.

An IMS can aid in the development and evaluation of a mission statement and related strategic objectives. Objectives can be written so as to take fuller advantage of available information in the system. An objectives matrix can be used to uncover potential conflicts among objectives and to test their viability. Additionally, the formulation of a mission statement and strategic objectives often requires a number of iterations. These statements can be stored in the IMS, permitting easy access for making comparisons and changes, and for recording comments of participants in the process.

Once a mission statement and strategic objectives have been determined (at least in preliminary fashion), the strategic planning process can identify possible directions that the organization should take in response to constituent or client needs in the broader environment. Two initiatives are important in this regard: (1) the search for possible new courses of action to improve the overall performance of the organization, and (2) a framework for resource management and control.

Strategies and technical innovations must be sought to improve the overall responsiveness of the organization. An organization's strategies must be a blend of deliberate and purposeful actions and as-needed responses to unanticipated developments and external pressures. Three different levels of strategies should be identified:

1. Strategies that relate to the overall development of the organization.
2. Strategies that focus on the management and delivery of new and existing processes and programs.
3. Strategies that address administrative and support needs and their impacts on the organization's efficiency and effectiveness.

Various "what if" scenarios regarding the proposed strategies may be tested through the analytical subroutines contained within the IMS.

The overall intent of the strategic plan is translated into more specific programs and activities through the management planning process. Without the consistent follow-through of management planning (Hoshin planning, programming, and budgeting), strategic planning is merely a set of good intentions with little hope of realization. Management plans are both information demanding and information producing. The budget process provides important managerial feedback in terms of evaluations of prior program decisions and actions. Feed forward information emerges from the various projections and forecasts required by cost analyses and the budgeting process.

The same system components used in the basic research and analysis phase can be applied in the formulation and analysis of program alternatives. Significant use can be made of the OLAP storage and query capabilities of the IMS. The results of previous decisions and program actions are combined through policy and resource recommendations. In this capacity, the IMS can be useful in the storage and retrieval of needed information and in report generation.

Management control activities draw on the memory banks of the organization in search for programmed decisions—decisions that worked successfully in the past. Timely resource evaluations also provide important inputs into the management control process. These evaluations include information regarding the current fiscal status of the organization (financial and cost accounting data), as well as the overall response capacity of other organizational resources (systems readiness). The management planning and management control processes provide critical feedback to the further refinement of objectives. In some cases, this feedback will require a recycling of analytical processes before proceeding to the next phase.

Resource management involves the application of the concepts and methods of process reengineering and continuous improvement programs (TQM) to produce improvement in the overall responsiveness and performance of the organization. The IMS becomes the repository for data and analyses regarding current processes and the recommendations for future processes—"quick wins" and longer-term improvements. Bold initiatives emerging from process reengineering should drive continuous improvements, which, in turn, should sustain periodic enterprise-wide efforts to re-evaluate basic processes that support the overall mission of the organization. Total quality procedures can be applied to work out bugs, perfect the process, and gradually improve both efficiency and effectiveness. Specific operations are detailed within the framework provided by the strategic plan, and responsibilities for carrying out these operations are assigned, as are the resources required by these operations.

Specific operations may be further detailed through the procedures of operations planning and control—including such techniques as program evaluation review technique (PERT) and critical path method (CPM). Programming and scheduling procedures usually require further information regarding resource capabilities. They also may precipitate a recycling of the management planning process.

A basic problem of organizations today—whether in the public or private sectors—is to achieve an appropriate balance in programs and decisions to ensure *systems readiness*. Systems readiness defines the response capacity of the organization in the short- , mid- , and long-range futures. Sufficient flexibility is required to meet a wide range of possible competitive actions. The development and maintenance of an IMS that includes the basic components outlined here can contribute significantly to meeting this challenge.

The final component of the IMS involves the information derived from performance evaluations. Performance evaluation draws data from the broader environment regarding the efficiency and effectiveness with which constituent or client needs are met, problems are solved, and opportunities are realized. Summary and exception reports may be generated by the IMS and become part of higher-level reviews and evaluations. These evaluations, in turn, may lead to further adaptations or innovations of goals and objectives. Subsequent management activities should reflect such feedback, and the entire process is recycled. Some writers view performance evaluation as a separate process outside the information management system. Others recognize the importance of incorporating the data and information developed through such evaluations by referring to a management information and program evaluation system [32].

Feedback is a basic requirement of any IMS. Feedback must be obtained in terms of quality (effectiveness), quantity (efficiency of service levels), cost, and so on. Programs must be monitored to maintain process control. Evaluations of resources (inputs) provide feedback at the earliest stages of program implementation.

Feedback data must be collected and analyzed at various stages in the implementation of programs and the maintenance of ongoing processes and operations. These analyses involve processing data, developing information, and comparing actual results with plans and expectations. Routine adjustments may be programmed into the set of ongoing procedures, and instructions can be provided to those individuals who must carry out specific tasks. Feedback from the operating systems provides an information flow within the management control procedures to initiate and implement process and program changes on a more timely basis. Thus, procedures are modified and files updated simultaneously with routine decision making and program adjustments.

Managers must seek data and information that will permit actions to be taken before problems reach crisis proportions. Historic data provided by conventional accounting systems may be insufficient to meet these decision needs (even when the time lag is only a few weeks). Resource evaluations on the input side and resource monitoring as programs or projects progress can provide the more timely information required to anticipate (rather than merely react to) problems.

An information system appropriate for strategic management must use *feed forward* as well as feedback. Feed forward anticipates lags in feedback systems by monitoring inputs and predicting their effects on output variables. In so doing, action can be taken to change inputs and, thereby, to bring the outputs into equilibrium with desired results before the measurement of outputs discloses a deviation from accepted standards. In time, an organization "learns" through the processes of planning, implementation, and feedback [33]. Approaches to decision making and the propensity to select certain means and ends change as the value system of the organization evolves.

4.2 Commitment of Top Management

Anthony and Herzlinger suggested that "the driving force behind a new system must come from top management . . . it is unlikely that a majority of operating managers will voluntarily embrace a new system in advance of its installation, let alone be enthusiastic advocates of it [34]." The support of top management means more than mere acquiescence to the system as a "necessary evil." Responsible managers in the organization must be willing to devote sufficient time and effort to fully understand the general concepts and objectives of the information management system. They must be able to explain to principal subordinates how these procedures will help them and the organization as a whole. If problems arise during the design and implementation phases, top management must listen to opposing viewpoints and then make decisions to resolve such problems and remove any impediments. The organization's leadership may also have to "do battle" with outside interest groups, which may otherwise seek to prevent the adoption of such systems. It often is tempting to fall back on the old saw, "We have no choice but to implement these new procedures to meet externally imposed requirements." In so doing, however, the ground has been laid for less-than-enthusiastic support (and perhaps organized resistance) from within the organization.

Top management must set the example in terms of the efforts to design the system. They must be willing to take time away from other pressing problems to clearly articulate goals and objectives, and to discuss information management needs and expectations. The participation of top management in these efforts will help to convince personnel at the various operating levels to devote the necessary and appropriate time and effort to the task (see Table 12.5).

4.3 Education Through Participation

Advocates of IMS "should understand that the installation of a new system is a political process. It involves pressure, persuasion, and compromise in proper

TABLE 12.5   Twelve Implementation Prerequisites

1.   Top management must actively participate in the implementation from start to finish.
2.   Scope of the project must be clearly documented and delivered to top management. Any and all changes to scope should be approved by top management.
3.   End-users should be involved early in the design process to ensure that the new system addresses their needs. A satisfied end-user will want to work with system.
4.   Key processes must be mapped and measurements should be developed to monitor critical performance issues.
5.   A gap analysis should be conducted to compare current conditions and practices to the vision of where the organization wants to be in the future.
6.   A determination should be made of the processes to be included in the information management system. It may not be feasible to include all processes in the initial implementation. Inefficient processes should be upgraded before being incorporating into a new IMS.
7.   Information technology that utilizes open architecture should be selected, making it easier to enhance and enlarge the system over time. It may be appropriate to select software that can be modularized and easily integrated into existing databases.
8.   The new IMS should be prototyped to facilitate phasing in of the new technology, allowing for experimentation on a smaller and less costly scale. Prototyping tests the system's functionality, highlights required changes, and demonstrates that agreed-upon objectives can be met.
9.   End-users should be thoroughly trained on the functions of the system before it is fully implemented. Training should include demonstrating how to access and utilize data, providing and maintaining understandable use documentation, providing a help line, and offering on-line tutorials that can be customized for each end-user.
10.   Critical performance issues should be reviewed on a regular basis by cross-functional teams that are empowered to make changes to operational processes to improve performance.
11.   An issue log should be established and regular meetings should be held with top management to solicit assistance to resolve open issues.
12.   A realistic implementation schedule should be established and the required resources made available. A unit should be designated to have responsibility for the maintenance of the system—for overseeing its continued welfare. This unit should include information "gatekeepers" responsible for ensuring that information is timely, relevant, easy to access, and serves user decision-making needs.

proportions as in the case with any important political action [35]." Operating managers will be more likely to support the new IMS if they are convinced that, on balance, it will benefit them in carrying out their assigned responsibilities. The new system should provide operating managers with better information about the activities and performance of those staff members for whom they are responsible. With this information, the operating managers should have a better basis for direct and controlling the efforts of subordinates. On the other hand, uncertainty about the manager's performance is also likely to be reduced. As a consequence, an operating manager may resist the new system depending on personal interpretations of how such information will be received by "higher-ups."

The preparation of a manual of procedures and other explanatory materials is a necessary part of the educational process. These materials are not the most important part of the process, however. Management at all levels within the organization must be convinced that the new system, in fact, is going to be used and that it will help them do a better job. The best way to "pass the word" is to have managers teach managers—that is, top management should discuss the new system with subordinates, who then carry the message to their subordinates, and so on. Since the teachers must themselves become more fully indoctrinated, this process assists in the education of all those involved. Once a system goes into operation, even on a trial basis, the use of the information that it generates is the best educational device available.

It may not be feasible to install a new information management system across the whole organization all at one time. Initial efforts may be concentrated on those segments of the organization where the results of such improvement will be most visible. Demonstrated success in one area often can lead to more general acceptance of the new system throughout the organization.

It is difficult to be specific about an appropriate period required to successfully design and implement an information management system. In a large, complex organization, two to three years may elapse from the time the decision is made to initiate systems development and the date that the system is implemented. The time available is never quite enough. There always will be worthwhile refinements that could be made. However, if enough time were allowed for all the fine-tuning efforts, the system may never go into operation.

4.4 A Final Caveat

It is important not to oversell the potential of the new system. Aaron Wildavsky offered a number of "rules" that are applicable to the implementation of any new information management system [36]. The *rule of skepticism* suggests that organizational officials should exercise a good deal of skepticism when presented with the initial concept of an improved information management system. The *rule of delay* cautions officials to give the system adequate time to develop and to be prepared to face periodic setbacks in its implementation. As Wildavsky observed, "If it works at all, it won't work soon." The *rule of anticipated anguish* is essentially a restatement of Murphy's Law—"most of the things that can go wrong, will." Wildavsky suggested that management must be prepared to invest personnel, time, and money to overcome breakdowns in the system as they occur. And the *rule of discounting* suggests that anticipated benefits to be derived from the new IMS should significantly outweigh the estimated costs of mounting the system. Much of the cost must be incurred before the benefits are achieved. Therefore, the tendency is to inflate future benefits—to oversell the system—to compensate for the increased commitment of present resources.

Even with the best information management system, data must still be analyzed and interpreted by managers. And based on this information, judgment must be exercised in decision making. Allowance must be made for the inadequacies or unavailability of data. Although the system can provide certain decision parameters, it cannot make decisions. Managers must continue to exercise judgment regarding the exceptions that prove the rules. Such caveats must be emphasized during the educational processes. Otherwise, managers are aware of such limitations and will regard the whole effort as the work of impractical theorists.

Around the turn of the century, Clerk Maxwell, an English physicist, suggested a very clever way to overcome the second law of thermodynamics. Maxwell envisioned a small, but very intelligent creature (a demon), who could see molecules and could serve as a "gatekeeper" between two containers of gas at equal temperature and pressure. By carefully opening and closing the gate, the demon could permit faster-moving molecules to pass into one container, while slower molecules remained in the other. Over time, one container would get hotter and the other cooler. The available energy in the system, as measured by the temperature differential between the two containers, would be increased without adding any new energy to the system (other than Maxwell's smart demon). Thus, the second law of thermodynamics would be circumvented.

Maxwell's demon is, of course, an allegory for anything that contributes *organization* to a disorganized or chaotic situation. In this context, the term "demon" refers to a positive genius, designed to address a host of problems within an organization. The objective is to reduce management costs as a percentage of total organizational costs and to satisfy the "increasingly voracious appetite for decision-influencing management information ... [37]." On the other hand, Maxwell's demon can become a resource-demanding devil—an organizational black hole that can absorb considerable energy with little apparent payoff. The careful design and implementation of an information management system can contribute significantly toward the demon-genius—or at least can help avoid the demon-devil.

ENDNOTES

1. A recent 1999 report by Hackett Benchmarking & Research indicated that more that 75% of the 1500 companies surveyed worldwide felt that their management information systems were inadequately integrated with transactional and operational

systems. Most companies continue to use the general ledger as their key information source, so that management reporting cycle time and decision-making information depend largely on the monthly closing of accounts. Since the average company takes two weeks to close and report, a problem could exist for 40 days or more before it became apparent to the management.

2. Richard A. Bassler. Data bases, MIS and data base management systems. Computer Science and Public Administration, compiled by Richard A. Bassler and Norman L. Enger. Alexandria, VA: College Readings, 1976, p. 203.

3. E. F. Codd. A relational model of data for large shared data banks. Communications of the ACM, Vol. 13, No. 6, June 1970, pp. 377–387.

4. E. F. Codd. The twelve rules for determining how relational a DBMS product is. TRI Technical Report EFC-6/05-16-86. San Jose, CA: The Relational Institute, 1986.

5. E. F. Codd. Relational completeness of the data base sublanguages. Data Base Systems. R. Rustin, ed. Englewood Cliffs, NJ: Prentice-Hall, 1972, pp. 65–98.

6. Nested tables are allowed when the constraint of the first normal form is removed. Extended or nested RDBMS support new relational operations that are not possible with a first normal-form database. Nested RDBMS simplify the logical structure of many databases by eliminating tables that map and record relationships among data tables.

7. For a comprehensive and at times humorous tutorial on the structure query language, see: Philip Greenspun. SQL for Web Nerds. www.arsdigita.com/books/sql/

8. Unfortunately, the power of the relational model often is significantly diminished by weak implementations. Most RDBMS engines are ad-hoc implementations that ignore key relational principles. This approach inhibits their ability to extend relational compliance and to provide the implicit benefits and performance to their users. A primary objective of the relational model is to provide practical solutions for problems in the real world. Inadequate support may eliminate these benefits for end-users.

9. Peter G. W. Keen. Let's focus on action not info. Computerworld. November 17, 1997; Marc Demarest. Technology and policy in decision support systems. DecisionPoint. Portland, Ore., 2000.

10. Walter J. Kennevan. Management information systems. Management of Information Handling Systems. Paul W. Howerton, ed. Roselle Park, NJ: Hayden Book Company, 1974.

11. Michael Hammer. Reengineering work: Don't automate, obliterate. Harvard Business Review, July–August, 1990, pp. 1–7.

12. Michael Hammer. Reengineering work: Don't automate, obliterate. Harvard Business Review, July–August, 1990, pp. 1–7.

13. Michael Scott-Morton and Peter G. W. Keen, eds. Decision Support Systems: An Organizational Perspective. Reading, MA: Addison-Wesley, 1978.

14. Samuel Solomon as quoted in: Martin Lasden. Computer-aided decision-making. Computer Decisions, Vol. 14, No. 11, November 1982, p. 157.

15. Ralph H. Sprague, as quoted in: Martin Lasden. Computer-Aided Decision-Making. Computer Decisions, Vol. 14, No. 11, November 1982, p. 157. For further discussion

of this point, see: Ralph H. Sprague and H. J. Watson. Decision Support Systems: Putting Theory into Practice. New York: Prentice-Hall, 1986.

16. Alan Walter Steiss. Public Budgeting and Management. Lexington, MA: Lexington Books–D.C. Heath Co., 1972, p. 79.

17. Steven L. Alter. Decision Support Systems: Current Practices and Continuing Challenges. Boston, MA: Addison Wesley, 1980.

18. See Chapter 2 for a further examination of these six phases of the decision-making process.

19. Clyde W. Holsapple and Andrew B. Whinston. Decision Support Systems: A Knowledge-Based Approach. St. Paul, MN: West Publishing, 1996.

20. Martin Lasden. Computer-Aided Decision-Making. Computer Decisions, 14:11, November 1982, pp. 160, 162, 168.

21. Alan Walter Steiss. Public Budgeting and Management. Lexington, MA: Lexington Books–D.C. Heath Co., 1972, pp. 79–80

22. Ralph H. Sprague and Eric Carlson. Building Effective Decision Support Systems. New York: Prentice Hall Inc., 1982.

23. Jeffery Moore and Michael Chang. Building Decision-Support Systems. John L. Bennett, ed. Boston, MA: Addison Wesley, 1983.

24. C. W. Holsapple and A. B. Whinston. Business Expels Systems. Homewood, IL: Richard D. Irwin, 1987.

25. Stephen A. Maclin. Going online: What public managers need to know. Public Administration and Management: An Interactive Journal, Vol. 3, No. 1, 1998.

26. Marc Demarest. Technology and policy in decision support systems. DecisionPoint. Portland, Ore., 2000

27. Often included as part of an ERP, but at times implemented as a "standalone," Customer Relationship Management (CRM) software is designed to automate a number of functions that relate to an organization's clientele or customers, including marketing, sales management, customer services, and e-commerce.

28. Mitchell Vaughn, as quoted in: Larry Marion and Erik Sherman. Systems Integration Moves to the Forefront. Newton, MA: Triangle Publishing Services Co., 1999.

29. Mitchell Vaughn, as quoted in: Larry Marion and Erik Sherman. Systems Integration Moves to the Forefront. Newton, MA: Triangle Publishing Services Co., 1999.

30. Donald F. Norris, Patricia D. Fletcher, and Stephen H. Holden. Is Your Local Government Plugged In? Highlights of the PTI/ICMA 2000 electronic government survey. Washington, DC: Public Technology, Inc., February 2001.

31. Baan, the fourth major ERP vendor, has not yet announced software specifically designed for public sector applications. The quotations cited are from the vendors' web sites.

32. For a further discussion of the concepts of MIPES, see: Alan Walter Steiss. Public Budgeting and Management. Lexington, MA: Lexington Books, D.C. Heath, 1972, chapter 10.

33. Richard M. Cyert and James G. March. A Behavioral Theory of the Firm. Englewood Cliffs, NJ: Prentice-Hall, 1963, p. 123.

34. Robert N. Anthony and Regina Herzlinger. Management Control in Non-Profit Organizations. Homewood, IL: Richard D. Irwin, 1975, p. 316.

35. Robert N. Anthony and Regina Herzlinger. Management Control in Non-Profit Organizations. Homewood, IL: Richard D. Irwin, 1975, p. 323.

36. Aaron Wildavsky. Review of politicians, bureaucrats and the consultant. Science 28. December 1973, pp. 1335–1338.

37. Robert C. Heterick. Administrative support services. Cause/Effect 4. November 1981, p. 29.

Appendix

Glossary

Action planning: Day-to-day planning at the operational level; also referred to as tactical planning. Usually does not exceed one year in duration; may be time constrained by operational factors or by a planning–budgetary process that runs from fiscal year to fiscal year.

Activity-based costing (ABC): Method for measuring cost based on the activities that an organization uses in producing its output. Cost pools or activity centers are identified and costs are assigned to products and services (cost drivers) based on the number of events or transactions involved in providing a product or service. (*See also* Cost drivers.)

Adaptive decisions: Seek to alleviate built-up pressures by removing more immediate sources of demand or by providing a satisfactory alternative solution. Provide a means of modifying established patterns of response and, thereby, re-establish a flow of productive activity on a more or less stable basis. (*See also* Strategic decisions; Tactical decisions.)

Appropriations: Amount of estimated resources provided by a governing body for expenditure during the period. Should be included on the liability and fund balance side of the accounting equation.

Associated costs: Costs involved in accessing or utilizing public services that must be borne by the recipient or beneficiary of the services. (*See also* Social costs.)

Arrow diagram: Provides the initial portrayal of a critical path network. Arrows on a network diagram represent the activities of a project. An event is a specific, definable accomplishment in an operations plan, recognizable at a particular point in time.

Authority relations communication network: Communication channels defined in terms of the legitimacy that one individual or group has vis-a-vis others with respect to the issuance of directives, commands, and decisions. Such networks have directionality—orders usually flow vertically, from a relatively few individuals at the top to many in the lower echelons of the authority structure. (*See also* Information exchange network.)

Autointelligence: Data about the component elements of a particular organization, including an evaluation of organizational resources and its capacity to respond to client needs. (*See also* Environmental intelligence.)

Balanced scorecard: Provides a framework for defining, implementing, and sustaining organizational strategy at all levels throughout the organization by linking that strategy to the performance measurement system. Monitors and controls key performance indicators useful in driving and sustaining performance in "best practice" organizations. Focus is on customer satisfaction and needs, organizational learning, growth, and innovation, and optimum performance of internal processes.

Barriers to change: Arise from four major sources: people, technology, infrastructure, and process.

Base/baseline: Performance level for a measure or index at the time that it was adopted or revised. May refer to establishment of a new reporting period for historical purposes or for additional emphasis.

Baseline funds: Support ongoing operations of the organization and are used to pay current operating expenses, provide adequate working capital, and maintain current plant and equipment in order to sustain (1) the same level of production or services, (2) the organization's "market share," or (3) a specified rate of growth. (*See also* Strategic funds.)

Benchmarking: Comparison of an organization's performance or of its processes with that of other organizations that represent "best practices."

Benefit–cost ratio: Present value of benefits divided by the present value of costs or average annual benefits over average annual costs. (*See also* Net benefits.)

Beta distribution formula: Deals with situations in which the variance of the distribution of cost approximates a bell-shaped curve and can be expressed as the square of the standard deviation. Variance can be estimated as roughly one-sixth of the range (i.e., the difference between the most optimistic and the most pessimistic cost estimate).

Bottom-up planning: Planning approach involving lower- and middle-echelon managers alone with little or no input from senior management, typically is lacking in external environmental information and analysis and generally is ineffective. (*See also* Top-down planning.)

Boundary conditions: Set of factors that define the field within which a feasible solution to a defined problem can and should be found.

Budgetary accounting: When a budget is used to make appropriations to government funds, generally accepted accounting principles (GAAP) require that budgeted expenditures and revenue be compared with actual expenditures and revenue. To facilitate this comparison, the budget and accounting classification systems are made equivalent through budgetary accounting practices. (*See also* Objectives of expenditure.)

Capital budget: Identifies expenditures to be incurred to meet long-term improvements needs (capital facilities) and the means of financing these commitments for the current fiscal period. (*See also* Operating budget.)

Capital facilities planning: Long-range planning of capital improvements, involving formulation of goals, objectives, and policies as to desired levels of services, staging of improvements based on a system of priorities, analysis of methods or sources of financing and the overall fiscal capacity of the organization, and the administration of debt obligations.

Cash flow analysis: Process to determine how current fiscal resources are allocated and to show where potential adjustments might be made to yield discretionary funds.

Cash management: Process of maximizing liquid assets of an organization by accelerating receivables and controlling disbursements. Assures that liquid assets are planned, organized, and controlled to meet immediate financial obligations in a timely manner and that temporarily idle funds are invested in safe and profitable securities from which they can be drawn quickly as the need arises.

Cause-and-effect diagram: Seeks to identify, explore, and display all the possible causes of a specific problem or condition. Designed to focus on the cause of the problem instead of the problem itself. Also referred to as a "fishbone diagram."

Certainty: A state of knowledge in which specific and invariable outcomes of each alternative course of action are known in advance. (*See also* Risk and uncertainty.)

Change management: Initiation of change in a planned or systematic fashion. Focuses on the more effective implementation of new processes, methods, and systems an ongoing organization.

Communications coordinator: Assigned the task of organizing and presenting a consistent flow of information regarding proposed changes in an organization's processes and structure.

Comparative advantage: The "competitive edge" or "differential advantage" that an organization has over other organizations offering similar programs to similar target groups and markets.

Compliance evaluation: Examines consistency of program objectives with broader legislative aims and attempts to ensure that public funds are allocated in accordance with policy guidelines.

Comprehensiveness: Concern for an organization as a total entity. An organization is a complex system composed of related and interdependent subsystems. To maintain direction and stability, information from one part of the organization must be linked to information from all other parts to create a comprehensive whole.

Conference room pilot: Demonstration directed to a small audience (15 to 20 participants) that affords participants with differing levels of expertise an opportunity to deal with and react to various aspects of proposed changes in procedures, processes, and operations. (*See also* Change management.)

Constraints: Limits within which an acceptable cost–benefit solution must be sought. Solutions that are otherwise optimal frequently must be discarded because they do not conform to these imposed rules.

Continuous improvement (CI) programs: Tend to focus on incremental improvements in existing processes or practices by identifying specific root causes of inefficiency and waste. Many small changes made by empowered teams of employees. CI programs often originate from the "bottom-up." (*See also* Total quality management.)

Core competencies: Set of the most significant and value-creating skills within an organization. Represent existing strengths and unique capabilities of the organization; should lead to competitive advantage, be growth oriented, difficult to imitate, and help to determine how the organization is different from all others.

Cost accounting: Involves the assembly and recording of the elements of expense incurred to attain a purpose, to carry out an activity, operation, or program, to complete a unit of work or a project, or to do a specific job. (*See also* Financial accounting; Managerial accounting; Responsibility accounting).

Cost approximation: Involves efforts to find predictable relationships between a dependent variable (cost) and an independent variable (some relevant activity), so that costs can be estimated over time based on the behavior of the independent variable.

Cost–benefit analysis: Seeks to identify and quantify (in dollar terms to the extent possible) benefits and costs associated with various alternatives. Examines constraints or limits within which optimal solutions must be sought, beneficial or detrimental side effects or unintended consequences, impacts of deferred benefits and future costs, and problems of risk and uncertainty.

Cost–constraint assessment: Examines the impact when strategies or programs are adopted that are not the most technically effective available. Cost of an alternative that may be adopted if no constraints were present is compared with the cost of the constrained alternative.

Cost driver: Any event that causes a change in the total cost of an activity through the conversion of inputs—resources consumed by activities (usually measured as costs)—into outputs—products (goods or services) that an activity supplies to its customers (internal or external). (*See also* Activity-based costing.)

Cost–effectiveness analysis: Economic concept of marginal analysis applied to determine additional resource requirements (inputs) to achieve some specified additional performance capability (outputs). Measures of effectiveness used to evaluate increments of output achieved relative to additional increments of cost. Supporting analyses include: cost–output studies to identify feasible levels of achievement; cost–effectiveness comparisons to assist in selecting the most effective program alternative; and cost–constraint assessments to determine the cost of employing less than the most optimal program.

Critical issues: Difference between the present position of an organization and its desired future position, identified during process mapping to determine the projected deficiency in performance at the process level. (*See also* Strategic planning gap.)

Critical success factors (*CSF*)*:* Set of factors essential for gaining and maintaining a competitive advantage; a barometer of the overall performance of an organization. Must be unique to the organization and essential to gaining a competitive advantage; should specify, at a high level, how major processes are best measured; and should be aligned with customer values and shared vision of the organization.

Cultural change management: Concerned with the ways in which people interact with each other in peer relationships and in superior/subordinate relationships. People behave in ways consistent with the culture of whatever society or community they are a part of, and by so doing, they perpetuate their culture. To change the culture, it is necessary to start to start by changing behavior.

Customer or user analysis: Evaluation of the level of services being provided to customers or end-users by an organization with the objectives of modifying and improving these services to achieve greater customer satisfaction.

Customer satisfaction: Determination that a product or service meets a customer's expectations, considering requirements of both quality and service.

Cycle time: Total amount of time taken from the point at which a customer requests a service or product until they receive it. Also referred to as elapsed time. (*See also* Process time.)

Data base management systems (*DBMS*)*:* Software that provides procedures for representing data, making changes in these data, for making inquires of the data base and processing raw data to produce information, and necessary internal management functions to minimize the user effort to make the system responsive.

Data warehouse: Maintains copies of transaction data specifically structured for querying and reporting. Main outputs are either tabular listings (specific queries) with minimal formatting or "formal" reports that adhere to predetermined formats.

Decision-support systems: Software systems that provide users with effective ways to access information on an interactive basis without intermediaries. Accommodates continuous changes and improvements in decision-making models.

Decision tree: Illustrates the various "paths" that influence problem outcomes by enumerating all possible outcomes of a sequence of events, where each event can occur in a finite number of ways. (*See also* Payoff matrices.)

Development change: Organizational change limited to improving what currently exists rather than making radical changes. Examples include team building, enhancing internal communications, increasing technical expertise or core competencies, or basic expansion of services or products. (*See also* Transformational change; Transitional change.)

Direct cost: Cost incurred for a specific purpose that is uniquely associated with that purpose. Direct cost components include labor (salaries, wages, and employee benefits), contractual services (services purchased from outside sources), materials and supplies (consumables), and equipment expenses (sometimes categorized as fixed asset expenses) (*See also* Indirect cost.)

Discount factor: Multiplier used to determine the equivalent present value of future streams of benefits and costs.

Dynamic programming: Mathematical approach to problem solving wherein a series of "best decisions" are identified by starting with the final decision and working backward to the initial problem statement.

Effectiveness: Measure of the ability of a program or project to produce a specific desired effect or result that can be qualitatively measured. Performing the right tasks correctly, consistent with organizational mission, vision, values, and in support of the organization's goals and objectives. (*See also* Outcome measure.)

Effectiveness measures: Scoring technique for determining the status of an organization at certain points in time. Indicators of both direct and indirect impacts of specific resource allocations in the pursuit of certain goals and objectives. Effectiveness measures can be defined by establishing levels and types of performance in discrete categories, estimating impacts of current resources on this performance, and then defining the desired levels and types of performance.

Efficiency: Measure of productivity relative to input resources. Efficiency refers to operating a program or project, or performing work tasks economically. Relates to resources expended or saved, not the effectiveness of performance. (*See also* Outcome measure.)

Encumbrances: Obligates funds for goods and services ordered but not yet received. Encumbrances are subtracted from the liability and fund balance side of the accounting equation.

Enterprise resource planning (ERP): Integration of enterprise-wide information systems, linking together all of an organization's operations, including human resources, financials, production, and distribution, and connecting the organization to its customers and suppliers.

Environmental analyses: Studies conducted to provide information about the broader environment of which a particular organization is a part.

Environmental intelligence: Data about the broader environment of which an organization is a part, including assessments of client needs. (*See also* Autointelligence.)

Evaluation: Assessment of the effectiveness of ongoing and proposed programs in achieving agreed-upon goals and objectives, leading to an identification of areas needing improvement through program modification (including possible termination of ineffective programs). Possible influence of external and internal organizational factors must be taken into account.

Externalities: Spillover effects or unintended consequences arising from a project or program that may be beneficial or detrimental. Often excluded from an analysis initially in order to make the problem statement more manageable.

Feedback mechanisms: Circular patterns or loops involving a flow of information from some point of action to a point of decision and then a return to the point of action with new information and perhaps instructions for modification.

Feed forward: Anticipates lags in feedback systems by monitoring inputs and predicting their effects on output variables. Action can be taken to change inputs and to bring the outputs into equilibrium with desired results before feedback discloses a deviation from accepted standards.

Financial accounting: Procedures to measure and record financial data and convert these data to information that is analyzed, interpreted, and reported to various groups both within and outside an organization. Concerned with results of fiscal transactions and the consequent financial position of the organizational entity. (*See also* Cost accounting; Fund accounting; Managerial accounting; Responsibility accounting.)

Fixed costs: Costs that do not change in total as the volume of activity increases, but become progressively smaller on a per unit basis. (*See also* Variable costs.)

Flattening: Process of reducing the organizational hierarchy through the intentional and calculated streamlining of processes by eliminating waste and redundant functions, often while decentralizing decision making. Often results in a reduction of the layers of management, which increases the span of control of managers at various levels to the point where efficiency and effectiveness may become compromised.

Focus group: Five to fifteen people, knowledgeable about, or impacted by a given process, who are organized to share ideas, discuss issues, and collaborate on defining activities and their relationships within processes. (*See also* Vision groups.)

Formative evaluation: Provides information necessary to design or modify service delivery systems and includes analysis of needs to be met or problems to be solved, determination of whether public programs should be initiated to meet such needs, and if so, how the program should be designed. (*See also* Summative evaluation.)

Full costing: Identifies all costs (direct and indirect) associated with some operation or activity. In the governmental and non-profit areas, full costs often are called program costs.

Functional process improvement: Variation of process reengineering developed and applied by the Department of Defense. Functional process improvement cycle is broken down into six different actions: define, analyze, evaluate, plan, approve, and execute.

Functional strategies: Serve as the initial steps toward the implementation of an overall strategic plan by focusing on critical issues related to organizational structure, finance, membership size and recruitment, human resource development, and facilities.

Fund: An independent accounting and fiscal entity to which resources are assigned, together with all related liabilities, obligations, reserves, and equities.

Fund accounting: Primary mechanisms for the control of governmental activities. Financial transactions are made between funds. Expenditures cannot exceed the dollar amount that has been appropriated or allocated to that particular expenditure category. Separate financial statements are prepared for each of the major funds and combined statements of funds with similar purposes often are distributed.

Futuring: Identification of a "preferred future" and the formulation of specific ways to realize that image. Provides an organization the ability to determine what it wants to accomplish, what it should become in the future, and how to get to those points.

Game theory: Attempts to provide a general theory of social interaction (primarily economic activities) by analogy with ordinary games of strategy such as chess or card games. Mathematical analysis is applied to problems of strategy, often using long and complicated chains of reasoning.

Gap analysis: Involves establishing performance targets and projections based on strategy and tactical applications to determine the projected deficiency in performance relative to established objectives. (*See also* Performance gap.)

General systems theory: Holistic approach that stresses similarities among the theoretical constructs of diverse disciplines rather than their unique properties. Principles, laws, and models that apply to generalized systems or their subclasses, irrespective of their particular kind, nature of their component elements, and relations of forces between them. Focusing on root causes and on their complex interrelationships can unite distinct sets of phenomena.

Goal management: Links goals from each strategic process (e.g., strategic planning, strategic training, operations management, performance measurement, etc.) to ensure that each process drives tactical performance.

Goals: Identify how an organization intends to address its critical issues, considering both its critical success factors and its core competencies, and in support of mission and vision. Goals are designed to drive actions and are intended to represent the general end toward which an organizational effort is directed. (*See also* Objectives; Strategies.)

Government Performance and Results Act (GPRA): Enacted by Congress in 1993 to improve the effectiveness, efficiency, and accountability of federal programs. Each federal agency must develop a strategic plan that covers a period of at least five years and is updated at least every three years. GPRA also requires that each agency prepare an annual plan to include performance indicators that will be used to measure the relevant outputs, service levels, and outcomes of each program activity in an agency's budget.

Heuristics: Ad hoc principles or general rules of thumb, applied in situations where more detailed, precise procedures (algorithms) cannot be used, either for reasons of economy or inherent difficulties in the problem situation.

Horizontal hierarchical structure: Form of management that focuses on common objectives that transcend traditional departmental boundaries to meet customer or stakeholder requirements. (*See also* Vertical hierarchical structure.)

Hoshin kanri: A system of planning and deployment that makes extensive use of quality management principles and techniques, and involves every part of an organization—in selecting and defining a small number of key targets and in contributing to the accomplishment of these targets.

Hoshin planning: An approach for achieving specific objectives developed in conjunction with management's choice of targets and means in terms of quality, cost, delivery, and morale. Uses a plan-do-check-act paradigm to involve all levels of management. Hoshin plans are communicated and conflicts between plans are identified and resolved through a process of "catchball."

Indexes/indices: Statistical compilation of multiple performance measures or metrics that are similar or related. Typically used to link related organizational issues, to evaluate interrelated leading or lagging indicators, or to effectively reduce the overall number of metrics or measures to a manageable level.

Indirect cost: Generally considered to be any cost associated with more than one activity or program that cannot be traced directly to any of the individual activities. In the public sector, the terms indirect cost and overhead often are used interchangeably. (*See also* Direct cost.)

Informal lateral networks: Develops when regular communication channels fail to function adequately. Informal communication networks often are not directly subject to management control and frequently are the result of natural social groupings.

Information exchange network: Messages in this communications network usually are concerned with internal operations and with the broader external environment. The flow is generally from the operational levels to the top of the organization. This network can be used to supply information for operational decisions—to establish guidelines or parameters with which such decisions can be made. (*See also* Authority relations communication network.)

Information management system (IMS): Provides processes by which pertinent information is organized and communicated in a timely and synergistic fashion to resolve organizational problems.

Inheritable asset: Previous investments that can be used to the particular advantage of one alternative over another. (*See also* Sunk cost.)

Input measure: Resources expended on a given activity. Useful for tracking status of available resources with no consideration of the results.

Intended strategies: Advance plans or actions undertaken in an effort to help an organization fulfill its intended purpose. Typically proactive in nature. (*See also* Reactive strategies.)

Interface management: Provides "flow support" to processes that pass between functional or operational areas within an organization.

International Organization for Standardization (ISO): A nongovernmental, federation of national standards bodies headquartered in Geneva, Switzerland, with one representative from each of approximately 130 countries. Established in 1947 with the mission to promote the development of standardization and related activities worldwide, to facilitate the international exchange of goods and services, and to develop cooperation in the spheres of intellectual, scientific, technological, and economic activity.

Intervention effect assessment: Attempts to establish the relation between program intervention and outcomes, or in some cases, the processes involved in producing those outcomes.

Irregular measures: Performance measures collected during special situations, certain conditions, or on a "demand-basis." Not always regularly tracked and may not be reported unless specifically requested on a demand-basis. (*See also* Regular formal measures; Regular informal measures.)

Investment costs: Expenses incurred to obtain future benefits. May be classified as sunk costs or actual project outlays, depending on their timing. (*See also* Sunk costs.)

Investment strategies: Criteria considered in selecting a specific security in which to invest, including safety/risk, price stability, liquidity/marketability, maturity, and yield.

Lagging indicators: Series of indicators that follow changes or movement in a given direction; typically associated with programmatic results. Examples include such indicators as customer satisfaction, employee growth and learning, and value added.

Leading indicators: Series of indicators that track movement in a given direction and which generally precede the movement of other indicators in the same or in a similar direction. (*See also* Output measures; Performance drivers.)

Legacy system: Existing information systems and technology in which an organization has considerable investment and which may be entrenched in the organization. May have been in place for many years and considered to be old or inadequate technology.

Line items: Budget appropriations may be made according to specific categories such as salaries, materials and supplies, travel, contractual services, and equipment. Legislative approval often must be granted for any expenditure that exceeds the dollar amount of these line-item appropriations.

Management audit: Involves an assessment of resource utilization practices, including an examination of the adequacy of information management systems, administrative procedures, and organizational structure. (*See also* Performance audit.)

Management controls: Measurement and evaluation of program activities to determine if policies and objectives are being accomplished as efficiently and effectively as possible. Provides the basic structure for coordinating the day-to-day activities of an organization, encompassing all those activities involved in ensuring that the organization's resources are appropriately used in the pursuit of its objectives. (*See also* Operational controls; Strategic controls.)

Management evaluations: Focuses on the efficiency and effectiveness by which available resources are deployed to achieve program objectives.

Management planning: Involves the programming of approved objectives into specific projects, programs, and activities; the design of organizational units to carry out approved programs; and the staffing of those units and the procurement of the necessary revenues to support the approved programs.

Managerial accounting: Involves formulation of financial estimates of future performance (planning and budgeting processes) and analysis of actual performance in relation to those estimates (performance evaluation and control). (*See also* Cost accounting; Financial accounting; Responsibility accounting.)

Memory: Repository for raw data, information concerning past experiences, programmed decisions, and for criteria by which "right" decisions can be tested for acceptability.

Mission statement: Statement of the role or purpose by which an organization intends to serve its stakeholders. Describes what the organization does (current capabilities), who it serves (stakeholders), and what makes the organization unique (justification of existence). (*See also* Stakeholders; Vision statement.)

Multidimensional measure: Category of measures that expresses a relationship between two or more fundamental units of performance, typically expressed as a form of ratio. (*See also* Performance measure; Single-dimensional measure.)

Multiple policy matrix: Mechanism used to record and analyze the range of policy statements—from long-term, general and educational objectives to more immediate, specific, and action-oriented programs—required in the identification and implementation of strategic objectives.

Net benefits: A measure of the difference between the present value of benefits and the present value of costs. (*See also* Benefit–cost ratio.)

Network analysis: Techniques for "mapping" various steps required to implement a project or program. Provides a basis for determining the order in which activities should be undertaken—either their sequence or priority—and the critical linkages among activities. Examples include the critical path method (CPM) and program evaluation and review technique (PERT).

Normalization: Determines how data should be organized to make the database as compact and as easy to manage as possible and to ensure that consistent results are produced. Normalization rules provide design guidelines by specifying how a relational database should be divided into tables and how these tables should be linked together. (*See also* Relational data base management system.)

Objective function: Involves identifying and quantifying (in dollar terms to the extent possible) the costs and benefits associated with each alternative in a cost–benefit analysis.

Objectives: Specific outcomes that an organization expects to accomplish within a given time frame. Should include sufficient detail to provide an overall sense of what exactly is desired without outlining the specific steps necessary to achieve that end. Objectives link "upward" to goals and "downward" to strategies, and also link directly to outcome/effectiveness measures.

Objectives matrix: Mechanism used to identify potential conflicts and areas of agreement and congruence among organizational objectives. Can reveal different levels of understanding regarding broader goals of the organization and provide information regarding conflicts among participants valuable in identifying levels of comprehension with respect to complex issues.

Objects of expenditures: Detailed listings of the categories of expense required to operate each program. Tabulations of the myriad items required to operate each program, including salaries and wages, employee benefits, rent, office supplies, travel, equipment, and other inputs. Provides the critical linkage between the budget and the accounting system.

On-line analytical processing (OLAP): Provides fast, consistent, interactive access to a wide variety of possible views of information. Provides an ability to conduct dynamic analyses of consolidated data, while supporting the analytical and navigational activities of end-users.

Operating budget: Principal document for the allocation of resources in support of the activities of an organization. Annual operating budgets are subject to periodic review and authorization and include estimates of expenditures in such areas as salaries, wages, contractual services, and materials and supplies.

Operational controls: Seeks to ensure that specific tasks or activities are carried out efficiently and in compliance with established policies. Involve a determination of program resource requirements and the order of commitment necessary to achieve specific program objectives. Focus on specific responsibilities for carrying out tasks identified at the strategic and management control levels.

Operational vision: Designed to translate the broader, more generic aspects of the strategic vision into specific applications within component processes and units of the organization. Seeks to organize and deploy resources effectively and efficiently to accomplish the organization's strategic objectives. (*See also* Vision statement.)

Operations scheduling: Involves determining the calendar dates or times that resources will be utilized in accordance with the total resource capacity assigned to the project or program.

Opportunity costs: Costs involved when resources are committed to a particular program or activity and, as a consequence, are pre-empted from being used elsewhere.

Organizational mapping: Diagnostic tool that focuses on providing a representation (model) of an organization's entire operations from a systemic or strategic perspective. Used to improve organizational efficiency and effectiveness. (*See also* Process management; Process mapping.)

Outcome-based (or results-based) budgeting: Requires the establishment of budget processes that link resource allocations to intended results, reallocating resources to the highest-priority results and demonstrating how public investments affect the achievement of agreed-upon outcomes and objectives. (*See also* Performance budgeting; Responsibility budgeting.)

Outcome measure: An assessment of the results of a program or project compared to its intended purpose to produce a specific desired effect or result which can be qualitatively measured. (*See also* Effectiveness.)

Output measure: Tabulation, calculation, or recording of activity or effort that can be expressed in a quantitative or qualitative manner. Useful for tracking volumes or levels of work when monitoring costs is more important than tracking quality or effectiveness. (*See also* Efficiency.)

Pareto diagram: Fundamental tool for determining which characteristic is causing problems in a given process. Constructed by categorizing data, ranking, and plotting frequency of occurrence in bar-chart form in descending order along the x axis. Sometimes dollars are plotted on the y axis to emphasize the cost factor.

Payoff matrices: Used in connection with decision trees to determine the probability of a given event (or decision) occurring in a sequence of events. Fundamental theorem is applied that conditional probabilities can be calculated by multiplying the probabilities associated with each event and that all probability paths leading to the same outcome are additive.

Performance audit: Extends focus of a management audit to include an examination of program results to determine whether desired benefits were achieved, program objectives were met, and alternatives were considered that might yield the desired results at a lower cost. (*See also* Management audit.)

Performance budgeting: Budget categories are stated in functional terms to evaluate the work efficiency of operating units, and work–cost measurements are required to encourage more efficient and economical performance of prescribed activities. A performance budget is built upon a series of work programs related to particular functions or activities.

Performance drivers: Quantitative measures of output that include such indicators as cycle time, defect rates, quality rates and ratios, and most financial metrics.

Performance gap: Difference between the present status of performance at the project or task level and its future desired position. (*See also* Gap analysis; Strategic planning gap.)

Performance indicator: Particular value or characteristic used to measure output or outcome. Detailed list of measurements to monitor and evaluate management strategies. Key performance indicators should be determined for each critical success factor.

Performance management: Involves the regular review of the performance measurement process flow to ensure that value is added and that the processes accurately reflect current stakeholder and customer requirements.

Performance measure (metric): Generic term used to describe a particular value or characteristic designated to measure input, output, outcome, efficiency, or effectiveness.

Performance target: Level of performance expressed by a tangible, measurable objective against which actual achievement can be compared. Represents the performance level that an organization expects to meet or exceed during a given period.

Planning horizon: Farthest point that can be anticipated based on an interpretation of what is known about existing conditions and emerging trends. Planning horizon of any organization can be determined through the application of both objectives (measurable) and subjective criteria.

Process: A structured, measured set of activities designed to produce a specified output. Specific ordering of work activities across time and place, with a beginning, an end, and clearly identified inputs and outputs. Method of accomplishing activities including all of the integral steps that are required; "how things get done."

Process champions: Individuals or groups with the power to promote a cross-functional initiative that transcends established lines of authority and responsibility. (*See also* Process owners.)

Process flows: Visual depictions showing the order of activities and the movement of information and other tangibles into and out of a process. (*See also* Process mapping.)

Process mapping: Diagnostic tool that focuses on providing a representation (model) of a specific operation or portion of an operation from a localized or tactical perspective. This model is then used to improve organizational efficiency and effectiveness. (*See also* Organizational mapping.)

Process owners: Individuals who are assigned responsibility for a process and accorded the authority to fulfill that responsibility. (*See also* Process champions.)

Process paradox: Refers to the phenomenon whereby process improvements may be significant and associated performance measures may be impressive, yet overall organizational performance may be well below expectations due to a failure to first make strategic decisions about which processes to improve.

Process profiles: Narrative descriptions that provide the detail behind process flow diagrams.

Process reengineering: Fundamental rethinking and radical redesign of organizational processes to achieve dramatic improvements in critical measures of performance such as cost, quality, service and speed.

Process time: Total amount of time that a service or product is having something done to it (other than waiting). Measured by defining the volumes and estimating the percentage of work on each path (sequence of activities); determining how much time is consumed at each step if the work goes down that path; and multiplying the total path time by the percent of work on that path and summing the results for all paths.

Productivity: Value added by a process, factored against the value of all labor, capital, or other resources consumed by the process.

Program: A group of interdependent, closely related activities or services that contribute to a common objective or set of objectives and bring together all costs associated with its execution. Fundamental building blocks for strategic planning.

Program analysis: Seeks to determine whether a program or proposal is justified, ranks various program alternatives appropriate to a given set of objectives, and ascertains the optimal course(s) of action to attain such objectives.

Program budgeting: Resource allocation procedures that incorporate basic objectives of accountability, efficiency, and effectiveness by presenting budget requests in terms of program "packages" rather than the usual object-of-expenditure format. Conscious effort made to state end objectives, seek a wide range of program alternatives, and link program and financial plans.

Program design evaluations: Test measurability of program assumptions, overall logic of program approach, and assignment of responsibility and accountability for program results.

Program evaluation: Focuses on actual performance of ongoing or recently completed activities. Seeks to measure the overall success and to identify areas where improvements may be made to more fully realize the projected program benefits.

Program impact evaluations: Deal with program delivery systems and the relation between program results and the legislated goals and program objectives.

Prototyping: Provides opportunities for simulating and evaluating reengineering potentials within the organization, as well as the systems development area. Also provides feedback on the progress and acceptance of the reengineering effort. Continuous prototyping enables necessary adjustments to be made before a final process design is chosen.

Purpose: Why an organization exists and what it seeks to accomplish. The main methods or activities the organization undertakes to fulfill this purpose defines its business.

Quality: Degree to which a product or service meets or exceeds a customer's requirements and expectations. (*See also* Service.)

Quality control circle: Small voluntary groups of key participants organized to discuss problems and plan for and implement actual solutions. Critical factors must be considered: management, employees and unions must be committed to this approach; measurements must be established to assess the work environment and productivity changes; and facilitative expertise must be provided to assist in organizing, focusing, and implementing the quality circle deliberations.

Quality function deployment (*QFD*): A systematic process for identifying customer desires, wants, and needs (the so-called "voice of the customer").

Data are translated into appropriate technical requirements that must be met at each stage of product development and production.

Quality improvement process (QIP): Variation on TQM that uses problem-solving teams established at various levels within the organization. Formal mechanisms are established for the systematic identification and deployment of policy. Plan-Do-Check-Act procedures are applied to involve workers at all levels in quality improvement on a day-by-day basis. (*See also* Total quality management.)

Rational decisions: Decisions that result from a sequence of acts or flow of choices that are mutually related to the attainment of some objective or group of objectives and require the orderly, systematic procedures of planning.

Reactive strategies: Refers to the actions that take place in response to events as they occur. Typically less effective than proactive and intentional strategies. (*See also* Intended strategies.)

Recurring costs: Include operating and maintenance costs that vary with both the size and duration of the program. They do not add to the stock of capital, but rather are incurred to maintain the value of the existing stock. (*See also* Investment costs.)

Regular formal measures: Organizational performance measures that are automatically gathered and tracked, often within an information management system.

Regular informal measures: Organizational performance measures that are gathered periodically, tracked on an individual basis, but not generally reported throughout the organization.

Relational data base management system: DBMS based on the mathematics of relations and first-order predicate logic to provide a rigorous definition of the "set operations" that supports the manipulation of tables, while maintaining the structure and integrity of the data.

Research and development (R&D) costs: Front-end costs that may or may not figure into the actual expenses of a given program or project. R&D costs that eventually benefit more than one program or project must be considered as *sunk* costs and should not be included in the direct cost estimate for a specific program or project.

Resource management: Ensures that each process has the necessary level of resources to meet its expected contribution to overall organizational goals and objectives.

Responsibility accounting: Emphasis is on specific costs in relation to well-defined areas of responsibility. Results (actual performance) are reported in such a way that significant variances from planned performance can be identified, reasons for variances can be determined, responsibility can be fixed, and timely action can be taken to correct problems. (*See also* Cost accounting; Financial accounting; Managerial accounting.)

Responsibility center budgeting: Seeks to assign greater accountability to those managers who can exercise significant influence over costs on a day-to-day basis. All pertinent direct and indirect costs and the funds necessary to support these costs are assigned to various organizational units designated as responsibility centers. Each responsibility center is held accountable for the specific outcomes that have occurred as a result of the total allocation of resources in support of its activities.

Responsibility costing: Assigns to an operating unit only those costs that its managers can control, or at least influence. Many argue that this approach is the only appropriate measure of the financial stewardship of an operating manager.

Risk: A state of knowledge in which each alternative leads to one of a set of specific outcomes, and each outcome occurs with a probability that is known to the decision maker. (*See also* Certainty and Uncertainty.)

Satisficing: Strategy for narrowing the search and screening process. When a decision maker finds an alternative that is good enough (one that suffices), they refrain from further search (that is, they are satisfied), thereby conserving time, energy, and resources.

Selective filtering: Systematic omissions of certain categories of information in order to reduce communication overload, which is a major problem in any large organization.

Sensitivity analysis: Measures the possible effects that variations in uncertain decision elements (e.g., costs) may have on the alternatives under analysis. Several values (optimistic, pessimistic, and most likely) may be applied in an attempt to ascertain how sensitive the results may be to variations in the uncertain parameters.

Service: Work performed by an individual or organization that benefits or provides advantage to a customer. (*See also* Quality.)

Service level analysis: Analytical technique that focuses on the resources required to deliver various levels of service. The objective is to identify essential service levels, so that an organization can maintain, deliver, and be held accountable for such programs in a more efficient and effective manner. Applicable to programs or activities in which some discretion can be exercised as to the course of action to be pursued.

Simulation models: Constructed as open systems to provide opportunities to study directly some dimensions of real-world problems and the effect of personal and social interaction on these problems.

Single-dimensional measure: Category of performance measures that indicate one fundamental unit (such as hours, dollars, errors, cycle time, etc.). (*See also* Multidimensional measure.)

Situational analysis: Involves research and analysis of both internal and external environmental factors, consideration of organizational success and failure, and the impact of the organization's past and present abilities to reach its goals. Includes the identification of a set of organizational strengths, weaknesses, opportunities, and threats (SWOT) both from a current and future perspective. Performance indicators are selected based upon an organization's past and present abilities to reach its goals as determined through success and failure analysis.

Six sigma: Set of strategies, tools, and statistical methodologies that emphasize business process improvement. Includes cost reduction, cycle-time improvement, increased customer satisfaction, and any other metric important to the organization. Objective is to achieve a high level of quality at reduced costs with a reduction in cycle time, resulting in improved profitability and a competitive advantage.

Social costs: Subsidies that would have to be paid to compensate persons adversely affected by a project or program for their suffering or "disbenefits." Such compensation rarely is made (except perhaps when affected individuals enter into litigation and are awarded damages). (*See also* Associated costs.)

Stability: Desire to reduce the effects of chance or randomness in the operations of the organization. Reflected in the need to establish order, sequence, and predictability, to anticipate events, and to establish procedures to deal with problems as they arise.

Stakeholders: Individuals and groups that either affect or are affected by the organization. Usually include all internal and external customers. Should be involved or consulted as part of the strategic planning process so that their views, needs, and concerns are given consideration during the development of goals, objectives, and strategies, and to provide input related to programmatic outcome measures.

Stakeholder survey: An opportunity for individuals and groups to state the importance of processes to their current activities or interactions with an organization. A determination is made as to where various internal and external stakeholders stand with respect to the retention of current processes and the implementation of target processes.

Standard costs: Relate service delivery costs or production to some predetermined indices of operational efficiency. If actual costs vary from these standards, management must determine the reasons for the deviation and whether the costs are controllable or noncontrollable with respect to the responsible unit.

Strategic choices: Alternative strategic plans available to an organization. The degree of choice is likely determined by the organization's resources, by such external factors as competition and environmental issues, and by managerial competence in terms of the ability to manage a new area of activity. (*See also* Strategic drift.)

Strategic controls: Used to evaluate the overall performance of an organization or a significant component of that performance. Assists decision makers in identifying when unanticipated changes occur in the broader environment and in determining appropriate corrective actions and should include measures of future performance focusing on efficiency, quality of service, innovation, and responsiveness to customers. (*See also* Management controls.)

Strategic decisions: Decisions with far-reaching implications. Decision-makers must determine what the problem situation is, identify what alternative courses are open to change the situation, select the most effective solution in light of available resources, and determine what additional resources might be necessary (and feasible) to achieve a more effective solution. (*See also* Adaptive decisions; Tactical decisions.)

Strategic drift: Limitations placed on strategic choice by assumptions made in the past and the application of previously tried remedies. May restrict organization from adopting the best strategies required to deal with a changing environment.

Strategic evaluations: Concerned with underlying causes of social problems and focus on "implicit theories" as a basis for broad ameliorative programs.

Strategic funds: Used to purchase new assets such as equipment, facilities, and inventory; to increase working capital; and to support direct expenses for research and development, marketing, advertising, and promotions.

Strategic funds programming: Fundamental approach to financial analysis that considers sources, flow, and uses of organizational resources in an effort to identify discretionary funds to implement new programs and strategies. Provides a future-oriented perspective on financial requirements and potential sources to meet those needs.

Strategic management: Process by which an organization determines its long-range direction and performance by ensuring that careful formulation, effective and efficient implementation, and continuous evaluation of strategy and performance takes place. Integrates various organizational functions and processes into a cohesive, broader strategy. Process that links the various other functions and strategic processes together in a dynamic and interactive manner responsive to the organization's changing environment.

Strategic marketing: Process of developing and maintaining a strategic fit between the organization's goals and objectives and its changing marketing opportunities.

Strategic processes: Primary value-added building blocks of an organization, comprising a number of process elements or major steps which, in turn, involve a series of functional activities that represent the input of a single functional group to a process element.

Strategic planning: Process by which an organization formulates long-range goals, selects activities to achieve each of those goals, and implements important decisions across different levels and functions to ensure that the organization is successful.

Strategic planning gap analysis: Involves performance projections based on an existing strategy, in a forecasted environment, to determine the projected deficiency in performance at the strategic level. (*See also* Critical issues; Gap analysis.)

Strategies: Specific methods, processes, or steps used to accomplish goals and objectives. Strategies impact resources (inputs) in some positive or negative way and are executed in a tactical manner so as to link goals and objectives to day-to-day operations. Strategies link "upward" to goals and objectives and also link directly to output and efficiency measures.

Strategy: General direction set for the organization and its various components to achieve a desired state in the future, resulting from the detailed strategic planning process. (*See also* Tactics.)

Structured query language (SQL): Industry accepted expression of the relational database management system. SQL interacts with relational databases but is not a full application development language. Well-defined foundation of a set-oriented database is kept distinct from less precise, procedural characteristics of existing programming languages.

Summative evaluation: Measures performance and program impacts, including an identification of input and intervening variables. Input variables provide information necessary to identify more clearly why a program may or may not be successfully implemented. Two kinds of intervening variables must be measured: (1) program operation variables, and (2) bridging variables (i.e., the intermediate steps selected as a means to achieve program objectives). (*See also* Formative evaluation.)

Sunk costs: Previous investments that cannot be used to the particular advantage of one alternative over another. (*See also* Inheritable asset.)

SWOT analysis: An analysis of an organization's strengths, weaknesses, opportunities, and threats. (*See also* Situational analysis.)

Systematic innovation (SI): Applies a contradiction matrix to identify characteristics that could be in conflict in any general technical system. Each cell of the matrix can contain up to five of the 40 principles of problem solving that represent possible solutions to the contradiction.

Systemic concerns: Desire to put things in order, to establish priorities, to relate specific activities to broader purposes, and to provide mechanisms for measuring success. Three elements are at the core of these concerns: purpose, stability, and comprehensiveness.

Systems readiness: Capacity of an organization to undertake proposed courses of action. Defines the response capacity of an organization in the short-, mid-, and long-range future.

Tactical decisions: Relatively routine decisions effectively handled through the use of precast responses. If both the underlying conditions of the problem and the requirements to be satisfied are known, tactical decisions can be reached through programmed problem solving. Decision criterion is usually one of economy (least cost). (*See also* Adaptive decisions; Strategic decisions.)

Tactics: Actions initiated to achieve more immediate objectives. (*See also* Strategy.)

Task expertise network: Provides technical know-how regarding the performance of organizational activities. Occupational groups and professions in unrelated islands of expertise use specialized jargon in handling the tools and techniques of their trade and provide norms concerning work standards and appropriate levels of performance.

Task interdependence: Extent to which essential steps in the process of change can be divided or modularized.

Team building: Involves a number of strategies designed to deal with intra- and intergroup competition, and structural rigidities and unresponsiveness within an organization. Employees are encouraged to address productivity and other operational problems by organizing flexible semi-autonomous work groups— operating teams, problem-oriented teams, or management teams.

Technology overload: Inability to utilize the technology that is available within an organization because of a lack of training and understanding of technology applications.

Theory of inventive problem solving (TRIZ): A systematic approach to the identification and solution of basic contradictions that are at the root of complex problems. Genrich Altshuller, while working in the Russian Patent Office, developed a series of algorithms for solving difficult problems, which forms the basis for TRIZ.

Timeliness: Measures whether work was done correctly and on time, usually based on customer requirements.

Top-down planning: Approach taken when senior management alone conducts planning activities with little or no input from the rest of the organization. Typically lacking in internal environmental information and analysis and, generally, is an ineffective planning methodology. (*See also* Bottom-up planning.)

Top-down/bottom-up planning: A "best practice" approach to organizational planning that draws upon the skills, strengths, and knowledge of the entire organization to maximize planning effectiveness through the successful integration of both internal and external environmental information and analysis.

Total quality management (TQM): Series of techniques for creating organization-wide participation in planning and implementing a continuous improvement process. Originated as a zero defects and statistical reliability measurement approach, it is also designed to train workers to recognize and adhere to organizational policy with regard to quality. TQM builds on four basic concepts: continuous improvement, customer focus, total participation, and social networking.

Transformational change: Organizational change that involves the implementation of an evolutionary new state, which requires major and often ongoing shifts in organizational strategy. Examples include major restructuring, reengineering, downsizing, consolidation, and major shifts in business focus. (*See also* Developmental change; Transitional change.)

Transitional change: Organizational change that involves implementation of a new state, which requires dismantling the present methods of operating and introducing new or replacement methods of operating. Examples include reorganization, minor restructuring, utilization of new operational techniques/methods/procedures, or introduction of new services or products. (*See also* Developmental change; Transformational change.)

Transition workshops: Structured presentations regarding proposed organizational changes to fairly sizable audiences (25 to 100 participants) with ample provision for question and answer sessions and audience comments and reactions.

Uncertainty: A state of knowledge in which one or more courses of action may result in a set of possible specific outcomes. The probabilities of these outcomes, however, are neither known nor meaningful. (*See also* Certainty; Risk.)

Unit cost: Cost of providing one unit of activity within an agency's realm of program responsibilities. Often determined simply by dividing the current budget allocation for a given activity by the number of performance units.

Update: Performance level achieved for a metric or index, current as of the time of generation or reporting.

Value-added analysis: Determines which activities in a process are most important to the customer or end-user and to the business strategy. Value-added activities usually meet the following criteria: related to doing it right the first time; moves the organization one step closer to delivering the product or service to the customer; and is something the customer is willing to pay for.

Value chain: Framework for examining the strengths and weaknesses of an organization and for using the results of this analysis to improve performance. Premised on the assumption that a basic purpose of an organization is to provide or create value for users of its products or services, and that value and customer satisfaction should be the primary customer drivers. Organizational activities are classified as either primary activities (that create, transfer, or support something of value) or as support activities (that assist primary activities by providing resources or infrastructure).

Values: Set of beliefs or standards that the organization and its stakeholders believe in and operate from, values are utilized to guide the day-to-day operations, serving as a linkage between mission (i.e., present operations) and vision (i.e., intended direction). Personal values allow organizational members to understand how their own beliefs fit into the organizational values and its intended operations and direction.

Variable costs: Costs that are more or less uniform per unit, but their total fluctuates in direct proportion to the total volume of activity. (*See also* Fixed costs.)

Variance: Difference between the amount budgeted for a particular activity and the actual cost of carrying out that activity during a given period. Variances may be positive (under budget) or negative (over budget).

Vertical hierarchical structure: Traditional organizational structure, vertically oriented, and using traditional concepts such as division of labor, standardization of parts and products, mass production, and control as basic or primary functions of management. (*See also* Horizontal hierarchical structure.)

Vision groups: Focus groups that are given license to be creative and to use divergent thinking to generate and evaluate new ideas, to challenge current assumptions, to break away from existing paradigms, and to throw out established rules to assist in formulating the future processes.

Visioning: Takes a forward look at the future by establishing an effective organizational vision that includes organizational performance criteria and ethical standards for employees and volunteers.

Vision statement: Identifies where the organization intends to be in the future or where it should be to best meet the needs of stakeholders. Incorporates a shared understanding of the nature and purpose of the organization and uses this understanding to move the organization toward a greater purpose. (*See also* Mission statement.)

Work breakdown schedules: Technique for developing a preliminary outline or "schematic" of the way in which supporting objectives mesh together to ensure the attainment of the major objectives. Total project is divided into major tasks, then subdivided into subtasks, activities, and so on according to their interrelatedness. Structure should be flexible enough that it can be expanded over time—in both depth and scope.

Workload measures: Time-and-effort indices such as number of persons served per hour, yards of dirt moved per day, or more generally, volume of activity per unit of time.

Zero-base budgeting (*ZBB*): Agencies are required to examine their budget requests below the current level of expenditures (the base). As part of its regular budget submission, each agency must specify the consequences of spending less money than the current year's appropriation.

Index